D1756524

Exile, Emigration and Irish Writing

To the memory of my parents: my father Packie, an exile, my mother Katie, an emigrant, and to my wife Jennifer, a long-suffering immigrant.

Exile, Emigration and Irish Writing

PATRICK WARD

IRISH ACADEMIC PRESS
DUBLIN • PORTLAND, OR

First published in 2002 by
IRISH ACADEMIC PRESS
44, Northumberland Road,
Dublin 4, Ireland

and in the United States of America by
IRISH ACADEMIC PRESS
c/o ISBS, 5824 NE Hassalo Street,
Portland, OR 97213-3644

Website: www.iap.ie

British Library Cataloguing in Publication Data

Ward, Patrick
    Exile, emigration and Irish writing
    1. English literature – Irish authors – History and
    criticism 2. Exile (Punishment) in literature 3. Emigration
    and immigration in literature
    I. Title
    820.9'9415

ISBN 0-7165-2658-1 (cloth)

Library of Congress Cataloging-in-Publication Data

Ward, Patrick, 1946–
    Exile, emigration, and Irish writing / Patrick Ward.
        p. cm.
    Based on the author's doctoral thesis (University College Dublin).
    Includes bibliographical references.
    ISBN 0-7165-2658-1
        1. English literature–Irish authors–History and criticism. 2. Exiles' writings,
    English–Irish authors–History and criticism. 3. Immigrants' writings, English–Irish
    authors–History and criticism. 4. Ireland–Emigration and immigration–History. 5.
    Emigration and immigration in literature. 6. Irish–Foreign countries–History. 7.
    Immigrants in literature. 8. Exiles in literature. 9. Home in literature. I. Title.

PR8722.E93 W37 2001
820.9'9417–dc21
                                                                        00-059791

Typeset by Vitaset, Paddock Wood, Kent
Printed by
MPG Books Ltd., Bodmin, Cornwall

Contents

Foreword

'HOME'–whenever my father spoke the word in his slow baritone, the sound of the 'm' seemed to rise and hum from the depths of his being. His instinctive relish for the sound of the word, the evident pleasure he took in his long slow delivery suggested to me an almost subterranean and sensual pleasure in its utterance.

In my childhood 'Home' for my father was Moree, The Rock, Pomeroy, Co. Tyrone. The enunciation of the address by my father was like some vaguely ritualistic, incantatory echo of things beyond my memory and experience, a deep satisfying rumble resonating in his mind's eye with evocations of past pleasures. Perhaps the rhythmic repetition of the full vowel 'O' suggested at some intuitive level a sense of completeness, circularity and return. In any event while he spoke little about Moree the mere mention of his homeplace lit up his eyes.

At that time–in the early 1950s–my father's memories of Ireland were still fresh and immediate. He received regular letters from his sister, who still lived at 'Home', telling him about her children, his brother and the latest on friends and neighbours and keeping him up to date with news about his sister in Brooklyn. She'd send huge bunches of shamrock over each year for St Patrick's day and a turkey at Christmas. He took an innocent delight in demonstrating his countryman's skills in plucking its feathers, separating the neck from the body and removing its inner organs–tasks his townie children recoiled from.

Every once in a while my aunt would send over the *Dungannon Observer* which he'd devour at a single sitting and re-read until it fell apart. At that stage the term 'home' for my father meant of course the place where he returned to each day, the place his wife and children were to be found; but 'Home' was where he wasn't–it was where he'd come from and where he wanted to return to–'Home' was 'Tyrone among the bushes', Moree, Knockavaddy, The Rock.

My mother came from the same area of Tyrone, a nearby townland rejoicing in the paradisal title of Edendoit. While she and my father often spoke of their shared background and mutual acquaintances, for her

'Home' was located in the here and now and 'Home' was intimately entwined with the future, while 'home' was to be found in the past.

During the 1950s emigration from Ireland resumed and surpassed its pre-war levels. At that time we were one of the few Irish families in the area to have a modern home equipped with a bathroom. As a result many of the young single Irishmen and women my parents knew through work and the Church visited on Sundays to bath and share the craic–and of course much of the talk was about Ireland, about 'Home' and leaving and returning.

For us children this emphasis on 'Home' by those we loved and admired was both intensely appealing and oddly alienating. It appealed at a primary instinctual level in that it gave us a history. We could make the connections in the narrative of our lives; we could identify and place ourselves in a community which was warm, witty and loving; we could chant almost liturgically the names of uncles, aunts, cousins and neighbours, most of whom we'd never met and many of whom were scattered across the English speaking world. It was a community and an extended family which validated our sense of a separate identity as Catholic, Irish, trans-national and local.

At the same time that involvement in the past of our parents was peculiar and estranging–their 'Home' was theirs–most of us had never been to Ireland. The Ireland we identified with was largely imaginary. It was an Ireland created out of nostalgia, sentimentality and stereotypes constructed and perpetuated both by the immigrant community and our English host society. Communal gatherings served to unite at one level but paradoxically confirmed our differences. References to 'Home', to the past, to those who remained in Ireland could by and large only be couched in politely enquiring terms, a distant kind of engagement which was reinforced aurally by delivery in English accents. In that sense we were there on the fringe, observers and partial participants, hybrids, neither fully English nor fully Irish–the Hiberno-English–a growing and distinct cultural formation which could relate to the communities we came from and the communities we lived in, but, in general, a group which felt most at home with ourselves and those from the English working classes who were, like ourselves, taking advantage of more open educational opportunities.

In later years, due to greater prosperity, the telephone and easier air travel, may of us became familiar with 'Home' and found it disconcerting to be unthinkingly referred to as English by our Hibernian cousins. This created a sense in us that our roots were somewhere just to the south of the Isle of Man–hyphenated Hibernians.

In the 1990s that sense of marginality is no longer embarrassing or disabling. In an increasingly pluralistic post-nationalist context, communication and diaspora, europeanisation and americanisation render Ireland and Irishness into mongrelised concepts. Essences become excrescences; anachronistic and irrelevant. In any case having grown up in an emigrant (or immigrant) community I have unsurprisingly an intense interest in how· my parents, uncles, aunts, cousins, here in Ireland, in England, America, Canada and Australia feel about Ireland, emigration and return and about how those emotions are expressed in everyday forms of communication and in art.

In artistic terms the spirit of Stephen Dedalus/James Joyce permeates this book; while the image of James Stephens, an underestimated genius in his own right, wandering alone and desolate in Trafalgar Square was never far from my mind. Joyce, in my view, towers above all artistic figures and wove his work literally and figuratively out of exile. Stephens, Joyce's nominee to finish *Finnegan's Wake* (a decision often thought of as a Joycean quirk but in reality a shrewd judgement on Joyce's part which acknowledged the knowledge and skill of Stephens) wrote nothing of consequence once he left Ireland in 1924. Thus for some, indeed, many artists, exile/emigration was liberating; for others, like Stephens, it was artistically emasculating.

The artistic and the personal connect for me in Liam O'Flaherty's *Going Into Exile* and *The Letter*, two of the most profoundly affecting things I have ever read. The world they evoke was the world my mother often spoke of; American wakes, convoying, young men disappearing from the fields, letters from America and returning 'Yanks'.

This book began its life as a doctoral thesis. Professor Declan Kiberd at University College Dublin supervised the work and shared with me his love of ideas and effervescent enthusiasm for literature and culture. Tony Crowley helped guide my early thoughts on the shape of the project and provided me with some very helpful advice. Anthony Roche undertook the daunting task of reading the completed text and drew my attention to errors for which I'm very grateful.

I should like to acknowledge a particular debt to my colleagues Austin Logan, Bobby Jennings, Dick Brennan, Brendan Cassidy and Marian Boyle whose active encouragement helped me to complete the work.

The Western Education and Library Board assisted by providing me with study leave. The Library Service of the WELB supported me throughout their endlessly patient efforts tracing books and articles and I am greatly indebted to the staff in Enniskillen Library in particular.

Saoirse Close undertook the unenviable task of reading my hand-writing, typing the text, and amending and correcting errors and revisions with patient professionalism, and I offer her my sincere thanks.

My most profound thanks, however, are expressed in the dedication. In the nature of things journeys undertaken may be metaphorical and literal, imaginative and actual, in any event my journey was inspired and supported by those I most love–and made a lot less lonely for that.

PATRICK WARD
Enniskillen, October 2001

Introduction

Exile is of course as old as written history and as an experience probably as old as existence itself. The very sound of the word 'exile' has embedded with it aural resonances of the primary human conditions of existence, experience, expulsion and excommunication. If we accept as a fundamental premise, the idea that human beings are first and foremost social creatures as opposed to loners and that as a consequence humans developed language to communicate and mediate between one another it follows that separation from the community should be painful. It follows too, that the articulation of that pain in language is an elemental constituent in any account, oral and/or written of that group's narrative of itself.

The concept of exile certainly forms an immensely powerful and enduring element in the tradition of western literature and those literatures which grew out of the european experience. Most foundational texts such as the *Iliad*, the *Odyssey* and the Scriptures deal with threats, separation, journeys and re-formations. Exile viewed metaphorically or literally has profoundly influenced the relationship of innumerable storytellers, artists and writers to their culture and it has contributed to the ways in which they have expressed that relationship in their works. In addition, exile has also profoundly affected the means by which texts are produced, transmitted and received by audiences in different places and at different times. The expectations, assumptions and perceptions of audiences have, in turn, fed the discourses and modes of expression employed–consciously or unconsciously–by writers. This is true whether or not they are categorised as producers of highly esteemed canonical works in the constructed tradition of 'high' culture or producers of less prestigious texts emanating from popular culture, from the folk tradition, or, in more modern times, a commercial tradition.

The idea of exile acquired force in the nineteenth and twentieth centuries as more individualistic philosophies deriving from Romanticism, Nationalism and Capitalism contextualised and shaped the discourses, patterns of action and reaction; and forms of oral and written communication available to cultures and writers.

This book begins by trying to clear the ground and examine how the term exile has been constructed by commentators on Irish writing. It goes on to question traditional perceived notions of artistic exile and to offer an alternative conceptualisation drawing on the work of Edward Said and Kerby Miller.

It argues that the term exile, the affective complex that surrounds it and the ways it is understood, expressed, resisted or ignored in oral and particularly in written forms, is a distinctive and distinguishing feature of Irish literary sensibilities and literary history.

PATRICK WARD

But remember that words are signals, counters. They are not immortal.
and it can happen–to use an image you'll understand–it can happen that
a civilisation can be imprisoned in a linguistic contour which no longer
matches the landscape of ... fact.

Brian Friel *Translations* (London 1981), p. 43

CHAPTER ONE

The Concept of Exile: Critical Constructions

INTRODUCTION

IT MAY be useful here to sketch the outlines of what this chapter attempts to deal with. It is not an attempt to survey the whole field of critical writing dealing with the subject of exile. There are books and articles (many of them originating from Comparative Literature Studies departments of American Universities) which do provide a panoramic historical view of the subject and offer very useful insights into the thematic and stylistic implications of exile.[1]

In broad terms these texts work out of traditions that privilege immanent criticism which in turn owes its ideological provenance to Romanticism, Symbolism and Modernism. They employ critical terms, categories and practices which originate in metropolitan centres and which are concerned with erecting national and international canons. In seeking kinds of archetypal commonality they tend to erase distinctions and minimise the impact of the extant cultural forces which shaped the various modes of thinking and expression available to the authors (almost invariably male) under discussion. They also axiomatically accept the author's self-imaging rhetorical position as an 'exile' and ascribe a romanticised exilic status to those whose absence from their homeland is entirely voluntary, and sometimes to writers who did not describe themselves as exiles at all.

This chapter, however, is more interested in examining a number of representative critical views on the nature of exile as it is used in relation to imaginative writing in the English language by Irish authors rather than to offer an encyclopaedic survey on all of the secondary writings which treat the subject exhaustively or in passing.

It considers a number of works of critical commentary produced by Irish critics and authors since Ireland became independent and continues examining its cultural identity in a post-colonial context. It also reviews literary critical texts produced by American critics and literary historians on Irish writing in English, thereby acknowledging the importance of the input to Irish literary studies of criticism originating in the USA.

The chapter concludes with a consideration of the meaning of the term 'exile', its construction and utilisation within colonial Ireland, and its representation in fictive discourses. To that end it draws on the writings of post-colonial theorists writing about Ireland and other colonised cultures. The text does not attempt to 'universalise' exile but to particularise it in terms of time and place and literary production. Therefore, the weight of emphasis is on the period of most intense cultural contestation in Ireland's social, political and literary history–the period between the Famine and Independence. Underpinning the discussion is the belief that all cultural artefacts and those constructed in language particularly, are the products of specific histories and that forms of feeling, association, expression and representation are always related explicitly and/or implicitly to the cirumstances that pertained at the time of their production. It follows then that while writers may inherit, borrow from, and modify themes and forms in the literary and critical tradition, they are never immune from the discourses and the material circumstances which prevail at the time they are writing. It follows too, that a materially grounded criticism has to look beyond a self-contained and inward looking set of critical practices and draw eclectically on a wider body of cultural criticism which acknowledges in Edward Said's term, the 'worldliness' of all texts.[2]

With that in mind, the book treats a number of 'popular' literary texts with the same level of seriousness as more highly esteemed 'canonical' works. It asserts their importance in the formation and transmission of beliefs and ideas, ways of thinking and expressing in terms of a general consciousness and in terms of their importance, consciously or unconsciously for the creation of 'élite' works.

The critical method adopted throughout this text is with concerned foreground questions dealing with the context out of which the text was produced. It is interested in relating authorship to time, place, prevalent discourses, available forms, codes, conventions, audiences, omissions and representations. It is also concerned with examining how the text was received and also how particular texts inform, cross-pollinate and mutate over time in the consciousness of differing groups.

CRITICAL COMMENTARIES BY IRISH AND AMERICAN WRITERS

Perhaps the most striking feature of an examination of the secondary literature concerned with exile, literature and Ireland over any period is how little there is generally and how little has been written by Irish commentators. An examination for example, of journals such as *The Crane Bag* and *The Irish Review*, both of which have provided forums for intense cultural debate in the recent past, reveal a noticeable neglect of exile and emigration in spite of the fact that it has been and remains a central fact of Irish experience for writers as well as for the population as a whole.

Similarly, a careful reading of bibliographies and chapter headings in otherwise comprehensive standard reference books such as: *The Field Day Anthology of Irish Writing* (1991); *The Macmillan Dictionary of Irish Literature* (1979); *A Short History of Anglo-Irish Literature* (1982, McHugh and Harmon), *Anglo-Irish Literature* (1982, Jeffares); *A Short History of Irish Literature* (1986, Deane); *Irish Literature: A Social History* (1990, Vance) and *Fictions of the Irish Literary Revival* (1987, Foster) shows an almost unanimous disregard of the subject.[3] Indexes to those texts rarely mention the word (except with reference to Joyce's play *Exiles*) and when they do as with Foster's *Fictions of the Irish Literary Revival*, there is a simple equation of the term with departure.

What references there are exist in articles and books which are by and large far more preoccupied with other matters. References to exile, or any of its cognates, are sparse and incidental. Few critics pause to examine the term, its meanings, or its impact thematically or stylistically. Yet the importance of the phenomenon is unquestionable–it has been an enduring and profoundly influential feature of life in Ireland since the time of Colmcille in the sixth century. There is, by contrast, a growing and well documented volume of writing by historians on the subject and a lively debate over its meanings and impact on Irish thought, feelings, and social and economic structures.[4]

In the period dealt with in this book, the population of Ireland fell by half, and as Daniel Corkery points out, the vast majority of writers using English as their principal medium were living elsewhere. In *Synge and Anglo-Irish Literature* (1931), Corkery pursues the narrow exclusivity of 'Irish-Ireland' into the literary sphere. He effectively casts adrift all of those writers then living outside Ireland from any affiliation with Irish culture or an Irish literary condition. The list of writers named ranges from Padraic Colum through Joyce, Austin Clarke, Seumus MacManus,

O'Casey to George Moore and G.B. Shaw.[5] Though later he reinstates Colum along with T.C. Murray to a provisional sense of Irishness on the grounds that they come from the people and not the ascendancy.[6] The Irish national being, he asserts, is different from the English national being in that it is dependent on '(1) The Religious Consciousness of the People (2) Irish Nationalism and (3) The Land'.[7]

In post-Independence Ireland, Corkery was of course staking out the territory for Irish cultural definition and addressing an internal audience of resident Catholic intelligentsia. In detached objective terms this cultural cleansing may be readily challenged and opposed. His argument is crudely selective and dependent on gross oversimplifications and purblind occlusions. A writer using English from an urban background, an atheist, agnostic or Protestant, a socialist or internationalist–in fact any non-resident, is relegated to some other, never defined, non-Irish, limbo of nothingness.

In Corkery's view, literature written in English by Irish (men), whether Protestant or Catholic in background, does not fulfil the demands of a distinctive national literature. It is not representative of the people either in terms of speaking for them or to them. It does not build on and utilise indigenous literary traits and it does not have the support of the nation's critical opinion. He goes on to ask:

> Can Anglo-Irish, then, be a distinctive literature if it is not a national literature? And if it has not primarily been written for Ireland, if it be impossible to refer it to Irish life for its elucidation, if its continued existence or non-existence be independent of Irish opinion–can it be a national literature?[8]

Here he is clearly articulating the narrow concerns of a restricted cultural nationalism which is striving for distinctive signifiers, and which borrows from and customises the preoccupations of nineteenth-century european Romantic nationalism with language, essence, ethnicity and territoriality in the creation of what Benedict Anderson has called an 'imagined community'.[9]

His argument has been vehemently attacked over the years yet the concerns he identified still form part of debates today about the nature of Ireland, Irishness and what constitutes Irish literature or indeed, if there is such a body of work at all. In terms of the concerns of this text he raises a particularly interesting question about the topos of exile. Another indicator of a national literature he argues, is that it is normal for a national literature to be judged by its own people rather than by critics from other cultures. In that sense 'normal and national are synonymous in literary criticism'.[10]

Taking that a stage further he says,

> a normal literature is written within the confines of the country which names it. It is not dependent on expatriates. The literary annals of almost every people will, of course, once in a while give account of their expatriate writers. In these cases the expatriation is hardly ever a life sentence, and expatriation itself is a rare phenomenon in the history of the literature. How different with us! Expatriation is the badge of all the tribe of Anglo-Irish literary men; and in nearly all cases it is a life sentence.[11]

He goes on to identify the reason for writers emigrating which is that the market within Ireland for their products barely exists. But he argues, Irish literary expatriates differ from figures such as Ibsen, Turgenev, Rolland and Unamuno in that they do not write for a home-based readership in the way that other expatriates write for their domestic markets. 'The typical Irish expatriate writer continues to find his matter in Irish Life; his choice of it however, and his treatment of it when chosen, are to a greater or lesser extent, imposed on him by alien considerations'.[12]

Leaving aside the reasons for other non-Irish expatriate writers writing as they did, there are numerous points of interest in his argument and several underlying assumptions which should be challenged. Implicit in his thinking is the notion that all those 'expatriate' writers left Ireland of their own volition in search of a livelihood elsewhere; that what unites–that is their search for a living, their Irish background and their use of the English language as their primary medium of expression–erases all distinctions between them. At no point in his discussion does he differentiate between these writers in terms of class, religion, political allegiance, cultural inheritance or gender. Nor does he attempt to explain where they went or why particular writers went to their various destinations. He also fails to explore and identify the audiences these writers addressed. Furthermore, his assertion that those abroad continue to find their sources in Irish life needs heavy qualification. Wilde, for example, or Shaw may have cultivated attitudes and styles which owed something to their background but little of what they wrote could be said to be 'matter in Irish Life'.

His deliberate choice of the appellation 'expatriate' is interesting however. He quite consciously denies the more highly charged and romanticised term 'exile' when referring to these 'wild geese of the pen'.[13] This opens up for consideration the ways in which those writers who did, for whatever reason, leave Ireland, write about the experiences (if at all) and the ways in which others whether in popular culture or academic criticism, represented their leavetaking, residence abroad and literary output. In conflating real differences between the backgrounds, experiences and intentions of all those who left and in consciously evading the romantic heroisation of the figure of the author, Corkery paradoxically aligns himself with English cultural constructions and perceptions. These saw Ireland as part of the Union and even after Independence as part of the cultural archipelago of Britishness, a province rather than a distinct nation. He makes the point in a footnote[14] that for writers such as Swift, Goldsmith and Shaw 'Ireland was never a *patria* in any sense'. Their home-land he implies, was England, and so too by extension it was the home of all those expatriates he names, regardless of difference, including Joyce.

The chapter continues by locating the development of Anglo-Irish literature in the colonial context of eighteenth and nineteenth-century Ireland and points out that it was produced to amuse a metropolitan audience; that all those books written by the ascendancy folk, 'those representatives of the motherland are nothing but travellers' tales'.[15] The leading theme of this literature has from the start been, 'the decline and fall of an Ascendancy "Big House"'.[16] It is a literature he says, 'all for their motherland, England, by spiritual exiles'.[17] It is a reversal of the usual ascription of the term 'exile' and unusually for Corkery, in the context of this argument, a metaphor-like, indeed hybridised employment of a designation normally associated with Irish Catholics when referring to 'Irish' Protestants.

In bringing to the foreground the colonial conditioning of literature written in English, drawing attention to the state of affairs whereby almost all of those writing in English were working abroad, and by going on to discuss the inchoate and unformed consciousness of a colonised people dispossessed of their language with a yet undeveloped critical autonomy, Corkery raises crucial questions about belonging, identity, authenticity and what David Lloyd refers to as, 'adulteration'.[18] It is in that context that representations are constructed and meanings contested, refuted, evaded, circumscribed and propagated and in that context too, that an examination of the concept of exile and its associated terms must be grounded. This book seeks quite consciously to avoid extended treatment or generalised comparison of the concept as applied to expatriates from uncolonised nation states such as Ibsen, Turgenev, Rolland and Unauno. This also applies to 'exiles' such as those dealt with by more traditional criticism like for example, Ovid, Dante, Conrad, James, Pound and Nabokov.

Corkery was writing at a time when a newly independent, post-partition Irish State was attempting to come to terms with its 'new' identity. Inevitably his thoughts reflect his commitment to the cultural struggle for supremacy and point to an essential cultivation of what he defined as the unique and distinguishing feature of Irish life and thought. The years between the publication of *Synge and Anglo-Irish Literature* and the publication in Dublin in 1950 of Benedict Kiely's *Modern Irish Fiction: A Critique*, saw the emergence of a considerable number of talented writers most of whom, in one way or another, came to oppose the prevailing cultural orthodoxy which imposed a prurient censorship on artistic endeavour and seemed intent on the manufacture of a spurious sense of nostalgia. The place of writers in the period leading up to the publication of Kiely's book has been comprehensively documented in numerous texts.[19] All of these point to the dispiriting narrowness of political, social and cultural life and to the subsequent attempts by writers and other intellectuals to change and resist the philistine and constricting hegemony being erected and enforced throughout the emerging polity.

Kiely, a graduate of the CBS Omagh, UCD, and a Dublin resident (hence a displaced but home-based literary migrant), rejects the distinctions made by Corkery regarding what is Irish or Anglo-Irish as an 'arid debate'.[20] He feels free therefore to devote an extensive chapter to those writers whom he calls 'Exiles'.[21]

He observes how from the time of St Colmcille down through the centuries, 'to the great starvation of the nineteenth century that sent thousands of the Irish wandering the earth, that same note of burning love for an impoverished and tormented country can be heard'.[22] He also notes how easy it would be in 1950 to compile a similar list to the one Corkery put together in 1931 mentioning a substantial number of contemporary writers then living out of Ireland. Unlike Corkery however, Kiely is unwilling to disown those working abroad. He in fact, accepts without any distinction their common right to exilic sentimentality:

> A writer may trace his origins to the peasants on the rocks of Aran, like Liam O'Flaherty or to the relics of the landed classes, like Elizabeth Bowen, or to the section of Ireland moulded by Trinity College, like L.A.G. Strong, or to Catholic Dublin, like James Joyce; he may abuse the island and stay away from the island but all the time the basic feeling is the nostalgia that has produced a hundred sentimental ballads.[23]

He continues by advocating that far from dwelling on the evils of 'expatriation':

> A small country with a minute reading population and limited publishing

opportunities should accustom itself to the idea of a very considerable
emigration of writers.[24]

The sentiments expressed by Kiely evince a generous catholicity to
all those abroad. He demonstrates an open-armed inclusiveness which
stands in obvious contrast to the attitudes of Corkery. He does not
however, exhibit any awareness of or accept any difference between the
terms 'exile', 'expatriation' or 'emigration'; they are used interchangeably
throughout. The first section of the chapter concludes with a rather more
overt and explicit recognition of the ambivalence which characterises the
concept of exile. This occurs when he alludes to centuries of nationalism
and emigration colluding to 'create the vague popular idea that an Irish
writer who lives out of Ireland has something nasty in common with
Carey the informer'.[25]

That often unspoken and unexpressed perception frequently exists also
as a residual deposit in the consciousness of those who left. This results in
an internalised dialogue between guilt and need, inhibition and ambition,
the pull of the hearth and the enticement of an enlarged and freer
existence. Kiely devotes little space to Joyce, the most celebrated of literary
exiles, and exhibiting a paradoxical, even contradictory elasticity says of
him:

> His country had not driven him into exile but he had deliberately chosen
> exile from the country and the creed in which he was born because he
> considered that exile necessary to his art.[26]

The most interesting discussion in the chapter however is devoted to
Seán Ó Faoláin, 'an Irish exile living at home'.[27] The chapter goes on to
deal with two texts of Ó Faoláin's *She Had To Do Something* (1937) and *Come
Back to Erin* (1940). Both are ostensibly concerned with people displaced
in some fashion which leads him to consider Ó Faoláin's uncomfortable
relationship with the state and culture. He sees Ó Faoláin as different from
other contemporaneous Irish writers such as Corkery, McLaverty and
MacManus who have 'never for a moment shown any signs of feeling
separated from their people'.[28] Ó Faoláin by contrast, feels intensely
nostalgic but estranged from the people. He is 'halfways to being an
exile',[29] and in Corney Crone the central figure of *Bird Alone* (1936), Ó
Faoláin has created one of 'the classical stories of exile–the exile of a man
from his people, of the soul in the world, the loneliness of the soul when
it is doubtful of God'.[30] He is for Kiely, 'that symbol of a revolutionary
without a revolution, of the exile from Erin who keeps on living in Erin

and thus sharpening the pain of exile because he has sacrificed the senti-mental memories that have consoled the generations of Paddies on the road to Philadelphia in the morning'.[31]

Kiely briefly alludes to Ó Faoláin's leading role as an opponent of censorship and to the provincial pettiness of Irish life as editor of *The Bell*; and possibly he has in mind biographies such as, *The Great O'Neill* (1942) which attacked the mythic pieties of the de Valeran settlement. The space he devotes to this 'inner-exile' and the warmth with which he writes suggests a genuine admiration for Ó Faoláin's iconoclasm and artistic integrity. It is as though he, Kiely, is applauding Ó Faoláin as a surrogate existential hero. In doing so he is perhaps unconsciously drawing attention to, celebrating and ironically deploying a trope long embedded in Irish Catholic and Gaelic symbology–the lonely guerilla of traditional resis-tance to military and proselytising Protestantism; the proscribed priest of penal times; the tory raider and the scholar poet of Gaelic poetic tradition. And in explicit association (though equivocal equation of Ó Faoláin and Modernism) he simultaneously and implicitly links him to twentieth-century ideas of artistic estrangement and alienation.

The chapter continues with a brief discussion of Kate O'Brien and her work. In reflecting on her role as an exile and referring to her novel *Pray for the Wanderer* (1938) he says:

> The result was more a pamphlet of protest than a nostalgic novel about the exile's pain of deprivation.[32]

Her evident refusal to acknowledge the patterns of exilic sentiment can for Kiely, only be reconciled on the symbolic plane when her image of herself as a 'homeless, evicted troglodyte' is equated improbably with Frankie Hannafy from Ó Faoláin's *Come Back to Erin*, the 'revolutionary without a revolution', as 'symbols of exile'.[33] Kiely is forcibly misrepre-senting O'Brien here to insist on compliance with his argument, which raises intriguing issues regarding female representation and authorship in the discourse of exile as well as residence in England.

His all-inclusive and all-purpose conceptualisation of exile extends to include Peadar O'Donnell, Patrick MacGill and Seamus Ó Grianna whose work deals with migratory and seasonal labourers in Britain. He refers to them as 'temporary exiles'.[34] It is a vital and neglected category for it poses queries about centre and periphery, short-term migratory labour, dual residence and exile and has, in the imaginative and in the secondary commentary been dealt with in a very ambiguous manner. In fact it is rare for any text produced in that particular period to refer to residence in

Britain as 'exile', at least in any meaningful and deeply felt way. His use of the term in this context signals perhaps, a shift in exilic imaginings and a loosening and slackening of applied meaning and categorisation.

Towards the end of the chapter he claims that 'There is hardly an Irish writer who does not touch somewhere on the exile or the idea of exile',[35] which in the broadest sense is true, but indiscriminate. It is true of course, if exile is figuratively applied to any author at any time, under any circumstances, who leaves Ireland and/or writes about the experience referentially or elliptically. It is also true if one considers the effect on those who remain in Ireland in terms of the emptiness they inhabit and the inevitable explicit or implicit dialogism which occurs between absence and presence. The point is illustrated albeit unintentionally, in his comments on writers who deal with returners, 'Yanks' or travellers, a much employed device to 'explain' Ireland to an uncomprehending, usually English, audience (and itself a distinctive feature of most colonial literatures).

In taking issue with Frank O'Connor's scathing criticism of and hostility to Ireland he enacts the pivotal tension between a home-based writer and one who has left. He suggests that O'Connor's conclusions in *Irish Miles* (1947) and *The Common Chord* (1947) are 'like pus from his own wounded sensibilities',[36] and that:

> Perhaps continuous material exile might have been better for Frank O'Connor, except that it would have separated him from the only material in which he has worked. His form of spiritual exile has something in it of the mentality of a boy living for years in a large house with rich relatives and then returning home to find that the house that shelters his people is a small, dark, poky place. He is so horrified by the defects in the house that he cannot see any of the genuine merits of his people.[37]

O'Connor's inescapable need for Ireland and Kiely's unavoidable kinship and entanglement with the community of Irish writers abroad mirrors the 'relentless reciprocity'[38] of the relationship between the coloniser and the colonised. Hidden beneath that strained bonding is perhaps the unspoken resentment of a writer who, when he did work elsewhere chose to work in America, against a writer who lived mainly in England and dared to voice his criticism from the (former) imperial centre. This was a form of betrayal unacceptable to one immersed in the nexus of Irish, and Irish-American cultural relationships.

The final category Kiely identifies, the Anglo-Irish, is represented by Elizabeth Bowen, Christine Longford and Francis Stuart. They too are prone to the same feelings of nostalgia and longing as those other representatives of the spectrum of Irish society and the artistic community.

His concluding remarks which suggest that 'the strongest force in the Irish soul is centripetal'[39] assume that there is such an entity or essence as the Irish soul–something pure, unique, quintessentially distilled by the experience of birth, spiritual inheritance and upbringing; an indelibility which marks out the Irish people from all the other peoples of the earth. That assumption effectively erases difference, history and culture, it articulates and echoes what Deane calls, 'the mystique of Irishness'.[40] It also effectively incorporates the whole linguistic and affective domain of 'exile' into that process of mythicism. Furthermore, it establishes and reinforces the simplistic sentiments, postures and vocabulary which almost all writings on the subject of literature, 'exile' and Ireland employ and inscribe both retrospectively and contemporaneously.

It is also remarkable how few of these individual souls made manifest in corporeal form, felt the centripetal pull sufficiently powerfully to actually return to live in Ireland on a permanent basis.

Like Kiely, Peter Costello, in *The Heart Grown Brutal: The Irish Revolution in Literature, from Parnell to the Death of Yeats, 1891–1939* (1978) rejects the atavistic monologism of Corkery in favour of a liberal pluralism, which accepts, in effect, all who were born and reared in Ireland as Irish. In doing so, he attempts a redefinition of the term 'expatriates' as used by Corkery:

> Those writers whom Corkery called 'expatriates' might have preferred to call themselves 'exiles', for among them were George Moore, James Joyce and Gerald O'Donovan. There is a psychological difference between the two states of mind: an expatriate is someone who sloughs off his country like an old skin; an exile, on the other hand, however far he may go, has his country always on his mind.[41]

He concludes his observations on the nature of exile so:

> Exile has always been an honourable fate in Ireland. From Columcille to James Joyce, those who left for other countries, might have echoed the saint's words: 'my mind is upon Erin, upon all the little places where my people are'. This old sense of exile dominates the mood of Irish writing after the revolution, in both the young and the old.[42]

The following two chapters are then entitled, 'Going into Exile (1): Drama and Poetry: Realistic Romanticism', and 'Going into Exile' (2) The New Novel: Romantic Realism'. Costello spends some time sketching in the background to the 1920s and 1930s and in the first of the two chapters deals primarily with O'Casey and Yeats. O'Casey after the rejection of *The Silver Tassie* (1928) he asserts, 'vowed to separate himself completely from the Abbey and from Ireland. He went to live in Devon, to become an exile. All writers are exiles of a kind, but a sense of exile does seem to permeate the slow dying fall of the Revival'.[43]

Apart from his simplistic and uncritical acceptance of O'Casey's obfuscatory myth-making concerning his arguments with Yeats and his departure from Ireland, Costello in the same manner as Kiely, substitutes 'exile' for any form of departure. His comments on Yeats' 'sense of exile'[44] and references to an 'internal state of exile'[45] flaccidly fail to engage with the constructions and deployment of the terms. While his definition of an expatriate is simply unsustainable, if we consider writers from England who wrote about their experiences in the Empire or those Americans who relocated themselves in Europe such as James, Hemingway and Fitzgerald. Far from 'sloughing off' their inherited ideological and experiential baggage, they took it with them everywhere and absorbed ideas and experiences from their host societies into what they already were. No doubt that process may have formulated a different consciousness than would have been the case had they remained at home, but no one can simply wipe out the matrix of feelings, values and attitudes they bring with them into adulthood.

There are serious questions to ask of the term 'expatriate' in a colonised or post-colonial society and within an imperial system concerning place and time. An examination of Corkery's list will reveal that some of those mentioned saw themselves as expatriates from England; others viewed themselves as expatriates from Ireland, some gravitated towards different metropolitan centres and not all considered themselves as exiles. Nevertheless, in highlighting the difference between exile and expatriation and the psychology inherent in those conceptualisations, Costello implicitly locates those concepts in culture. However, simply substituting 'exile' for 'expatriate' replaces one unitary and absolute categorisation and way of thinking, for another.

Most general histories of Irish writing and intellectual life work within the same loose linguistic framework. Absence is described in very similar terms by McHugh and Harmon, Jeffares, Deane, Cairns and Richards, Vance, and Goldring.[46] In much the same way the term is accepted unproblematically throughout the contributions to a recent volume of essays entitled, *Irish Writing: Exile and Subversion* (1991).[47]

American academics also take the term at its face value. James M. Cahalan applies the word liberally throughout *The Irish Novel* (1988) without pausing to consider its relevance or applicability. Charles Fanning entitles his anthology of nineteenth-century Irish-American fiction, *The Exiles of Erin* (1987) without further explanation or qualification, and Richard Fallis in *The Irish Renaissance: An Introduction to Anglo-Irish Literature* (1978) labels a chapter devoted to Anglo-Irish poetry from 1923 to 1940, 'Doors Open On Exile'.[48] He acknowledges that most of the poets dealt with in the chapter–F.R. Higgins, Yeats, Austin Clarke and Patrick Kavanagh–did the best of their work while in Ireland, but then goes on to muse on the nature of exile:

> Yet exile is a state of mind as well as a state of the body, and every valuable Irish poet in this period became some sort of exile.[49]

Higgins he claims, exiled himself in the West of Ireland, in the Yeatsian, Celtic Twilight. Some of the younger poets of the 1930s exiled themselves in the world of Modernism (Beckett, Devlin, McGreevy and Coffey presumably). Yeats exiled himself 'in his imagination',[50] Clarke in medieval Ireland and Kavanagh 'when he wandered off from the pubs to the banks of the Grand Canal, found exile and himself'.[51] He concludes:

> The fullness of the exile chosen was in direct proportion to the fullness of the poetic vision accepted and the final greatness of the achievement.[52]

An argument which is self-fulfilling in its circularity it seems to be saying that the great writers are great exiles or that the most significant writers are those who are most fully estranged. In this particular discursive formation exile is optional, even a matter of degree. The artist is the originator of his (*sic*) own exilic creation and the perpetuator of his own self-made myth. On the other hand the critic, the assessor of achievement, takes as a key index in his evaluative range of indices the distance a writer puts between himself and the society from which he emerged.

As with Kiely, Costello and previous critics referred to, Fallis feels no need to ask what exile is, what forms it takes, or why it is accepted as apodictically self-evident. It seems reasonable to assume that he, like the critics referred to earlier, is working out of a critical tradition which sees its role primarily as explication, exegesis and evaluation. It is moreover, a tradition which tends to accept the myths of artistic creation, genius and difference arising out of Romanticism and Symbolism. In the case of Cahalan, Fallis and a large number of American commentators there is also an additional contributory element to their attitudes. This is inherited from the ways in which the Catholic Irish-Americans imaged and represented their departure from Ireland–invariably as exiles–and the needs of Irish literary studies within the American academy.

George O'Brien, an Irish academic and writer working within an American university, has written elegantly in this vein in his essay 'The Muse of Exile: Estrangement and Renewal in Modern Irish Literature' (1988).[53] He sees exile as a 'movement–essentially of the mind'. It 'proceeds from absence to realisation, from estrangement to intimacy'[54] which he claims, links Joyce and Yeats. He says:

> The consciousness of the Irish artist, as embodied jointly by Yeats and Joyce, is estranged from the reality that is its subject. Indeed, if that reality–the constituent elements of which are cultural, political, racial, historical and religious–is to be apprehended artistically, a condition of withdrawal, displacement, and alienation must be undergone.[55]

They, like their successors Francis Stuart, Denis Devlin, Flann O'Brien and Thomas Kinsella 'are united–quite possibly, against their will–in the history of a posture. They are all the more brothers-in-art by virtue of the formal strategies and accidents of temperament that individuate them'.[56] His argument continues with reference to the Censorship of Publications Act of 1929; a piece of legislation which 'confirmed all Irish writers as Shelleyan "unacknowledged legislators" speaking, in Yeats' phrase "the language of the outlaw" and constituting by virtue of their heterodoxy, a government in exile'.[57]

O'Brien effectively elides the terms outlaw, withdrawal, displacement, alienation and estrangement in pursuit of a monological, overarching, historically transcendent, artistic unity which establishes a brotherhood-of-art, set against the quotidian philistinism of Irish life.

A very similar mind-set informs Hallvard Dahlie's, 'Brian Moore and the Meaning of Exile' (1988).[58] This paper, presented to the Canadian Association for Irish Studies, begins with a brief discussion of the terms exile, émigré and expatriate. He finds exile to be the most inclusive and useful of the three. Émigré when applied to writers refers to those compelled to leave their homeland for political or ideological reasons. They are free to return to practise their art when more favourable conditions arise. Should they remain within their host society and adapt to its customs and community they then become, in effect, indigenous to that society.

Expatriates are distinguished by the temporary nature of their absence from home. 'They are little more than extended tourists who leave their homeland temporarily because they believe that certain possibilities for living or for art are more favourable elsewhere'.[59]

The paper then proceeds with an absolutist definition of exile which would certainly exclude writers such as Brecht and Alexander Solzhenitsyn from any exilic pantheon:

> Exile is a process which both in its genesis and in its unfolding is irreversible, and there is a kind of inescapable definition that controls this term: because this displaced individual continues to be at odds with both the world he has rejected and the one he has moved into, he remains physically, spiritually, and intellectually an exile forever.[60]

Quoting a distinction made by Brian Moore between the writer in exile and the writer as exile; he equates the émigré and the expatriate with the former state of being, and the latter with a position where the writer 'is permanently an outsider'.[61] Given Moore's freedom to travel, to visit or to live in Ireland as he chose, (a right all Irish writers have had throughout the period of the nineteenth and twentieth centuries), Dahlie can only apply this definition as a metaphor. It leaves unanswered supplementary considerations such as whether the role of 'outsider' is self-ascribed, imposed by the community he inhabits, or the one he has left. In addition, it recasts the writer solipsistically as his one and only begetter; a product of his own imagination, unknown and unknowable, (except presumably by such acolytes as Dahlie), a self-sufficient isolate and a hero of consciousness.

The essay 'Emigration and Exile' (1988)[62] by Chris Curtin, Riana O'Dwyer and Georóid Ó Tuathaigh tantalisingly reviews literature and the theme of emigration as an additional section to a more general historical review of the nature and impact of emigration on Ireland over the past one hundred and fifty years. They do not however, take the opportunity to fully integrate an examination of 'literature' with the phenomenon of mass emigration. Their treatment of imaginative writing is in fairly conventional literary critical terms. This tends to isolate the artist and the artistic community from the discourses surrounding cultural and social circumstances and formations.

They offer a useful breakdown of the principal ways in which writers have dealt with the theme of exile and suggest that there are four 'phases of relationship to Ireland, within the context of the exile theme'. First of all, there is 'the exploration of Irish identity' which involves an examination of community and attachment to place. Secondly, a 'contrary theme of alienation and separation'.[63] Thirdly, there is the literature written outside Ireland which strives for objectivity and integrity and which also deals with the effect of separation on those who have departed.

The fourth category is concerned with return; and within this cycle of departure and return may be included those texts which concern themselves with internal exile and return to the homeplace.

The remainder of the essay goes on to illustrate this typology and refers mainly to prose, poems and plays written since Independence. As with almost all of the critical texts referred to in this survey of the secondary literature, Curtin et al. simply fuse the terms exile and emigration and assume an identity of meaning between exile, emigration, alienation, separation and isolation. They also assume that exile may be 'self-imposed'.[64]

The essay offers a succinct restatement of the range of relationships embodied within the discourse of Irish exile and literature, and it encapsulates types of experience described by Benedict Kiely very neatly. It does not however, historicise the language used and in eliding the various cognates within the linguistic community it acknowledges kinship, but fails to respect etymology and specificity.

Throughout the whole discursive field, but particularly within the secondary literature there is an overwhelming and uncritical obeisance to the image of the artist as an exile. The language is applied like a palimpsest over virtually all of late nineteenth and twentieth-century imaginative literature. In fact, taking the typology outlined by Curtin et al., it would be extraordinarily difficult to find an Irish writer, male or female, who could not be described as an exile whether or not they thought of and described themselves as such.

It is as though the commentaries are in such awe of the images, representations and stereotypes of individuals, artists and resistance, which were seized, manipulated and represented during the period and immediately afterwards, that they can only obey and proselytise. They seem not only to acquiesce in acceptance of the self-created images of exile, particularly the posture adopted by Joyce, but to propagate those constructions to encompass the whole differentiated and diverse body of fictive writing produced by Irish writers. In applying this kind of totalising and canalising perceptual framework they impose a spurious unity on genuine difference. They efface variety to create in the critical sphere, a kind of epistemological and interpretive fusion which aims to transcendentally harmonise diversity. It is an hibernicised version of the Republic of Letters standing against the twentieth century's morass of crass vulgarisation and insensitivity.

If all Irish artists are exiles they form a community separate from the real class, religious, political, cultural and gender differences which mark

Irish life. They are made to unite in adversity and in effect, they are realigned with the occidental diaspora of artistic exiles in an aesthetic opposition to nationalism and bourgeois materialism–Irish yet somehow above, detached from, and superior to, indigenous Ireland.

ALTERNATIVE VIEWS OF EXILE

Numerous commentators have drawn attention to the contributions made to western culture by displaced artists and intellectuals–whether described as exiles, émigrés or refugees in the twentieth century.[65] Many fled the threats of fascism, communism and authoritarianism. Large numbers found their way to America and consciously or unconsciously reinforced and perpetuated romantic individualism and its associated connotations, which clustered around the notion of the lonely exile, thereby affecting American perceptions and reproductions of the image.

Edward Said, himself a displaced Palestinian and Professor of Comparative Literature at Columbia University, has written sensitively on the subject of displacement, deracination, exile and what he calls 'filiation' and 'affiliation'–the relationship of the author to his homeplace and its culture and to other, sometimes non-national cultures.[66] His essay 'The Mind of Winter: Reflections on life in exile' (1984)[67] begins with a definition:

> Exile is the unhealable rift forced between a human being and a native place, between the self and its true home. The essential sadness of the break can never be surmounted.[68]

It has such prominence in the twentieth century because of its scale, modern warfare and imperialism. The 'quasi theological ambitions of totalitarian rulers' have created 'the age of the refugee, the displaced person, mass immigration'. He takes issue with the view that exile is somehow heroic, romantic or 'a spur to humanism or to creativity'. Such a view he suggests, is to 'belittle its mutilations'. To fully comprehend exile he believes, it is necessary to 'map territories of experience beyond those mapped by literature. It is necessary to set aside Joyce and Nabokov and even Conrad, who wrote of exile with such pathos, but of exile without cause or rationale'.[69]

The essay continues with a reflection on nationalism and exile, pointing out how all nationalisms have their own histories, heroes, canonical texts, versions of truth, lies and enemies. Just outside that nationalist construct is 'the perilous territory of not belonging'. The terms nationalism and exile are inextricably entwined he asserts. Neither can be discussed objectively on its own 'Because both terms include everything from the most collective of collective sentiments to the most private of private emotions, there is no language adequate for both, and certainly there is nothing about nationalism's public and all inclusive ambitions that touches the truth of the exile's predicament'.[70]

In locating the affective complex surrounding the concept of exile in actual social, emotional and cultural conditions and at the same time drawing attention to the ambivalence, inadequacy and interdependence of the idea with a wider set of meanings, which may exist 'contrapuntally', Said detaches exilic discourse from the vaguely idealist and ethereal constructions which image all displaced people, artists and intellectuals in particular, as exiles.

He offers some distinction between the various terms frequently utilised in the lexicon of exile. An exile he says, is a person who is 'prevented' from returning home. He associates exile with banishment in this case and it carries with it a 'touch of solitude and spirituality'. The idea of the refugee he points to as a twentieth-century creation. It has political connotations, suggesting large numbers of 'innocent and bewildered people' requiring assistance. Émigrés by contrast are people who emigrate to a new country–choice characterises their condition rather than banishment. Similarly, expatriates 'voluntarily live in an alien country usually for personal and social reasons'. He names Hemingway and Fitzgerald as examples. In the context of the line taken in this text his elaboration on the term 'expatriates', is pivotal. He say: 'Expatriates may share in the solitude and estrangement of exile, but they do not suffer under its rigid prescription'.[71]

This attentive distinction regarding the difference in experience when applied to Irish writers and intellectuals and the leaving of Ireland is particularly helpful in 're-reading' Irish writing and examining its (re)-formations and imagery. It is assumed throughout therefore, that there are similarities between exile and expatriation; that there is a degree of overlap and that the two conditions may give rise to patterns of thought, behaviour, themes and forms which are culturally specific formulations of common exilic perceptions and reactions. That understanding however, rests on the belief that writing in the English language produced out of the circumstances of Ireland, which utilises the imagery and narrative strategies commonly characterising exile–whether it be imaginative, critical or historiographical–does so metaphorically.

Said draws attention to some of the features and implications of exile for those who conceive of themselves as exiles. The new world of the exile he claims, is unnatural–and its 'unreality resembles fiction'. Using the arguments of George Lukacs, he asserts that the novel is *the* form of 'transcendental homelessness'.[72] He also maintains that the european novel emerges from instability and changing circumstances in which the principal character attempts to create a new world that resembles his/her former home. The novel as opposed to the epic 'exists because other worlds may exist, alternatives for bourgeois speculators, wanderers, exiles. No matter how well they may do, exiles are always eccentrics who *feel* their differences (even as they frequently exploit it) as a kind of orphanhood'. They may exhibit characteristics such as 'the right to refuse to belong', intransigence, willfulness, exaggeration and overstatement. They also lack composure and serenity. 'Artists in exile' he says, 'are decidedly unpleasant, and their stubbornness insinuates itself into even their exalted works'.[73]

The literature of exile he goes on to argue, draws on the 'Christian and humanistic tradition of redemption through loss and suffering'[74] wherein exile has to be endured prior to a restoration of identity and achievement of a better existence. It is also implied that even those who are not exiled may benefit redemptively. He focuses too on the fundamental human need for a sense of rootedness and warns against 'the kind of narcissistic masochism that resists all efforts at amelioration, acculturation and community. At this extreme, the exile can make a fetish of exile, a practise that distances him or her from all connections and commitments'.[75]

In more positive terms he notes that the exile is uniquely gifted with the insight into at least two cultures. This gives rise to a plurality of vision which creates 'an awareness of simultaneous dimensions'. He concludes his essay in the following manner:

> Exile is life led outside habitual order. It is nomadic, decentred, contrapuntal, but no sooner does one get accustomed to it than its unsettling force erupts anew.[76]

There is a great deal here which resonates with Irish experience in terms of the postures he describes and attitudes exhibited by Irish writers. There is a very obvious tendency by artists to refashion their natal communities and memories fictively and to stand apart from the communities they find themselves resident in after leaving Ireland. There is also, a similar doubleness of vision which may well be explicitly worked out, but is frequently implied dialogically rather than fully and openly stated. His comments on the Christian and humanist traditions and rootedness have particular force when applied to Irish culture. However, they are equally applicable to a consideration of emigration as they are to a study of exile and just as relevant to the consciousness of those who left in droves as well as to those whose self-appointed artistic mission led them to leave.

Literary critical tradition has by and large ignored popular culture within Ireland. There is as we know, a huge critical industry devoted to those canonised as the leading literary figures of the early twentieth century–most notably Yeats, Synge, Joyce and O'Casey. They have been dealt with exhaustively by creative artists operating as critics and by an enormous international community of academics. By contrast, little attention has been paid by this particular interpretive community to texts produced by 'popular' writers. Not much secondary literature exploring the relationship(s) between specific historical moments, cultural formations, discourses, popular literature and 'élite' culture exists either. This is especially true concerning the field of emigration/exile and literature.

Traditional critical treatment of the subject links exile with canonical literary figures. When it mentions emigration, which is rare, it is usually only in passing and it is treated as a minor theme applied to minor characters. It is necessary to look elsewhere therefore, for serious and sustained exploration of the connectedness of emigration, exile and literature within Irish thought and tradition.

There is a growing body of historiographical work on the experience of emigration from Ireland[77] which often refers to literary texts for purposes of illustration and notes with brief comment that Irish emigrants viewed their departure as 'exile'. The American historian Kerby Miller has gone beyond those relatively superficial and tentative observations to explore in depth why emigrants to America in the pre-Famine period and most significantly in post-Famine times, viewed themselves as exiles. His investigations and thesis are chronicled in his monumental *Emigrants and Exiles: Ireland and the Irish Exodus to North America* (1985),[78] a work of cultural analysis as much as a work of linear or narrative history. He has extracted and rewritten his central thesis in essay form as 'Emigration, Capitalism and Ideology in Post-Famine Ireland'(1990).[79]

Miller's ideas provide a very helpful cultural context within which to study literary treatment of the subject. It is a context moreover, in which the insights of Said may be grounded and made specific and the formation of the literary critical concept of exile and its treatment in imaginative works may be examined. He notes the scale of Irish emigration during the second half of the nineteenth century and the modernising commercial imperatives such as: the decline of cottage industries, crop failures, falling prices, impartible inheritance, consolidation of holdings and so on. These contributed both to the expansion of the Catholic middle classes and to movement away from the land to urban centres within Ireland, Britain and the industrial centres of the USA.

He also describes how the interpretation of these migrations and specifically the movement to North America was viewed by Catholics as 'involuntary expatriation' or exile and attributed to colonial oppression in the form of British malevolence, the tyranny of landlords and Protestant ascendancy. This misperception, he argues,

> was integral to Catholic Irishmen's sense of individual and collective identity and most important, it was crucial for maintaining 'social stability'and bourgeois hegemony in a Catholic society whose capitalist institutions and social relationships made mass lower-class emigration imperative.[80]

The idea of emigration as exile he explains, had deep roots in the Irish literary and historical tradition. Gaelic poets, he says, usually used the word 'deoraí', which literally means exile, to describe anyone who left for whatever reason. It was obviously applicable to those who left under the pressure of defeat, banishment and proscription in the conflicts of the seventeenth and eighteenth centuries; those whose departure was lamented as the 'Flight of the Earls' and the 'Flight of the Wild Geese' in poetry of the time and in subsequent historiographical and literary re-tellings. For later generations of Irish Catholics, still living under the dispensation of the descendants of those victors in an era of rampant nationalism, the O'Neill and Sarsfield figures provided heroic models of dignity in defeat and emblematic hopes of recovery, return and restitution. Furthermore, he asserts that the Irish language makes definite distinctions between active and passive states of being. It classifies a broader 'range of phenomena into an area in which action and self-assertion are inappropriate'. Emigrants described their decision to leave in impersonal and non-volitional terms. Thus, the common form employed by emigrants translates as 'I *had* to go to America' or 'going to America was a necessity for me'.

That linguistic categorisation of emigration as exile was reinforced, he argues by a

> prevalent tendency in the traditional Irish Catholic worldview to devalue individual action, ambition, and the assumption of personal responsibilities–especially when actions, such as emigration, seemed innovative and

threatening to customary patterns of behaviour and thought which enjoined, by example and precept, passive or communal values such as duty, continuity and conformity.

The Irish Catholic community he goes on to say, in both pre- and post-conquest periods, was 'hierarchical, communal, familial and traditional'. The Church's structures and demands reinforced secular constraints which diminished scope for individual and independent thought or action. That general view of emigration as exile he continues, masked the 'contradictions and tensions which characterised a society in rapid transition'.[81] It allowed for a transference and displacement of responsibility, from those who benefited within the emergent Catholic hegemony, onto the traditional figures of repression. Traditional ways of categorising and thinking thus externalised and 'explained' the disruptive forces of modernity without creating conflicts within Catholic families, communities and institutions.

Miller argues that 'compromises between tradition and innovation were psychological necessities' and that the various ideological representations of those compromises were determined by the needs of the post-Famine, the strong farmer type of rural family, the Catholic Church in its devotional revolution mode and by Irish nationalism. Each of these essentially modern social institutions 'demanded absolute conformity and proscribed deviations as familial ingratitude, religious apostasy, or even national treason'.[82] They needed to regenerate the old trope of emigration as exile to obviate and deflect responsibility for mass emigration, from its beneficiaries (within what Joseph Lee calls 'the possessing classes')[83] onto their rhetorical others, the British and the Protestant Irish.

His essay goes on to deal with the resultant tensions, ambivalence and contradictions in this Catholic nationalist conceptualisation of 'exile'. He registers the recognition among some Catholic leaders that poverty necessitated emigration, and the way in which this was imaged glorified those emigrants as 'holy missionaries', fulfilling a 'divine destiny'.[84] But most clerics viewed the flight from Ireland negatively. They regretted their loss of power over the emigrants and at the same time saw emigration as tragic and threatening to the emigrant's physical and spiritual well-being. America was seen as a godless, materialistic antithesis to Ireland where innocent young Irish men and more particularly young women, would be corrupted, shamed and degraded. Some blamed the emigrants themselves for their selfishness in deserting Ireland while most priests and nationalists recognised the material benefits which derived from the emigrant trade, from remittances and Irish-American support for church building and opposition to England. Catholic and nationalist perceptions of history which stressed British attempts to 'exterminate' the native population, politicised the issue in terms of colonial relationships. This reinforced the imagery of exile, the sense of loss, the antagonism towards their enemies and the sense of guilt and obligation of those who contemplated leaving.

Catholic nationalism, Miller continues, led to the ideological construction of a 'semimythical holy Ireland'[85] fashioned out of what England (and the USA) was not. Holy Ireland was spiritual as opposed to materialistic, conservative as opposed to modern, agricultural and rural as opposed to industrial and urban. It celebrated hierarchy, stasis, organicism, it prized patriarchy, purity and piety and it opposed 'landlordism, Protestantism, secularism, socialism'.[86] It demanded ideological policing through control of education, reading matter and resistance to anglicising influences and in such an edenic formation, the desire to leave could only be explained in terms of wilful betrayal, stupidity, or British oppression. Thus, the anger and frustration of those 'forced' to leave could be refocused onto others and their feelings for Ireland retained intact and even intensified by their exile.

For Miller, the importance of the motif

> lay in its symbolic resolution of the discrepancies between the reality of social fragmentation and the ideal of organic community. After all, if England could yet be blamed for emigration's causes, for the inability of 'holy Ireland' to support all her children, then both the emigrants and those who profited by their departures could be absolved of culpability while the consequent resentments against England could themselves reinforce the outlooks and allegiances which held Catholic Ireland together in the place of the disintegrative and potentially demoralising effects of commercialisation and anglicisation.[87]

At a time when literacy in the English language was expanding rapidly; when relatively new mass markets were developing in the Irish diaspora; when mass production methods of print communication were making Irish and Irish-American producers less dependent on English material sources; and against a background of emergent mass democracy, nationalism and massive emigration, literature whether 'popular' or 'élite', could hardly but be implicated and engaged in the dominant discourses of cultural nationalism. Miller's thesis therefore, whether or not accepted in its entirety, strips bare the ideological processes at work in nineteenth and early twentieth-century Ireland and provides a valuable contextual framework within which literary texts may be situated and scrutinised. Nevertheless, the cultural and historical frame he provides needs to be widened for the purposes of this study, to allow for consideration of the Irish in Britain and the literary inter-relationships of Irish writers with the traditions, themes and forms available in the English language. The argument also aims to take acccount of borrowings from continental Europe as well as the means by which literary loans from both Europe and England translated and mutated into Irish idioms, literary sensibilities and written expression.

In rendering historic and documenting the (re)formations of the language of exile and highlighting its uses, abuses and ambiguities, Miller has outlined the centripetal, monologising tendencies of Catholic national-ist thought and linguistic behaviour which attempted to impose con-straints and imperatives in the service of pro 'Holy Ireland' and 'Irish Ireland' aspirations, values and lacunae. And of course, it was a tense and contested ideological and linguistic arena; inhabited not just by politicians and churchmen but by writers too. Many chose to reinforce the imagery of exile in support of nationalist and anti-colonial aims; others sought to challenge and redefine exilic definitions and classifications and to promote the centrifugal heteroglossia implicit in artistic choice and individualism in opposition to the univocal impulses of communal conformity.

CONCLUSION

Homi Bhabha in his essay 'DissemiNation: time, narrative, and the margins of the modern nation' (1990)[88] has written, 'how fully the shadow of the nation falls on the condition of exile'[89] and of how we need to be 'alive to the metaphoricity of the peoples of imagined communities–migrant or metropolitan' in order to see that, 'the space of the modern national people is never simply horizontal. Their metaphoric movement requires a kind of "doubleness" in writing; a temporality of representation that moves between cultural formations and social processes without a "central" causal logic'.[90]

In introducing his reflections he refers to Said's concept of 'worldliness' and Fredric Jameson's notion of 'situational consciousness'.[91] Both con-cepts locate cultural consciousness in specific times and particular geo-graphic locations. In examining the idea of exile, then within the context of an emergent nationalism, the interpreter is enjoined to attend to the conditions that prevailed at the time within Ireland; to examine the residual cultural sedimentation of contributory indigenous tropes, motifs and forms as well as those absorbed, borrowed and adapted for internal use from other cultural formations.

Miller's analysis articulates the longevity and mutability of the idea of exile in the Gaelic, Catholic and nationalist traditions and associates it with the rural, economic and political imperatives of bourgeois Catholicism. Such concentration however, on masculine perceptions, needs and emotions minimises and marginalises the experiences of women. In its nineteenth-century hibernicised form, the idea brings to the foreground rural experience at the expense of urban perceptions. It also excludes Protestants, mistrustfully dispossesses those who leave, and erects borders of suspicion, even hostility, against those who return.

Paradoxically therefore, the conceptualisation of exile in these terms, negates the homogenising impulses of nationalism. In its literal and figurative representations it becomes, as Timothy Brennan says, 'nationalism's opposite'. Brennan argues:

> Exile and nationalism are conflicting poles of feeling that correspond to more traditional aesthetic conflicts: artistic iconoclasm and communal assent, the unique vision and the collective truth. In fact many words in the exile family divide themselves between an archaic or literary sense and a modern, political one: for example, banishment vs deportation; émigré vs immigrant; wanderer vs refugee; exodus vs flight. The division between exile and nationalism, therefore, presents itself as one not only between individual and group, but between loser and winner, between a mood of rejection and a mood of celebration. Literarily, the division is suggested by the tensions between lyric and epic, tragedy and comedy, monologue and dialogue, confession and proclamation.[92]

The case here assumes a problematic and even contradictory relationship between exile and nationalism. Consequently space is given, not only to the inherited thematics of exile and the cognates that the term metaphorically subsumes, but also to the aesthetics of exile as manifest in terms of content and form. It also assumes throughout, that ideological, social and cultural formations and representations (and repressions) of the idea of exile are contrapuntal, hybrid and dialogic. It argues that preoccupation with, or avoidance of the concept, marks a definite and distinguishing feature of imaginative writing by Irish writers in the English language within the period under review.

Exile, literary achievement and Ireland are symbiotically interfused into what Seamus Deane calls 'The oppressiveness of the tradition we inherit'.[93] The principal aim of this argument therefore, is to question that kind of casual coagulation and easy transference into the literary sphere and to consider the implications for representative literary works which accepted the truth value of Catholic nationalist representations; those which (re)deployed the language of exile and those which evaded serious treatment of the phenomenon at all.

Said contends that the job of the cultural intellectual is to refuse to 'accept the politics of identity' and 'to show how all representations are constructed, for what purpose, by whom, and with what components'.[94] The arguments advanced in this text attempt to work within the rescriptive remit of that injunction.

Exile in the Irish Language Tradition and the English Language Tradition prior to the Famine

INTRODUCTION

Said, as has been noted, argues that the literature of exile draws on Christian and humanistic traditions of redemption through loss and suffering and Kiely, in a commonplace and widely accepted observation, has located the idea of exile in Irish culture as far back as the time of St Colmcille. The idea and perception of exile therefore, has deep roots in the Irish psyche and in the Gaelic language tradition. It precedes nationalism, industrial capitalism, colonisation and the Reformation. As a corollary of its pre-existence to those epoch shaping movements it predates expression in the English language.

Therefore, before a serious examination of its thematic and stylistic forms in English in the nineteenth century can be undertaken it is necessary to contextualise, as far as is possible, the origins and evolution of the term in the recorded Irish language tradition. It is essential to consider how the idea was dealt with, by whom and for what purposes in formal literary modes and in more prosaic and less consciously crafted popular cultural constructions.

It is also vital to examine how and why those native English speakers who settled in Ireland in the aftermath of conquest used the term in both ordinary and literary discourse as a preparation for a consideration of attitudes and artistic formulation in the period with which this book is primarily concerned.

A third major concern of this chapter will be to analyse the conceptualisation of the idea of exile in English in the years prior to the Famine. This was a time when large numbers of native Irish became bi-lingual and significant pressures combined to create a monoglot, English speaking, native Irish section of the population.

This chapter attempts to work explicitly within the spirit of Jameson's exhortation to 'always historicise'.[1] It aims to lay bare the ideological formulations and leitmotifs of exile in pre-Famine culture as a prelude to an inquiry into its use or misuse and avoidance in post-Famine representations and cultural rivalries.

St Colmcille, one of Ireland's three patron saints, has by tradition long been regarded as the archetypal if not the first exile from Ireland. The traditional explanation for his departure centres on a quarrel he had with Finnian, abbot of Moville, over a copy he made of a psaltery. Finnian objected to the copy being made and demanded that Colmcille hand it over. The dispute led to the judgement of the High King Diarmuid who said: 'To every cow its calf and to every book its copy'. Colmcille rejected the decision and the argument escalated into armed conflict and the battle of Cuildreimhne in 561. There are alternative versions as to what then occurred. One suggests he was condemned by a synod at Teltown Co. Meath and sentenced to exile, another that he sought the advice of St Molaise, who told him that he should attempt to expiate his offence by winning as many souls for Christ in foreign lands as had died at Cuildreimhne.[2] In any event, he left on his mission to Iona and in time he succeeded in establishing numerous monasteries and in christianising much of Scotland.

The story may or may not be apocryphal. It certainly has elements of the allegorical within it which reflect the reasoning behind the *consuetude peregrinandi* or passion for exile in foreign lands–a dominant feature of the devotional activities of the early Irish Church.

The Church in Ireland was spared the persecutions experienced elsewhere in Europe and compensated to a large extent by inventing and imposing its own. It devised a threefold classification of martyrdom, each stage of which represented an intensification of suffering and hence brought the supplicant a degree nearer to God. The first stage was known as white martyrdom wherein a man (*sic*) parted with everything he loved and suffered fasting and labour. The second was green martyrdom, which involved labour in penitence and repentance, and the third stage was red martyrdom, which demanded submission to the cross. White martyrdom thus underpinned a doctrine of penitential exile which imitated the experience of the Lord and the apostles. Pilgrimage and exile could take two forms. The first was in terms of actual corporeal departure for which most credit could be gained; the second theologically authorised the notion of inner-exile, in which a man might leave his fatherland in soul, if not in body. This inner-exile manifested itself in the harsh rigours of Irish monasticism, and in a more extreme form of ascetic anchoritic existence. It provided for many a model of sacrifice and devotion in the iconography of Irish Christianity.[3]

Colmcille though not the first missionary, became 'the prototype to later generations of the patriotic exile, thinking longingly in a foreign land of the little places at home he knew so well'.[4]

Liam de Paor suggests that, that psychically disabling way of picturing displacement was bound up with the kind of social structures that the monks left behind them:

> In a society where there was not a clear concept, in most matters of abstract and impersonal justice or of police in any sense, the well being of each person was so bound up with status, with membership of tribal and kin groups and of a particular *tuath* that exile involved a stripping away of protection and rights and probably a psychological trauma. It appears to be so regarded in the texts. There were no citizens. There were no autonomous individuals: people belonged to families–although this dependence was mitigated by the universal custom of fosterage, … The monastery itself was thought of as a family; but separation from foster–or kin–or family, as the most severe of penances was behind the impulse to exile.[5]

As a complement to those deeply ingrained familial and communal obligations the poets

> cultivated with an unremitting assiduity a study to which they gave the name *dindshenchas*, the lore of the high places, until by the accretion of centuries there came into existence a large body of literature in prose and verse forming a kind of Dictionary of National Topography, which fitted the famous sites of the country each with its appropriate legend.[6]

The reverse of such intense love and psychological attachment to one given locality was dislocation and deracination; the fear of which seems to form part of a distinct dialogue in the theological and hagiographical writing, as well as in the more personalised lyric prose and verse of the time.[7] It finds less obvious, but equally substantial form in the redactions of the ancient Gaelic epics and mythological tales.

Thomas Kinsella's translation of the *Tain Bó Cuailnge* (1969)–The Cattle Raid on Cooley, is based on *Lebor na huidre*–The Book of the Dun Cow, which was compiled in the monastery of Clonmacnoise in the twelfth century and from a partial version in the fourteenth-century *Yellow Book of Lecan*. The origins of the *Tain* however, predate those sources and may in fact be eighth-century in part. Most Gaelic scholars believe the *Tain* had a long oral history before it acquired a perceptible patina of Christianity in transcription by the monastic scribes.

Kinsella's version impresses by the way in which flight from danger and separation from home is axiomatically signified as exile–in fact, the term and its cognates permeate the text throughout. Its earliest mention is in the most famous and often treated *remscela* or pre-tale in the whole epic, the *Exile of the Sons of Uisliu*. The tale relates how Derdriu defies the will and concupiscent intentions of Conchobor, the King of Ulster. She elopes with Noisiu, Uisliu's son, and accompanied by his two brothers flees Ireland to escape the vengeance of the lustful king. Their stay in Alba is self-evidently and implicitly assumed to be 'exile'. The term itself is never applied to Derdriu and her companions but the condition or state of exile is subsumed under the title of the tale. Conchobor lures them back to Ireland with a false series of guarantees involving Fergus the former King of Ulster whom he–Conchobor–has previously cheated out of his king-ship. Once on Irish soil the sons of Uisliu are killed by Conchobor's mercenaries. It is perhaps the earliest instance of betrayal in Irish writing and as such the progenitor of a literary and cultural trope which was to take root in the public and private consciousness of Ireland–reinforced, of course, by Christian teaching which stressed the betrayal of God by Adam and Eve, and Jesus by Judas Iscariot.

Fergus, learning how he has been manipulated, launches an armed attack on Conchobor then leaves Ulster for Connacht accompanied by a retinue of soldiers or as it is put in the tale 'A full three thousand the exiles numbered'.[8] As the cattle raid progresses these 'Ulster exiles'[9] side with Medb the Queen of Connacht and throughout the remainder of the saga are invariably referred to as exiles. Thus, the term continues to be used unquestioningly and it coexists with a heavy stress on topography which forms an extremely large part of the *Tain*. The topographical emphasis suggests it was composed or grew by oral and later written accretion in accordance with the *dindshenchas*. The heavy and persistent emphasis on the pre-eminence of place, with its accumulated freight of legend, lore and loyalty, seems justification enough in the context, for the manifest acceptance of exile as clearly given. The term thus generically subsumes and incorporates a range of related concepts such as separation, banish-ment and voluntary departure. It operates linguistically then, as a literal description as in the case of Derdriu; a metonymic device suggesting a part of a wider complex of ideas such as deceit, cunning and betrayal, and as a metaphor for sacrifice, martyrdom and the human condition in relation to the divine.

Buile Shuibhne, the story of Mad Sweeney the King of Dal-Arie (now South Co. Antrim and North Co. Down) explores the consequences of human defiance of God. Seamus Heaney in the introduction to his version of the tale *Sweeney Astray* (1983) briefly sketches the history of the text pointing out that the manuscript may have been composed at any time between twelve hundred and fifteen hundred. Heaney goes on to say: 'the *Buile Shuibhne* which we now possess is a development of traditions dating back to the time of the Battle of Moira (AD 637), the battle where Sweeney went mad and was transformed, in fulfilment of St Ronan's curse, into a bird of the air'. In commenting on the story Heaney says that: 'the literary imagination which fastened upon him as an image was clearly in the grip of a tension between the new and dominant Christian ethos and the old recalcitrant Celtic temperament'.[10] A tension which is treated explicitly in the opening pages in the clash between St Ronan and in the coda to the tale when Sweeney after years of restless wandering and pursuit, reconciles himself to Christianity and death in St Moling's monastery. In addition, however, to that thematic overlay, there is an underpinning of assumptions which help to explain why Sweeney's plight is so dire. Apart from the obvious inconvenience of being metamorphosised into a bird, thus becoming the prey to all manner of more powerful and predatory life forms, and the monotony of a diet of unadorned watercress, Sweeney's principal punishment has been that 'God had exiled me from myself'.[11] After a year of vain adventures and escapes Sweeney finds himself in Glen Bolcain among the annual convocation of Ireland's madmen.

There, 'exhausted and beaten', he speaks a poem which laments the loss of his former corporeal configuration, status, comforts, companionship and sense of well-being. His initial reaction is a kind of self-pitying sorrow for the material losses he has suffered as well as the loss of self-esteem, but those understandable feelings are built on a growing awareness of a more profound dislocation. When homesick for Dal-Arie Heaney has him speak the following verses:

> I pined the whole night
> in Derville's chapel
> for Dal-Arie
> and peopled the dark

with a thousand ghosts.
My dream restored me:
the army lay at Drumfree
and I came into my kingdom,

camped with my troop
back with Faolchu and Congal
for our night at Drumduff.
Taunters, will-o'-the wisps

who saw me brought to heel
at Moira, you crowded my head
and fade away
and leave me to the night.[12]

His isolation, psychic and physical, his immediate circumstances and the disorientating darkness leave him open to the persecutory phantasms latent in the Christian (Catholic) consciousness. Displacement engenders derangement, disobedience and defiance generates alienation, and alienation is imaged as exile. In addition, the sentiments expressed by Sweeney suggest a deep ambivalence towards women on the part of the monks who wrote down and organised the old original oral and fragmented written versions of the story. This probably echoed their ascetic misogyny. However, that coupling of the notion of betrayal and femininity was not original nor was it a momentary historical and cultural phenomenon.

In the context of Sweeney's travails however, it contributes to his estrangement from all things human, familial, communal and supportive. It contributes also to his perception of punishment that is divinely inflicted. He says he has 'endured purgatories'[13] since Ronan placed his curse on him. His wanderings and pain can be seen in much the same way as the penitential peregrinations of Colmcille, for like Colmcille he has experienced exile and exile is thought of as punishment; the interregnum between the moment of banishment and death as purgatory. Resolution in these circumstances is a kind of homecoming, a restitution of wholeness. In that return to 'home' is peace and salvation. It is as though 'home' is a synonym for 'heaven' and the eternal where body, soul and place are seen as spiritually and physically organic and indivisible. While the story may be seen as an allegorised journey from paganism into Christianity given the predisposition of the monks to employ allegory as a narrative mode, it can also be read as an allegory on exile emphasising as it does the tendency towards topographical detail. For instance, the naming of Glen

Bolcain, sketching in the story behind the naming of 'The Madman's Well', stressing the dislocation following on migration, describing Sweeney as a 'pilgrim' and resolving fragmentation and discontinuity in the closure which (re)integrates Sweeney's body and soul into a Christian cosmos which clearly equates psychic and corporeal wholeness with home, and home with the Church.

In his introduction Heaney suggests another way of reading *Buile Shuibhne* or *Sweeney Astray*:

> insofar as Sweeney is also a figure of the artist, displaced, guilty, assuaging himself by his utterance, it is possible to read the work as an aspect of the quarrel between free creative imagination and the constraints of religious, political and domestic obligation.

A reading which perhaps, helps explain why the displaced poet Heaney, is attracted to the figure of Sweeney sufficiently so to re-work the tale.

Colmcille, as we know, left Ireland to establish his mission abroad which was considered to be the most severe penance an Irishman could undertake. Others however, found alternative means of mortifying the flesh in the service of God.

One form of extreme asceticism involved seeking out lonely places and remote islands where monks could spend their lives as hermits free from worldly distraction. Many such places were located on the edge of Ireland or on offshore islands. In time, stories were told of the adventures of these monks on the seas:

> In this way developed the *Navigato Brendani* which purports to be an account of St Brendan's sea-wanderings but is actually a skilful piece of fiction, having *Immrain Maile Duin* as its prototype.[14]

In Christianising the *Immrama*, the scribes of the early Church effectively incorporated them into their developing exilic discourse. If 'white' martyrdom represented the state of penitential exile and leaving everything one loved, self-denying abnegation–voyaging for Christ, enduring all the danger and hardship the imagination could create–formed an effective complement to the kind of image of exile associated with anchorite asceticism and 'imprisonment' overseas as in the case of Colmcille. It added to the amoeba-like, shape-changing accretions around the conceptualisation of exile emphasising the heroic, the dynamic and the adventurous in the service of God. Viewed in this way, journeying out into the unknown could be seen as glamorous and exciting, a necessary supplementary motivation perhaps, for the missionary explorers and a kind of ideological seedling for the idea of the Church militant.

Colmcille, the prototype of the penitential exile, was followed by others such as Fursey of East Anglia and north-east Gaul; Killian who was martyred at Wurtzburg in 689; Fergal, Bishop of Saltzburg; Aidan of Lindisfarne; Finan and Colman who converted Northumbria; Gall of Switzerland and the most famous of all, Columbanus. His most notable foundations were the monasteries Luxenil in France and Bobbio in Italy–hundreds of later foundations were said to be directly or indirectly influenced by those he founded. Those pioneering monks had secured their reputations by the seventh century. By the ninth century, the numbers of the Irish abroad had been added to by many Irish scholars–often fleeing from the Viking invasions–who served Charlemagne and helped establish France as a centre of learning. Probably the most noteworthy of these scholars were the geographer Dicuil, the philosopher and theologian Sedulius Scotus and the most important, the man often thought of as the most influential scholar and philosopher of his age, John Scotus Eriugena.

We can see in this movement the beginnings of that image of Ireland as the land of Saints and Scholars–a cultured european society different from and perhaps superior to its nearest neighbours.

After the twelfth century the majority of manuscripts that have come down to us were written by

> a new class of men, the hereditary bards attached to the noble families of
> Ireland, whether the families of the Old Gaels or those Anglo-Norman lords
> who came afterwards to be known as the Old Foreigners. These literary
> families were the guardians of the tradition as it was arranged and stored
> in the older manuscripts by the scribes of the great clerical schools.[15]

There is common agreement among commentators that writing in Gaelic between this time and the end of the seventeenth century was extremely conservative–backward looking, as Frank O'Connor put it. Kinsella says:

> Originally the bardic order of poets had developed in close relationship with
> a conservative ruling class. They fulfilled a largely social function in a stable
> society; their poetry became and remained a standardised medium, with a
> high respect for precedent, with rigorous requirements as to syllable count,
> alliteration, and the like, and with a fixed array of formal phrases and
> references.[16]

The effect as James Carney points out, was that 'linguistic consider-ations are alone no certain guide to either date or place of composition'.[17] A view supported by Seamus O'Neill:

> The file (poet) was so tightly bound by the traditions of his craft–in metre (*sic*), in language and in subject–that for four centuries, from 1250 to 1650, hardly the slightest change or development is discernible in this type of official verse.[18]

The poets were, as Flower describes, governed by a system of rules which had been formally codified and written as a series of treatises at the time of Brian Boroma, the High King of Ireland in the eleventh century. These formed the system which governed the teaching and practice in the Bardic schools.[19] The themes and subjects they adopted were eulogies to their patrons, genealogies of the aristocracy and elegies on the death of a member of the family. They gathered there in family poetry books or *duanaires*. They wrote satires on their rivals, those who were in conflict with their overlords, and on social practices and behaviour that deviated from custom and tradition.

Confined then as it was by the castle building Normans and under pressure directly and indirectly by the success of this second wave of invading strangers, Irish civilisation withdrew into itself and cultivated its own tradition–a defensive reaction to colonising aggression, a 'with-drawal' from the world of everyday reality' into 'a culture of dreams'.[20]

The Tudors of the sixteenth century were more successful than the Normans had been in subduing Ireland. Like the Spanish in their exploita-tion and conquest of the indigenous peoples of the Caribbean and South America, they characterised Irish culture as archaic, barbarian and uncivil-ised; a world in need of re-making in the image of Protestant England. The image of the Irish as savages led to ruthless massacres as on Rathlin Island in 1574, to plans to transfer the whole of the Irish population to England to provide a helot class, and to Governor Mountjoy's plan to make Ireland 'a rased table' on which the English State could 'transcribe a neat pattern'.[21]

An immediate effect of periodic revolts and their suppression was flight. From the 1530s when the Geraldines of Leinster were banished and exiled after the failure of the rebellion of Silken Thomas, through to the 1580s when another Norman or Old English family, the Desmonds of Munster rose and were crushed, hundreds of defeated Old English and Gaelic rebels went into military service in Europe. Some went as soldiers of Leicester serving in Flanders, some to Lisbon, then later, others travelled to

France.[22] Their numbers added to the considerable swell of Irish on the continent who had, under increasing pressure and circumscription, left Ireland for the priesthood[23] or to obtain a Catholic higher education which was impossible in Ireland. They went to: Salamanca, Rome, Paris, Bordeaux, Douai or Louvain. Their membership was drawn from the Gaelic community and from among the Old English. There, they absorbed the teachings of the Counter-Reformation before, in many cases, returning to Ireland. Ireland lacked political and administrative cohesion. Attachments and loyalties were to the locality and to the extended family grouping and the bardic families accordingly identified with and received protection from their hereditary patrons.

Ireland represented a poetic abstraction. It had a mythic identity. It could be *Fodla*, *Banba*, *Erin* or metonymically it was 'Connla's Plain', 'Uisneach's land', 'Fal's High Plain', 'The Plain of Lugh' while metaphorically it might be the 'Isle of Saints' or in a reallocation from the *Immrama*, the 'Isle of the Blest'. This mythic overload could at once suggest or allude to a spurious cultural and racial idea of unity on the poetic level, while at the same time obfuscating and deferring indefinitely any kind of movement to material and practical implementation. It was a psychologically sustaining myth of Ireland; 'Ireland' held in perpetual promise and suspended in linguistic vacuity. It was also an enfeebling imaginative construct predicated on a 'historical' fiction. It sanctioned Irish civilisation and superimposed an image of an ancient time–a weak dialogic response to the aggressive nationalism of England–on institutionalised fragmentation. In masking or distorting reality it helped create the conditions for invasion and exploitation by a stronger, more technologically advanced neighbour. A neighbour which was ideologically and militarily ordered and driven by a providential teleology; a teleology that was composed of elements that were modernising, supremacist, mercantile and Protestant.

Native Irish poets and chroniclers reacted to the advance of the New English Tudor settlers–the 'Upstarts'–by recourse to traditional models of absorption. The popularity of new editions of the *Leabhar Gabhála*, the Book of Invasions, a twelfth-century text which told the story of the peoples who supposedly occupied Ireland in pre-historic times from Caesar before the Deluge through the invasions of Partholon, Nemed, the Firbolg, the De Danaan and the Milesians who came from the Iberian peninsula, indicates a belief that these new invaders would be absorbed as the Old English and the Norsemen had been before them.[24] The renewed preoccupation of the poets with reworking of the old tales and the long-standing antiquarian tendency to re-copy glossaries, genealogical and historical material, points to a reluctance to accept new realities. This also indicates an inability to react to exigencies not contained within the traditional framework of understanding and perception. In part, their failure to take a lead against the imposition and encroachment of the English language, English thinking and organisational methods was a cautious response to official sanctions aimed at curbing the use of the Gaelic language, and the hostility directed towards encomiastic poetry in particular.[25] Panegyric poetry was seen as a propagandistic threat to the values and credibility of the new order, an explicit acknowledgement of the power of discourse and the pre-eminent position then held by the poets and bards in Gaelic society, and increasingly amongst the Old English, the descendants of the Anglo-Normans. In attempting to silence the bards the Tudor invaders were of course, employing one of the fundamental stratagems of colonialism. This was to eliminate as far as possible, the space for the dominant native discourse and fill the gap with their own 'superior' ideological language complex and value system. The relative success of the policy is of its nature unquantifiable–it was not for example, always applied consistently everywhere. But it is reasonable to assume that that sort of pressurised proscription, combined with the poets' propensity to introspective conservatism, helped channel protest and dissent into a sort of exorcistic, self-lacerating and politically disabling self-criticism characterised by paganistic appeals to totemistic shibboleths and legendary precedents.

They were prevented by a lack of comprehension, a haughty aristocratic disdain for the mores, fashions and behaviour of the newcomers and bound by traditional modes of thinking and expression which prohibited, or at least militated against innovation and flexibility. As a result the poets responded to changed circumstances by working within established forms and for the most part turning in on their native culture in a mood of narcissistic despair and hopelessness. An anonymous poet of the sixteenth century wrote the following poem which illustrates his sense of shame, and his contempt for those Irish chiefs who had submitted to the King of England:

> Shame for the grey foreign gun,
> Shame for the golden chain,
> Shame for the court without language,
> Shame for the denial of Mary's son.

Nobles of the island of Art of old,
Ill is the island of Art of old,
Ill is the change in your dignity,
O weak cowardly lot,
Henceforth say nothing but 'shame'.[26]

Opposition was thus intoned in metrical chants, it was as though the resort to rhythmic, incantatory repetitions would ward off reality and render Ireland unto the Gael. Others such as Laoiseach Mac An Baird compensated by glorifying in his poem 'Two Sons', the image of the unmaterialistic patriot inspired by noble visions of the past glories of Celtic/Irish civilisation. A hero prepared and eager to raid and harass the powerful, the dominant, the corrupt, the complacent and the effete–a lonely hero living in a kind of self-imposed internal exile. Such images began to form powerful consolatory and enduring motifs in the history of colonial Ireland. The culmination of the Tudor conquests came in 1601 with the defeat of the Irish armies at Kinsale. This was a cataclysmic event, sometimes explained in self-exculpatory polemics by monocular national-ists in a variation of the 'betrayal' motif, as a consequence of the treachery of an Irish captain, Brian Óg McMahon. It is alleged that he gave infor-mation to the English commander, Mountjoy, about Hugh O'Neill's plans. Sometimes the defeat is blamed on the 'perfidy' of the Spanish leader Don Juan del Aquila. After the ignominious rout, Mountjoy pursued and harried O'Neill who like a wood kerne took refuge in the woods and hills of Ulster–an exile in his own territory. The new overlord took possession of Dungannon, which became an English fort and then in the words of Ó Faoláin the

> final symbol, the crowning-stone of Tullyhoge, where O'Neills had been inaugurated from time immemorial, was smashed to pieces. The old Gaelic world fell there like an idol on the grass.[27]

Defeat and humiliation was followed in 1607 by the 'Flight of the Earls'. Hugh O'Neill the 'Prince of Ireland' accompanied by Rory O'Donnell, Red Hugh's brother, the Earl of Tyrconnell and their closest relatives: sons, nephews, sisters, friends and followers, some ninety-nine in all–the 'noble shipload'–sailed down Lough Swilley into exile and more significantly, into the iconography of Irish historiography and culture. For the poets and chroniclers it signalled the death of the old Gaelic order and with its destruction and the dispersion of their aristocratic sponsors their patronage, security and privilege disappeared too.

Fear Flatha Ó Gnimh in his grief-stricken monody 'After the Flight of the Earls', written in the early seventeenth century, speaks of Ireland as an abandoned corpse where 'only their leavings linger' and 'a craven host remains'.[28] Aindrais MacMarcuis' poem 'This Night Sees Ireland Desolate', from the early seventeenth century, identifies Ireland with scriptural representation of Israel. His conceptualisation of exile is broadened into exodus; the complexity of exilic discourse is correspondingly widened to incorporate mass movements of people out of Ireland. Therefore, the discourse can contain the idea of departure as a self-volitional act (although conceived and presented as forced) and as diaspora, resulting from the action or actions of some external agency. The immediate cause is, of course, the 'foreigner' but the English in this formulation are intermediaries; in the rhetoric of persecution and suffering they are a 'visitation' or a 'plague'. As intermediaries their importance, superiority and power is in a sense diminished. The 'real' agent, the prime actor or motivating force in their drama is divine–it is God who is chastising the Gael. The Christian imagery of the final verse suggests the punishment that has been imposed and it echoes the martyrology of previous centuries; while the explicit evocation of the fate of the Israelites invokes associations with dispossession, captivity, homelessless and wandering– divine retribution for the worship of false idols.

The flagellatory impulse in Gaelic writing at the time is within the tradition of the self-scourging monks of medieval Ireland and it was a dominant feature re-accentuated by returning clerical historiographers and poets of the Counter-Reformation. Catholic Ireland pre-Kinsale had, it was believed, grown notoriously lax in the practice of the Church's teachings. Divorce was easy under brehon law, probationary marriages common and there was no taboo on sexual relationships within degrees of affinity that would have been forbidden by Catholic (and Protestant) orthodoxy.

Since the mid 1500s there had been a strong Irish identification with continental seminaries such as Salamanca, Alcola, Douai, Louvain, Paris and St Isidoes in Rome:

> Between such centres and the strongholds of Gaelic Ireland a network of Catholic publicists plied to and fro; emigrant Irish culture was preoccupied by the necessity to renew Catholicism in Ireland. This was also true of exiled Irish lords and their retinues turning up as clients at Hapsburg Courts. Most of all, the growing commitment of exiled scholars in Catholic intellectual centres to the memorialising of Irish history established an early connection

between Catholic zeal and the Gaelic identity that would be seen, at least in retrospect, as 'nationalist'.[29]

Catholic intellectuals like Geoffrey Keating, Michael O'Cleary, Pádraigín Haicéad and Peter Lombard, drawn from both the Old English and Gaelic communities, were instrumental in fusing Catholicism and patriotism and particularly in the case of the first three who wrote in Gaelic, in linking Catholicism and patriotism into an elemental trinity with the Gaelic language. As publicists rather than aristocratic acolytes, they had to reach out to a mass audience and mobilise the majority against their Protestant overlords. They employed the new techniques of printing, which as Deane points out aroused national feelings all over Europe.[30] They used colloquial Irish in order to reach as many people as possible and they frequently communicated in verse for the benefit of the illiterate. Thus, they contributed to the destruction of the old of the bardic schools and the literary conservatism they embodied. However, paradoxically, in their militant appeal to pre-Reformation traditions, they reinforced the traditional in ideological terms and underpinned immobility linguistically through recourse to simplistic mnemonics.

Each was concerned in his own way with the refutation of the anti-Irish works of Giraldus Cambrensis, Spenser, Fines Moryson and John Davies. Keating in his *Foras Feasa ar Éirinn* (1631), the first narrative history of Ireland in Irish and O'Cleary with *Reim Rigraidhe* (1630), a list of Kings and their pedigrees with lives and genealogies of the saints. *Leabhar Gabhála* (1631), the book of Invasion, and *Annala Rioghachta Éireann*, the Annals of the Four Masters (1636), Haicéad's polemical poetry and Lombard's *De Regno Hiberniae Commentarius* (1632), which portrays O'Neill's rebellion as a war defence of Catholicism. All were concerned to defend and idealise a doomed civilisation. As Roy Foster says:

> In Irish life historiography and poetry did the duty of political manifestos and would continue to do so.[31]

It is also a comment that could be employed as a headquote for Brian Friel's *Making History* (1989). His play deals with O'Neill, the passing of the Gaelic world, the Counter-Reformation, the fictive nature of history and much else besides. Towards the end of the play when O'Neill, a drunken melancholic failure now in exile in Rome, is protesting to Peter Lombard, his biographer about the distortions in his account, Lombard replies:

Think of this (book) as an act of *pietas*. Ireland is reduced as it never has been reduced before–we are talking about a colonised people on the brink of extinction. This isn't the time for a critical assessment of your 'ploys' and your 'disgraces' and your 'betrayal'–that's the stuff of another history for another time. Now is the time for a hero. Now is time for a heroic literature. So I am offering Gaelic Ireland two things. I'm offering them this narrative that has the elements of myth. And I'm offering them Hugh O'Neill as a national hero. A hero and the story of a hero.[32]

Lombard like Keating, O'Cleary and Haicéad experienced exile– Keating doubly so in that much of his work was done in hiding in the glens of Aherlow–and it seems understandable in terms of his own, O'Neill's and Gaelic and Catholic experience that he should romanticise his subject as an exile. It is probable that he first suggested the heroising image of 'The Flight of the Earls'. In fact, it is difficult to see how, given the purpose of his project, he could do otherwise. Exile in the nature of his narrative had to be idealised, it had (in addition to the profound sense of sadness and loss) to carry within it the possibility of return–if not the restitution of this hero then some other and later reincarnation of 'The O'Neill'. Out of this hope and need grew the preoccupation with 'lost leaders' and 'leaders overseas' and with the recurring search for a saviour from abroad.

Exile therefore became politicised in a way that it hadn't before. With O'Neill's departure and in its reconstruction in historiography and poetry it accrued ideas of deferred leadership, daring and secular sacrifice. It also held within it the possibility of redemption for an impoverished and oppressed people in some postponed, never-quite-tangible future. 'The Flight of the Earls' mattered then on the symbolic level. It acquired a mythic significance, which was to permeate Catholic and later nationalist consciousness in a way that was to transcend actuality. As Lombard addressing Hugh O'Neill in *Making History* says:

> You lost a battle–that has to be said. But the telling of it can still be a triumph.[33]

Friel's play, he tells us, was based on Ó Faoláin's biography of O'Neill. Ó Faoláin concludes his preface so:

> Indeed, in those last years in Rome the myth was already beginning to emerge, and a talented dramatist might write an informative, entertaining, ironical play on the theme of the living man helplessly watching his translation into a star in the face of all the facts that had reduced him to poverty, exile and defeat.[34]

'Informative, entertaining and ironical'; Friel, the 'talented dramatist', is of course doing what Lombard and Ó Faoláin were doing in their time. He is 'making history', re-fashioning events in ways he judges appropriate and necessary and 'those ways are determined by the needs and the demands and the expectations of different people and different eras'.[35]

That recursive dialogue with thought-shaping historic or historio-graphically conceived motifs is constitutively indicative of an unresolved history; one that is still in the making or possibly one that may be perceived as being imprisoned in a sort of cognitive dissonance. In the case of Lombard the literary re-creation may well have been necessary as an attempt to re-constitute and make whole a version of Gaelic culture. It also served as a reassuring palliative aimed at restoring a sense of organic continuity. There was within it a suggestion that the intolerable present was an aberration and implicit within that, that the natural order would reassert itself sometime–sometime in the not-quite-discernible future. The effect of the efforts of Lombard, Keating, Haicéad, O'Cleary and others was to perpetuate the traditional. Their conservatism, which essentially reacted against English characterisations of the Irish, ensured that much of Ireland remained 'Trapped in the Old Gaelic paradigms of thought'.[36]

Conquest, plantation, the abolition of the brehon laws and the image of the mendicant missionary of the Counter-Reformation conducting outdoor Mass on an altar stone–sharing his experiences of exile, while inculcating a sense of guilt–reinforced the feeling of loss and abandon-ment which the native Irish felt after 'The Flight of the Earls'.

Tom Dunne has pointed out how the *dánta deoraíochta* of Haicéad and Keating 'revealed a love and concern for the country as a whole, which transcended the local or conventional'.[37] In doing so, they also established in the colonial context an affective pattern of association between 'Éire', patriotism, defeat, guilt, loss and exile. They also popularised through their preaching and the use of the vernacular in print that connective complex in their proselytising on behalf of the Counter-Reformation. This Counter-Reformation discourse stressed obedience, sacrifice, sub-mission to the authority of the Church, and a link between a Celtic golden age and Catholicism. It also underwrote subservience to the social order which, according to the shifting emphases of the time, was nominally the Gaelic aristocracy, those remaining and those abroad or more pragmati-cally those descendants of Elizabethan settlers who were considered to be noble and anti-Protestant, reserving a particular detestation for the Calvinist variety.

Nicholas Canny argues[38] that the poets and priests actively colluded with the Catholic aristocratic landowning classes to uphold an aristocratic culture and to repress the lower ranks of Irish society through insult and mockery. It is an argument that would help explain the apparent contradiction between the concern felt by the poets for those exiled in Europe–aristocrats, priests and soldiers–and the lack of concern, indeed the total absence of comment in the surviving translated texts, about those who were transported to the plantations of Virginia and the Caribbean in the aftermath of the Cromwellian wars. Their voices are unrecorded in contemporary accounts although traces or echoes of their experiences are surely to be found in the oral storytelling and in the ballad traditions of the eighteenth and nineteenth centuries.

After the defeat of the Irish forces some 34,000 'swordsmen' followed what was by then a long established practice by enlisting in continental armies. Such a practice effectively rid England of the potential threat they represented while adding to the difficulties of their rivals, France and Spain, who were still at war:

> Others left less willingly, being transported to the English plantations in America. Contemporary accounts would claim that vast numbers were rounded up in organised slave-hunts, and this version of events has become part of the Irish legend.[39]

There were two principal categories of people transported: first of all, those considered a danger to the state, frequently including younger priests, and secondly, the poor and vagabonds. Transportation was a penalty applied in England also. Nevertheless, the circumstances in Ireland ensured that far more people were categorised in this way and of course the numbers of those who were destitute and rounded up for expulsion far exceeded those in the first category. P.J. Corish and other historians such as Foster argue that the numbers involved have been greatly exaggerated. However, the reality of transportation, buttressed by proposals such as that in 1655 to transport 2,000 Irish boys and girls to Jamaica; the experience, whether real or vicarious, of the manhunts; the memories of the massacres at Drogheda and Wexford; the brutal public executions; the savage dehumanisation of the defeated and their denial of a legal and religious being inevitably scarred the Irish psyche irreparably and engendered a sense of impending genocide. Such degradation was justified ideologically by Cromwellian soldiers, administrators and slave trade adventurers in terms of their innate superiority and 'civilising' mission in much the same way that they justified the African slave trade. In legalistic

terms the transported Irish were indentured servants. In their own eyes
and in the perception of the Irish at home, to their new masters and to the
Negroes on the plantations they were 'white slaves'.[40] Conor Cruise
O'Brien has pointed out in reference to later historical comparisons with
the oppressed black slaves of America how the Irish indignantly rejected
any such analogy. He underlines the fact that they saw themselves as an
ancient civilised and european people and that any comparison with non-
white peoples was a bitter insult.[41] It is understandable that in such a
context the Irish should cling to what few shreds of psychological comfort
they had and that they should reassert the values and beliefs which had
sustained them. Exile therefore became associated on the one hand with
an (in)voluntary departure in which the subject retained his self-respect
and dignity and nursed hopes of a conquering return. On the other hand
it became connected with a forced removal or banishment, whereby the
victim defines himself in terms of that from which he came–in this case
Gaelic Catholic Ireland–against that which he was forced, quite literally,
into. But in either case, exile is associated with oppression, the colonising
power, subjugation and defeat. Leaving Ireland is imaged as a consequence
of brutal dispossession. 'Home', by contrast, is idealised and entwined in
that idealisation is a submissive unquestioning longing for the imagined
security of the old order. Corish[42] estimates that there were some 12,000
Irish people in the West Indies in the late 1660s (not all of whom would
have been transported) and that approximately 8,000 of them were in
Barbados working on the sugar plantations in intolerable conditions
which were totally alien and with little hope of ever returning to Ireland.
It is little wonder then, that to be 'Barbadosed' injected so much fear and
loathing in the Gaelic Catholic community and that the 'New World', full
of unknown terrors, should be thought of as an earthly hell.

Connaught was the alternative destination planned for the remainder
of the indigenous Irish population. The conquering Puritans intended to
clear most of Ireland of native and old English Catholics and confine them
to Connaught and Clare. The Shannon would form a natural quarantine
boundary, effectively imprisoning them in the most infertile and moun-
tainous areas of the island. As Corish says, the consequence of this policy
was that 'Catholics almost without exception ceased to be property
holders east of the Shannon'.[43] In these circumstances of defeat and expulsion the identification of the dejected Irish with the displaced Israelites
now became commonplace–and more acceptable than comparison with
Black Africans.

Fear Dorcha Ó Mealláin in his only extant work, invoked the only response available to the defeated Catholics–prayer. *Exodus to Connacht* (c. 1650) begins by imploring the help of the Holy Trinity, Mary, the Apostles and numerous local saints. He describes the 'possessions' and 'rations' they carry as their 'faith in God'. Lacking material sustenance the hope he offers 'to his fellow travellers is that of trust in divinity; their plight is like that of 'Israel's people, God's own'. They, like the Irish were driven from their ancestral homes and were watched over and protected by the 'King of Heaven' and the Irish like the Israelites will one day come into their heavenly inheritance if only they endure and pray to God.[44]

Ó Mealláin it seems, may have been a native of Co. Down and may have been a priest. In any event, all that he can offer is quiescent acceptance and the hope of a deferred reward in the afterlife–and the consolation that though they are suffering, they like the Jews will be led out of the wilderness and into the Promised Land in some indeterminate future. It was the sort of stoic fatalism that was to be preached down through the centuries which encouraged the passive acceptance of misfortune attributing it to the sins of the Gael, the superior cunning and might of the English or to the inscrutability of Providence. It was probably the only response possible short of incitement to violence. But it added to and underpinned the idea and reality of dispossession and exodus with helplessness and deracination.

Not all Catholics moved to the west however, a substantial unpropertied class of labourers and tradesmen remained to service the needs of the victors. In pragmatic terms there were insufficient numbers of Protestant yeoman farmers. It was therefore in the interests of new landowners to press for the retention of tenants, some of whom were the former proprietors. So in reality the vast majority of Catholics, three-quarters according to Corish,[45] remained more or less as they had been before the holocaust. However, crucially, they like those who were actually expelled, suffered severe psychological displacement.[46] Inevitably the dispossessed, both those who experienced banishment and those who remained where they were, came to see themselves as exiles within their own island. Their faith provided what little solace they had and no doubt they derived some consolatory pride from the guerrilla resistance of the 'tories',[47] bands of Irish soldiers who refused to surrender, dispersed to the woods and mountains and continued to fight as others had done in previous moments of armed resistance to the colonising forces. The exploits of the rapparees[48] seem to be unrecorded in the translated verse of the seventeenth century but their heroics and frequently their deaths are captured in song and story.

The point of the creation and continued existence of such stories and songs was the comfort they provided in themselves and the comfort they provided as models of resistance. Their central characters frequently personify admirable courses of action and embody sustaining myths. Their disregard for illegitimate authority is founded on more fundamental ideas of natural justice which oppose the arbitrary inhumanity of the Penal laws; while their insouciant devil-may-care demeanour contrasts vividly with the dour, humourless cruelty of their Protestant oppressors. The resolution of such tales is however, extremely revealing. Most tend to end with the hero trapped, captured, betrayed, imprisoned, executed or transported. This suggests how narrow the options were for resistance and how inevitable and inexorable was the power of the state.

The mythic power of these embryonic stereotypes grew as the English control of Ireland became more complete. As images they could form a male counterpart to the female personification in Ireland in the *aisling* poems of the trained poets from the formal tradition. Like that female personification, the images could shift and slide into relatively optimistic representations when Irish fortunes seemed to be improving, usually when France or Spain seemed about to offer aid, or pessimism when hopes were dashed once more. These images found a tangible expression in a whole series of secret agrarian organisations in later centuries. These included Oakboys, Steelboys, Rightboys, Defenders, Whiteboys, Rockites and Ribbonmen which in a sense 'articulated' in a crude inchoate form, the refusal of the suppressed to accept the legitimacy of the 'stranger'. Thus, the idea of opposition, subversion and rebellion attached itself to images of dispossession, secrecy, cunning and inner-exile.

It is unknown how many priests were killed or executed and no doubt many of the stories that spread were distorted, apocryphal, the stuff of legends. That many were there is no question and by 1654 it had become general policy to banish all Catholic priests. Their presence in Ireland was regarded by the authorities as treasonable and sheltering them became a felony. To enforce the policy a reward of £5 'head money' was given to those who aided a priest's capture. Many priests did go abroad–those who refused 'voluntary' exile were to be transported to Barbados. Their presence there was unwelcome as they formed a focal point of potential rebellion for the other Irish transportees. Therefore, they were banished to the western islands of Aran and Innisbofin–exiled within Ireland. Many of those who did leave for Europe never saw Ireland again. The poet-priest Pádraigín Haicéad had to settle down in the Irish College of Louvain and a simple quatrain of his describes the exiles' heartache:

Awake, I am here in France.
When I sleep I'm in the Island of Conn.
Who would choose to watch and wake?
I am watchful–to suckle sleep.[49]

The disturbance he described derives from being wrenched from Ireland and relocated in an alien space, a dislocation which disrupts his spatial co-ordinates and his grasp of a linear temporality. His perceptual framework is located in the remembered past and subject to the transmogrifications of dream and the distortions of memory. His articulated desire for home is innately conservative in that he can only think, feel and be, within that ontological paradigm which predates his present. He is thus the archetypal Irish exile, the avatar and the model for millions from later generations.

By the latter half of the 1650s it is clear that priests were returning to Ireland–coming into exile from exile:

> They had to walk very warily. It would have been too dangerous, both for themselves and for their hosts to have tried to depend on the laity. Some sought safety in the fastnesses of bogs or mountains, others moved around in disguise or settled as farmers or labourers. The tradition of a local 'mass-rock' is very widespread in Ireland and in many places it may more probably be traced to this period than to the opening decades of the eighteenth century.[50]

It was out of such experiences and discourses that the opinions, ideas and values of the Catholic clergy with their attendant connotations of flight, persecution and suffering became inextricably woven into the consciousness of the people, into their symbology and iconography. The harassment and pursuit experienced by the priesthood became a kind of re-enactment of the narratives of the early Christian martyrs. It conferred on them a validating moral legitimacy which empowered them to propagandise to congregations which accepted their authority and the power of their word in the absence of any other indigenous leadership. Consequently, the mass and the mass-rock became powerful physical and cultural emblems of the native Irish community; additions to the lore of the *dindshenchas* and elemental signifiers of the opposition to their Protestant conquerors and clandestine cultural markers, signalling a profoundly different world-view.

The colonisers' project demanded the silencing of all voices of opposition. They were thus equally zealous in their pursuit of Irish schoolmasters who like the priests could help shape opinion. That little is recorded of these hero-victims, even within an extant and latter-day historiography, is testament to the power and the predominance of priestly discourse and the access they had to external channels of communication in a pan-european institution which heroised the missionary martyr in his opposition to the heretic. Teachers, by comparison, lacked a cohesive centralising organisation. However, it seems reasonable to infer that their experiences and allegiances would tend to create a compensatory discourse looking to Gaelic values, a golden age in pre-conquest Ireland and hope invested in the secular and religious images of lost leaders and potential saviours in much the same way as the poet-priests.[51]

There was a form of secular sanctification in the culture of the defeated. Leaders like Rory O'More, Owen Roe O'Neill and Pierse Ferriter, the latter the embodiment of the poet as a man of action, echoed the reactions of the priests and poets who memorialised the 'Flight of the Earls'. Yet, on this occasion the defeat was so comprehensive as to be beyond consolation. Dispossession, the denial of civil status, the destruction of the old Gaelic order, proscription of Catholic ritual and banishment found a metaphoric mirror in the devastation of Ireland itself. In their desire to create a *tabula rasa*, it seemed as though the parliamentary forces were intent not only on the obliteration of Gaelic civilisation but, on some occasions, on the rasing of the very topography of the island itself.

They had adopted as a military tactic a scorched earth policy which deliberately laid waste forests and fields. Contemporary accounts describe areas of up to thirty miles in which there was no sign of life at all. Woods were systematically destroyed, partly to deny hiding places to guerrilla bands, partly to create more arable land and partly to provide charcoal for smelting. Huge areas of fertile land went untilled. Inevitably the poor suffered chronically from hunger, disease and were total immiseration. One observer saw people

> feeding on carrion and weeds, some starved in the highways and many times poor children, who have lost their parents or deserted by them, are found exposed to, and some of them fed upon by ravening wolves and other beasts of prey.[52]

William Petty, Physician-General of the army and the author of *The Political Anatomy of Ireland* (1691) the only source of figures of the period, estimates that in 1641 the population of Ireland was 11,448,000 of whom 616,000 had died by 1652. Of these 504,000 were natives (native Irish and old English) and 112,000 were colonists and English troops. He also estimated later, that some 40,000 Irish soldiers (and by definition mostly young) had gone to serve in european armies and that 100,000 men, women and children had been transplanted to the colonies in the Americas.[53] Historians tend to be sceptical about how precise the figures are but, what is not in dispute, is the absolute devastation left in the wake of the conquest. Dystopian images of destruction, sterility, emptiness, of conqueror and vanquished pervade the aftermath of the Cromwellian settlement and occupied the consciousness of coloniser and colonised; while exile became on one level indissolubly associated with dispossession, degradation and shame for the defeated Catholics.

On another level however, what little hope there was for the Gael was invested in those abroad. In fact it was their only hope as their plight was attributed to their own sinfulness in conformity with the teachings of the Counter-Reformation and their acknowledgement of the superiority of the *Sasanaigh*. In projecting their hopes onto some *deus ex machina* they were recognising their own powerlessness and inferiority. In what in a sense was a coda to the English Protestant subjugation of Ireland–the Williamite Wars–the Catholic Irish, and the poets in particular, attached their desires for a return to the old hierarchies and conservative certainties to James II and the Jacobite succession. The failure of that project produced a substantial addition to the pantheon of failed heroes.

Patrick Sarsfield embodies all the virtues expected in a leader of the Irish in the late seventeenth century. He symbolised a healing union, a coming together of two previously opposing elements into a newer and more ennobled version of Irishness. Received wisdom and popular opinion suggests that the Irish were betrayed by James II or *Séamus an chaca*,[54] James the excrement as he came to be called, and the French who failed to send sufficient military aid in time. Responsibility for defeat therefore, is effectively shifted onto the deviousness of the English monarch and the indifference of foreigners; while Sarsfield and the Irish are absolved of any shame or blame. Defeat is presented as dignified withdrawal and the signing of the Treaty of Limerick as a negotiated settlement between equals. But as so often in Irish history, cruel irony counter-points heroism for 'Scarcely was the ink dry when a great French fleet came up the Shannon, with a real army on board, but it was too late for Sarsfield to go back on his word, and in any case he was a man both of valour and honour'.[55]

Edmund Curtis here, is of course dealing with received images created out of the need for a creditable version of history. Defeat therefore becomes a consequence of the incompetence, self-interest and deceit of others. The Irish in this version of events are the innocent victims of their own chivalry, decency and honour and victims too of the arbitrary disjunctions of fate. Sarsfield the hero-exile, carries with him the aspirations of his people, which in turn imposes upon him and the 'Wild Geese' the obligation to return and liberate his enslaved compatriots. The term 'Wild Geese' first appeared in an Irish poem in the mid-eighteenth century[56] and was applied retrospectively to the eleven thousand or so Irish Soldiers who sailed with Sarsfield to France under the terms of the Treaty. Their presence there as a military force offered hope for the future and established a significant channel of communication and haven for the Catholic Irish. France was both sanctuary and inspiration, the place from which deliverance would come when, like the wild geese, the exiles would return and redeem Ireland. The exile then is burdened with a crippling weight which links him in an umbilical manner with Mother Ireland, Home, the Past and with succeeding generations.

The psychic burden figures such as Sarsfield came to bear is exemplified in Richard Murphy's eponymous elegy. His virtues are celebrated and his successes abroad are vicariously honoured; the final four verses read as follows:

> You stood, while brother officers betrayed
> By going, and six thousand Irish died.
> Then you assumed command, but veered about
> Choose exile in your courteous conqueror's boat.
>
> 'Change Kings with us, and we will fight again,'
> You said, but sailed off with ten thousand men:
> While women clutched the hawsers in your wake,
> Drowning–it was too late when you looked back.
>
> Only to come home stronger had you sailed:
> Successes held you, and the French prevailed.
> Coolly you triumphed, where you wanted least,
> On Flemish cornfield or at Versailles feast.
>
> We loved you, horseman of the white cockade,
> Above all, for your last words, 'Would to God
> This wound had been for Ireland'. Cavalier,
> You feathered with the wild geese our despair.[57]

Out of this sort of elegiac idealisation exilic heroes often came to be enshrouded in a sort of rhetorical aureole of hopes and dreams; a kind of penumbra of projected wishes which mingled, refracted and distorted according to the needs of the moment. It was a process that mutated easily into the spheres of the mythic and the religious. In time, consoling representations such as this mutated into nationalist symbology as heroic, salvationary, exemplary icons–redemptive emblems for a fallen race.

The poets reacted to the events of the seventeenth century with impotent rage and they railed against the Cromwellian settlers on cultural and social grounds. They inverted the 'barbarian' stereotype the English had created and pinned on the native Irish. The English conquerors were described as 'low-bred, boorish, and heretical'. They were 'English speaking churls', 'bastards', a 'grimy rabble of churlish artisans' or 'wolves and wild dogs'.[58] The poets lamented the loss of their aristocratic patrons and what they deemed to be their virtues–refinement, talent, grace and generosity. They also bemoaned their own descent into insecurity and poverty by turning on the lower orders in savage polemics and caustic mockery. The unknown author of *Páirlimint Cloinne Tomáis* (c. 1650) satirises tenants of English planters who have prospered. They are described as 'coarse and brutish peasants, gluttonous and quarrelsome, aping the gentry, trying to dress fashionably, too low to understand the meaning of refinement, but lost in admiration of a man who could talk broken English'.[59]

Such invective directed in vitriolic fashion at segments of the same conquered culture typifies the fragmented consciousness of a colonised people. Nevertheless paradoxically, as Ó Cuív points out, it is a text saturated in slang, the demotic is utilised as a device to mock the 'churls' and 'rabble' which the composition satirises. In this way, the vernacular of the uneducated and unprivileged entered into the literary tradition. It suggested at least that the professional learned classes acknowledged their existence and that a dialogic interchange between the literary and oral traditions existed and was consciously manifesting itself in the written, as well as the oral texts of Gaelic culture.

Liam de Paor notes that in those areas where the literary tradition maintained a hold on life

> there was extraordinary activity in the copying and circulation of manuscripts. It was a kind of samizdat publication, except that most of the contents were traditional. The copying was a means both of publishing new work (mainly poems) and of providing farmhouses throughout the area with anthologies of material old and new, including tales and romances, poetry, genealogies, religious matter, lives of saints, charms, spells, medieval texts, histories, prophecies, and other lore.[60]

This activity complemented the continued vigorous survival of folk-music, folk-poetry and the folk-tale throughout the whole of Ireland. This suggests that there had been a kind of subterranean continuity within native Irish culture that survived the demise of the formal literary tradition and preserved the modified concerns and poems of the *file* in the folk tradition. Many poets had of necessity to support themselves by transcribing and copying manuscripts and by becoming hedge-school masters and as Kinsella says: 'By the eighteenth century the distinctive role of the poet in Irish was that of outcast'.[61] The poet cast in this mould could hardly help but view himself as an estranged exile. His sense of loss inevitably included a collective keen as a reaction against the disappearance of his privileges and position; a motif which embedded itself not just in the scholarly tradition of literature but in the traditions of the people too.

Dáibhí Ó Bruadair, whom many consider to have been the finest of Gaelic Irish poets, exemplifies in his life and work the alienation and ambivalence of the displaced and out of favour professional poet. He rages against the limitations of the common people, mourns the loss of the 'high poets', composes threnodies for lost patrons, epithalamiums, praise and religious poems, maledictions for those who fail to grant him his due, panegyrics for heroes such as Sarsfield, cries for a second Brian Boru and castigates the Irish for creating their own purgatory. His most famous poem was 'An Longbhriseadh' (The Shipwreck c. 1691). The translated title reads: 'The Shipwreck of Ireland, composed by Dáibhí Ó Bruadair on the misfortunes of Ireland in the year of the Lord 1691 and how the sins of her own children brought ruin and dispersion upon her in the month of October of that year: *Regnum in se divisium desolabitur*'.[62]

It entwines the disasters of his own diminished status with those of Ireland, combining the personal and public, formal literary and contemporaneous speech forms, in a manner his predecessors in the bardic orders would have considered impure or improper. Such a break with tradition almost certainly occurred over a considerable period and suggests that in the absence of secure patronage, there was a need to adapt to other audiences which meant finding forms which might prove accessible to what was in effect the only audience available. Hence a modification of the traditions, entailed an awareness and employment of the song-metres and speech patterns of the people.[63] But as Dunne observes, his poetry as a whole 'revealed a traditional outlook which was weak on analysis and explanation, and content with a pessimistic account of destruction and defeat'.[64]

Aogán Ó Rathaille, most of whose surviving work was written after 1700 (he died in 1729), shared Ó Bruadair's disgust and despair. Dunne comments:

While he detailed the human and local impact of the new colonial system, his mood was one of profound fatalism, offering no real hope for the reversal of the revolution which had destroyed his world and no articulation of Gaelic or Catholic solidarity which might achieve it.[65]

While Ó Bruadair looked to actual corporeal contemporary and histori-cal aristocratic male figures for psychological sustenance, Ó Rathaille increasingly developed the identification between Ireland and an histori-cally unspecified femininity. That sort of personification was not new in Gaelic poetry. He however, re-accentuated the trope and constructed entire poems around the vision of the woman/Ireland and the poet's dialogue with the self-created illusion.[66] Such vision poems or *aisling* could portray Ireland as a faithless mother or shameless hag *meirdreach*, who lifted her skirts for the *Sasannach*'s pleasure;[67] or a visionary daughter in 'Brightness Most Bright' (c. 1709) and as the Goddess Éire in 'The Redeemer's Son, Mac an Cheannaí' (c. 1720). The latter was written in popular eighteenth-century song rhythms which suggests perhaps, Ó Rathaille's recognition of the need to communicate in a form accessible to the people and thus offer the possibility of its acceptance and incorpora-tion into their repertoire of memories and attachments. These accentual song metres 'could draw a response from an audience which shared their sorrows, hopes and joys. The value attached to this poetry by the society from which it came is reflected in the amount of it that was written down and also preserved through oral tradition.'[68]

The shift into this form of allegorical allusiveness could be attributed to the need to encode opposition to the repressive philistinism of the new order, while simultaneously registering the death of hope. In this sense it becomes a poetic palliative or stylised placebo and an implicit acceptance of the impotence of poetry–a nihilistic retreat into retrospection, ritual and memory.

Variations on the *aisling*, encoded the feminisation of Ireland with attachment to place. Art MacCumhaigh from Creggan in Co. Armagh concludes *Úr-Chill an Chreagáin* (The Churchyard of Creaggan) with this response to the dream maiden's invitation to him to join her in 'that honey-sweet land still untouched by alien rule':

O pleasant sweet princess, if you're fated to be my love,
a compact-a promise-ere I take the road West with you:
though I die by the Sionainn, in Man, or in mighty Egypt,
bury me under this sand with Creagan's sweet Gaels.[69]

The poem also registers the tension experienced by the poet between his dream aspiration for Ireland and his loyalty to his wife and friends–between ideal and reality.

Ireland in this kind of formulation is virgin and seductress, temptation and reward, dream projection and wish fulfilment. In later re-formations she is fertility and motherhood 'the very personification of an idealised passive female, beautiful in form and in harmony with nature' and as Ó Tuathaigh goes on to say: 'The dominant motif is important and constant–the passive female is dejected and sad until a *male* poet brings her the good news that a *male* deliverer is coming over the water to free her from bondage'.[70] But she is always there, oedipally, romantically and earthily tugging on the links that bind the exile to his (*sic*) homeland.

It is hardly surprising then, to find that the language, preoccupations and power of the prevailing and continuing patriarchal ideology determine the concerns and forms of exilic discourse. Women as lovers, wives, mothers and sisters are there to lament the leaving of lovers, husbands, sons and brothers. For the male in the discourse they stand totemistically for all it is that they are sacrificing by departing. Perhaps it was the predominance of the religious/military elements in the various waves of outward bound migration that created the overwhelming impression that all who left were men. In any case, women whether abroad as missionaries, wives, followers, indentured servants or at home remained voiceless and departing men sailed away with their eyes fixed firmly on the shores of Ireland and their backs to the future.

Jerrold Casway has estimated that there were about 602,000 pre-nineteenth-century emigrants from Ireland–of whom thirty per cent were women.[71] Men left to serve in the armies of Europe throughout the eighteenth century for the Jacobite cause. Some left to be educated abroad in Irish seminaries, some went out to the colonies in the New World and many went to England as seasonal migrant labourers or vagrants. Others enlisted in the British military like the *spailpín* poet Eoghan Rua Ó Súilleabháin–the archetypal wandering poet-playboy. Ó Súilleabháin refined the *aisling*, matching theme expertly to melodies[72] and Brian Merriman parodied it in *The Midnight Court* (c. 1780). Eibhlín Dhubh Ní Chonaill in the only formal, culturally acceptable means open to an Irish woman, lamented the death of her husband in *Caoineadh Airt Uí Laoghaire* (Lament for Art O'Laoghaire c. 1783).[73] It provided a model for countless other such keenings in the folk tradition on the occasion of the death or departure of a close family member–though how many lamented the loss of a close female relative in formal verse is unknown.[74] The absence of genuine women's voices in the years prior to the twentieth century, as opposed to assumed voices and representations of women in P.L. Henry's anthology of writing in the Irish language *Dánta Bán: Poems of Irish Women* (1991)[75] would suggest that women had some degree of independence but that nevertheless their role was essentially subordinate. Poems such as 'Donal Óg' and 'My Grief on the Sea'[76] ventriloquised–as was the convention in Gaelic poetry with the poet adopting the speaking voice of the female protagonist–or not, testify to the utter dependence of women on absent men and the decision they took as to whether women could leave Ireland. The idea that a woman might depart of her own volition was clearly incomprehensible to the male psyche–poetic or otherwise.[77]

The poetry survived and as part of the oral tradition it remained strong.[78] However, without a forward looking intelligentsia experimenting with new ideas and forms it existed vestigially, preserved in a reactive, downtrodden, oppressed and conservative consciousness, endlessly recycling itself in each generation of resentful and dispossessed native Irish. As Canny says: 'the form no less than the content of these poems indicates that the Gaelic outlook which flourished in the eighteenth century was a deeply pessimistic one, because in rejecting the existing political system the Gaelic poets held out no realistic prospect of an improvement upon their position other than a vague hope of a fortuitous return to a lost golden age'.[79] In fact, Irish Jacobite poetry synthesised millenarian appeals and projections with Catholicism and an oppositional form of Gaelic psychic resistance which united master and servant, aristocrat and peasant, literate and illiterate, the dispossessed within Ireland and the dispossessed overseas in a restorative fantasy which of necessity excluded the conquerors.[80]

Canny goes on to argue that ironically the Catholics and the Protestants were both working out of a providential paradigm. The Catholics as has been established, attributed their misfortunes to their own failings while the victorious Protestants ascribed their triumph to the vengeance of God and to the belief that they were the elect, the chosen people.[81] The Protestants consolidated their success with a series of legislative measures that came to be known collectively as the Penal Laws. The Penal Laws attempted to reinforce Protestant dominance by excluding Catholics from public life and preventing them from accumulating any economic power. They were not allowed to vote, carry arms or own a horse above the value of £5, Catholic clergy were banished, intermarriage was made the grounds for disinheritance, inheritance between Catholics was disallowed and leasing rights restricted. They were excluded from the professions and in common with the Dissenters, Catholics were subject to sacramental tests, oaths of allegiance and adjuration.

Corkery's picture of a 'hidden Ireland', a peasant society homogeneously flat, depressed and poverty stricken, has been challenged by Louis Cullen[82] and other historians. No doubt the Gaelic Catholic reality was more differentiated than his picture would suggest, but as Foster says:

> The Penal Laws reflected Protestant fears and affected Irish mentality, creating a tension of resentment born of enforced deference as well as necessitating the elaborate concealment and stratagems of Catholic political activity. Here, at least, the concept of a 'hidden' Ireland has a real meaning.[83]

The political, social and economic alienation thus institutionalised forced the native Irish back onto their own resources. Class, economic and regional differences were minimised and paradoxically their interests coalesced around a much greater sense of unity as they defined themselves inevitably against their Other–the Protestant possessors. It was a Manichaean dualism which the process of colonisation ineluctably ordained: 'colonialism ... is in fact the organisation of a Manichaean world, a world divided up into compartments' according to Frantz Fanon,[84] 'a world of statues' where 'The native is a being hemmed in'.[85] The Gaelic Catholic self-image formed and modified itself against the Protestant perception of the native Irish and against their own perception of English (primarily) Protestant actions, behaviour, values and beliefs. While both coloniser and colonised were operating within a Christian and eurocentric world-view, Catholics consciously and intuitively identified and sought differentiating signifiers which distinguished them from their oppressors and conferred a sense and image of difference upon themselves and their culture. In doing so they were attempting to recover on the psychological level some dignity and pride. In their horrific present all they had, had to be excavated out of history–albeit an imagined or fictive version of their origins, evolution and resistance. Among the most obvious markers of distinctiveness were: their religion, their language, their shared experiences of the present such as the emblematically communal alienation of the 'stations', gatherings at traditional shrines, the cult of the holy wells and their perceptions of the past. The priests, poets and schoolmasters were all principal movers in creating a counter-hegemonic discourse. They were concerned to propagate a particular view of the Gaelic past which was hierarchic, privileged and introverted.

Integrated into that very partial representation was the notion that leaving Ireland constituted a form of exile, that to leave the homeplace and travel within Ireland was itself 'unnatural' and dislocating–an experience many were obliged to undergo as they followed seasonal/migratory work patterns often in the wake of famine as in 1740–41.

Given that context as hopes of a Jacobite restitution faded and as Britain and the ascendancy began to react to the political challenges inherent in the American and French Revolutions, it was entirely predictable that the Irish should begin to identify with ideas like democracy, independence and nationalism–that Jacobitism should mutate into Jacobinism. The ideological predisposition to look to Europe for salvation on the part of the Catholic Irish meant that they regarded the 'New World' in a negative light. Their experience of North America, actual or vicarious, linked it with forced transportation, kidnappings, hard labour and dissolution of identity. As Miller points out, there were few attractions in substituting one form of Protestant ascendancy for another.[86] Nevertheless, the received image we have of a monolithic movement of Protestant Presbyterians to America in the eighteenth century oversimplifies the reality– there were Anglicans, Quakers, Methodists and Catholics who left Ireland in substantial numbers. But, the Ulster-Scots (a designation adopted in the nineteenth century to distinguish them from the Catholic Irish), some 200,000 of whom emigrated between 1700 and 1776, stood out. This was partly because they remained separate from their host communities and perhaps more importantly because Ulster women also emigrated,[87] which enabled them to preserve a distinct familial and communal identity.

THE ANGLO-IRISH TRADITION

Like the Catholics the Ulster-Scots Presbyterians saw themselves as exiles. They employed similar biblical rhetoric to describe their condition and they too were discriminated against under the Penal Laws. That superficial similarity however, overlay profoundly different realities and perceptions. Economic considerations such as rack-renting, payment of tithes to the Anglican clergy, poor harvests, fluctuations in the linen trade and competition from Catholic tenants who were often willing to outbid Protestants for leases, were underpinned by a shallowness of memorial ties to Ireland and a sense of betrayal by King, Parliament and the landowning classes. They felt too, the counter-attractions of an edenic New World as described in letters by those who had gone before, the appeal of a 'Promised Land' as promoted by the shipowner's agents and the promise of support by Puritan clergymen already there:

> Finally, and most important, Ulster Presbyterians viewed history as if it were a morality play–with themselves in the role of the old Testament Israelites–which would end in the prophesied millennium when they would be delivered from their enemies; consequently, they regarded the secular and the supernatural–economic, political and religious causation–as inseparable, Presbyterian countrymen saw themselves as 'exiles' already in an Ulster where they laboured under the harsh authority of Anglican pharaohs, and they interpreted the adverse consequences of commercialisation not as the inexorable workings of impersonal market forces but as evidence of a villainous campaign to suppress their civil and religious liberties.[88]

The fixation on the idea of themselves as the elect, predestined to inhabit a heaven on earth sustained the Presbyterian emigrants through their experiences as indentured servants. The hostility they encountered in New England from their Calvinistic cousins and the hardships they endured in establishing communities in outlying areas were subsumed under the power of that belief. It also precluded any sustainable retrospective longing for Ireland. Ireland for them was merely a staging post, a trial on their journey–home, destiny, deliverance and destination were in the future. It was out of such experiences and self-perceptions that the descendants of the Ulster Presbyterians and other commentators on America like Woodrow Wilson, created the myth of the Scotch-Irish whose 'rugged individualism', attachment to liberty, freedom and conscience and entrepreneurial energy epitomised the spirit of capitalist America. Qualities which at the same time distinguished them from the native and emigrant Catholic Irish.[89] In that kind of configuration there was no space for the notion of forced exile or any sense of loss. Departure had to be viewed as voluntary, self-interested and positive. It was an elemental constituent of a teleology predicated on success, which goes some way to explaining the absence of the concept in most Protestant discourse and the relative silence in historiography and literature about Protestant emigration.

About a quarter of those Protestants who emigrated in the eighteenth century were from the poorer sections of the Anglican community–although some of those from the ascendancy who did not go to make a career in England went to America. Unlike the Presbyterians and the Catholic Irish they quickly assimilated and became indistinguishable from other white, Anglo-Saxon Protestants, whether newly arrived or long established settlers.

The Anglo-Irish ascendancy, the possessing classes, had no meaningful alternative but to look to and identify with England and the Empire. In aligning themselves accordingly, they enhanced and protected their reflected self-esteem while ensuring a continuation of their social, cultural, economic and political privileges. At the same time, the alliance, unequal though it was, guaranteed their military security.

In placing themselves ideologically at the heart of the Empire and having of necessity to accede to the pre-eminence of the metropolitan centre, it was impossible to represent themselves and their peripheral position as exile. Therefore, their unbalanced dependency necessitated a substantial and unavoidable degree of self-deceit which manifested itself in what Memmi calls the dialectics of 'exaltation-resentment'.[90] They oscillated between a glorification of England and the Empire in all their outward achievements and bitter resentment at what they judged to be its neglect of their contributions to its wonders. Their condition was, according to J.C. Beckett, characterised by

> a kind of ambivalence, or ambiguity of outlook, arising from the need to be at once Irish and English, and leading sometimes to detachment, some-times to a fierce aggressiveness that may, on occasion, mark an underlying sense of insecurity.[91]

That internalised and irreconcilable conflict produced a form of psychic isolation bounded by a nexus of justifications and special pleadings arising out of rights based on conquest and coercion, and weakness emanating from the absence of consent and independent power. Jonathan Swift, 'the archetype of the colonial in Ireland', who 'embodies the contradictions and uneasiness of the Anglo-Irish tradition',[92] in his career and in his writings exemplifies in many ways the perverse inconsistencies and occlusions of the ascendancy mind. An outsider in the land of his birth, and like the poet Spenser before him, a self-imaged exile from England, he describes his feelings on his return to Ireland and the ailing Stella in *Holyhead Sept 25 1717*, written after he'd given up hope of an appointment in England. The poem opens with a choleric and dyspeptic expression of irritation at the forced delay in sailing and concludes:

> I never was in haste before
> To reach that slavish hateful shore
> Before, I always found the wind

To me was most malicious kind
But now, the danger of a friend
On whom my fears and hopes depend
Absent from whom all climes are curst
With whom I'm happy in the worst
With rage impatient makes me wait
A passage to the land I hate.
Else, rather on this bleaky shore
Where loudest winds incessant roar
Where neither herb nor tree will thrive,
Where nature hardly seems alive,
I'd go in freedom to my grave
Than rule yon isle and be a slave.[93]

Ireland, for Swift, was 'a land of slaves and fens' inhabited by 'A servile race in folly mired, who truckle most, when treated worst'. Writing about himself in the third person he says:

In Exile with a steady heart,
He spent his life's declining part;
Where, folly, pride and faction sway,
Remote from St John, Pope and Gay.[94]

London was clearly considered by Swift to be the cultural epicentre of the known world and Ireland, Dublin, peripheral and by implication provincial; an uncivilised, unfashionable remote outpost of the Empire. Yet at the same time, he asserted the irreconcilable parity of Ireland as a sister kingdom entitled to the same status and privileges as England under the Crown. As J.C. Beckett put it:

His attacks upon English policy towards Ireland are inspired by jealousy, not by contempt or hatred, and the claim that he puts forward on behalf of Ireland is essentially a claim to be treated as the equal of England. In all this there is a strong personal element. Swift, the Irishman in England, is aggressively conscious of his status as one of a ruling group, very insistent on the respect in which he feels he should be held. Swift, in Ireland, can achieve the same end only by insisting on the status and rights of the country in which he is compelled, however unwillingly to live.[95]

This frustration is built into something like a climax in the fourth Drapier's letter, 'To the whole People of Ireland' (1724), when he asserted

the rights of the Irish against the impositions of the English Parliament.
In what was to him a self-evident transparent truth he said:

> For in *Reason*, all *Government* without the Consent of the *Governed* is the *very*
> *Definition of Slavery*: But in Fact *Eleven Men well armed, will certainly subdue*
> *one single Man in his Shirt*. But I have done. For those who have used *Power*
> to cramp *Liberty*, have gone so far as to resent even the *Liberty* of
> *Complaining*; although a Man upon the Rack, was never known to be refused
> the Liberty of *roaring* as loud as he thought fit.[96]

And he goes on to express his resentment at the way in which the
English look on his people as 'a Sort of *Savage Irish*'.[97] In Swift's eyes of
course, the 'Savage Irish' were the Catholic Irish, those 'rightly' suppressed
by the Penal Laws–they were not included in his address to the 'whole
People of Ireland'. He was in fact addressing the Protestant nation, approximately a quarter of the inhabitants of the island and even more specifically, he was speaking to the middling sort of Anglicans, those loyal to the
Crown and the established Church. It was a rhetorical slight of hand shot
through with the inescapable contradictions of his position and symptomatic of his class frustration at the lack of discrimination on the part of
the English. Their failure to distinguish between the native Irish and the
'English-Irish' was to Swift, not only a form of ingratitude, but profoundly
insulting.

Imprisoned as he was by the prejudices and interests of his people he
was utterly incapable of conceiving of Ireland as a colony–colonies for
him were in the Americas or elsewhere overseas. He was thus unable to
acknowledge and accept the subservience of Ireland to England or to
comprehend the English indifference to what he considered to be reasonable and natural:

> Swift's writing implied the need for radical change but dreaded the
> prospect. His Protestantism held itself up as the supreme example of stoic
> loyalty, but was forever dissatisfied. Caught between roles of mastery and
> servitude, loyalty and betrayal, it struggled for some liberating sense of
> identity, based on consensus and freedom. The rhetoric was usually heroic,
> but the reality was often farcical.[98]

It was out of the clash between the desire for order and the chaotic
irrationality of the Irish experience that Swift and others such as Burke
attempted to find language and forms which could encompass those
disparities. That search led to a partial projection of Ireland's particular
problems onto a more generalised human plane as in *Gulliver's Travels*
(1726) and the desperate and despairing mock innocent savagery of *A*

Modest Proposal (1729) with its logical but inhuman calculations, for 'Where Nature and Reason have been defeated, Madness rules'.[99] Swift it seemed, occupied a cognitive no man's land in which he experienced an oxymoronic estrangement as he oscillated between the metonymic polarities of London and Dublin. It is not hard to see how the linguistic and stylistic innovation generated by the attempt to deal with alienation, absurdity and 'madness', inaugurated a tradition and culture given to experimentation and exploration of the marginal and the irrational.

The process of elision whereby the distinct self-images which the principal groups within Ireland had of themselves as conflated in English eyes into a simple nebulous image of Irishness was paralleled in Ireland by the imaginative needs of later generations of nationalists. Swift ironically became a founding figure in the struggle for nationhood, an heroic example to those such as Grattan and Yeats concerned with constructing a lineage of Anglo-Irish independence. He came to be seen as one of the first Irish patriots along with Molyneux–a designation he would have almost certainly rejected. Nevertheless, his incorporation into the pantheon of Irish Protestant (and later nationalist) heroes served a need as the ascendancy began to assert its independence from England and demand self-government. In that ideological reconstruction and appropriation he became what in Memmi's paradigm was termed a 'coloniser who refuses' having been throughout his life a 'coloniser who accepts'. A similar kind of fate overcame other figures from the ascendancy who in their own time and lives had identified themselves as English and/or had spent much of their active working lives in England. Such figures included Thomas Southerne, Richard Steele, George Farquhar, Thomas Parnell, George Berkely, Oliver Goldsmith, Richard Brinsley Sheridan and Edmund Burke. Individuals such as these never wholly assimilated into metropolitan society. Though drawn to the centre by ambition and the absence of opportunity in Ireland, they remained to a greater or lesser extent on the margin psychologically (and often socially too) and developed in many instances a mocking–sometimes affectionate, sometimes savage–distance from what they observed and experienced. A corollary to that marginalisation was that some, like Farquhar, connived with and pandered to the basic needs of the imperialist audiences to produce stereotypical representations of Irish characters. They invariably conflated grossly caricatured images drawn from the Catholic population which of course, helped confirm and develop English ideas of superiority.

Wolfgang Zach in his essay, 'Oliver Goldsmith on Ireland and the Irish: Personal Views, Shifting Attitudes, Literary Stereotypes' (1982), has described the protean ambivalence inherent in the Anglo-Irish writers' position. Goldsmith he asserts, is

> emotionally attached to Ireland, though at the same time intellectually drawn towards the polite English world of learning and literature. It is much more difficult to determine the position he takes in his literary oeuvre, as he does not overtly refer to Ireland in his major poetical works and even in his accounts of Irish matters in his minor writings he is averse to acknowledging his Irishness, rather sheltering, behind fictional 'English' masks and 'impersonal' typification. Nevertheless, we can see his point of view shifting from extreme anglocentricity to Anglo-Irish attitudes and even pro-Irish propaganda, which may lead us to suspect that an oscillating allegiance for England and Ireland can be discerned from his literary works ...
>
> Goldsmith, influenced by the classicist tradition and under the pressure of 'writing for bread', tends to exclude his personal experiences and individual impressions rather keeping to the learned tradition, to the 'universally' valid views, and to the literary expectations of his English reading public instead—at least overtly.[100]

His dilemma is that of the prototypical cultural hybrid—neither fully English nor fully Irish. He was privileged and marginalised within Ireland; on the periphery and provisional within England. His writing and criticism (and acceptability) was contingent on his ability to amuse, entertain and mock within the unspoken boundaries of English establishment sensibilities. It was also dependent on his ability to absorb, deflect and negotiate the preconceived, patronising stereotyping attendant on any immigrant, at whatever social level, endemic within the centripetal and self-regarding culture of the metropolitan centre. In that sense the role he adopted in attempting to earn a living and make a literary reputation was archetypically Anglo-Irish. He was the lineal antecedent of equally gifted Anglo-Irish progeny, like G.B. Shaw and Oscar Wilde, neither of whom could escape the cultural constraints and deformations he experienced, though each in his own way tried.

In striving for control of their own affairs it was of course necessary for the ascendancy to emphasise their differences from the English. In the latter part of the eighteenth century they did by developing the idea of the 'Irish Nation' as a distinct but equal polity under the Crown. The conception had to be supported by markers which clearly signalled their uniqueness. They obviously stressed their history, ways of thinking and separate economic needs. However in addition, in the linguistic and cultural spheres, they had developed speech patterns which resembled those of the native Irish and some among the intelligentsia began to take an active interest in Gaelic Irish history, antiquities and literature. Around the middle of the eighteenth century some of the surviving Catholic gentry began to rehabilitate Gaelic culture in an attempt to show that their ancestors were not uncivilised and savage and that Catholic Ireland was worthy of admittance to the political nation. Charles O'Conor, John Curry and Sylvester O'Halloran wrote pamphlets and papers to progagate their views. In do so they opened up an area of distinctive Irish interest which caught the imagination of Joseph Cooper Walker who published his *Historical Memoirs of the Irish Bards* in 1786. Henry Brooke, and his daughter, Charlotte prepared a collection of Gaelic poems with verse translations entitled *Reliques of Irish Poetry* which was published in Dublin in 1789 while Edward Bunting was asked to transcribe the airs played at the Belfast Harp Festival in 1792 by the last of the Irish harpers. Such activities received the support of many individual Protestants and of the Royal Irish Academy as they lent credence to the formation of a separate Irish identity. Their enthusiasm and needs led to the attempt to appropriate the remnants of aristocratic Gaelic culture which may ostensibly have seemed disinterested and motivated solely by scholarship. But in effect and in time, it enabled the nascent middle-class intellectual Protestant nationalists to shift allegiances without relinquishing privileges held or hoped for:

> For them the old language and culture was valuable because through its recovery they could realign themselves with the past of the country they lived in and (decreasingly) governed; because through it they could more effectively proselytise the Catholic Irish of the West and, finally, they could find in its revival a powerful counter to the egalitarian mass democracy which it was in the interest of the Irish Catholics to realise.[101]

A view endorsed, refined and confirmed by Norman Vance, when he says:

> The Irish past which was largely a literary diversion for Anglican intellectuals like William Preston was a vital political and literary weapon for presbyterian writers like William Drennan.[102]

Presbyterian radicals like Drennan, inspired by the American revolution, and Tom Paine, infused antiquarianism with 'moral and political passion'[103] and added a democratic dimension to the restoration of Ireland's history.

Part of the cost of that identification with native Irish culture was however, the partial loss or blurring of distinct and discriminatory images and the linguistic terms that conveyed differences. If they were not lost to the unconscious of Protestant dominance, they had at least to be suppressed during the struggle against the English. Within Ireland therefore, among those Protestants seeking a form of cultural and ideological synthesis, any kind of affective or rational challenge to the conceptualisation of exile in Catholic thinking became inadmissible. It was an issue on which they were effectively silenced if indeed they comprehended or considered the idea at all. That so few understood or thought about exile or emigration for that matter, is evident by its absence from the literature produced in the English language in Ireland in the eighteenth century. A volume such as *A Georgian Celebration: Irish Poets of the Eighteenth Century* (1989) [104] edited by Patrick Fagan, an anthology of English language poetry written primarily by Protestant graduates of Trinity College Dublin, contains no mention of the terms or reference to the ideas at all. Their concerns and forms by and large mimic the poetry being written in England at the same time. This was inevitable given the pattern of thought that saw Dublin as the second city of the Empire and the colonialist as the embodiment of the essential virtues and values of the mother country. For 'the coloniser who accepts' to borrow Memmi's term, the home country constitutes a 'remote and never intimately known ideal' and it is necessary that this 'ideal be immutable and sheltered from time; the colonialist requires his homeland to be conservative.[105] Basking in the reflected exaltation of their imagined homeland and perceiving himself to be its ideal representative his circumscribed view of the world attempts as far as possible to denigrate and exclude the problems and concerns of the colonised. The concept of exile, at least as it was conceived by Irish Catholics, was therefore completely absent from the consciousness and poetry of the Anglican neoclassicists of TCD.

The attempt to unite Catholic and Protestant interests in the cultural sphere through antiquarianism was paralleled in the political domain by the efforts of the United Irishmen to form a common bond in adversity and unite in opposition to the English. Wolfe Tone describes in his autobiography how he analysed the three principal denominational groups. He felt no need to address the Protestants as their interests were inextricably linked with the preservation of the status quo or the Catholics, as 'there existed in the breast of every Irish Catholic an inextricable abhorrence of the English name and power'. His famous pamphlet, 'An Argument on behalf of the Catholics of Ireland' (1791) was

> to convince them that they and the Catholics had but one common interest and one common enemy; that the depression and slavery of Ireland was

produced and perpetuated by the divisions existing between them, and that, consequently, to assert the independence of their country, and their own individual liberties, it was necessary to forget all former feuds, the consolidate the entire strength of the whole nation, and to form for the future but one people.[106]

Tone, Russell and ten Belfast Presbyterian merchants–'colonisers who refused' in Memmian terms–founded the first club of the Society of United Irishmen in August 1791. Membership was overwhelmingly Protestant, though links were sought with the Catholic Committee and as the Society moved to a position of militant republicanism, with the Defenders.

Government proscription and repression induced the United Irishmen to redefine their organisation into a tighter cellular form to preserve secrecy. This however, had the adverse effect of restricting the flow of ideas and information and their goals. This in turn increased their distance from the Catholic masses–now they aimed for a 'republican government with separation from England'.[107] Tone's association with William Jackson, an emissary from France who was arrested for treason, led to his effective banishment. Faced with the choice of arrest or leaving the country, he accepted the inevitable and with the authorities' permission made plans to go to America as a stepping stone to France where, delegated by the new United Irishmen's leadership, he was to seek the assistance of the French in the search for independence. Tone viewed his leaving unproblematically. In his autobiography he tells how he 'was obliged to quit my country, and go into exile in America' [108] and that 'undoubtedly, I was guilty of a great offence against the existing Government; that, in consequence, I was going into exile; and that I considered that exile as a full expiation for the offence, and consequently felt myself at liberty, having made that sacrifice to begin again on a fresh score.[109] During his period in France from 1796 to 1798, Tone found himself among a cosmopolitan and amorphous society of revolutionary exiles from other European countries such as Russia, Poland, Holland and Savoy; the loosely knit and fissiparous community of Irish radicals who, like Tone, had fled Ireland; and the older generation of Irish émigrés, Catholic, aristocratic, monarchical for the most part, who formed the Irish Brigade.

Unlike the survivors and descendants of the native Irish in France and the Catholic Irish in Ireland, Tone and the other Protestant radicals thought of exile in a qualitatively different form. Exile for them was in a sense a means to an end, a determinate sentence from which one could redeem oneself. It was as if the mantle of 'exile' were in itself honorific and in the age of Romanticism it resonated with newly charged meaning. It was as though the revolutionary exile formed a political counterpart to the romantic artist–a visionary singled out by the Gods or Providence to fulfil a given destiny beyond the capacities of lesser mortals. Tone's idea of exile was inspirational, cosmopolitan and modernising. It formed part of a transcendent vision in the spirit of the rights of man, brotherhood, liberty and equality. Significantly, it contrasted sharply with that embedded in the consciousness of the Catholic Irish which emphasised place, community, a numinous organicism and the weight of tradition. Urban, urbane, ahead of his time and ignorant about Irish realities, Tone and the United Irishmen inaugurated a tradition which could transcend the entrenched antagonisms of colonialism, just as socialism aimed to do later in the nineteenth and early twentieth centuries. But, it was a tradition that nevertheless assumed implicitly, that those from the Protestant community would take on leadership in the new Ireland.

After Tone's death, the defeat in 1798, the Union in 1800 and Emmet's failed rebellion in 1803, the continued presence of former United Irishmen in France

> attracted the periodic pilgrimages of Irish nationalists and republicans, reminding them of the mission left unfinished, of 'the account they keep open'. The contributions of surviving United men to debates in the Irish press, and the frequent resurrection of the United Irish bogey by the authorities, kept their memory alive for much of the nineteenth century. Honourable exile in what Irish nationalists recognised as the traditional 'asylum of the banished Irish insurgents' had endowed the former United leaders with a nobility and an authority which would have most certainly been submerged in Daniel O'Connell's crusade for Catholic emancipation and repeal of the Union, had they been permitted to return.[110]

Most of the leaders of the United Irishmen however, either fled to America before their capture, accepting the failure of their enterprise, or bargained for their freedom with the Dublin authorities exchanging prison and possible or probably execution for 'voluntary' exile in the USA. Throughout the sixteenth, seventeenth and eighteenth centuries America had seemed welcoming to Protestants but alien and hostile to Catholics. However, in the aftermath of its own revolution, the revolution in France, the events of 1798 and Protestant reprisals, the USA seemed less threatening. Miller sums up the consequences of the actions of the United Irishmen for Ireland and Irish perceptions of America in the following manner:

the United Irishmen, their ideals, and their abortive revolution had ultimately profound effects upon Catholic Irish Society and Catholics' perception of emigration to America. First the horrors of '98 became part of the peasants' bitter heritage, modernising and reinforcing the legends of Elizabethan and Cromwellian persecutions: 'Before I was ever able to read a book', remembered a late nineteenth century Catholic rebel, 'I heard stories of Irish women ripped open by English bayonets, and of Irish infants dashed against walls'. Second, through their propaganda the United Irishmen bridged the ideological gulf between Dissenter radicalism and Gaelic tribalism, melding both into a future-oriented and at least theoretically inclusive Irish nationalism couched in the language of American and French republicanism. Thus the United Irishmen gave Catholics old anti-*Sasanaigh* traditions a new medium of expression–born in urban Anglicised Ireland–which could flourish despite the inexorable decline of Gaelic culture. Third, by fleeing abroad after their defeat, the United Irish leaders preserved and perpetuated the Gaelic tradition of emigration as political exile; banished to a foreign land, these first republican nationalists inherited the mantle of O'Neill and Sarsfield, and so established continuity between past and present persecutions. Finally, by making the United States–rather than Europe–their asylum, the United Irishmen helped transform Catholics' hitherto negative perceptions of the New World. Just as the flights of the Ulster earls and the Wild Geese had directed Catholic attention to Spain and France, the experiences of Emmet, Macneven and countless other fugitives demonstrated that–even if emigration was 'exile'–at least the United States was a land of refuge, abundance, and equal opportunity for Irish Catholics as well as Protestants.[111]

Miller goes on to point out that the exile motif itself was like the Irish versions of Catholicism and history, Gaelic Irish music and poetry, part of the cultural luggage imported into what was to become Irish-American discourse and self-imagery. Further infusions of Catholic Irish experience in later waves of emigration renewed and revivified the discourse. It acquired its own dynamic and was refracted by time, by the institutionalisation of Irish identity in organisations like: the Friendly Sons of St Patrick of Philadelphia (1771), the Friendly Sons of St Patrick (1784), the Shamrock Society of New York (c. 1812) and the Hibernian Societies of Charleston (1803), Baltimore (1816) and New Orleans (1817),[112] and by immersion in the heteroglot culture of an assertive, self-confident and increasingly powerful political and industrial world power. 'Irishness' in the ethnic multiplicity of nineteenth-century America, became simplistically essentialised as Catholic and Gaelic and saturated with images of wild abandoned beauty, spirituality, rebellion and dispossession. Images such as these helped define and describe protean Irish-American ideas of Ireland and the Irish. Unlike other immigrant groups of comparable size such as the English and the Germans who assimilated rapidly,

> with the Irish, new arrivals interacted with the Americanised and the American born in such a way that assimilation in manners, livelihood, and education neither opened all doors to social acceptance and career advancement nor snapped the links forged by churchgoing and pride of ancestry between the poor and the better-off or those men born in Ireland and those born in the United States. A common outlook and appearance, however imponderable, survived the loss of Irish accents and customs and even survived American birth.[113]

Protestant liberals it seems, continued to leave Ireland for the USA for some years after the Union, attracted no doubt, by the ideals and opportunities represented by America. That in turn had the effect of diminishing non-Catholic opposition to the rampant growth of Orangeism and sectarian oppression within Ireland. In addition, many emigrant Protestant conservatives and loyalists began to find enthusiastic American republicanism profoundly unattractive and alienating. Many such emigrants in the early nineteenth century began to emigrate to Canada. In these pre-famine years the total numbers of Protestants emigrating still exceeded the total number of Catholics.[114]

Canada was an extension of 'home' where the precepts of Orangeism could be preached and practised and the idea of exile was irrelevant and psychologically insupportable. Canada also represented a context wherein the Protestant Irish whose lineage as 'Irish' was relatively recent, could shed the appellation 'Irishman' to become a new being, a Canadian, while retaining and renewing their fundamental value and belief systems as earlier generations of emigrants had in the context of colonial America. Emigration for Protestants frequently resolved their problematic sense of identity. It received ideological underpinning from the increasingly bourgeois nature of Irish Protestantism. This itself was bound up with the urbanisation and industrialisation of the North East and the development of the Protestant work ethic which emphasised and legitimised individualistic achievement. Emigration in pursuit of a better material (and spiritual) life thus came to be seen as positive, optimistic, offering opportunities for personal fulfilment and conversely, leaving Ireland was seen as a form of escape or release–often from the perceived threat of a resurgent Catholicism.[115]

The ease with which Protestants were assimilated into the cultures of

North America contrasted vividly with the experience of the Catholic Irish. That ready absorption left the discursive field free for the Catholic Irish to develop their distinctive exilic discourse unchallenged. That discourse had profound and far reaching consequences when allied to, or subsumed under, the dominant romantic nationalist discourse which formed and guided so much political and aesthetic activity in the nineteenth and twentieth centuries.

Within Ireland the aftermath of the upheavals of the 1790s and early 1800s induced a realignment of Protestant society into a relatively homogenous ideological bloc. Industry, commerce and agriculture were increasingly dependent on British links. Informal and institutional social and political hegemony manifested itself through the rapid rise of Orangeism. This unified disparate Protestant interests in opposition to republicanism, Catholicism, constitutional reform and in support of the 'New Reformation' a militantly proselytising Protestant movement incorporating Anglicans, Methodists and Presbyterians. The 'New Reformation' failed in its intent to eradicate Catholicism, but

> successfully sublimated denominational and social differences among Irish Protestants, marshalling them in defence of both the Ascendancy and the union with their British co-religionists. However, by emphasising the exclusively *religious* aspects of group identity, the New Reformation effectively divorced Irish Protestants from the bulk of their countrymen who were demanding repeal of the union under the slogan 'Ireland for the Irish'. Unable or unwilling to be 'Irish' by that definition, yet not really 'British' despite their proclamations of loyalty to the Crown, Ireland's Protestants were in a sense, a 'nation' bereft of a homeland.[116]

They were thus obliged to subliminally reject or repress deracination and ally themselves with each other, primarily, and subserviently with Britain. Hence Protestantism became synonymous with unionism[117] while 'The colonial élite were absorbed into the metropolitan system'[118] becoming substantial providers of the 'servants' of the Empire such as military men, judges and administrators.

Ecumenical reformers and adherents to a more generous and encompassing Enlightenment philosophy such as William Drennan the United Irishman, doctor and poet, and Maria Edgeworth, were effectively marginalised if not silenced by the emigration of so many liberals and the shift to a reactionary, monolithic conformity amongst the minority Protestant community on the occasions when any real or perceived challenge came from the Catholic majority. If the Catholics had ever listened, which seems highly unlikely, then the assumption implicit in such offers of *rapprochement* that their offer of enlightened leadership was the way forward for Ireland was bound to be received with at least indifferent scepticism and most probably uncomprehending hostility. Yet, the Blakeian rhythms and Franciscan appeal of Drennan's elegy 'The Wake of William Orr' (1797) testifies to the possibilities inherent in the historical moment. Out of the dystopian chaos of irrationality, arbitrary injustice and casual cruelty, he prays for a new creation:

> God of mercy! God of Peace!
> Make this mad confusion cease;
> O'er the mental chaos move,
> Through it SPEAK the light of love.
>
> Monstrous and unhappy sight!
> Brothers' blood will not unite;
> Holy Oil and holy water
> Mix, and fill the world with slaughter.
>
> Who is she with aspect wild?
> The widow'd mother with her child–
> Child new stirrings in the womb!
> Husband waiting for the tomb!
>
> Angel of this sacred place,
> Calm her soul and whisper peace–
> Cord, or axe, or guillotine,
> Make the sentence–not the sin.
>
> Here we watch our brother's sleep:
> Watch with us, but do not weep:
> Watch with us thro' dead of night–
> But expect the morning light.[119]

Drennan's appeal is to a shared future rather than a fragmented, nightmarish and mythologised past from which he was necessarily excluded. His past, his history, had to be in a sense erased to effect any kind of union with the Catholic oppressed. This meant that freedom and harmony inevitably had to be projected onto a millenarian future. He was perhaps naive in his aspirations and like Edgeworth ignorant of the depth and difference of native Irish feeling. Like most of the United Irish leadership however, he survived the rising and its savage reprisals with his life and limbs intact and his liberty unimpaired.

THE NATIVE IRISH AND THE CONCEPT OF EXILE IN THE
ENGLISH LANGUAGE

The peculiar class formations within the Irish colonial context precluded any real or worthwhile interchange between middle-class radicals and lower-class rebels. Class differentiation took on extreme cultural forms. For example, Catholic Gaelic disenfranchised as against Protestant 'English' subjects having voting rights with no immediate, meaningful or straightforward lines of transmission between the elements opposed to the status quo. It is unsurprising that each absorbed the ideologies of the French and American Revolutions in different ways, assimilating them to their own traditions, preoccupations and aspirations which meant in effect that they were received into the Gaelic Catholic tradition and into the Irish Patriot tradition. In that way the same terms, concepts and icons came to have different connotations and resonances according to the background of the speaker/writer and the context in which they were spoken, written or visualised.[120] What had always been a tentative and provisional alliance between Protestant and Catholic United Irishmen, and particularly between the 'Gentlemen' and the lower-class Catholic Defenders, crumbled and disintegrated. The ordinary Catholic people felt themselves misled, betrayed and abandoned by the Protestant middle-class leaders and henceforward looked to their own for leadership, among whom were local priests who had been prominent in the rebellion. Their importance grew significantly throughout the nineteenth century as the Catholic community asserted its claims to equality in the age of emergent mass democracy, involving themselves with O'Connell's Catholic Association[121] and (at times ambivalently) with the nationalist movements. As their strategic importance grew, so too did their power and influence on the thought forming processes of all classes of Catholics, including Ribbonmen, which linked overt and covert protest and subversion to a general sense of alienation. As we have seen from the days of the Counter-Reformation, their sacerdotal imagery frequently stressed obedience, sacrifice, fatalism and the distance between heaven and earth in figurative language–as exile.

In suppressing the Rising and punishing those deemed to be rebels the Protestant (and Catholic) militiamen employed savage and barbaric methods including house burnings, hangings, half-hangings, pitch capping, picketing, floggings with the cat-o'-nine-tails, indiscriminate shootings and transportation.[122]

Most rebels thus punished were sent to Prussia to serve in its armies or to work in the mines. The remainder were pressed to serve in British army regiments overseas or they were transported to Australia. Inevitably transportation, as a term and fear, quite clearly and unequivocally came to be thought of as identical with exile and Australia with its utterly alien topography with alienation–the Siberia of the British Empire.[123] The experience of the banished was deposited into Irish-Australian consciousness to condition the developing self-definition of the Irish-Australian and his reactions to other ethnic and social groups within Australia. Patrick O'Farrell has described the cultural inheritance of the Irish-Australian in the following terms:

> What was Gaelic continuous, what was preserved, nurtured, passed on was not language, or modes of building or curious folkways, but something more elusive, much less tangible, more central–mind-sets, mentality, values, mental furniture, ways of thought, attitudes, dispositions, slants and tangents. In those deep fastnesses of mind and heart the real Gaelic person long continued to live.[124]

In general the Irish experience of Australia at the time confirmed the profoundly conservative feelings of the indigenous Catholic Irish–leaving Ireland was a form of temporal purgatory as the medieval monks had known. The heightened tensions of the period, the now almost universal use of spoken English (less than five per cent of the population spoke Irish alone by 1851),[125] the identification of nationalism and modernity with English meant that

> a new type of Irish Nationalism began to be diffused throughout the country and it was propagated almost entirely in English. In Leinster they sang of 'The Croppy Boy' of Father Murphy and of Billy Byrne of Ballymanus, and all over Ireland they sang 'The Wearing of the Green' and 'The Shan Van Vocht' … Ballad sheets appeared at the fairs with the words of 'Bold Robert Emmet', 'I am a true born Irishman, John Mitchel is my name', or 'My Name is Pat O'Donnell, I was born in Donegal', and hundreds of similar songs … These, and speeches from the dock, and the songs of Thomas Moore, and the ballad poetry of the Nation group and their successors, became the prevailing nationalist diet.[126]

To suggest however that this 'new type of Irish Nationalism' was a radical break with the dreams and longings of past generations is to overstate the case. It differed from the aristocratic values and views borne by the learned Gaelic tradition but as Michelle O'Riordan argues:

> Gaelic Ireland like most other European communities enjoyed a variety of
> social difference, the stimulation of contact with other languages, religions
> and cultures and a strong sub-literary culture, but one which did not enjoy
> official patronage as did the official learned culture which for us is repre-
> sented by the bardic tradition.[127]

The 'sub-literary culture' in a society which spoke Gaelic but did not
write it, manifested itself in oral stock forms which 'often provided a
vehicle for updated versions of folk songs ballads etc. and where a declining literate middle order mediated between the monoglots and the
bilingual communities'[128] and

> The poems and songs which had a vital existence in the Gaelic-speaking
> community can be seen to conform in a general way with what we have
> came to expect from the so-called folk song and folk ballad; individual
> works, linked with specific occasions and transient fashionable motifs also
> turn up. Such material can be found in most European communities and it
> plays a very important part in the literary history attached to any
> language.[129]

This Gaelic popular culture co-existed in the latter half of the
eighteenth century and the first half of the nineteenth century with the
growth of literacy and that in turn affected many more than those who
could read and write. It touched those who listened to others reading texts
such as newspapers, pamphlets, proclamations and ballads and as Dunne
points out, this literacy was almost entirely in the medium of English:

> Thus the poor person, illiterate in both languages but functionally bilingual
> and with aural access to manuscript or printed texts, could be exposed
> simultaneously to the relatively static seventeenth and early eighteenth-
> century perspectives of Gaelic poetry and the comparatively volatile
> response to the contemporary scene in street literature, and even more in
> newspapers and proclamations. The interaction of the new and largely
> English world which literacy introduced with the old and largely Gaelic
> world of folk belief and folk (and residual aristocratic) literature was to
> produce unexpected and sometimes bizarre political patterns.[130]

The interrelationship between oral traditions and popular printed
literature evolved out of impersonal commercial concerns and found
expression through a set of formulae and motifs which reflected immediate popular concerns.[131] Read, sung or declaimed in an emotionally
charged manner, context and tone, they served to reinforce beliefs, channel
feelings and bind individuals into mnemonically inscribed patterns of

thought, reaction and behaviour. As oppositional texts emanating from the unprivileged and excluded, they inevitably spoke of the experiences and sympathies of Catholics. Dáithí Ó hÓgáin for example, points out that one of the most popular booklets of the period was *Irish Rogues and Rapparees* which 'exerted a strong influence on the rich lore of outlaws in Irish oral tradition'.[132] He also describes how the spread of stories and ideas from mainland Europe influenced the manner in which the image of Irish poets was created and perpetuated. He quotes a formulaic valediction attributed to a priest on the death of Eoghan Rua Ó Súilleabháin, which clearly suggests the privileged position the poet held in popular estimation:

> His death is a greater cause of sorrow than the death of a hundred priests. Money would make a priest and it would make a bishop but neither Eoghan Rua or his kind will ever be there again.[133]

Ballads and folk songs printed on broadsheets and in chap-books were often composed by bilingual folk-poets many of whom were hedge-school masters and *spailpíns* like Eoghan Rua and many of whom formed an important link between a Gaelic oral culture and a written English one. In such a position they had the capacity to relay, to translate and to propagate images and ideas in a two-way flow. In addition, as many were at least sympathetic to nationalist aspirations and familiar with English literary forms, they were able to influence the way thinking and forms, feelings and thoughts were expressed in among the people they were closest to. In their migratory lifestyles they personified the disenchanted, idealised figure of the wandering poet.

Rootless, unencumbered by material ties and the obligations attendant on patronage, an inverted image of the *scholaris vagans* of pre-conquest Ireland, many such embittered and deracinated 'truant scholars' contributed significantly to the sedition of the 1790s.[134] Hundreds of songs appeared each year many of them new, but many drawn from the traditional fund of anonymous ballads. Once printed they were taken over by ballad singers who sang and sold the broadsheets in towns, at fairs, races and elections. Therefore, they were able to reach large audiences and according to accounts of the time, excited tremendous interest particularly among the poor.[135]

The 'political' songs had stereotypical heroes and villains and recurring themes which testified to the longevity of their oppression, to their unsatisfied aspirations and to their unchanging self-perception as victim-heroes unjustly imprisoned in an arbitrary polity run by demonic aliens. In that sense, English language ballads and songs though no doubt reaching a wider audience–among whom would be monoglot Catholic Irish from all classes and liberal nationalist Protestants–merely recycled the suppressed resentments of 'hidden' Ireland. This ensured a continuity of ancient thought processes modified marginally by the transition into the monoglossia of the coloniser's tongue and the selective appropriation of terms belonging to discourses of mass democracy and republicanism. These texts celebrated the subversive and valorised the outlaw. The spirit of the wood kerne, the tories and the rapparees found life in stories which narrated the exploits of highwaymen and bandits. Others sympathised with 'the man on the run' from the police and a vindictive magistracy–a motif which was to be re-worked throughout the succeeding years to enable artists to register their distance from the expectations and impositions of society. Many described the honest farmer who kills a rapacious or lascivious bailiff and is then banished or executed. In such tales the hero figure is seen as a judicial victim, his crime as natural justice, a rightful execution of a tyrant or a traitor and his refusal to inform or betray his comrades an emblem of simple nobility. The villains were those the peasants dealt with at firsthand: landlords, parsons, peelers, agents, bailiffs, proctors, land-grabbers and 'emergency men', that is, those who took over the land of an evicted family. The most vehement execrations were however, reserved for the informer. The force of hundreds of years of Gaelic Irish tradition packed the maledictions that were placed on the betrayer who caused eviction, imprisonment, transportation, separation from loved ones, forced flight, unjust punishment or execution. The peasant Irish having acquired the language of their masters were in a sense 'calibanised'. The profit they had derived from their entry in English was that they knew how to curse, and they did so, with feeling and within the relative safety of their own discursive and social formations. Like Caliban they had to resort to a double voiced discourse in their dealings with their colonial overlords. This induced a kind of social and psychic schizophrenia, a propensity to assume assorted personae in relation to different power figures and to adopt a variety of voices or vocal postures according to varying social and power contexts. In their powerlessness the people continued to look to liberation through the agency of some powerful overseas ally. Just as the poets of the eighteenth century looked to the Jacobites for deliverance, the ballad makers of the early nineteenth century pinned their hopes on Napoleon, France, and a little later, Irish-America. The allegorised representative of Ireland the *Shan Van Vocht* (the poor old woman) stands as an exemplar of the type. A version thought to be from around 1797 begins:

> The French are on the Sea! says the Shan Van Vocht;
> The French are on the Sea! says the Shan Van Vocht;
> The French are on the Sea! they'll be here without delay,
> And the Orange will decay, says the Shan Van Vocht.

and it concludes:

> Shall Erin then be free? says the Shan Van Vocht;
> Shall Erin then be free? says the Shan Van Vocht;
> Yes, old Erin shall be free, and we'll plant the laurel tree,
> And we'll call it liberty, says the Shan Van Vocht.[136]

Ireland in this case is personified as *Erin* as well as the *Shan Van Vocht* but it could also be *Banba, Fodla, Sheela na Guira, Sile Ní Ghadra, Caitlin Trial, Caitlin Ní Uallachain* and most commonly in the ballads, *Granuaile*–a beautiful young girl or a grey-headed old woman. The proliferation of nomenclature articulates an ontological confusion. But, whatever the form of the presentation, the allegory almost invariably presents female-ness as passive. The female figure grieves, watches, waits, laments, accompanies, inspires and prophecises–as she had since the time of Aogán Ó Rathaille and before. That passiveness arises of course, out of the subjection of Ireland and a patriarchal ideology which projects men as leaders, initiators and adventurers. If Ireland is fixed in time and space as popular representations suggest, then so too is Woman–and it is the man's role and purpose to rescue, renew and redeem if not in the foreseeable future, then through the intervention of succeeding generations of exiled sons and allies.

Prophecy as a rhetorical device was not something new. It had been embedded in pre-conquest consciousness and was the particular prerogative of saints, seers and poets throughout the history of conquest and colonisation. It represented hope at one pole in a continuum which had as its other opposing pole nihilistic despair. The collective feelings of the native Catholic Irish oscillated between the two over the centuries refusing any kind of stability, sense of progress, or completion. Thus it was (and is) that a story can go so far without any possibility of a teleological resolution; that a narrative becomes self-absorbed, reflexive, millenarian and prone to open-ended 'closures', arbitrary conclusions or cyclical return to origins. The story of Ireland at this time lacked the structural certainties of liberal bourgeois imperialism with its inbuilt notions of hierarchies, progress, self-determination and ends operating out of the fixed and naturalised certitudes of the metropolitan centre. In

the absence of any clear narrative model from their own history which
might motivate, direct and sustain their struggle, the ballads of the peasants
fell back on analogy, as their poetic predecessors of the seventeenth century
had, in stoically accepting the realities of conquest and Cromwellisation.
Like their predecessors they regularly invoked the experiences of the
Israelites in bondage and compared them to their own misfortunes. They
tended to differ from earlier analogies with biblical precedents however, in
being less quiescent. Their assertiveness was no doubt, due in part to the
strength they drew from a sense of affiliation with the emergent powers
of France and America and the cultivation of a derogatory and demeaning
counter image of the Englishman. He was a 'faithless Philistine',[137] one of
'Harry's breed', or 'Calvin's bloody race', 'a heretic of England' and therefore a suitable case for conversion / extirpation in a 'holy war' in the service
of the Pope and Roman Catholicism. Conversely Daniel O'Connell, the
leader of the Catholic Association whose formation and success induced
self-belief and pride, was sometimes referred to as 'The Moses of Erin'.[138]
Such anti-English and anti-Protestant images were predictable, defensive
responses in the language of the ruling caste to the stereotyping endemic
in the colonial enterprise. They mark the increasingly sectarian nature of
representation in the early nineteenth century which the ballads often
record, particularly in their accounts of party fights.

The intuitive identification with the Israelites worked on the conscious
level as the Catholic Irish saw themselves as a persecuted race of true
believers in the same way as their Old Testament antecedents had done.
It also worked on a slightly more subliminal plane for both ancient races
had experienced conquest, dislocation and diaspora. That affective association did not on the whole however, extend to the nineteenth-century
descendant of the Israelite, the Jew, or to those like the American Negroes
who lived and worked as the legally validated chattels of plantation
owners. In such cases Irish popular opinion reflected the eurocentric
prejudices of the time, in the same way as the Citizen in *Ulysses* (1922)
spoke of the widespread popular racism of early twentieth-century
imperialism even while denouncing the British presence in Ireland.

Perhaps just as revealing as the themes and ideas that are to the fore in
the ballads and songs are the omissions, the absences and the briefly
alluded to. Zimmerman points out that apart from a few anti-clerical songs
written in response to the Church's condemnation of the fenians and
later Parnell–none of which proved popular–there was an 'almost total
absence of anti-clerical feeling in Irish popular literature',[139] a fact which
distinguishes it from many other european countries. But, unlike other

european societies, the Catholic Church in Ireland was not part of the dominant hegemonic superstructure. It aligned itself, if not always unequivocally, with the counter-hegemonic forces of nationalism. This was unsurprising given that the Penal Laws had only been relaxed in the last quarter of the eighteenth century, that Maynooth had only been established since 1795 and that it was still regarded with fear, hostility and loathing by the Protestant establishment. In addition, the Catholic population resented the payment of tithes to an alien institution and had looked to the priesthood since the early days of colonisation for leadership, a leadership now to some extent secularised in the form of the Catholic Association under O'Connell. The Church nevertheless, was still intimately entwined in the administrative and political structures of Catholic interests and institutions. Most local agents of the Association for example, were parish priests.[140] The authority and respect they enjoyed imbued their voices with particular force in all areas of anti-colonial discourse. The collective experiences of the priesthood, their theology permeated as it was with religiose images of exile and their proselytising mission to spread Catholicism made them an extremely powerful–if ambivalent–cultural and thought-shaping force, particularly in the post-Famine period.

The Irish language was the object of official hostility by the British. It was viewed as subversive, 'barbarous', a mysterious marker of difference and potential disorder. Government and official transactions were conducted in English. It was necessary therefore for Irish speakers to acquire English in both oral and written form if they were to protect and promote their interests in the struggle against excessive rents and tithes and numerous other injustices visited on them. The Church, though tacitly supporting Irish through the interest of individual churchmen, who could only communicate with parishioners through the medium of the indigenous language, and those involved in scribal and literary activity, 'made little positive contribution towards maintaining the language–such as using it rather than English as far as possible as their normal means of communication, both spoken and written'.[141]

Neither the Church nor the national schools promoted the use of Irish in education and Daniel O'Connell actively advocated the acquisition of English as an aid in the political struggle. His attitude and that of the peasantry in general was expressed by Máire in Friel's *Translations* (1981). As part of a discussion with the hedge-schoolmaster Hugh, she says:

> I'm talking about the Liberator, Master, as you well know. And what he said was this: 'The old language is a barrier to modern progress'. He said that

last month. And he's right. I don't want Greek. I don't want Latin. I want
English. I want to be able to speak English because I'm going to America
as soon as the harvest's all saved.[142]

In this kind of thought configuration Irish is represented as archaic, a
barrier to modernity, a badge of shame and English as the Liberator
suggested, liberating, a passport to the New World. It was also of course,
the bearer of old myths and legends. The government had no interest in
sustaining or providing a conquered rebellious and 'barbaric' people with
any kind of legitimating cultural antiquity and the Church no desire to
revivify a pagan past. Most Irish speakers could not read Irish[143] (Ó Cuív
estimates that out of an Irish speaking population of 1,500,000 in 1806
only 20,000 could read the language) and even if they could, the literature
existed vestigially in manuscript form and was inaccessible. Where the
stories did survive in peasant communities they were presumably of little
interest to the ballad-makers, those chroniclers of their times who needed
new up-to-date material for their broadsheets if they were to sell them.
The myths and legends being old and outmoded were probably considered anachronistic, irrelevant and vaguely degrading. Like the language
that bore them they were rejected and suppressed by the native Irish
majority in a painfully recursive adaptation to the nineteenth century
which 'rent the fabric of Irish life (and) effected a breach between its past
and present, and an alienation between the speaker and his speech'. An
alteration felt by 'the majority of Irish people as a kind of loss, an exile
from an original whole and good place or state.[144]

As the nineteenth century wore on and as more Catholic Irish settled
in America, it was to be expected that popular culture should remix
traditional elements and re-present ancient concerns. The songs and
ballads produced out of the exodus to the New World prior to the Famine
differed from the writings of the eighteenth century poets and their predecessors in that they were written for and by representatives of the
common people of Ireland. These emigrant texts usually attributed the
leaving of Ireland to some imperial (divine or secular) imperative beyond
their control: poverty, slavery, hunger, fear of imprisonment or execution.
The language of the ballads and songs was simple and repetitive. Ireland
is 'poor', 'old', 'distressed'. Heroes and sons are 'bold', 'undaunted',
'gallant', 'noble', 'true'. Enemies are 'cruel', 'bloodthirsty', 'strangers' and
'saxons'. Maidens are 'fair', mothers are 'tender', fathers 'aged' and sisters
'loving'. Prisons are 'dark' and 'cold' while the people are 'persecuted'
in 'captivity', 'bondage' or 'slavery', wearing 'chains', 'irons' or 'fetters'.

Irishmen are 'martyrs' who are frequently 'banished', 'transported' or 'betrayed' by 'informers', 'spies' or 'traitors' and forced to 'flee' their 'native land' by 'oppressors' and 'tyrants'. Some are 'felons' 'condemned to the scaffold high' or to 'Van Diemen's land', or forced to leave for 'freedom's shore' or the 'land of liberty'.

The opening verses of 'The Banished Defender' exemplify a number of post '98 preoccupations, fusing Catholicism, nationalism, anti-Protestantism, betrayal, persecution and exile:

Poor Catholics of Erin give ear unto these lines I write,
I've fled to the mountains, for ever I am banished quite,

For the sake of my religion I was forced to leave my native home,
I've been a bold defender, and a member of the Church of Rome.

Then woe attend those traitors who forced me from my native soil,
Those perjured prosecutors, that banished me in exile;
They swore I was a traitor and a leader of the Papist band.
For which I'm in cold irons, a convict in Van Diemen's Land.

Right well do I remember when I was taken in New Ross,
The day after the battle, as the Green Mount Ferry I did cross.
The guards they did surround me and my bundle searched upon the spot,
And there they found my green coat, my pike, two pistols and some shot.

The reason that they banished me, the truth I mean to tell you here,
Because I was a head leader of Father Murphy' Shelmaliers,
And for being a Roman Catholic I was trampled on by Harry's breed,
For fighting in defence of my God, my country, and my creed.[145]

Unlike 'The Banished Defender' Patrick Brady escaped capture and transportation, but nevertheless felt himself to have been banished. In the 'New Song on the Banishment of Patrick Brady' the first person narrator fuses love of Ireland, his mother, his faith and the malice of the 'sons of Luther' with forced departure. After describing how he joined with others in resisting the plans of 'tyrants' to pull down a Catholic chapel, a union in defence of 'the Pope and poor old Granuale', and how they defeated 'those perpetrators'–a term resonantly suggestive of treachery and betrayal–the final two verses restate and encapsulate the simple certainties of ballad discourse. They link the private and the public, the intensely familial and the overtly political:

Farewell my aged mother, I'm bidding you adieu,
And likewise to my comrades boys that always did stand true
If e'er your foe dare to oppose as they had done before,
In triumph say: now clear the way for Paddys evermore.

Now since those lines I must conclude, no more I have to say,
I hope the Lord will bring me safe unto America,
For Patrick Brady is my name, a patriot so bold
No heretic of Calvin's breed will ever me control.[146]

Zimmerman commenting on the structure and effects of the texts says:

> The ballad-writers probably devoted little time to the composition of their texts. To fill up the lines they had at their disposal a stock of tags, of recurring phrases frequently employed to express similar ideas. The use of commonplace expressions is indeed common to folk poetry in general; it has been observed that sub-literary poetry preserved a mode of composition fundamentally different from that of more learned literature: it used as its elements whole passages rather than isolated words. For the authors of Irish street ballads this technique was not as essential and highly developed as it had been for epic singers and story-tellers belonging to an entirely oral tradition still, it had two advantages: it facilitated the writing and the memorising, and it also pleased the audience. Unlike the sophisticated public, the traditional or semi-traditional poet and his listeners are not particularly interested in novelty and originality; on the contrary, they eagerly welcome familiar phrases occurring over and over again, the popular taste in the matter of art and poetry being essentially conservative. Such conventional phrases also avoided distraction from the story, which was the main thing, and repetition of the same words and formulae might have in some way the magical effect of an incantation. Those stock phrases contribute more than anything else to the archaic tone of the real street ballads.[147]

If they were not original they were effective. Translated or adapted from the Irish or written in English they were printed and disseminated throughout Ireland among a population which now had access to the medium of the world's most influential language. Ireland moreover, was in the first part of the nineteenth century experiencing a population explosion. It is estimated that there were some eight million people in Ireland on the eve of the Famine. The dispersion of Irish people around the world, in the USA and Britain principally, but also in Canada, Australia and in the imperial forces–about one million people left between 1815 and the Famine carrying with them their experiences and prejudices–meant that exile was embodied in their existence. In addition, their identity was

expressed in forms of sentimental attachment which demanded continued obedience to traditional paradigms of thought and expression.

Songs and ballads emanating from popular Protestant Orange culture
were equally reductive and conservative though much narrower in
thematic and emotional range. As Zimmerman says: 'They certainly are
less numerous, expressing the sentiments of a stern-faced minority
defending its privileges and therefore mostly deprived of the easy romantic appeal of rebel songs'.[148] Like the texts of the nationalists, Orange
songs and ballads were transmitted through the oral tradition in booklets
and broadsides. They drew from the Bible, the history of Protestantism
and the folk memories of the Williamite wars. They commemorate and
celebrate victories and persecutions of Protestantism and Protestant
people, incorporate descriptions of conviviality, sentimentality and party
fights and they deal with the rituals and mysteries of Orangeism and
similar organisations.

Zimmerman alludes to the inclusion of emigrant songs in the Protestant corpus[149] yet fails to provide examples. In the light of Miller's analysis
of Protestant attitudes to emigration,[150] the absence of any political
imperative and their symbiotic dependence on England, the 'mother' of
the Empire, it would be psychologically inconceivable that emigration
could be sentimentalised as 'exile'. Viewed as a form of internal migration
and/or as a means of self-advancement Protestant departure could not
bear the psychic and cultural weight attached to emigration by Catholics
leaving Ireland. Their freedom, liberty and right to self-determination was
already inscribed and institutionalised in colonial government and privileged practice–in return they offered loyalty.

The popular ballads and songs were simple, direct and prejudiced. They
arose out of and reflected the instincts and interests of two mutually
antagonistic and irreconcilable traditions and as such they were indifferent
to the opinions of the English. Writers from Ireland writing in England
however, lacked the relative freedom of expression of the ballad-makers.
They had to work out the problems of audience, tone, form and dissemination if they were to be read and if they were to make a living from
writing. All writers from Ireland writing for English audiences had to work
through the realities of colonial domination and political acceptance in a
post-Union landscape–in that world England defined reality and Ireland
deviated from it. Deane sums it up in the formulation:

> The English audience lives in the everyday world; the Irish writer and the
> Irish culture belong to a surreal world. The artist, as mediator between

these two, even as apologist for one to the other, is beset by a plight which is a political as well as an imaginative one. A favoured explanation for the difference between the two worlds is the national character of each.[151]

THOMAS MOORE

Thomas Moore, Ireland's 'national' poet, typifies the problem of the Irish (or any colonial) writer in the metropolitan centre. Like those writers from the eighteenth century, most of whom came from Protestant back-grounds, Moore had to appeal to an English audience which when it turned its attention to the periphery, to Ireland, failed to distinguish between coloniser and colonised, Protestant and Catholic, unionist and nationalist. Moore, a product of the emergent Catholic bourgeoisie, had been educated at Samuel Whyte's English Grammar School in Dublin, the overwhelmingly Protestant Trinity College and the Middle Temple in London. His experiences and entry into English literary life led him to project 'himself as a scholar and a gentleman in the English mode'.[152] His first work as a translation of Greek lyrics attributed to Anacreon. This established him as an English poet in the tradition of Cowley and Herrick and foreshadowed his subsequent career as a translator and transmogri-fier; one whose ambivalence necessitated the adoption of the role of mediator between uncomprehending and unbalanced epistemic power positions.

His reputation and enduring appeal as Ireland's national poet rests primarily on his *Irish Melodies* which were published in ten numbers between 1808 to 1834. The music which his lyrics accompanied came from Bunting's *A General Collection of the Ancient Irish Music* (1796) and it was arranged by Sir John Stevenson to fit Moore's words. In turn, many of the ideas and sentiments in the *Melodies* were derived from Moore's readings of the antiquarian researchers Walker, Brooke, O'Halloran and Vallancey. The success of the *Melodies* earned Moore £500 per annum for many years and at the same time they attracted favourable critical attention and ensured his fame and success. Moore was extremely adept at exploiting the 'infantile romanticism'[153] of the time for a drawing-room audience and he was acutely conscious of doing so. In a letter to the Marchioness Dowager of Donegal, an aristocratic absentee from Ireland, prefixed to the third number of *Irish Melodies*, he outlines in a pre-Arnoldian formu-lation his view that Irish music is the truest of all comments upon our history. The tone of defiance, succeeded by the languor of despondency–a burst of turbulence dying away into softness–the sorrows of one moment lost in the levity of the next–and all that romantic mixture of mirth and sadness, which is naturally produced by the efforts of a lively temperament to shake off, or forget, the wrongs which lie upon it–such are the features of our history and character, which we find strongly and faithfully reflected in our music.[154]

This contrasts markedly with the utilitarianism developing in industrial-ised, urbanised (and Protestant) Britain and is, as Terence Brown points out, an aspect of 'the Celticism that had flowered in the fertile soil of the Ossianic enthusiasm'.[155] Brown goes on to argue that Celticism was a vogue closely allied to the vogue for the Orient (which Moore himself was to exploit with *Lalla Rookh* (1817), and for the Gothic which produced a version of Irishness emphasising wildness, tenderness and originality. Such characteristics were equally applicable (and equally facile) to the inhabitants and regions of the Orient. To English audiences particularly those of a vaguely whiggish disposition, such qualities contrasted strik-ingly with developing self-images of Englishness. There was an imagina-tive allure surrounding such images of otherness that fulfilled affective desires within some part of the English psyche; a charm and appeal which extended the English emotional range and notions of being–provided of course that they remained subservient, distant and unthreatening. Within England the exotic, the alien and the exile could be utilised imaginatively against the dominant orthodoxy as long as they remained unfocused and unspecified. It was inevitable therefore that Romanticism in Ireland should be mediated principally through England. 'English Romantic modes, notably the picturesque and the gothic were an obvious feature of Irish writing in this period'[156] and Moore 'attempted to evoke a painful histori-cal experience through a combination of sense and sound, of carefully pitches sentimental lyrics matched to modified musical tradition. They were meant as he said 'rather to be sung than read'.[157]

Working within an English climate of receptivity Moore had to produce a homogenised, sanitised Irishness which evaded or avoided offending English sensibilities. He had to select appropriate voices, gestures and subject matter which highlighted the sentimental and acclaimed the Celtic–a kind of cultural cartography which fringed the core, the essence and heartland of Englishness and faded away into misty outer regions. A literary parallel to the economic peripheralisation of Ireland, Scotland and Wales, the Celtic fringe.

In defending himself against the accusation that he had chosen these airs 'as a vehicle of dangerous politics,[158] he describes exactly who the *Melodies* are aimed at:

> I beg of these respected persons to believe, that there is no one who deprecates more sincerely than I do, any appeal to the passions of an ignorant and angry multitude; but that it is not through that gross and inflammable region of society, a work of this nature could ever have been intended to circulate. It looks much higher for its audience and readers–it is found upon the pianofortes of the rich and educated–of those who can afford to have their national zeal a little stimulated, Without exciting much dread of the excesses into which it may hurry them.[159]

The poems in Moore's *Irish Melodies* deal with an Ireland created out of romantic melancholy; one which is suffused with romantic languor, whose mystical function is to inspire a spiritual revitalisation of patriotic aspiration. In numerous poems death becomes triumph, in 'Remember the glories of Brian the Brave', 'Oh breathe not his name', 'The Minstrel Boy', triumph co-exists with despair, glory; with defeat.

It is an Ireland of 'lost battles, silenced harps, the silent tear, the muted bard' and a collection which is 'interspersed with poems which evoke the personal sorrows of a poet whose present gaiety disguises the depths of his own sorrows'.[160] Thus, the lachrymosely lyrical harmonised with the plangently political, the tear and the smile, Ireland's and everybody's. He made

> the cause of Ireland the dream of perfect love sacred causes, spiritualising each as an enterprise for the sake of which life itself was not too great a price. In fact it was the only price worth paying. So even his evocations of Irish landscape, of the remembered valley or home of the exile, are evocations of place that the spirit never leaves, of an Ireland that persists through all changes and catastrophes as the beloved place. This charismatic rendering of traditional affections was perfectly suited to the ardent, exclusive spirit of nationalism.[161]

Though the spirit in Moore's evocations of place never leaves, the body almost invariably does. Moore's speakers speak from a distance or speak on the point of departure. They are effectively positioned outside Ireland rather than within as is the case with speakers in Gaelic poetry and in the ballads. They deliberately eschew the specific and the named to evoke an unfocused and generalised impression of sadness and alienation–it is an historically unspecified Ireland cut loose in time and space. It was a poetry suited to an emergent Irish bourgeoisie in that it civilised the Gaelic tradition preserving and modernising it simultaneously. In time the success of Moore also came to provide an authenticating model for wandering bards and literary 'outlaws' predisposed to lead and / or oppose national sentiment. If the anapaestic rhythms, allegorical readings and mesmeric numinosity inspired the Irish middle classes to protest if not rebellion, the absence of the Irish historical memory which formed the *Melodies* allowed the British to hear them musically, romantically and nebulously. Vague references to 'saxons', 'tyrants' and 'foes' offered no threat, and stirring appeals to 'liberty', 'swords', 'glory' and 'nobility' could be just as appealing to the unflective British Romantic as to the self-sacrificing martyr-hero. Moore's themes of loyalty to the betrayed and his heroes who were pure and honourable opposing 'the sweet-natured against oppression' [162] were inspirations, and the Ireland he popularised embedded itself in the English consciousness also.

The Irish 'exile' from Moore onwards became as much a fixture in English perceptions of Ireland as the shamrock and the shillelagh. It became a distant and oversimplified representation which registered all Irishmen abroad (though rarely women), nationalist and unionist in the same way. Within Ireland however, this two dimensional idea of Irishness linked the iconography of Celticism with a nascent Catholic nationalism and the affectivity of Romanticism. This effectively excluded the *sasanaigh*, the settler and the Protestant from any legitimate historical or affective claim on Ireland or identification with it. Writers and artists from both major traditions had to negotiate, modify, evade or accept externally conceived and imposed stereotypes while at the same time internalising if not fully acknowledging differentiating ideologies arising out of conquest and submission. Moore's life, work and fame in England ironically blurred the distinction between dominant and subaltern Irish discourses within English culture which came to accept his versions of national essence at the expense of the potential exploration of other constructions of legitimate and acceptable fictive representations. The power of the images he generated and the hold they achieved on the imagination of both the English and the Catholic Irish effectively foreclosed on any meaningful counter-representation by Irish Protestants. They had to utilise, dilute and transmute such images for their long term strategic needs. What they could not do in an age increasingly dominated by the drive to mass democracy and the hegemony of the ideal of a 'national genius' resident in the people, was to challenge such representations head on. For the nationalist middle classes, however, Moore sentimentalised an acceptable kind of iconographic nationalism which idealised the past without challenging the present. Nevertheless, as Heaney points out, the

Irish Melodies 'were a potent carrier of the tradition of exile from the first and good Gaelic place'.[163]

'Oh, Ye Dead', one of Moore's best known poems, works out of the sense of desolation he inherited from the culture of the colonised. It frames the interconnected psychic association of time, memory and place among the living and the dead, the indigenous Irish and those who like himself are categorised as exiles:

> Oh, ye Dead! Oh, ye Dead! whom we know by the light you give
> From your cold gleaming eyes, though you move like men who live,
> > Why leave you thus your graves,
> > In far off fields and waves,
> Where the worm and the sea bird only know your bed;
> > To haunt this spot where all
> > Those eyes that wept your fall,
> And the hearts that bewail'd you, like your own, lie dead?
>
> It is true–it is true–we are shadows cold and wan;
> It is true–it is true–all the friends we lov'd are gone;
> > But oh! thus ev'n in death,
> > So sweet is still the breath
>
> Of the fields and the flow'rs in our youth we wander'd o'er,
> > That ere, condemn'd, we go
> > To freeze 'mid Hecla's* snow,
> We would taste it awhile, and dream we live once more!

The invocation of the long tradition of absence in exile in the poem re-inscribed the rootedness inherent in the native Irish inheritance as far back as the *dindshenchas* of the early Gaelic poets. It reiterates the appeals of the post-conquest bards and balladeers to lost leaders and to putative saviours, and as James Joyce suggests in his story 'The Dead', (1916) it signals unconsciously perhaps, the tensions and threats immanent in the resurrection of the past and the return of the departed. Themes which Joyce himself and others in the neo-realist tradition like George Moore, Ó Faoláin and O'Connor were to explore at length in reaction to the Celtic Twilight.

---

* Paul Zealand mentions that there is a mountain in some part of Ireland, where the ghosts of persons who have died in foreign lands walk about and converse with those they meet, like living people. If asked why they do not return to their homes, they say they are obliged to go to Mount Hecla, and disappear immediately.[164]

CONCLUSION

In *Emigrants and Exiles* Miller elaborates on his argument that Catholic Gaelic linguistic and cultural formations and practices shaped the semantics of exilic discourse. He describes how in Old Irish *deoraid* was a legal term under *brehon* laws, meaning a person without property. This in the context of communal relationships and attachment to place, carried the implications of disassociation and estrangement–lack of belonging. The language also employed the term *dithreabhach* meaning one who was homeless and *dibeartach*, one who suffered banishment:

> Thus, the Irish language, when combined with the poets' interpretation of postconquest Irish history, provided both linguistic patterns and heroic models to predispose the Catholic Irish to regard all those who left Ireland as unwilling and tragic political exiles.[165]

His argument receives panoptic reinforcement from Walter J. Ong who in *Orality and Literacy* (1982) examines the nature of oral modes of communication and the ways in which written communication differs from and changes patterns of thought and expression. Ireland, prior to the introduction of national education and the linguistic upheavals deriving from the Famine and post-Famine emigration, was largely an oral culture and:

> In a primary oral culture, to solve effectively the problem of retaining and retrieving carefully articulated thought, you have to do your thinking in mnemonic patterns, shaped for ready oral recurrence. Your thought must come into being in heavily rhythmic, balanced patterns, in repetitions or antitheses, in alliterations and assonances, in epithetic and other formulary expressions, in standard thematic settings (the assembly, the meal, the duel, the heroes, 'helper', and so on), in proverbs which are constantly heard by everyone so that they come to mind readily and which themselves are patterned for retention and ready recall, or in other mnemonic form. Serious thought is intertwined with memory systems. Mnemonic needs determine even syntax.[166]

Ong goes on in the same chapter to consider several other features of oral culture and how such features may affect writing either in calligraphic or typographic forms. He describes cultures with a massive oral residue as having tendencies to build narratives through additive layering where the text frequently employs listing techniques such as 'and' to add to that which has gone before. They are aggregative as opposed to analytic, they do not dispose of epithetic accretions as disciplined writing might so the princess remains, 'the beautiful princess'. Oral discourse retains, indeed because of its ephemerality needs, repetitions of strictly redundant terms and phrases to ensure that the listener's understanding is retained and reinforced. Oral cultures are constitutively conservative and inevitably resistant to new formulations, as they involve so much effort. Originality resides not in making up new stories, but in varying the received and traditional narratives to create interactivity with each unique telling and audience. They are lacking in abstract analytic categories and are therefore closer to the concrete and the lived and characterised by oppositional combative dynamics where in others are engaged in verbal and intellectual conflict – the obverse of such name calling is the expression of praise and 'praise goes with the highly polarised, agonistic, oral world of good and evil, virtues and vice, villains and heroes'.[167]

Other features of oral cultures include expression through communal as opposed to individual understanding and interpretation. They exist in the present and 'meanings come continuously out of the present, though past meanings of course have shaped the present meaning in many and varied ways, no longer recognised'.[168]

Thinking in such cultures tends to be situational, that is closely related to lived experience and expression is never merely verbal since it involves the totality of the spoken, the body language employed, the environmental and cultural contexts and the interaction between those elements within a given temporal situation.

Gaelic Catholic culture exhibited to a greater or lesser extent all of those denominators in the literary tradition and in the songs and ballads passed down and reformulated in the English language. The idea of exile may well have lacked the noetic logic and reasoned literalness attached to writing which Miller suggests. It nevertheless carried over into the language of the coloniser the communal consensus and protean pervasiveness of native Irish perceptions. By the 1840s the idea of exile had effected the transition from the Gaelic Irish mind to the Catholic Irish, English language consciousness and established itself in both the popular and the literary traditions.

The solidification and incontestability of the fusion of departure and exile in the minds of Catholics and its tacit acceptance in the consciousness of nationalist Protestants was reinforced and assured by the horrors of the Famine and the experiences of the Young Irelanders after the failure of the 1848 rebellion.

CHAPTER THREE

Nationalist Constructions: Famine and Fenianism; Feelings and Forms

INTRODUCTION

IN HIS 'General Introduction' to the *Field Day Anthology of Irish Writing*, Seamus Deane notes how writing came to be narrowly conceived as 'literature' under the sign of Romantic Nationalism in the late eighteenth century and the early nineteenth century. Prior to that he says, writing was thought of in more inclusive terms: subsumed under the term for example, might be forms such as philosophy and history.

He goes on to point out how national vernacular literatures came to be seen as 'articulators of the "national tradition"', suggesting that in embodying the national essence the greatest national literature at the same time provided 'a local instance of the human spirit'.[1] His argument continues with a consideration of the ways in which literature as a detached autonomous field of expression and study has attempted to resist and deny nationalism in the context of Ireland, claiming for itself–in its institutional forms–both authority and authenticity.

Such claims however, rest on self-interested appropriations of rights and legitimacy and necessarily involve processes of foreshortened and partial definitions of what literature is, what constitutes 'good' literature and what may be defined as and incorporated into the national canon. Arbitrary and inconsistent attempts to erect canons of privileged texts and detach them from the discourses of the political and the popular, inevitably involve the marginalisation and denial of texts which overtly challenge the assumptions of the canonisers and stand outside a consensual, non-conflictual arena of the apolitical. The tendency is therefore, to valorise texts which do not threaten, in a profound sense, the loose 'liberal' ideological concurrence, texts which do not endanger due to their antiquity and/or texts which may be corralled into the aesthetic domain– imaginative literature for the most part.

Modern critical theory involving the 'destruction and deconstruction of author(ity)'[2] grounding the canonical in the quotidian, reinstates eighteenth-century inclusivity and abrogates late nineteenth and twentieth-century canonicity. It opens up for consideration a far wider range of texts which may have been perceived as commercial or popular and classified as histories, polemics, travelogues, memoirs or street ballads.

In the context of nineteenth-century colonial Ireland where the most fundamental questions of identity, belonging, power and control clustered around nationalism in its various forms, written modes of nationalist expression and feeling inevitably attempted to utilise literary forms such as poetry, drama and prose fiction. But, those were not always the most immediate or useful modes of opposition given the relatively small market in Ireland for such genres and the dependence of Irish writers on English publishers. To make themselves heard or to find a readership, proponents of nationalism had to by-pass English sources of production and speak and write directly to their assumed audience and in ways their audience would understand, feel and react to.

In seeking to establish a counter-hegemonic discourse[3] nationalists in Ireland, like their colonised counterparts elsewhere in the world, employed forms of writing which spoke directly of their experience in autobiographies, articles, ballads, prison memoirs and histories written from within Irish nationalist discourse. This was a discourse which did not recognise distinctions between politics and literature. Ironically however, writing in the language of the metropolitan centre involved borrowing and imitating forms, codes, conventions and epistemologies which frequently replicated modes of apprehension, comprehension and representation employed by the English and the Anglo-Irish in their writings about the native Irish, and indeed, natives anywhere in the Empire.

This chapter therefore, is concerned with examining the interplay between the concepts of nationalism and exile in the emergence and hardening of nationalist attitudes and postures in a number of seminal and varying texts and to point up the resistance of the idea of exile to a simple and unvarying monologic reading of the term.

THE FAMINE AND YOUNG IRELAND

The Cataclysm of the Famine of the late 1840s has been likened to the Bolshevik Revolution in Russian history or the Great War in British experience.[4] The scale of the disaster is framed starkly by Mary Daly when she comments:

In the century prior to the famine Irish population quadrupled; in the
following century it was halved.[5]

Population loss on such a scale, and at a time when most other european countries were experiencing population growth, irreversibly
penetrated all aspects of life within Ireland: material, spiritual, perceptual
and all those relationships with the world beyond Ireland's shores.
Estimates vary as to how many people died or fled Ireland but most
commentators seem to accept that around one million men, women and
children died as a result of the failure of the potato crop and diseases
related to malnutrition during the years of the Famine. In addition, one
and a half million left Ireland in the same period, the vast majority of
whom embarked for the United States, though large numbers also went
to British North America, Great Britain and Australia. Miller claims that
more people left Ireland in eleven years than had left in the preceding two
hundred and fifty.[6]

Within Ireland itself, the condition of the poor, labourers, Irish speakers
and small farmers particularly in the west, north midlands and the south[7]
was terminal. Cecil Woodham Smith has detailed the phantasmogoric
horror reported in first hand accounts of the time as the third horseman
of the apocalypse rode the land.[8] The Famine was accompanied by
incompetent and parsimonious official response, by petty restrictions and
officious insults and in part, at least, informed by a Malthusian *laissez-faire*
ideology which held that the Famine was inevitable and a necessary
corrective to economic imbalance.[9]

Many landlords took the opportunity to evict tenants compounding the
misery of the poor in another wave of dispossession–there were some two
hundred and fifty thousand evictions between 1849 and 1859. Those who
surrendered possession for a workhouse ticket or subsidised emigration
were excluded however.[10] Like the evictions, Protestant proselytising
further hardened the sectarian divisions embodied in social, economic and
cultural relationships,[11] while the coffin ships that carried the Irish to the
New World were assumed to be full of Catholics. Miller estimates that
more than ninety per cent of those fleeing Ireland in these years were
Catholic and that a very large number were Gaelic speakers.[12]

The conceptualisation of emigration as exile did not by and large figure
in the cultural mind of those writers grouped under the label 'Young
Ireland' in the pre-Famine years. The contributors to *The Nation, The
United Irishman* and *The Irishman* were in the main young middle-class
professionals. Some, like Thomas Davis and John Mitchel were Protestant, others like John Blake Dillon and Charles Gavan Duffy anglicised

Catholics. As nationalists they at first allied themselves with O'Connell and the Repeal Movement which necessitated the suppression of any differences they might have had with the overwhelming Catholicity of the Repeal organisation and its leaders and the promotion of a transcendent cultural unity. A unity which differentiated itself from and opposed itself to perceived ideas of Englishness and English civilisation.

Literature was seen as a crucial vehicle for the development of a unifying Irish spirit, one that could express itself in the language of the possessing classes and appeal at the same time to the Catholic masses. Nationalists were therefore enjoined to 'saturate' themselves in Irish feeling through absorption in the Irish language, peasant life and Irish history in order to create a distinctive Irish future. The role of the ballad in this enterprise was judged to be essential. It was seen as an integral part of the cultural foundations necessary for the building of a national literature–individuality in terms of authorship and expression was thus judged to be unimportant:

> Total immersion of the writer's identity in that of the nation was seen as the first condition of a process that sought to fabricate a foreshortened literary history in which the development that had hitherto been thwarted might speedily be made up. For if, in the first stage of that missed development, the ballad would have been the anonymous voice of the people, in the attempt to forge the trace of a never-existent literary history an *impersonal* balladry becomes the necessary first step. The spirit of the nation may thus manifest itself uncontaminated by a subjectivism which would be the mark of English civilisation and be kept pure for future emergence in a fuller growth of the literary tradition.[13]

Lloyd goes on to point out that 'the programme of Young Ireland comes to replicate the very aesthetic history that legitimates the subordination of the Celtic races'.[14] In that sense it differs little from the projects of Samuel Ferguson and the antiquarians of the eighteenth century in seeking out a means by which a minority may legitimate its right to leadership in an emergent mass democracy. The popularity of the message can be measured in the readership figures of *The Nation* estimated to be around 250,000 in 1843[15] and the success of *The Spirit of the Nation* (1843), a compilation of songs and ballads which outsold Moore's *Irish Melodies*.[16] Like the *Melodies*, many of the songs and ballads originally printed in *The Nation* became woven into the cultural consciousness of Ireland and Irish-America to be revitalised periodically, assuming a heightened sense of continuity and relevance at succeeding moments of hope and aspiration.

Thus, though 'artificially' engendered, they achieved a congruence with pre-existing popular cultural forms which their relatively 'anonymous' authorship intended and contributed to the politicisation of the masses. The people ironically, absorbed and naturalised them into the amorphousness of their everyday lives denying in effect the origins and ownership of the ballads to their authors. Apart from editors of anthologies and cultural historians, few would be interested in knowing that John Kells Ingram wrote 'The Memory of the Dead' (1843) or that 'O'Donnell Abu' (c. 1843) was written by Michael Joseph McCann and 'The Rising of the Moon' (1866) by John Keegan Casey. Though 'force fed' as part of a consciously constructed and implemented cultural nationalism, the constraints of the form as Zimmerman has pointed out, inevitably restricted the range of feeling that could be conveyed. The balladry of Young Ireland channelled emotions and responses into pre-constructed models and to a large extent pre-determined and constrained the affective sphere within which Irish people, and usually Irish men, could react.

In Gramscian terms the Young Irelanders were seeking to establish a counter-hegemony, one that challenged the dominant colonial/imperialist model through consent as opposed to coercion. Their nationalism was however, as Lloyd points out, linked closely to imperialist ideology:

> If an explanation for this phenomenon is required, it may be found in the fact that Irish nationalism, in its early theory as in its later practices, has always sought to be an instrument of bourgeois hegemony.[17]

As such it had difficulty accommodating the traditional Gaelic view of the world where exile, destitution and famine were written into the tradition normatively, or the English language popular tradition which had come to bear the weight of those normative experiences and expectations. As a result the Great Famine of the 1840s left these middle-class poets 'abandoned by tradition'. They were working in a medium–English–which had no memory or forms capable of handling such catastrophes. Many

> turned to the all-embracing lyric, choosing to focus on emotional expression of their own reactions to individual instances of suffering. Of those who tried to take a wide view, there was a contrary tendency to sidestep the physical realities of starvation by placing the Famine in a religious or mythological context.[18]

Bourgeois nationalism had as its objective an internalised teleology which attempted as far as it was able, to exclude or gloss over the historical irreconcilabilities of Irish experience and promote a mystic militancy:

> Culturally and politically the concern of Young Ireland is precisely to articulate the 'otherness' of Ireland around its *own* centre, both geographically and politically, and in relation to the myth of a unified and coherent cultural past.[19]

That concern was undoubtedly more true of those working out of a Protestant background. As a result the lawyers, doctors and minor aristocrats of the 1840s who were striving for a greater degree of autonomy from England had a great deal of difficulty in coping with the idea of exile. Unlike the native Gaelic aristocratic and peasant traditions, their cultural consciousness had no experience of the realities of non-volitional mass movement from Ireland. When they left, they left as an act of individual will, usually in order to advance their careers and enhance their reputation and lifestyle.

They therefore, approached the exodus of the poor and the undeniable involuntary nature of that external migration with a substantial element of ambivalence. When the term is used it tends to be employed hesitantly, ambiguously or metaphorically as in the poems of Aubrey De Vere such as 'Widowhood: 1848'[20] where 'exiled honour' sits on 'a cold hearth, on a stranger's floor'.

Usually however, the concept of exile is diluted and displaced onto that of emigration, diffusing the collective and generalised bitterness, despair and rage felt by the Catholic poor onto a personalised and subjective plane. Lady Dufferin in one of the most famous poems of the Famine, exemplifies the kind of rhetorical strategies at work in the period when she adopts the persona of a newly widowed emigrant lamenting the death of his wife, Mary. In a superficially emotional identification of his wife, Ireland and personal happiness, the unnamed and friendless speaker says:

> I thank you for the patient smile
> When your heart was fit to break
> When the hunger-pain was gnawin' there,
> And you hid it for my sake:
> I bless you for the pleasant word
> When your heart was sad and sore–
> Oh! I'm thankful you are gone, Mary
> Where grief can't reach you more.
> I'm biddin' you a long farewell,

My Mary–kind and true!
But I'll not forget *you*, darling,
In the land I'm goin' to:
They say there's bread and work for all,
And the sun shines always there–
But I'll not forget Old Ireland
Were it fifty times as fair!

Patrician sympathy thus masquerades as empathy. It is as though her direct poetic voice is unable to conceive of any circumstances in which she as Lady Dufferin, could imagine herself as an emigrant, let alone an exile, or that she can admit that a peasant could view himself as such. In its written form, unaccompanied by the powerfully evocative force of its musical accompaniment, the relative pusillanimity of its emotional expression reveals the lack of complete identity between writer and subject where the pathetic passivity and paucity of aspiration attempts to compensate for the death of his wife and child.

The holocaust is then sanitised and rendered subjective and emigration envisaged as a natural and positive response to an externally ordained calamity. It is in effect the lot of the peasant to suffer and the aristocrat to lyricise (sympathetically). Once in America Ireland becomes a fond memory for the emigrant where

I'll sit and shut my eyes,
And my heart will travel back again
To the place where Mary lies;
And I'll think I see the little stile
Where we sat side by side,
And the springin' corn, and the bright May morn
When first you were my bride.[21]

In Lady Dufferin's meretricious imaginings the ties with Ireland felt by the peasants seem easily cut when Ireland can be distanced and reduced by time and geography to little more than romantic nostalgia. Her failure to comprehend is indicative of much of the writing of the period which attempts to project onto the peasantry the attitudes and sentiments of a modernising and alien minority who were set on creating a modern political state. But that state paradoxically, could not be achieved without the majority of the population supporting the ideology espoused by the putative leaders of this 'new' Ireland.

Some writing therefore, engages with the drain of human beings from

Ireland on a sympathetic human level recognising the necessity for survival, like Lady Wilde's poem 'The Exodus'.[22] On the other hand some castigate those who flee as, in effect, traitors–presaging the latent tension between those who stayed and those who left in subsequent nationalist discourse. Such an instance is provided by Thomas D'Arcy McGee in 'The Woeful Winter: Suggested by Accounts of Ireland in December 1848':

> Yea! they are flying hither, breathless and pale with fear,
> And it not the sailing time for ships, but winter, dark and drear;
> They had rather face the waters, dark as the frown of God,
> Them make a stand for race and land on their own elastic sod.[23]

But neither McGee nor Lady Wilde had any meaningful access to the thoughts and attachments of those most immediately threatened by famine, disease and eviction. The 'national consciousness' they and like-minded bourgeois reformers constructed was

> constituted at the expense of historical political consciousness and at the cost of denying the full subjective and cultural dislocations undergone by a colonised people.[24]

Their reactions were second-hand, vicarious and of necessity couched in language and forms which attempted to control and contextualise chaos out of a kind of cultural dysphasia. Their attempts to speak for and to the victims were impaired by, and refracted through their deracinated unconnectedness with the Catholic rural masses and their urbanised, romantic nationalist aspirations.

As the rhetoric of 'high' and middle-class culture failed to reflect the realities of the Famine, millenarianism filled the space.

In resorting to prophecies, visions, revelations and biblical analogies the poets were paralleling the instinctive reaction of people who invoked comparisons with the Israelites in song and in Gaelic poetry to provide some kind of historical explanation for their plight. Christopher Morash's anthology *The Hungry Voice: The Poetry of the Famine* (1989) is filled with allusions to 'bondage', 'slavery', 'tyrants', 'spectres' and images of devastation, and desolation, famine and fever, which quite consciously evoke associations with the Israelites, God's chosen people. It is a discourse of despair which contains within it more modern and bourgeois notions of freedom arising out of Young Ireland's commitment to Romantic Nationalism and echoing, though never directly, referring to the abolitionist debate in America. The silence on the position of the American-Negro was, it seems reasonable to infer, a horrified reaction to the apeing of the Irish and their equation with Negroes in the English press and in English political rhetoric.[25]

Millenarianism arises out of contexts where despair follows closely on hope and expectation.[26] Ireland in the years of the Repeal movement and the expansion of european nationalism had appeared to be making advances. In the era of the Famine the devastation of those hopes was all the more cathartic since the hopes had seemed realisable.

JAMES CLARENCE MANGAN

Morash points out that James Clarence Mangan, more than any other poet of the time, established the millenarian idiom with 'The Warning Voice', 'The Peal of Another Trumpet', 'A Vision: 1848', and 'A Voice of Encouragement–A New Year's Lay'.

Mangan uniquely found in millenarian interpretations of the world forms which reflected his personal obsessions. He, unlike middle-class contributors to the nationalist press, resisted the sublimation of the self into the nationalist cultural project. In refusing to ally himself with any particular movement and denying any organic bonding of the individual to the whole, he refuted nationalist expectations of the poet which identified him as 'the highest representative type of the race'.[27] Mangan was in society though not of it. He was an isolated city dweller, alienated, estranged, yet surrounded by humanity, leading an 'unallied existence' where suffering can only be met by endurance and resistance in an unfathomable cosmos and a chaotic moral order.[28]

His attitudes were no doubt derived principally from his biography. Born in Dublin in 1803, his life is shrouded in a miasma of mythification generated in part by himself and in part by the needs of later nationalists for literary heroes. There seems little doubt that the impoverishment of his family's fortunes and the inadequacies of his father engendered a disposition to solitariness. This was reinforced by his experiences in the scrivener's office which he entered at the age of fifteen–an experience he represented as claustrophobic confinement. Descriptions of his physical appearance dwell on his singularity. His contemporary, Gavan Duffy, provided the following pen portrait:

> When he emerged into daylight, he was dressed in a blue cloak, mid summer or mid winter and a hat of fantastic shape, under which golden

hair, as fine and silky as a woman's, hung in unkempt tangles, and deep blue eyes lighted a face as colourless as parchment. He looked like the spectre of some German romance rather than a living creature.[29]

The attire, Lloyd suggests, may have been modelled on that of Charles Maturin author of *Melmoth the Wanderer* (1820). The cloak both attracts and obscures, it draws the eye of the observer, yet hides that which is beneath it and it establishes the persona of the poet-prophet but elusively obscures any manifestation of reality behind it. It is as though, 'Identity becomes disguise and simultaneously elicits and deflects the gaze of the other, which would seek to identify the appearance with the authentic figure of man which should underlie it'.[30]

His demeanour in social gatherings has been described by his biographers as a form of melancholic self-absorption and he habitually marginalised himself in 'convivial evenings' with other writers and journalists.[31] That he was an alcoholic there seems little doubt, and in all probability an opium user too. He was in fact, Ireland's first *poète maudit*. As an employee of the Ordnance Survey Office which was responsible for mapping the Irish landscape and translating Irish place names into their English equivalents and as a translator of 'Persian', German and Irish texts, Mangan was immersed in the problems of transliteration and the consequent difficulties of rendering the essence of the originals into the English language. His translations inevitably became transmutations, versions, condensations and extensions refracted through his own personalised conscious or unconscious predispositions. As such they could approximate to the original yet could never merely replicate it. His practice therefore, like his non-alliance, challenged simple notions of cultural or spiritual transmission, absorption and reproducibility and in doing so also questioned unproblematic equations of the self and the national essence. Mitchel, in his introduction to Mangan's poems (a production aimed at an American market and published in New York in 1859), attributes the neglect of Mangan's work to the hegemony of British criticism and 'the law throughout the literary domain of that semi-barbarous tongue'.[32] He goes on to explain that neglect in the following terms:

> For this Mangan was not only an Irishman, not only an Irish papist, not only an Irish papist rebel, but throughout his whole literary life of twenty years he never deigned to attorn to English criticism, never published a line in any English periodical, or through any English bookseller, never seemed to be aware that there was a British public to please. He was a rebel politically,

and a rebel intellectually and spiritually–a rebel with his whole heart and soul against the whole British spirit of the age.[33]

He continues with an appeal to his American audience to ignore British opinion in the essential belief that

> there is in these United States quite enough of the Celtic blood and warmth of temperament, enough too of the true Gaelic ear for melody, to recognise in the poems of Mangan that marvellous charm which make him the household and heart-enshrined darling of many an Irish home.[34]

Mitchel is of course, incorporating the image of Mangan and a particular nationalist reading of his work into his own version of developing cultural nationalism. His interpretation of Mangan's work assumes a transparent referential quality which identifies writer and text as one and the same. Mangan, like Ireland, is saint and sinner, victim and genius. The duality of his existence emblematically mirrors and allegorises the spirituality and the degradation of Ireland itself:

> No purer and more benignant spirit ever alighted upon earth–no more abandoned wretch ever found earth a purgatory and a hell.[35]

The essay continues with an outline of Mangan's career and while acknowledging that Mangan took no active role in Young Ireland's project, claims his fidelity and commitment to the cause of Ireland:

> for his history and fate were indeed a type and shadow of the land he loved so well. The very soul of his melody is that plaintive and passionate yearning which breathes and throbs through all the music of Ireland. Like Ireland's his gaze was ever backward, with vain and feeble complaint for vanished years. Like Ireland's his light flickered upward for a moment, and went out in the blackness and darkness.[36]

Writing out of the experiences of Young Ireland, the Famine, the failed rebellion of 1848, his own transportation and settlement among the diasporic community of Irish-America, such a construction of Mangan's life and work is plausible and understandable. Mitchel's reading may be supported readily by reference in particular to Mangan's 'translations' from the Irish. As both Mitchel[37] and Donoghue[38] make clear, Mangan renders the sense and spirit of the originals into English rather than attempting to literally transcribe the Gaelic language text. In doing so, he is however, constrained by the need to present a believable approximation to the Gaelic language version and thus employs forms and tropes familiar from seventeenth and eighteenth-century Gaelic Irish literature. Examples of these include: the *aisling* in 'The Dream of John MacDonnell',[39] 'Kathleen Ny-Houlahan',[40] 'The Dawning of the Day',[41] 'The Captivity, of the Gaels'.[42] Also included were variations on dream projections such as 'Dark Rosaleen',[43] 'Welcome to the Prince of Ossory'[44] and 'The Geraldine's Daughter',[45] keens, odes and laments like 'O'Hussey's Ode to The Maguire',[46] 'The Woman of The Three Cows',[47] 'Lament for the Princes of Tyrone and Tyrconnell (Buried in Rome)',[48] 'Lament Over the Ruins of The Abbey of Teach Molaga',[49] 'Lament for Banba',[50] 'Cean Salla',[51] 'Lamentation of MacLiag for Kincora',[52] 'The Sorrows of Innisfail',[53] 'Owen Reilly: A Keen',[54] 'Lament for Owen Roe O'Neill',[55] 'A Farewell to Patrick Sarsfield' and 'Earl of Lucan'.[56]

His versions relay and reactivate the language of loss, dispossession, abandonment and conquest in mock-medieval, chivalric idioms borrowed from the English Romantic ballad tradition. At the same time they survey and audit the genealogical and topographic features of a vanished civilisation. Poems such as the 'Woman of the Three Cows', 'Laments For The Princes of Tyrone and Tyrconnell', 'Lament over the Ruins of The Abbey of Teach Molaga', 'Prince Alfred's Itinerary Through Ireland',[57] 'Lamentation of MacLiag for Kincora', 'The Sorrows of Innisfail' and 'The Fair Hills of Éire, O!'[58] register the imagined glories of an idealised neo-Arthurian, indigenous aristocracy inhabiting a mythicised, uncultivated, unspoiled, virgin landscape in distorted modalities eerily echoing Tennysonian poetics.

Inevitably in this representation of dispossession, loss is pictured as exile in traditional style. In 'The Dream of John MacDonnell' a dream-vision appears before the speaker and says:

> 'Draw near, O mortal!' she said with a sigh,
>   'And hear my mournful story!
> The Guardian–Spirit of Erin am I,
>   But dimmed is mine ancient glory;
> My Priests are banished, my warriors wear
>   No longer victory's garland;
> And my child, my son, by beloved Heir;
>   Is an exile in a far land.'

The child in question, according to Mangan's footnote, is the Young Pretender.

In 'Kathleen Ny-Houlahan' the nobles of Ireland

> wander to and fro, proscribed, alas! and banned;
> Feastless, homeless, altarless, they bear the exiles' brand

And in 'The Ruins of Donegal Castle' we are told that

> our Kings, Lords, and men of mark and might
> Are nameless exiles far away![59]

'The Ruins of Donegal Castle' and 'A Vision of Connaught in the Thirteenth Century',[60] typify the kind of strategies at work in many of Mangan's poems. They evoke a vision of past Gaelic splendour against a landscape of ruin and decay to create a mental view of desolation and despair. It is a movement from the imprecise particular to the general, from a romanticised glow to a phantasmogoric and hallucinatary horror-scape. It may well be a movement which analogously parallels Mangan's imaginative projections and displacements. Mitchell informs us that he never left Ireland 'never perhaps penetrated farther into the country than the hills of Wicklow'.[61] In the absence then of actual experiences, Mangan could only offer visions and images drawn from an imagination fuelled by his experience of Dublin, his reading, drink and opium. The lack of objective specificity, of detailed observation in his work springs perhaps from a self-denying unwillingness to write about Dublin and the immediate world of experience, sensation and reflection which he inhabited. Those forms of lyric expression were in a sense displaced, repressed or censored out of indigenous Irish sensibilities by the perceived need in the 1840s to create a national literature. Mangan's response was, it seems, to personalise those imperatives.

Themes that had long featured in Gaelic Irish writing–defeat, desolation, prophecy and exile–are in Mangan's poetry not merely re-worked in the context of the Famine and reified for another albeit larger English speaking audience within Ireland, rather they are subjectivised in a way which internalised and aestheticised them. The poem 'Siberia', written in 1846 as the Famine entered its second year, incorporates imaginatively the public and the private, petrification, hopelessness and existential desolation–narcosis and nightmare:

> In Siberia's wastes
>   Are sands and rocks
> Nothing blooms of green or soft,

But the snowpeaks rise aloft
And the gaunt ice-blocks

And the exile there
   is one with those;
They are part, and he is part,
   For the sands are in his heart,
And the killing snows.

Therefore, in those wastes
   None curse the Czar.
Each man's tongue is cloven by
   The North Blast, who heweth nigh
with sharp scymitar.

And such doom each drees,
   Till, hunger-gnawn,
And cold-slain, he at length sinks there,
   Yet scarce more a corpse than ere
His last breath was drawn.[62]

The rhythmically shifting sibilants liminally suggest the casual and inexorable indifference of a malevolent and inhospitable force of nature perfunctorily overwhelming a puny and impotent humanity; whose existence is barely distinguishable from his (*sic*) non-existence, whose isolate and indeterminate being is equated with, and subsumed under the signifiers, starvation and exile.

In standing apart from the collective and distancing himself from the communal, Mangan inaugurated a tradition in Irish English language writing of inner-exile, where the poet-prophet outlaw speaks in the wilderness. It matters little whether or not the wilderness was created by an external agency or simply given. Imbued with the 'other' exotic imagery of Romanticism and the Neo-Gothic, the exile comes to incorporate the spiritual and the ontological and on occasion the oneiric. It becomes a state into which one may be born, rather than one into which one may be sentenced. It is characterised by enervation, etiolation and estrangement. Exile as imaginative projection becomes almost synonymous with alienation; denotation slides into connotation, the overtly anti-colonial into the subversively artistic.

Mangan as the poetic avatar of the alienated Irish artist detaches art from propaganda; art is traumatised into Art; he opens up a space for Romantic/Symbolist modernists of succeeding generations to enter. His versions of original Gaelic poems intensify the allegorical representations of Ireland as beautiful, suffering and female. Yet, at the same time they resist the particular topographic specificity of the *dindshenchas* and the regional associations of the Irish language poets of the seventeenth and eighteenth centuries. Mangan, like Moore, Dubliners both, lacked the rurality of the Gaelic poets and writing out of the ethos of Romanticism and Romantic Nationalism, it is hardly surprising that his representations of Ireland were more generalised and less clearly delineated than those of his more rooted predecessors.

Mangan, again like Moore and other poets of High Romanticism, was fascinated with the Orient. Exotic locations in the Near and Far East real or imagined, served as sites where the artist could displace his immediate concerns as he did in dream sequences or prophetic projections onto an aesthetic plane. In 'The Caramanian Exile', an original rather than a 'translated' poem, he adopts the persona of a pressed soldier captive; an exile in the service of the Turks forced to oppose his own (and other) oppressed people. In his exile the speaker inverts all normative judgements and associations. Karaman, 'home', 'The hot bright plains, the sun, the skies', seems 'like deathblack marble to mine eyes'. Home, his originary presence, exists only in dreams. Ripped from the security of his birthplace and stained with the blood of those he has killed in the service of his colonial masters, all natural feelings and affections are reversed. They are 'withered, like young flowers uptorn', his 'burning eyes are dried to horn' and he hates 'the blessed light of morn'. Moreover, the future holds no relief as the tyrant plans to destroy Karaman and on the once edenic homeland where 'dews and ruins' nourished and fertilised the landscape, 'poison–dews and bloody rains' will nourish the infertility of this new dystopia.

In such circumstances death is a release and a relief, and revenge wrought at the hands of Azreel, the avenging angel, the only consolation. Compensation however, can only be deferred onto the indefinite and the prophetic. The imminent reality is that the forces of desecration have sounded the muster call while 'the foe! the foe–they scale the walls'.[63]

Morash suggests that like the Karamanian exile the world Mangan inhabited in the 1840s

> came increasingly to resemble the desert of his nightmares in the final years
> of his life, the themes which had long haunted his work, themes of isolation,
> spiritual exile, and metaphysical terror, found their objective correlatives in

the state of Famine Ireland. It was as if the spiritual malaise of one man had been realised in the landscape of a nation.[64]

In the last poem he published before his death in June 1849, 'The Famine', Mangan addresses the reader directly without the mediation of an assumed persona:

> Despair? Yes! For a blight fell on the land–
>   The soil, heaven-blasted, yielded food no more.
> The Irish serf became a Being banned–
>   Life-exiled as none ever was before.
> The old man died beside his hovel's hearth,
>   The young man stretched himself along the earth
> And perished, stricken to the core!

To be Irish then is to be an exile; and exile is axiomatically encoded in art.

In his millenarian mode, Mangan invested what hope he had for the future in the young men of the nationalist movement and just as in the Old Testament and the Book of Revelations, the élite or the chosen, achieve their sanctification through experiencing the ordeals of conquest, exile, famine and pestilence. The self-selecting middle-class reformers of Young Ireland were in a sense ordained and anointed to serve the cause of Ireland. The weak will perish but the élite survivors have thrust upon them the obligations of leadership:

> Ye True, ye Noble, who unblenching stand
>   Amid the storms and ills of this dark Day,
> Still hold your ground! Yourselves, your Fatherland,
>   Have in the Powers above a surest stay!
> Though Famine, Pest, Want, Sickness of the Heart,
>   Be now your lot–all these shall soon depart
> And Heaven be yet at your command![65]

There is an uncomfortable fusion here of the sufferings of poor, voiceless, Catholic, rural peasants with the discomforts, crises of conscience and political powerlessness of the articulate urban bourgeois leadership of nationalist Ireland. It is as though the life-denying realities of peasant experience are 'devoiced' and subsumed under, or transfered to, the collective complex of bourgeois feeling and aspiration, enabling nationalist poets and politicians to envisage themselves as having undergone a rite of passage or ritual suffering, legitimising their self-appointed leadership. An ambivalent legerdemain enables the relatively privileged to absorb the sufferings of the uneducated and to reproduce the material afflictions visited on the masses in intensely individualised, sensitised bourgeois forms. Actuality is metamorphosed into metaphorical representation of middle-class nationalist Romantic angst, and paradoxically, the paradigms of colonialism are replicated among the colonised. The denial of individualised sensitivities to the peasantry and the ascription of highly developed feelings and sensitivities in the forms of famine, exile, persecution, fever and desolation to the materially secure (or at least the non-starving) effectively apes and mimics the cultural representations of the Irish by the English and the ascendancy. It is a position from which the indigenous aspirants to political and cultural power like Mitchel, could assume a lofty superiority and castigate the docility and instincts for survival of the poor as they refused to rise in 1848; the Catholic priesthood, which refused to sanction armed rebellion; and the hundreds and thousands who fled rather than starve nobly in the cause of Ireland, sword in hand, attacking the mechanical might of the Empire as McGee and Thomas Francis Meagher would seem to have wished.[66]

Mangan however, unlike most of his Young Ireland contemporaries, resists the crude categorisations of bourgeois colonialism, simple-minded nationalism and unthinking adherence to the diktats of devotional Catholicism. His art refuses the exterior authority of fixed univocal meanings and explores the possibilities of diversity. His work fuses notions of artistic isolation, existential acceptance and spiritualised exile. Behind the various masks and personae there may not be an authentic identity as Lloyd speculates,[67] but, in ventriloquising dysphoria he manifests the divisions and uncertainties inherent in a colonial subject. As an artistic chameleon at a juncture of crisis he embodies the centrifugal and fragmentary propensities in a dislocated, discontinuous and reiterative historical experience.

The work and his life juxtapose past and present; the self-abasement, resignation and acceptance of the inexplicable, amplify and re-echo the despair of the Gaelic poets and co-exist with a post-Enlightment proto-modernist sensibility which erases distinctions between the real and the fantastic and highlights the grotesque as the quotidian. Epistemological categories are reversed and intermingled as nihilism, surreality, the hallucinatory and the apocalyptic, interweave in a pre-Kafkaesque or pre-Beckettian horrorscape.

George Petrie's 1855 description of Ireland in the wake of the Famine forms an appropriate topographic and social context for the disembodiment and despair of much of Mangan's work:

Of the old, who had still preserved as household gods the language, the songs and traditions of their race and localities, but few survived. Of the middle-aged and energetic whom death had yet spared, and who might for a time, to some extent, have preserved such relics, but a few remained that had the power to fly from the plague and panic-stricken land; and of the young, who had come into existence, and became orphaned, during those years of desolation, they, for the most part, were reared where no mother's eyes could make them feel the mysteries of human affections–no mother's voice could soothe their youthful sorrow and implant within the memories of their hearts her songs of tenderness and love–and where no father's instructions could impart to them the traditions and characteristic peculiarities of feeling that would link them to their remotest ancestors. The green pastoral plains, the fruitful valleys, as well as the wild hillsides and the dreary bogs had equally ceased to be animate with human life. 'The lang of song' was no longer tuneful; or, if a human sound met the traveller's ear, it was only that of the feeble and despairing wail for the dead. This awful unwonted silence, which during the famine and subsequent years, almost everywhere prevailed, struck more fearfully upon their imaginations, as many Irish gentlemen informed me, and gave them a deeper feeling of the desolation with which the country has been visited, than any other circumstances which forced themselves upon their attention.[68]

Mangan, the unattached artist, was writing out of the margins of his time and experience. He was a lyricist of the liminal, inhabiting the borderlands between day and night, light and dark; literary modes and forms emanating from the metropolis and resisted, reworked and imitated from the periphery; between the past and the present, drug dependency and self control–being and nothingness. Like the speaker in the 'Nameless One', existing, enduring–an isolate on the fringe, a voice from the abyss.

The myth of the Romantic outsider, which he came to symbolise for later generations of nationalists and literati, served numerous interests and the plurality of positions he adopted allowed for disparate forms of cultural appropriation. Mitchel incorporated him into his pre-capitalist dream world of yeoman farmers. Yeats, of the 1890s was intrigued by the multiple play of personality and his 'poeticised' exterior, and Joyce the archetypal modernist, the alienated urban artist, and 'priest of the eternal imagination' was also fascinated by the man and his work. As an image of the persecuted Irish artist Mangan came to assume an iconic significance in the development of a distinct Irish literary corpus. He was Ireland's Baudelaire or Edgar Allan Poe, a prototype and precursor whose work and life osmotically synthesised alienation, art and exile.

His death in the cholera epidemic of 1849 as the Great Famine ended, provided an appropriate conclusion to the life and the myth. He was 'one of its ancillary victims and thereby, one of the most perfectly pedigreed of the Irish literary heroes'.[69]

POST-FAMINE CONSTRUCTIONS

The psychopathology of post-Famine Ireland and of the diaspora could barely countenance the brute realities of a malevolent or indifferent Nature–to accept cruel and casual catastrophe normatively was to reject history as meaningless. A teleology predicated on an analogy with other european states; progression to independence and citizenship would have had to be abandoned reducing all Irish nationalists, Protestants and Catholics, to a pre-human ontology, 'white niggers' to be disposed of at the whim of an imperial master rendering them rightless and dehuman-ised–slaves of philistines. It was therefore, imperative psychologically, to seek explanations which transferred guilt onto some 'Other' in an exculpatory shift which exonerated Ireland and alleviated the profound sense of shame felt by the Irish. They perceived themselves as having being defeated without having fought and being reduced to sub-human degra-dation without ever having achieved the status of the fully human. Mortification in this historical instance differed from that of previous moments when it was internalised and considered to be self-induced. In the second half of the nineteenth century the humiliation was no less keenly felt but explanations were readily to hand. Whether they accepted Mitchel's genocide charges against the English or not, it was abundantly clear that the Union had brought absolutely no benefits to Catholic rural Ireland. The rhetoric of constitutional equality merely masked the exploi-tative imbalance in cultural, social and economic spheres and mocked the existential immediacies of starvation and despair.

The Revd. John O'Rourke in his popular account of the Famine published in Dublin in 1875,[70] resurrects the Catholic fears of whole-sale dispossession derived from the Cromwellian policy of 'To Hell or Connaught'. He describes in detail the proposal in 1847 by the 'so called Irish party'[71] to launch a gigantic emigration scheme whereby two million Irish Catholics were to be transferred to Canada in three years–ostensibly because Ireland could not sustain its population. The scheme, he goes on to say, was 'regarded as a plan for getting rid of the Celt by wholesale'.[72] He quotes the reaction of the Right Revd. Dr Maginn, Coadjutor Bishop of Derry, which encapsulates and articulates the fears and anger of Catholics in general and the Church in particular:

> In sober earnestness, gentlemen why send your circular to a Catholic bishop? Why have the bare-faced impudence to ask me to consent to the expatriation of millions of my co-religionists and fellow countrymen? You, the hereditary oppressors of my race and religion,–you, who reduced one of the noblest peoples under heaven to live in the most fertile island on earth on the worst species of a miserable exotic, which no humane man, having anything better, would constantly give to his swine or his horses;–you, who have made the most beautiful island under the sun a land of skulls, or of ghastly spectres–you are anxious, I presume, to get a Catholic bishop to abet your wholesale system of extermination–to head in pontificals the convoy of your exiles, and thereby give the sanction of religion to your atrocious scheme. You never, gentlemen, laboured under a more egregious mistake than by imagining that we could give in our adhesion to your principles, or could they have any, the least confidence, in anything proceeding from you.[73]

The Famine was a 'primordial trauma' which fixated Irish development at one level while it continued at another. It represented irrevocable loss, cataclysmic catharsis, regressive teleology. As Terry Eagleton puts it, it was the marker of the modern period out of which flows

> an origin which is also an end, an abyss into which one third of the population disappears. This deathly origin then shatters space as well as time, unmaking the nation and scattering Irish history across the globe.

And what was lost on the material and cultural level re-formed itself in time and in other locations 'on the alternative terrain of myth'.[74]

Eagleton, like Morash,[75] draws attention to forms and structures that failed to encompass chaos and meaninglessness. Morash recognises the inadequacies of pre-modernist idioms in dealing with experience that (quoting George Steiner) like 'The World of Auschwitz lies outside speech as it lies outside reason'.[76] He nevertheless defends the efforts of those represented in the anthology as a collective attempt to comprehend the incomprehensible and come to terms with atrocity. All those represented in *The Hungry Voice* however, were reacting at the time of the Famine or immediately afterwards. Eagleton, working out of a much longer temporal frame of reference points to repression and evasion at work throughout Irish literary culture. He asks where

> apart from the two or three obvious texts–is the Famine in the Irish novel or drama, or in the literature of the Revival? Where is it in Joyce? There is

a question here, when it comes to the Revival, of the politics of form: much of that writing is programmatically non-representational and thus no fit medium for historical realism.[77]

Repression and evasion as silent markers of literary response are probably explicable in terms of the backgrounds of most of the contributors to the Revival (Anglo-Irish, Protestant, landowners and urban dwellers mainly from Dublin and London) and in the nature of their project which was of course to establish Ireland as a legitimate claimant to independence (or at least Home Rule). This was on the grounds that it was an ancient european nation and thus entitled to the same privileges and status as other western nation states. Implicit in that position was the assumption that they would provide the leadership in any new Irish polity and that they would lead Ireland away from crass commercialisation and modernisation into a pre-Catholic future–a movement that might be characterised as forward to the past. The imperatives propelling that project were thus incompatible with a culture of shame and degradation and required the suppression of experience that testified to meaningless oblivion.

The optimism and pride implicit in emergent literary nationalism could not co-exist with despair and annihilation. Even if its progenitors had the capacity to comprehend the holocaust it seems improbable that they could feel it and admit it to a privileged élitist consciousness. Celticism then, was incapable of incorporating the catastrophic realities of the Famine or the consequences which emanated from the post-Famine experiences of massive emigration, depopulation, spiritual Catholic renewal and antipathy to colonial rule. It reacted in the only way it could. It occluded what it would not assimilate, by-passed history and the contemporary reality of Catholic rural Ireland. It was not in fact until the post-Revival era of the Catholic realists and their successors that the Famine came to be featured in 'high' literary culture.

It was registered, however, in the popular literary tradition, in texts such as Canon Sheehan's *Glenanaar* (1905), Peadar O'Laoghaire's *Mo Scéal Féin (My Story)* (1915), in the poetry of the *Nation* published in the best selling *The Spirit of the Nation* and in Hubert O'Grady's melodrama *The Famine* (1886). More significantly it was preserved and relayed in the oral tradition in both Irish and English. Roger McHugh presents a picture of the Famine as it has come down to us. Writing in the 1950s he says:

> During the past century such experiences have been told and retold around the firesides of the farming and fishing communities of the districts which bore the brunt of the famine, they have been firmly linked to associations

of place, of family and of language; in many places they are as real to the inhabitants today as are the events of last year.[78]

The tenacity and vivacity of the events and memories he records testifies to their centrality in the Irish folk memory and to the huge gulf separating their memories and experiences from those of their 'superiors', proselytising Protestants in particular, to their dependence on local priests, on family groups and the intimacy of the Gaelic language with the landscape where local place-names evoke daily reminders of the Famine for many:

> For example Stirabout in *Lios a Londuin*, Co. Galway, and *Pairc and tSuip* (Soup Park) in *Gurran na Fola*, West Kerry, are named after food centres, and places similarly named are to be found in many Irish counties. Still more derive their names from association with relief schemes; Brochan Road, *Bealach an Breachain* (Porridge Way), *Droichead na Mine* (Meal Bridge), Stirabout Quay, Stirabout Drain, local people often use those dating from the famine. Often such names arise from the association of individuals with famine relief-schemes; thus *Bealach Mór Cheallaigh* (Kelly's big road) in north-west Donegal has been christened after the engineer in charge of it making; *Bealach an athar Domhnall* (Father Donal's Road) in Rannafast, Co. Donegal, after the priest who sponsored it; a road into a bog in Co. Leitrim is called 'Barton's Line' after a local landlord.[79]

Conversely place-names also narrate a history of erasure:

> These are sometimes names of places–*Baile an Tobair, Loch lar an bhaile, Sean-bhaile*–where no village now exists but where tradition records that villages stood in the famine times. Sometimes they are names of fields and houses–*Paircon Hector, Garrai Mhichil, Máire Bhuidhe's* old house–which are said to bear the names of tenants of a century ago. Sometimes they are the ruins of old cabins, the remains of ditches, gate-pillars and fences–*Maireann na cuaili criona ach ní mhaireann an lámh a shin iad* (the old posts remain but not the hand that set them)–sometimes old potato-ridges overgrown with grass and barely discernible on the slopes which no man tills to-day.[80]

The Famine is then inscribed in what for many was already a sacral landscape, and the ground itself sanctified (and sometimes defiled) by the mass burials of the innocents in what might be read as a rough symbiosis between the living and the dead, the womb and the sepulchre. 'Taking the emigration' in this context is a phrase redolent with the ambiguities inherent in the consciousness of most reluctant emigrants. The ritual surrounding the going reinforced the sense of involuntary departure for most, particularly those from the Gaelic speaking districts. It was a form of living death, a journey from which they and their neighbours knew they would not return. The oral tradition as recorded by McHugh in Donegal recalls the similarities between the rituals of emigration and the rituals of an Irish wake:

> On the night before the departure, people would crowd into the house of the emigrating family and would try to cheer them by making forced merriment until morning; but for all that the house would be '*comh bronach le teach faire*' (as sad as a Wake-house). When the time for departure came, the emigrants would make ready and would bid farewell to the company, which would accompany them to where the car for Derry was waiting; ... 'Some of the women would fall fainting when they saw any person going, others would hang out of the car to keep back the departing one; but when it would go, the whole lot, men and women would raise a cry of grief that would wrest an echo from the peaks.'[81]

For the Revd. O'Rourke the purgatorial trials of the Famine emigrants enduring as they did the inhuman conditions of the voyage, and the assaults by armed gangs prior to embarkation, and on arrival in America, testified implicitly to the wicked material godlessness of modern commercialism outside Catholic Ireland. Yet, at the same time their sufferings and continued devotion to Mother Ireland validated the right of the Catholic Irish to assert their full occidental citizenship and the fullness of their humanity. Referring to the period up to 1870 and reacting to the English and Anglo-Irish criticism that the native Irish were feckless and irresponsible, he concludes his chapter on emigration so:

> For the lengthened period of three and twenty years, something like £1,000,000 a-year have been transmitted to their relatives and friends by the Irish in America. In three and twenty years, they have sent home over TWENTY MILLIONS OF MONEY. Examine it; weigh it; study it; in whatever way we look at this astounding fact–whether we regard the magnitude of the sum, or the intense undying, all pervading affection which it represents–it STANDS ALONE IN THE HISTORY OF THE WORLD.[82]

The orthographical assertiveness embedded in the passage obviously attests to a developing counter-image being erected by the Catholic Irish against the prevailing English stereotype of the sentimental and childlike in the form delineated by Matthew Arnold.[83] It challenges the fenian monster representation propagated by some writers in *Punch* and the English press after the attempted rising of 1867 and the incidents surrounding the Manchester Martyrs. The passage asserts the essential obedience and Catholicity of the emigrant and his (*sic*) loyalty and love of hearth, home and Holy Ireland. It also bears within it the notion that alone among the peoples of the modern world, the Irishman abroad preserves his virtues intact in exile and in the service of Ireland.

JOHN MITCHEL, THE *JAIL JOURNAL* AND FENIANISM

The failure of the 1848 rebellion and the subsequent fate of the leaders of Young Ireland dramatically altered middle-class nationalists' notion of exile. Ethereal impressions generated by Moore's verse became actuality for almost all of those who participated in the events at Ballingarry Co. Tipperary and those who supported armed resistance to English rule. Some were fortunate and evaded capture. Michael Doheny, Thomas D'Arcy McGee and Richard O'Gorman escaped to the United States of America. James Stephens, John Blake Dillon and John O'Mahoney fled to France. The leader of the rising, William Smith O'Brien, together with Thomas Francis Meagher and Terence Bellew McManus were arrested, tried, found guilty of treason and sentenced to transportation to Tasmania. They were later joined by John Mitchel who had been arrested and sentenced to fourteen years earlier in the year, as a result of his advocacy of a 'holy war' against the English, in his newspaper *The United Irishman*.

As gentlemen prisoners they had their own houses and a relative freedom of movement and some, like Mitchel brought out their wives and children. Their exile and treatment was invested with notions of honour and gentlemanly behaviour derived from English polite society. Some were pardoned and others like Meagher, McManus, O'Donohue and Mitchel (having withdrawn his word not to escape), escaped to America when the opportunity arose. Australia for them, represented tyranny, degradation and oppression, and America symbolised freedom. Mitchel recorded his experiences in his *Jail Journal* which was originally published for an Irish-American audience in his New York newspaper *The Citizen* in 1854. Commenting on his experience in Australia and his record of it in the *Jail Journal*, the Irish-Australian historian Patrick O'Farrell says:

> Exile in Tasmania had the effect of immensely enhancing the international reputation of Young Ireland ... It also formed the core of an Irish revolutionary masterpiece, John Mitchel's *Jail Journal* ... Mitchel invested his exile with an extraordinary mythical power which clung in the mind to its Australian setting, but which also seemed to capture the sense of internal exile, even within their own country, which tormented many Irishmen.[84]

Masterpiece or not, his *Jail Journal* became an exemplary text in the Irish revolutionary canon 'reintegrating Irish writing with the radical separatist tradition from which it has been so carefully disengaged since the early days of the Union'.[85] It went further however, and was different in kind from the writings which emanated from the United Irishmen such as Tone. The literary historian Thomas Flanagan says:

> The *Jail Journal*, which provided extreme Irish nationalism with an entire arsenal of attitudes and ideas; has rightly been called the Bible of republicanism, and like other scriptural revelations it derives its authority from its bleak and unyielding singlemindedness. Like Mitchel's own life, it is shaped on the single principle of rebellion against British rule, and it is with Mitchel that hatred of England, a passion raised to a principle, makes its appearance in the thought of modern Ireland.[86]

Unlike Tone's republicanism which seemed motivated by the inherent attractions of democratic republicanism, Mitchel's writings seem animated not just by a hatred of British rule, but by a hatred of the modern world in its entirety. Britain, as the most powerful urban industrialised country in the world and geographically the closest such society to Ireland, became the obsessive paranoiac focus of all that Mitchel despised in the nineteenth century.

The intensity of that loathing is superficially reminiscent of the sense of self-disgust that the Gaelic poets expressed in the seventeenth and eighteenth centuries. However, the rage and disgust expressed by Mitchel is Swiftean in its externalised displacement onto the subservience of the Irish and the monolithic power and philistinism of the British. It contrasts with the internalisation of guilt and shame characteristic of Catholic native Irish consciousness. It may perhaps, derive from the irresolvable tensions inherent in the mix of Mitchel's Presbyterian upbringing, Romantic Nationalism, his proto-fascistic commitment to Ireland and a sense of utter powerlessness as a cultural 'alien' speaking out of the margins of a traumatised, impoverished, Catholic, rural community. The awesome, apoplectic fury he manifests, may have its origins in contradictory impulses which are unable to reconcile a supercharged ego formed out of an intensely individualistic ideology, with a communalistic tradition which refused his leadership and denied him the crusade or messianic mission he had ordained for himself. Speaking of his motivation he said:

> I have found that there was perhaps less of love in it than hate–less of filial affection to my country than of scornful impatience at the thought that I

had the misfortune, I and my children, to be born in a country which
suffered itself to be oppressed and humiliated by another; less devotion to
truth and justice than raging wrath against cant and insolence. And hatred
being the thing I chiefly cherished and cultivated, the thing which I specially
hated was the British system–everywhere, at home and abroad, as it works
in England itself, in India, on the continent of Europe, and in Ireland. Living
in Ireland, and wishing to feel proud, not ashamed of Ireland, it was there,
first and most, that I had to fight with that great enemy.[87]

As Lloyd points out Mitchel portrays himself as a 'representative' of
Ireland. In his version of nationalist ideology 'the integration of the
individual subject is achieved through his integration with the nation'.[88]
That integration however, could not be realised while Ireland was a slave
of England. Ireland as a reified property, a colony, was unable to achieve
a sense of fulfilment physically or spiritually. It was denied the possibility
of achieving a fundamental sense of identity, of realising its essence in the
same way that other european communities were attempting to in 1848.

His arrest, trial, transportation and exile personified and epitomised the
state of Ireland. Just as Ireland was denied the rights of self-determination,
so too was he. Exile was for Mitchel intrinsically dehumanising in that he
was arbitrarily denied basic human rights:

> So my moorings are cut. I am a banished man. And this is no mere *relegatio*,
> like Ovid's at Tomi; it is utter *exsilium*–interdiction of fire and water; the
> loss of citizenship, if citizenship I had; the brand of whatsoever ignomiy
> law can inflict, if law there be. Be it so; I am content. There are no citizens
> in Ireland; there is no citizenship–no law. I cannot lose what I never had; for
> no Irishman has any rights at present.[89]

Mitchel's conception of exile is thus clearly formed out of the rhetoric
of democratic republicanism and in this instance refracted through the
language of the classics. His style, generally borrowing from the Bible, the
classics, Swift, Cobbett and Carlyle,[90] ironically highlights his anglicised
education. This in turn suggests that his assumed and understood etymology of the concept owes more to the traditions of his opponents than
to the indigenous native social formation. Unlike the Catholic Irish peasants
who subsumed themselves in the totality of an organic communal identity
and for whom exile was a kind of spiritual amputation, Mitchel absorbed
and internalised the state and idea of exile into a complete identification
of the individual with the state. Ireland's wrongs are Mitchel's wrongs,
and his wrongs are Ireland's too. The act of composing the *Jail Journal* was

a means by which he could remind himself of his origins, his history and his own identity. He

> reconstitutes the *continuity* in which his personal identity resides and thereby re-enacts on the individual level the practices of the nationalist who attempts to discover the identity of his nation in his history.[91]

In composing and narrating this image of himself his exile becomes an appropriate emblem of Ireland's alienation and it is 'as though with him the conscience and intellect of Ireland itself has passed into exile'.[92] In the model of the dedicated revolutionary Mitchel came to represent to later generations of fenians and their successors; alienation and exile were inextricably bound up in the image of the exiled rebel. It was also interwoven with Mitchel's accusation of genocide against the British authorities and their Irish acolytes the landlords; a charge which echoed those made by the Catholic Irish against Cromwell. The extirpation of the Irish masses was, he believed, to be achieved through '*killing* as many people in Ireland as might be needful to preserve the sacred landlord property untouched'[93] and by driving out as many as was necessary. Writing of an Ireland against the background of the impending Crimean War, an Ireland 'broken and destroyed', he said:

> To America has fled the half-starved remnant of it; and the phrase that I have heard of late 'a new Ireland in America', conveys no meaning to my mind. Ireland without the Irish–The Irish out of Ireland–neither of these can be *our country*. Yet who can tell what the chances and changes of the blessed war may bring us? I believe in moral and spiritual electricity; I believe that a spark, caught at some happy moment, may give life to masses of comatose humanity; that dry bones, as in Ezekiel's vision may live; that out of the 'exodus' of the Celts may be born a Return of the Heracleidae.
>
> Czar, I bless thee, I kiss the hem of thy garment. I drink to thy health and longevity. Give us war in our time, O Lord![94]

The *Jail Journal* was a seminal text in the evolution of Irish separatism whose fierce negative obsessiveness obscured its lack of any reasoned or formulated social philosophy (fortunately perhaps, given Mitchel's barbarous attitudes to criminals and slavery). It was a kind of autochthonous scream emanating from a psyche constitutively prone to schism and dissent. It speaks out of a cultural schizophrenia whose consciousness was formed out of conquest, privilege and a sense of the elect–a mindset constitutionally unable to cope with subjugation and impotence–

whose only apparent integrative principle was a rancorous fixation with modernity and imperialism.

But it was that very lack of any logic and consistency which generated its mythopoeic force. Its anger 'articulated' the inchoate frustrations of many nationalists and in some ways Mitchel paradoxically represents the classic exile raging from the zone of exclusion. As a Protestant individualist convinced of his superiority, he was unable to submit to an imposed communal identity and at the same time equally unable to effect change directly or assume leadership–a Nationalist in opposition to Britishness rather than because of his hibernian heritage. But his vision of an avenging and liberating army of exiles sustained hope in Ireland and contributed to the maintenance of an exilic self-image among Irish-Americans. Its very lack of specificity enabled its assimilation into post-Famine nationalist discourse but paradoxically its genesis out of Romantic Nationalism aligned Mitchel with a nationalism that was increasingly sectarian. Oliver MacDonagh commenting on the inheritance of Young Ireland has said:

> There were apparent similarities in the cries in different generations to break the connection with England and to regard Catholic, protestant, and dissenter as forming a single flock. But these appearances should not blind us to the reality, to the revolution that romanticism had wrought. The new emphasis was on *cultural* division and *cultural* hostility; on emotion rather than rationality; on group, rather than individual, rights; on a subjective and creative rather than a formal and negative concept of independence; and of course, in the very long run, on race and language.[95]

It was inevitable that the increasing polarisation that manifested itself in a Catholic nationalist, Protestant unionist division should express itself in distinctive discourses and that Mitchel's particular experience and representation of *exsilium (sic)* should attach itself to the already long formed discourse of Catholic Irish exile. In fact, it was an elementary signifier of difference which acquired added significance in the emergent nationalist rhetoric as the failed leaders of Young Ireland were celebrated in America as heroes.

There, their celebrity and image were diffused rapidly through new and very effective transmission systems, such as the newspapers and railroads, which spread their explanations and interpretations throughout the United States within a relatively short period. They encouraged the Famine victims and later generations of emigrants to view themselves as persecuted victims of English rule. In doing so, they met a pychological need among many Irish immigrants. Those who attributed the catastrophe of the Famine to God's will, or who fled in panic defying the intense communalistic tradition binding the Irish to the soil, found consolation and justification in explanations which shifted responsibility onto the oppressive genocidal rapaciousness of the English and the landlords. Such explanations absolved the immigrants of guilt and modernised traditional perceptions of emigration as exile. In addition the presence of the Young Ireland leadership and their growing band of supporters in Irish-America offered a redemptive, if deferred, solution to Ireland's problems. By uniting behind the nationalist leadership they could effect a kind of restitution, establish a democratic republic of Ireland and take revenge on the Carthaginian philistines of England, like Mitchel's Heracleidae. Those unifying aspirations reinforced a continuing sense of racial distinctiveness which distinguished the Irish from other immigrant groups and reinforced that sense of themselves as banished exiles.

Militant Young Ireland mutated in the late 1850s into the Irish Republican Brotherhood and its transatlantic counterpart the Fenian Brotherhood. The fenians in Ireland recruited from among craftsmen and factory workmen, a membership whose religious affiliation reflected that of the leadership in that they were overwhelmingly Catholic. Irish-American fenians agreed to supply money, arms and trained soldiers. Memories of the Famine, the coffin ships, the landlords; evictions suffused with Gaelic tradition; and Young Ireland's rhetoric reinforced by hostile American nativism, combined to make revenge on England a psychic imperative. Irish-American rhetoric categorising all movement to the USA as 'exile', underwrote Irish communal traditions and helped generate a circular, transatlantic justification, rationale and explanation for migration.

Emigration seen as exile was thus historically reinforced in Irish Catholic and Irish-American consciousness at what was undoubtedly the most profoundly pivotal moment in Irish historical experience. The association of exile, anti-Englishness, loss, memories of Ireland and adjustments to the fiercely individualistic ethos of capitalist America became for Irish-Americans, indelibly fixed in the moment of their departure and their early experiences in America. Inevitably such powerful and affective memories and images permeated community values and perceptions for generations to come.

Malcolm Brown has recorded how Irish Americans came in effect to colonise fenianism.[96] An act of possession which initiated a whole series of manoeuvres in various spheres, as the relationship between America and Ireland developed in the remainder of the nineteenth century and throughout the twentieth century. The imbalance in the relationship and the dependence of Ireland as an impoverished colony on an imperial power and later as an impoverished dependant on a neo-imperialist power, ensured a subordination of Ireland's economic, social and cultural independence to American expectations. A great deal of the iconography, imagery and discourse employed in the description and analysis of Ireland and its culture derives from the expectations and distorted memories of the American-Irish and their cultural organs and institutions of production. Irish images served American needs, and those American images of racial memories were frequently inherited from static or half remembered pictures of 'home'. Irish realities were to a large extent entrapped and canalised in Irish-American perceptions and psychic needs. Irish-America defined Irishness, leaving little room for plurality. Ireland was 'traditional', rural, Catholic and anti-English; while the Irish in America were invariably 'exiles'.

Paradoxically, the most significant moment in the nine years of fenianism occurred in the heartland of the Empire when three young Irishmen were hanged publicly for the murder of a guard during the rescue attempt of two fenians from a prison van. William Allen, Michael Larkin and Michael O'Brien were the 'celebrated Manchester martyrs, one of the crowning exhibits of Irish patriotic symbology'.[97] The widespread belief that the trial was rigged, that the sentence was completely unjust and that the English authorities took a ghoulish delight in the pageantry of the execution, sanctified the actions and imagery of the three in Irish nationalist consciousness. The mood of Ireland, of Irish-America and the emotive legacy of fenianism was encapsulated immediately in probably the only form open to the defeated, the martial ballad. 'God save Ireland' (1867) was a ballad that might have been produced by Young Ireland but was in fact (ironically) written by T.D. Sullivan the brother of Arthur Sullivan the then owner of *The Nation* and arch opponent of the fenians. The third verse reads:

> Girt around with cruel foes,
> Still their spirit proudly rose,
> For they thought of hearts that loved them far and near;
> Of the millions true and brave
> O'er the ocean's swelling wave,
> And the friends in Holy Ireland ever dear.
> 'God save Ireland!' said they proudly;
>   (Chorus).[98]

The song became in effect the national anthem of pre-Independence Ireland. It asserted the links between Ireland, nationality and Catholicism with the quasi-religious antiphonal response of 'God save Ireland', a remark made by one of the defendants at the trial which was picked up and echoed around the courtroom. Rhetorically it opposed might and power with bare unaccommodated dignity, patience and an inviolable belief in the sanctity of the cause. It imaged execution as beatification; death as martyrdom. In it death is mystified and sacrifice glorified while 'Holy Ireland', home and abroad, is unified across time and oceans into a seamless assertion of the superiority of the communal to the private, of the nation to the individual and of the spiritual to the material.

It is a song which looks backwards through Thomas Davis to Thomas Moore and forwards to the 'blood-sacrifice' hyperbole of early twentieth-century Europe which permeated the discourses of rival imperial powers, of coloniser and colonised. Moreover, in the context of the second half of the nineteenth century, it is a text which implicitly excludes those who are unwilling to adhere to a rigid nationalist ideology which unites the 'sea-divided Gael' in active military opposition to English imperialism. Its language and imagery are saturated with a Nationalist/Catholic religiosity which admits no qualification or addition and which effectively registers the tacit expulsion of non-Catholic thought, religion and/or secular modes of being from definitions or assumptions about what it is to be Irish.

The treatment of those sentenced to long penal terms in English prisons differed markedly from that meted out to the Young Irelanders. The brutalities and indignities that they suffered were recorded by O'Donovan Rossa in *Irish Rebels in English Prisons* (1874),[99] a memoir which endorsed Mitchel's genocide accusation and provided further evidence of the malice of the English authorities towards Irish rebels. Rossa, like Devoy, Luby and O'Leary had his imprisonment commuted into formal banishment. O'Leary took up residence in Paris, joining James Stephens who had left the USA after disagreements with the American fenians and Luby. Devoy and Rossa chose to go to America where they became actively involved in Irish-American politics. Rossa records how in opposing Tammany Hall he exposed the self-interest of Irish-American politicians who, in many instances, were less concerned with Ireland and her freedom than they were with their own interests.[100] This verifies the potentially exploitative and distorting misuse of Irish hopes and aspirations for Irish-American ends.

Nevertheless, like the Young Ireland leaders and the leaders of the

United Irishmen the presence of exiled–banished–fenian leaders and rebels personified the relationship between oppression, rebellion and expulsion. As heroes they served as models for the Irish on both sides of the Atlantic who were themselves increasingly politicised and therefore prone to see all emigration as involuntary–the result of exploitation by an alien power.[101]

A.M. Sullivan, the younger brother of T.D., opposed the physical force nationalism of fenianism and rejected Mitchel's charges of genocide against the English. However, he contributed significantly to anti-imperialist feeling through his immensely popular *Story of Ireland* which was published in 1870 and dedicated to 'My young fellow countrymen at home and in exile'. It was a victorianised and highly sentimentalised version of Irish history written from the standpoint of a constitutional and Catholic home-ruler. He gathered together in a linear narrative the key episodes in Irish history highlighted and implicitly understood and defined against England. They included those heightened moments when martyrs and heroes left Ireland unwillingly, to serve God in the case of Colmcille, or as a consequence of defeat and betrayal in the case of the Flight of the Earls; the transportations to the West Indies and the exodus of the Wild Geese after the surrender at Limerick. It is a narrative which presupposes involuntary departure, which inscribes such partings as exile and unquestioningly assumes that those exiting Ireland are Catholics and that England and the colonialist Protestants are the agents of their expulsion.

Commenting on the flight from Ireland in the aftermath of the Famine, he accuses the landlords and the English and the English press in particular of callously promoting the evictions of 'surplus population' and stigmatising those who left as 'assassins, creatures of superstition, lazy, ignorant, and brutified':[102]

> Pages might be filled with extracts of a like nature from the press of England; many still more coarse and brutal. There may, probably, be some Englishmen who *now* wish such language had not been used; that such blistering libels had not been rained on a departing people, to nourish in their hearts the terrible vow of vengeance with which they landed on American shores. But *then*–in that hour, when it seemed *safe* to be brutal and merciless–the grief-stricken, thrust out people
>
> 'Found not a generous friend, a pitying foe'
>
> And so they went into banishment in thousands and tens of thousands, with hands uplifted to the just God who saw all this; and they cried aloud, *Quousque Domine? Quousque?*[103]

Sullivan's 'story' confirmed, reinforced, perpetuated and propagated a near unanimous Catholic/Nationalist interpretation of Irish history. The weight and space he allocates to pre-Norman Gaelic civilisation; its emphasis on 'Saints and Scholars'; its condemnation of Cromwell, the celebration of the Irish abroad; its silence on issues which portrayed and celebrated Protestant achievement and difficulties inevitably fed the developing monoglossic master narrative of Catholic nationalist discourse. The 'story' contributed to the (re)formation of a distinct and oppositional (un)consciousness which intuitively (though not always overtly) resisted imaginative affiliation with non-Catholic nationalists whether Protestants, atheists or socialist. At this moment, it underwrote an unambivalent attachment and subsequent dependence on Irish-America as a haven, a source of material support–and for a reflected image of self-esteem which could sustain masculine Ireland in its traumatic present and offer an image of what might be in a resurgent future.

CHARLES KICKHAM: *KNOCKNAGOW*

Charles Kickham, arrested in 1865 along with other fenian leaders, was tried and sentenced to fourteen years hard labour. He served part of his sentence in Pentonville and was released from a gentler regime in Woking in 1869 due to chronic ill-health.

His fiction rehearses a narrow thematic range dealing with a romanticised heroic 1798 past in *The Eagle of Carryroe* (1920), the landlord issue, eviction, seduction and madness in *Sally Cavanagh* (1869) and *The Tales of Tipperary* (1926); and quasi-religious, political and militant commitment in *For the Old Land* (1886). The work for which he is best remembered however, is *Knocknagow, or The Homes of Tipperary* written shortly after his release from prison and published in 1873. It first appeared in serial form in *The Emerald*, New York and *The Shamrock*, Dublin, aiming at the expanding emigré market and an increasingly literate domestic middle-class audience. It has probably been reprinted more times than any other Irish novel and it (together with *The Collegians*, 1829) was almost certainly the most popular Irish novel of the nineteenth century. It was 'the most important single literary work ever written by a leading Irish revolutionist',[104] and Kickham was for years in Ireland 'a national piety'.[105]

The novel describes rural Catholic life, middle-class and peasant, in the period between the Famine and the Land Wars. To a large extent it reproduces the stereotypes of victorian sentimental fiction in a sub-

Dickensian form[106] within an Irish context. The novel is populated with virtuous, home-bound, suitor-seeking, middle-class heroines; various virile, chivalrous and manly young men; wiser and more reflective parent figures; amusing and persecuted peasant types whose intrinsic merits almost qualify them for fully adult status and a band of black-hearted villains led by Isaac and Beresford Pender, the land-agents supported by the hiss inducing blackguards, the bailiffs Darby Ruadh and Wat Corcoran. 'England, "the stranger", exists in the novel as an invisible, malignant, presence, hostile to the settled way of life that the book cherishes and celebrates'.[107] In the course of a ramshackle narrative it delineates almost all of the problems and grievances of Catholic rural life which were to inform, exacerbate and underpin the thought patterns and attitudes of the Catholic Irish within Ireland and the Catholic Irish of the diaspora. Kickham employs the well-worn convention of introducing Ireland to a visiting outsider, the Englishman Henry Lowe, who attempts to come to terms with Irish Catholicism and Irish customs. Like so many other figures in Irish fiction, Lowe is created out of an Arnoldian mould. He is beguiled, disarmed, enchanted and fascinated by the warmth, hospitality, humour and beauty of Ireland and the Irish. At this point Kickham appears to be pleading for understanding, for tolerance. It is as though he is appealing to the better nature of the English in the belief that comprehension will engender compassion, and that affection will lead to an amelioration of the injustices Ireland labours under.

As the novel progresses however, the role of Lowe is diminished. Kickham appears to lose interest in addressing England as he focuses on the brutalities of the evictions of Mick Brien and more particularly of the Hagan family. Lowe ceases to perform any stuctural function and the authorial voice takes on a more urgent and insistent note in depicting evictions, near evictions, the tumbling of cottages, the destitution of the dispossessed, the separation of families, the flight from the land, the fear of the poorhouse and the relationship Ireland is developing with the USA. The authorial stance registers an anger and despair at the uncompre-hending indifference and cruelty of blind power and seeks redress by a shift of focus which speaks to a sympathetic readership across the Atlantic.

Kickham, like many other middle-class nationalist leaders, combined 'fenian beliefs with an intense social conservatism and a deep religious piety'.[108] A combination which enabled the production of an idealised pastoral, an Ireland of the imagination; a pre-de Valeraian eden, where happiness is equated with land tenure and ownership. The reflective Dr Kiely says 'Give a man a rock with security and he'll turn it into a garden'.[109] It was a tension that generated the ambivalence that Kickham displays towards the landlord question. Sir Garrett Butler the new but absentee owner of much of the land in the district is in a sense absolved from most of the blame for the miseries of the tenantry; responsibility is displaced onto the land-agents and their minions. Thus, the Penders are portrayed as stock melodramatic cowards and villains, a shift which in effect suggests evil and betrayal are latent within the colonised body itself. In the case of the Penders there is a hibernocentric, anti-semitic coloration which mirrors anglocentric mid-victorian racism in the naming of Pender Senior as Isaac, and a distancing of racial origin which implies a notion of the 'alien within'; which poisons the purity of Holy Ireland.

Garrett Butler is positioned between two polar extremes; Sam Somerfield, the old foxhunter, who cleared his property for grazing and Bob Lloyd who 'gives good lases at a fair rent'[110] according to Phil Lahy. Like Lord Colambre in Maria Edgeworth's *The Absentee* (1812), when acquainted with the realities of Ireland he becomes a model landlord. By this time however, the text has in a sense 'forgotten' its putative audience of English and Anglo-Irish readers and turned towards America. It drives towards a denunciation of the Irish landlords who 'were encouraged to exterminate the people' and as Dr O'Connor goes on to say 'when the work was done many of themselves were exterminated. England cares just as little for them as for the people'.[111]

The attitudes of the evicted and dispossessed tenantry who flee Ireland are witnessed by the peasant hero Matt 'The Trasher' Donovan, when he sails to America in search of Bessie Morris, the love of his life:

> The vessel was crowded with Irish emigrants and many an 'o'er-true tale' of suffering and wrong did he listen to during the voyage. But as they neared the free shores of America, every face brightened, and the outcasts felt as if they seen the end of their trials and sorrows.[112]

Warming to his theme, Kickham reintroduces Phil Lahy his fenian alter ego to comment on the Irish leaving Ireland in a speech which anticipates Joyce's Citizen[113] in its clichéd resuscitation of formulaic nationalist rhetoric:

> If they are ... it is because the invader won't allow them to live there. The Celts are gone with a vengeance says the London *Times*. And the English Viceroy tells us that Providence intended Ireland to be the fruitful mother of flocks and herds. That is why our people are hunted like noxious animals, to perish in the ditchside, or in the poorhouse. That is why the floating coffins are crossing the stormy Atlantic, dropping Irish corpses to the sharks

along the way, and flinging tens of thousands of living skeletons on the shores of this free country. That is why the last sound in the dying mother's ears is the tooth of the lean dog crunching through the bones of her infant.[114]

The conflicts inherent in Kickham's narrative stance are inevitably exposed as the text struggles through its denouement. Closure can be achieved in the traditional, romantic-sentimental sense by the union of many of the young couples in matrimony and by providing for their security and that of the older generations through the *deus ex machina* device of Sir Garett Butler's enlightened provision of security of tenure and the institution of the Incumbered Estates Court. A particularly Irish variation on this form of closure is provided by Bessie Morris' long-lost father, now a rich and successful Irish-American, who is able to provide an assured romantic future for Bessie and Matt–a motif which recurs throughout much of Irish fiction. That closure however, can only be partial and provisional while Ireland's problems are unresolved, suspended in the purgatory of colonialism; in the irresolution between the profound aspiration to independence and the determination of the English and the ascendancy to retain their power and privileges.

A text emanating from the interstices of the irreconcilable cannot conclude–it can only project or reflect. Thus, when Tommy Lahy, now a successful Irish-American businessman, returns to his parents after a trip to Europe and Ireland, inspiring tearful reminders in his mother of the bathetic death of her daughter Norah (a literary clone of Dickens' little Nell) and when she keens 'will I ever again kneel down on the green grave on the ould churchyard where my own darlin' is sleepin'–at home in beautiful Ireland?' Phil Lahy her husband replies:

> You will … There are bright days in store for beautiful Ireland, as you call her, and she deserves to be called. There is a spirit growing up among the outcast children of beautiful Ireland that will yet cause another English monarch to exclaim 'Cursed be the laws that deprived me of such subjects'. The long night of her sorrow is drawing to a close. And, with God's blessing we'll all be in beautiful Ireland again.

Tommy Lahy endorses his father's sentiments and speaks for all the 'exiles' of Irish-America in his remarks which conclude the conversation:

> 'You are right, father', returned the fine young Irish-American. 'We will never forget old Ireland.'[115]

As dialogue this is embarrassing, as exhortatory encomium however it was inspiring. Like a set piece out of a patriotic painter's portfolio or a stylised tableau from a nationalist melodrama, it attempted to dignify, ennoble and counter the scurrilous and demeaning representations of Irishmen in English newspapers and magazines. It signalled the pride that could be engendered in 'serfs' when liberated and allowed to prosper by the efforts of their own endeavours; the gravity, seriousness and fixity of purpose of the Irish (bourgeois) overseas. Nevertheless, it remained a pose, an oratorical flourish, the hollow rhetoric of a fixated 'exile' entrapped by racial memory and recent history.

The troubled nature of the text and its inability to conclude satisfactorily is encapsulated in the final conversation between the two 'articulate' protagonists of middle-class Catholic rural Ireland; a conversation which echoes Mitchel's accusations and is redolent with the fears of generations and the unchallenged beliefs of the vast majority of the Catholic Irish:

> 'The Irish people will *never* be rooted out of Ireland. Cromwell could not do it; the butchers of Elizabeth could not do it.'
> 'But there is a more deadly system at work now', returned the doctor. 'The country is silently bleeding to death.'
> 'Not to death', rejoined Hugh Kearney. 'Those of her people who are forced to fly are not lost to Ireland.'[116]

In attributing all emigration to a malignant imperialism, Dr Kiely, Hugh Kearney and Charles Kickham were undoubtedly voicing the belief of most Catholics. In investing their hopes in the return of the exiles they were expressing the hopes of nationalists in the only way acceptable within the emergent discourse of the time. Their dependence on Irish-America, financially and psychologically, necessitated that posture and investment in the future for the Irish present offered nothing. The corollary of that subordination to their children abroad and to the future was however, a kind of evasion of the here and now. It was a silencing and suppression of elements, needs and contradictory truths (potential or otherwise) which challenged the simplistic communal account of experience and which they themselves could logically and rationally control. The text is, for instance, silent about the power of the Catholic Church, which is represented by Father McMahon, a kindly but vague figure in the background; nor does it deal with inter-familial conflicts about inheritance arising from the predominance of large families and familial pressure on younger siblings to leave Ireland and remit substantial sums home to subsidise the natal household. It is silent too, on the 'failures' in Irish-

America and on the Irish in England. Kickham's positioning is then symptomatic of the bourgeois nationalist conservative he believed in his idealised vision of an Ireland remembered from his childhood with its stratifications, deference and religiosity.

It was a stance that ironically brought him into an imaginative conspiracy with Matthew Arnold's characterisation of the Celt. Arnold sentimentalised the Celt and denied him parity; Kickham sentimentalised the peasant whilst implicitly denying him equality. The essential nature of the peasant, his innate generosity and kindliness provide sufficient explanations for the remittance of huge sums from America and therefore evades the more complex reality of a mendicant Ireland. 'The Irish peasant is a being of sentiment' we are told by Dr Kiely. 'The millions of money they have sent from America to their relations at home is a wonderful proof of the strength of their domestic affections.'[117]

The 'sentimental' Irish peasant was a fiction of the powerful image-makers of victorian England, employed situationally to categorise and place the poor. The image also served the Anglo-Irish in their self-appointed and self-justificatory roles as rulers and leaders. In the 1860s and throughout the remainder of the nineteenth century the image was exploited by middle-class nationalists in part to counter the caricatures of the Irish in the British press. L.P. Curtis[118] has detailed the kind of processes at work in mid-victorian Britain and how the Dublin based press countered such stereotyping with their representations of Ireland and Irish people in general. Ireland was personified as Erin:

> Erin was a stately as well as a sad and wise woman, usually drawn in flowing robes, embroidered with shamrocks. Her hair was long and dark, falling well down her back; her eyes were round and melancholy, set in a face of flawless symmetry. Occasionally she wore a garland of shamrocks and appeared with a harp and an Irish wolfhound in the foreground. Erin suggested all that was feminine, courageous, and chaste about Irish woman-hood, and she made an ideal Andromeda waiting to be rescued by a suitable Perseus.

The 'Perseus' might be England rescuing Ireland from fenianism, America freeing Ireland from British rule or masculine Ireland itself. The figure of Erin was complemented in the Irish press by that of Pat who was

> the epitome of Irish masculinity. His face was long but full, his forehead high, his chin square, and his nose and mouth straight and firm. There was a twinkle in his eyes and an easygoing smile, marking him as a man prepared to trust anyone of equal good faith.[119]

Kickham's peasants, particularly Matt the Thrasher, are clearly written with such ennobling models in mind; yet the portrayals position the rural poor in much the same way as sympathetic treatments by Anglo-Irish writers. They are assigned their place in the 'natural' order of things and the articulate middle-class construct and ventriloquise for them. Kickham, by this time a Dublin resident writing out of his nostalagia for his Tipperary childhood, a nostalgia mediated by his nationalism, fixes his specimens through the social subservience he ascribes to them. The disempowering dialectal presentation underwrites the status quo and he also erects his own speech borders in an implicit acceptance of the naturalness of the relations of dominant and dominated within Irish-Ireland.[120] Phil Lahy for example, is granted the normative power of standard written English to express his nationalist views as are the middle-class figures who populate the novel while Kickham as omniscient narrator, reserves similar rights to himself. The lower classes however, have their speech represented orthographically in a demeaning rendition of Tipperary dialect. Their expression in direct speech is almost invariably confined to the personal, to the relay of information or comic utterance, while anything more profound, philosophical or reflective is given to the reader through authorial commentary.

Kickham acknowledged his debt to Charles Dickens as a writer and it is obvious in his sentimentalisation of the inhabitants of Mullinahone. It is also apparent in his imitation of Dickensian play with language, which almost invariably fixes or pins the poor and the different in place in the social order like a lepidopterist's specimen in a manner informed perhaps, by half understood notions from mid-century ethnography. The peasant whether at home or abroad is expected to accept his position as ascribed to him by the conventions, codes and restraints of nationalism, Catholicism and family obligations. He (*sic*) not only sends money home to assist those who remain, he is expected to do so and expects it of himself–and, in addition, he is expected and expects to continue to submit to the prevailing demands of Ireland itself.

Given his (ironic) opposition to the indigenous new middle-classes and his antagonism to England and their colonial progeny in Ireland, Kickham could only idealise the past, accept its discourses and project his desires onto the only autonomous group available–the emigrants. In order to realise those hopes in any way at all it was essential that he and those like him, image the emigrants as unwilling exiles; eager to return at the first opportunity to re-create a kind of pre-lapsarian wonderworld populated by comely maidens and hurley-wielding heroes out of Gaelic mythology.

That imaginative imperative results in the strange uneasy and incongruous juxtaposing of the 'happy families' of Billy Heffernan and Matt Donovan against a depressed, desolated and depopulated landscape as the novel draws to its end. The reality that the text speaks to however, is that 'KNOCKNAGOW IS GONE',[121] and that there is no possibility of recreating that rural Gaelicised eden. A conclusion which subverts and contradicts the conventionalities of victorian certainties and confounds the expectations of narrative harmony, making it in many ways untypical of the victorian novel as it evolved in England but typical of similar productions in Ireland. A clumsily written though 'memorable exposure of colonial misrule, encased in a tawdry context of victorian melodrama'[122]–the product of a colonised and peripheral culture. That it was so popular in its time and for the later generations in Ireland and America testifies too, to a communal need. It represents an imagined community and stands for a kind of retrospective generational wish fulfilment, a lost innocence; a representation and affirmation of aboriginal virtue in a fragmented, disorienting and destructive modernity.

CONCLUSION

The version of exile created out of Catholic nationalist discourse was predicated on the widely accepted belief that England consciously and malevolently sought to drive the Irish out of Ireland. It could not admit the possibility that people wanted to go elsewhere and to the USA in particular, to escape Ireland and create an alternative way of life.

Public oppositional texts created an overarching diachronic master narrative in forms borrowed and adapted from a (relatively) stable and ordered British society which in turn assumed a patriarchy, a class hierarchy and goal–nationhood, which was natural and inevitable. Mass emigration viewed as exile enabled bourgeois politicians and writers

> to pursue nationalist goals largely without hindrance from lower-class-based movements which threatened collective purpose as well as the privileged status of nationalist leaders themselves.[123]

Nationalism was reinforced and complemented by the Gaelic linguistic inheritance and the power of 'Holy Ireland'–'Irish' images which engaged with dominant British attitudes; sometimes in collusion and sometimes in conflict with those images which were situated to the fore. Such representations efface and oppose representational mass democracy, industrialisation, urbanisation, gender and class divisions arising out of eurocentric racial epistemologies. They offer straightforward linear narratives which reconstruct history from the point of view of the subaltern, creating a difference in emphasis, yet replicate British hierarchies and ways of knowing and seeing in 'hibernicised' forms.

For those who could not or would not subscribe and submit to the counter-hegemonic imperatives of Catholic, nationalist Ireland there remained the margin–a territory of the imagination peopled by the disaffected and rebellious; the individualistic and increasingly the artistic. Benedict Anderson has suggested how intimately nationalism with its mythification of an 'immemorial past' and its assumption of a 'limitless future'[124] is linked to religious modes of thought, how both cultural systems provide 'taken-for-granted frames of reference!'[125] In the context of Ireland in the second half of the nineteenth century, nationalism and Catholicism provide overlapping 'frames of reference' and exile is for the most part viewed as involuntary; the result of external forces, England or Providence, landlords or intrinsic individual perversity.

CHAPTER FOUR

Holy Ireland: Constructions, Omissions, Evasions, Resistance

INTRODUCTION

IN THE decade 1846–1855 during the Famine and in its immediate aftermath, about two and a half million people left Ireland. This human torrent diminished to an annual flood in the years between 1856 and 1921 when (partial) Irish Independence was achieved. Around four to four and a half million Irish women and men emigrated to North America–the vast majority to the USA–around 289,000 to Australia and New Zealand, 60,000 to South Africa, Argentina and other destinations and a large but unknown number to Britain; many of whom subsequently moved to the USA, Canada, Australia and elsewhere.[1] In 1890 as David Fitzpatrick points out 'only three-fifths of those born in Ireland were still at home ... The United States contained nearly two thirds of the overseas Irish and one quarter of all Irish natives.'[2]

Emigrants from Ireland differed from those from other european countries in that they tended to emigrate as single, unattached men and women. They were young, in their teens and early twenties, unskilled 'servants' and 'labourers', often barely literate, largely from rural environments, predominantly Catholics from Munster and Connaught (and to a lesser extent Leinster) where the old traditional folkways, culture and the Irish language survived–and unusually, approximately half were unmarried women.[3] Those going to urban employment in the USA 'were drawn from the surplus of a rural population which had formerly subsisted upon potato production before the coming of the blight'.[4] Emigration for young Catholic rural westerners 'was integrated into the life-cycle of both sexes'.[5] Even those remaining in Ireland were deeply involved through their kinship with departing brothers and sisters, daughters and sons, lovers and neighbours. As Sir William Wilde put it in 1864, those left behind were 'a legacy upon our charity, the caput mortuum of the population–the poor, the weak, the old, the lame, the sick, the blind, the dumb, and the imbecile and insane'.[6]

Emigration from among the Protestant section of the population in the same period it is estimated, constituted less than twenty-one per cent of the total, though religious allegiance was not recorded. Miller points out that the early nineteenth century was a peak period for Protestant emigration[7] and it was also of course a time when Catholic nationalism was gaining political and economic ascendancy in Ireland. Most Protestants left for Canada, Scotland, New Zealand and Pennsylvania following lines of communication and association long established within the milieu of the British Empire. But, as Fitzpatrick comments:

> To alien eyes and ears, it often mattered little whether an Irish emigrant was from Dublin or Mayo, a Protestant or a Catholic, a labourer or an artisan, a parent or on the loose. To their great indignation, the Irish overseas tended to be lumped together as ignorant, dirty and primitive Paddies or Biddies.[8]

In all, at least eight million men, women and children left Ireland in the period 1801 to 1921 and very few returned. Inevitably such a massive and enduring social phenomenon had profound effects on those who stayed in terms of the politics, economics and social formation of Ireland; on those who left and though to a lesser extent, on the societies which received them, however willingly or begrudgingly. Population haemorrhage on such a scale over such a period inherited, generated and perpetuated images and leitmotifs which reverberated through Irish culture actively and surreptitiously, structuring thought patterns and determining modes of expression consciously and unconsciously. The experience of emigration ineluctably shaped and differentiated Irish (and Anglo-Irish) cultural products from those of other English speaking societies and those of other european cultures.

This chapter is primarily concerned with the representation of exile (and emigration)–omissions and evasions, in the popular and literary traditions as they developed, reflected and reacted to the powerful cultural dynamics of a mythicised 'Holy Ireland'.

POPULAR SONGS AND THEATRE

Irish Catholic nationalist songs and writing were saturated with motifs that harked back to pre-Famine community, rebellion, rural innocence, the landlord issue, clearances, emptiness, devitalisation, stasis, paralysis, 'American Letters', remittances, chain migrations, lovers parting, family separation and intra-familial conflicts of conscience and responsibility particularly with regard to the land.

They also deal with: millenarian projections, obeisance to clerical authority, returning 'Yanks', venerations of aged parents (mothers most noticeably) and most evocatively affecting the American Wake. All of these were articulated in simplistic forms like the ballad, letters home, reflections, recordings of oral reminiscences, autobiography and stories written or performed in the shanachie tradition. Such forms are in themselves innately restricting, formulaic and conservative; bearers of traditional perceptions, feelings and values.

Post-Famine emigration songs and ballads emerging out of the popular tradition invariably attributed the leaving of Ireland to secular imperatives identified particularly with landlords and oppressive English rule. The Famine, Fenianism, the Devotional Revolution and the Land War provided an indigenous rationale within the context of occidental nationalism for an increasingly simplified version of Irishness which was by and large Gaelic, rural, Catholic and male. England was contrasted to the USA. It stood for repression, cruelty, injustice and slavery. America was the land of opportunity; figuratively personified as Columbia beckoning the young Irish male to 'freedom' or to 'liberty's shore'. The songs habitually assume that the emigrant is 'forced' or 'driven' to leave, that he 'must' go, that he is 'banished', 'compelled', an 'outcast' and even like the speaker in 'The Emigrant's Farewell to Ballyshannon' 'doomed to leave'.[9]

They ritually invoke eulogies to birthplace, childhood memories of youthful companions, hearth and home. They castigate the ruling classes, informers and landlords, and they describe hardships during the voyage and in trying to make a future in America. Others celebrate rebel and fenian heroes such as Mitchel, Meagher, Stephens, O'Donovan Rossa, Michael Hayes and martyrs such as Phillip Allen, Michael Larkin and Michael O'Brien.

Most emotive, however, are those ballads which evoke memories of final partings with aged parents, particularly mothers. Lachrymose lyrics and plangent melodies unashamedly equate home, Ireland, motherland and filial obligation in traditional fashion. They incorporate the emigrant into a memorial and communal psyche which validated the notion of emigration as exile–which was in fact, incapable of viewing and feeling it in any other way.

Emigrants carried thousands of songs and ballads with them to the 'New Island'. Many were in Irish and English and all were potentially subject to modification and adaptation in the context of their emigration and reception in America.

The antiquarian tradition within Ireland had infused the spirit of

Moore's *Melodies* and stimulated the collection and transposition of songs from the Gaelic in Edward Walsh's *Irish Popular Songs* (1847), George Petrie's *Ancient Music of Ireland* (1855), and Patrick Weston Joyce's *Ancient Music of Ireland* (1873). The experience of Mangan demonstrates the impossibility of simple transliteration transferring the essence of Gaelic experience and expression simply and unproblematically into English. The process of rendering the songs of the Gael into an equivalent English mode was inevitably infected with the attitudes and psychological pre-dispositions of the translators. The result was that the whole enterprise was permeated with and surrounded by Victorian sentimentalism; the music, the drawing-room ballad in particular became enormously popular. The music and its audiences generated and reflected 'cultural nostalgia' within Ireland itself which reinforced notions of the destructiveness of modern industrialisation and urbanisation amongst the urban masses of the Irish diaspora in England and perhaps more significantly, in the USA. They were 'removed in time and space from their heritage and, on that account, were more spectacularly than others the victims of the iron age of political economy and the factory system'.[10]

The 'sentimentalising and bowdlerising' process that Deane refers to acquired a momentum of its own in America where the demands of the music hall, the variety stage and vaudeville–the principal sources of popular entertainment for immigrants–were driven by their own impera-tives. The songs and dramas produced by the music hall artistes such as Harrigan and Hart, Irish-Americans both, and by first generation Irish entertainers catered for the simplistic needs of their audiences. Senti-mental representations and parodies which attempted to fulfil the demands of Irish audiences for idealised images of 'old Ireland' reinforced stereo-typical ideas of the Irishman for the benefit of other wider native-American and immigrant audiences.

Irish-Americans thus colluded with and acquiesced in their own misrepresentation and added to the developing divergence between the interests, needs and self-perception of those now resident in America and those at home in Ireland.

Nevertheless, the wealth, political weight and glamorous allure of Irish-America ensured that their versions of Ireland and Irishness as depicted in popular literature, magazines, music hall and drawing-room songs were received uncritically by newly arrived immigrants and by those remaining in Ireland. There was a sense in which the Irish in Ireland acted to please the Irish abroad. This was partly no doubt for the heightened sense of self-respect that may have been engendered. However, it was also probably to avoid offending people who were their financial benefactors and in a limited sense the guarantors of cultural distinctiveness and an alternative source or model of authenticity; one that opposed the powerless and dependent construction of Irish identity erected and imposed by the English.

Irish popular opinion within Ireland, aided by the advent of the phonograph and assisted by the ease of transport between Ireland and America in the late nineteenth century and the early twentieth century, absorbed and reproduced the fictions created out of Irish-American circumstances. Songs and ballads which had their origins in Ireland such as Moore's *Melodies*, Samuel Lover's songs, the balladry of *The Nation* were mediated through Irish-American culture and became superficially indistinguishable from the 'Oirish' products of Tin Pan Alley. The interaction between the two cultures went a long way to producing that kind of impersonal balladry advocated by the Young Irelanders in terms of popular literature and song. It requires careful reading to distinguish between the origins of songs embedded in notions of Irishness on both sides of the Atlantic. Therefore, someone who popularises this hybrid cultural collage like John McCormack, can quite happily incorporate Chauncey Olcott's 'Mother Machree' into a repertoire which includes traditional songs by Moore, Lady Dufferin, Balfe, T.D. Sullivan and Francis Fahy;[11] and Olcott's 'My Wild Irish Rose' and 'When Irish Eyes are Smiling' are accepted in Irish communities and by other ethnic groups throughout the world as part of the Irish heritage.[12]

The comic Irish songs produced for the Irish-American audiences of the 1860s and 1870s established a tradition within which Percy French chose to work.[13] Like the American songwriters of that time[14] who wrote about the Irish, French chose to employ dialect for comic effect in songs such as 'Are Ye Right There Michael'[15] and 'Phil the Fluter's Ball'.[16] The kind of homogenised Hiberno-English he deploys owes more perhaps to the English, Canadian and American audiences he performed before and to their expectations and aural receptivity, than it does to any recognisable dialect within Ireland. It is obvious nonetheless that he had a genuine affection for the Irish peasantry and some insight into their attachment to place, their self-ironic humour and their heartache in contemplating emigration. 'Come Back Paddy Reilly',[17] 'The Emigrant's Letter'[18] and most famously 'The Mountains of Mourne',[19] all set to music by his collaborator Dr Collison, are essential items in any Irish singer's repertoire and were as popular in Ireland as the diaspora at the time.

French, the son of a Protestant landowner from Roscommon, who was educated at Windermere College in England, Foyle College in Derry (an independent Protestant school for the Anglo-Irish) and Trinity, was in many ways typical of his class and background. That he chose to write about emigration at all was an acknowledgement of how deeply embedded it was in Irish rural experience in the late nineteenth century, and the manner he employed was tolerant and sympathetic. He was clearly trying hard to understand and to express what was to him an alien state of being. His recognition of the seriousness of peasant alienation in addition to their comic potential may perhaps have been forced on him in his work around the countryside of the north midlands in the 1880s when landlords like his father felt threatened by the activities of the Land League. Like others of his class and background predisposed to a liberal unionist paternalism, French seems implicitly to be reaching out in a fumblingly belated attempt to comprehend the grievances and humanity of the poor, those with no land and the emigrant. But, in a manner reminiscent of his predecessor Lady Dufferin, his sympathy stops short of real empathy. He is effectively distanced beyond comprehension by the chasm that separates the landlord from the peasant. The term and the conceptualisation of exile, the profundity of the psychic wrench experienced by the emigrant departing from his family and home are fundamental constituent elements which are displaced outside his perceptual frame. Within those borders we are offered a picture of modified Englishness; of sadness tinged with nostalgia, feelings checked by emotional control which contrasts vividly with the raw pain and unashamed display of emotion of the American Wake.

It is not surprising that he chose to leave Ireland in 1890; in part to pursue his career on the stage where the greater population of urban, industrialised England provided non-threatening audiences; in part because the deteriorating political condition in Ireland and the Land War presaged the decline in power and status of his class. It seems reasonable to infer that he went to England in particular because his upbringing and education focused his mind and vision on England, the Imperial Mother, as 'Home'. He was of course following in a long tradition stretching back to the seventeenth century in which the Anglo-Irish sought to make their name or seek refuge in the metropolitan homeland. There in the 1890s he was like so many before him–Farquhar, Sheridan, Lover, Lever and Maturin as well as his contemporaries Wilde and Shaw. He escaped provinciality and left behind him the remnants of his class, such as Somerville and Ross and the instigators of the Irish Literary Revival.

The preoccupation of critics and commentators with the major figures of the Revival and questions of value and canonicity has until recently obscured the products of popular culture, whether they be ballads, plays or novels. Few literary historians for example have paid heed to Irish drama before the founding of the Irish Literary Theatre in 1897. Stephen Watt has pointed out however, that there were three very popular theatres in Dublin in the late nineteenth century. These were the Theatre Royal, the Gaiety and the Queen's Royal Theatre[20] which produced commercial Irish melodramas on a regular basis.[21] He also drew attention to the fact that the Irish plays of Boucicault were particularly successful. Watt claims that the 'lives of O'Casey's and Joyce's Dubliners are to a great extent determined, not merely influenced, by popular drama'.[22] He also advances the argument that they and 'many of their most important characters as well–in crucial respects–"see" and "know" the world in ways determined by popular dramatic and theatrical conventions of the turn-of-the-century stage'.[23]

Dion Boucicault, born in Dublin with French Huguenot antecedents, was educated in London. He was an atypical Irishman in life story and lifestyle who challenged the conventional pieties of nineteenth-century victorian morality and reinvigorated the drama as spectacle in the latter half of the century. In 1853 he moved to American and achieved success as an actor, manager and playwright with *The Poor of New York* (1857), *Jessie Brown, or, The Relief of Lucknow* (1858) and *The Octoroon, or, Life in Louisiana* (1859). *The Octoroon* dealt with the highly contentious issue of slavery in a theatically sensational manner without alienating either side in the abolitionist debate. According to David Krause,[24] the success of *The Octoroon* convinced Boucicault he had to concentrate on local colour and he turned to Ireland for inspiration–mindful perhaps, of the large potential of New York's immigrant Irish as an audience.

His first Irish play *The Colleen Bawn, or, The Brides of Garryowen* owed its name to a popular ballad 'Willie Reilly and the Colleen Bawn' and its plot to Gerald Griffin's *The Collegians*. The play, first performed in 1860 in New York,[25] inaugurated within the popular melodramatic stage tradition a shift from the stage Irish stereotypes erected by previous generations of English and Anglo-Irish dramatists to representations more appealing to transatlantic Irish and Irish audiences. It was a process he continued with *Arrah-na-Pogue or, The Wicklow Weddings* his second Irish play set in 1798 and first performed in Dublin in 1864. A more explicitly political text than *The Colleen Bawn*, it was hugely successful and 'Boucicault became the idol of the people. He was cheered in the streets, he gave a command performance for Dublin Castle, and he appeared at all the literary salons in Merrion Square, often visiting such notables as Sir William and Lady

Wilde and Sir Samuel and Lady Ferguson.'[26] The third of his Irish plays was written in 1874 and first performed in New York. *The Shaughraun* (The Vagabond) is generally considered his best play and is overtly his most political, dealing as it does with the activities of the Fenian Brotherhood of the time–an organisation which of course had its origins in the USA– within the conventions of popular melodrama.

The plays challenged the image of the stage Irishman and 'He remodel- led the stage Irishman to portray a more realistic gallery of types. What had once been a foolish, drunken butt of English wits, he transformed into a clever, courageous and resourceful descendant of the tricky slave of ancient comedy.'[27] In inverting the image, Boucicault was appropriating and idealising the representation described by L.P. Curtis[28] and substitut- ing a more attractive alternative which Irish-Americans could sympathise with. This was one which flattered the indigenous Irishman and yet remained for the most part unthreatening to English and Anglo-Irish audiences. The political challenge to colonialism embodied in *Arrah-na- Pogue* and *The Shaughraun* was muted by the demands of commercialism, the conventions of melodrama with its demands for moral simplicities, Boucicault's propensity and talent for sensational stage effects and his own need to identity himself as an Irishman. Yet, there is undoubtedly a heightened historical and political awareness in those texts when com- pared to his first Irish play *The Colleen Bawn*, Watt points out that the world of *The Colleen Bawn* does not include police spies, exiled nationalists, fears of atrocities to prisoners and 'in short, no deep chasm between England and Ireland'.[29] He argues that Boucicault pre-empts divisive reaction by advancing a myth of reconciliation between those who hold power and those who oppose them. In part, this is achieved by representing the colonial power in softened and sympathetic ways, for example, in *Arrah* the centre of power is distanced and kept off stage while its representative Colonel Bagenal O'Grady is also *The O'Grady*, the titular head of all the O'Gradys, a native Irish clan. He is, moreover, a tolerant (if patronisingly benevolent) friend of the lovable natives who instinctively sides with them in their love of life and identifies with nationalism by obtaining a pardon for Beamish MacCoul, a local rebel leader. In *The Shaughraun* the English officer charged with keeping order in the district, is carefully de-anglicised. His name Molineux, is linguistically allied to that of the fenian leader Robert Ffolliott. He falls in love with Claire, the fenian fugitive's sister and allies himself with Conn in the rescue of Arte O'Neal and Moya Dolan after they have been abducted by Corry Kinchela, a gombeen man, and Harvey Duff a police agent. As in *Arrah* where the villains of the melodrama are the overzealous, English officer Major Coffin and the cowardly Irish process server Michael Feeney, Boucicault displaces the conflict between ruler and ruled onto the stock villain figures of popular Irish demonology. He also of course suppresses differences arising out of oppositional religious adherences by making Father Dolan selectively myopic in overlooking Robert Ffoliat's membership of a violent secret society:

> underlying both plays resides the history of Ireland's struggle and a mythology that Ireland can be unified socially, politically, and religiously. This myth is usually transmitted in plays whose narrative posits the peaceful co-existence of England and Ireland–and implicitly asserts the power of humanity and truth to topple national, social, and economic barriers.

As a myth of 'optimism and cohesion' it offered 'a nostalgic, in part politically conservative retreat to Dubliners'.[30] It echoed previous attempts at cultural conciliation and behind the comic elevation of Myles-na-Coppoleen, Shaun the Post and most convincingly Conn the Shaughraun into psychologically assertive comic archetypes, it deployed a romantic notion of exilic heroism which is suffused with a Thomas Moore like nostalgia for a lost pastoral eden. The Wicklow and Sligo settings are wild, spectacular landscapes saturated with a kind of elemental pantheistic and universal 'Irishness'. They are decorated with architecturally archaic peasant cottages and neo-Gothic ruins, while numerous action scenes are lit by moonlight which dramatically highlights the romantic and the sentimental. Beamish McCoul, believing himself to be on the verge of capture, apostrophises his departure in a passage that reads like a hybrid collage of lines and images from the *Irish Melodies* and popular balladry:

> See the morning is beginning to tip the heights of Mullacar; we must part. In a few hours I shall be on the sea, bound for a foreign land; perhaps never again shall I hear your voices nor see my native hills. Oh, my own land! my own land! Bless every blade of grass upon your green cheeks! The clouds that hang over ye are the sighs of your exiled children, and your face is always wet with their tears. Eirne meelish, Shlawn loth! Fare ye well! And you, dear abbey of St Kevin, around which the bones of my forefathers are laid.[31]

The myth was also subverted from within the same text by Boucicault's own version of the traditional ballad 'The Wearing of the Green'. Perhaps driven by the conventional dynamics of traditional balladry; perhaps unable to resist the temptation to create a moment of heightened theatricality or perhaps appealing to the sentiments of an Irish-American audience, the ballad noisily and unequivocally proclaims the cruelty, injustice and oppression of Ireland by England. In defending Erin's right to demonstrate its Irishness emblematically through the 'Wearing of the Green', the ballad intuitively links nationalism, exile and freedom with America and repression and opposition with England:

> But if at last our colour should be torn from Ireland's heart,
> Her sons with shame and sorrow from the dear old isle will part;
> I've heard a whisper of a country that lies beyond the sea
> Where rich and poor stand equal in the light of freedom's day
> O Erin, must we leave you, driven by a tyrant's hand?
> Must we ask a mother's blessing from a strange and distant land?
> Where the cruel cross of England shall nevermore be seen,
> And where, please God, we'll live and die still wearing of the green.[32]

It is little wonder then as Krause points out, that after the play was performed in London, 'an official government edict banned the singing of the song in future performances'.[33] Thus, a text which formed part of a larger text, which in itself and its conventions proclaimed a form of romantic conservatism and underwrote an image of idealised rurality, could pose a threat to the conservatism of a wider set of established/imposed relationships. It attests to the perceived threat from popular culture and the limits of tolerance that constructions and associations of exile meant within the matrix of imperial relationships. Exile within a fenian political landscape was at once radical and reactionary, regressive and rebellious.

The enduring appeal of his plays to late nineteenth-century and early twentieth-century Dublin and Irish-American audiences was in part due to the taste for melodrama and sensationalism, to their sheer comic exuberance and reaffirmation of the eternal verities. But, in addition

> dramas like Boucicault's evoked, profound nostalgia for a rural or 'green' world of community and cohesion, a utopian world, regardless of real economic concerns, in which dispossession or emigration, foreclosure or familial ruin, could be delayed or interrupted through the goodwill and works of one's neighbours or priests. Secular and imperial law, a weapon in the hands of avaricious or lecherous process servers or barristers could be subsumed under a broader, more potent ethical law—or comically overturned in a carnivalesque inversion of established order, the stock-in-trade of Wild Irish Boys and Boucicault's Irishmen alike or England's

colonial power could be resisted more directly by young nationalists and their comic sidekicks, hence the coterminous radical and conservative dimensions of Boucicault's and O'Grady's melodramas.[34]

A little like Memmi's 'coloniser who refuses', Boucicault chose to 'affiliate'[35] himself with Irish nationalism and publicly supported the release of Irish political prisoners from English prisons. This may or may not have been opportunistic publicity seeking, nevertheless, the effect was to identify his Irish plays as cultural icons in a developing nationalist symbology and to legitimate the efforts of successors like Synge and O'Casey who both imitated and reacted against the forms and stereotypes he localised.

Hubert O'Grady according to Watt,[36] was just as popular in his day as Boucicault was with Irish audiences and his play *Famine* (first performed in Dublin in 1886) was considered the most popular drama of the 1890s. Like Boucicault he accepted and adhered to the social hierarchies of his time and society and again like Boucicault his cowardly, lecherous and treacherous villains, are those who betray their positions as middlemen between the upright paragons of natural authority and the weak and dependent.

Unlike Boucicault however, O'Grady highlights the historic specificity of the play as a primary (or primal) determining factor of the dramatic action that ensues. Therefore, he quite consciously roots the play in the Great Famine when a destitute small farmer Vincent O'Connor, incurs the hatred of the villain Sackvill, the overseer of relief, for his (anachronistic) refusal to pay rent in obedience to the 'No Rent Manifesto'. He also incurs the wrath of his henchman Sadler who hates O'Connor, as O'Connor, a patriot, prevented his sister from marrying Sadler, a 'loyal subject'.[37]

O'Connor's wife dies of hunger and he is imprisoned for stealing bread to feed his children—the bread is literally removed from the starving family to use in evidence against him. The play then moves forward fifteen years when we discover that Sackvill has 'ruined' Nelly O'Connor, the daughter of Vincent, and now wants rid of her in order to marry Lady Alice, the virtuous, innocent and benevolent daughter of Sir Richard Raymond, the good and noble government inspector. The villains conspire with the aptly named Dr Kilmore (while deceiving one another) to incarcerate Nelly in the local lunatic asylum and then convince Alice that Nelly's accusations are groundless. Her brother John O'Connor, returned from military service, seeks satisfaction, but finds himself falsely accused of murdering Lumley Sackvill, a deed committed in fact by Sadler. He escapes with the

aid of a band of local patriots and is instrumental in the eventual apprehension of the two real culprits. The play concludes with John O'Connor's
innocence established and his rehabilitation with his sister, freed from the
asylum by the good offices of Lady Alice.

O'Connor then speaks the final words of the play:

> Thank you, Sir Richard and Lady Alice, for the kindness shown to my sister
> in my absence. And if you will only look back to the years gone by, you
> cannot but be convinced that all our trials and troubles can be traced to the
> great distress during *The Famine.*
> Picture-Curtain. End.[38]

As Literature this is risible in much the same way as *Knocknagow*, and
to read it in the same context as Boucicault's work is to appreciate the
latter's wit, skill and theatrical nous. However, O'Grady was writing from
within the emergent Catholic nationalist consciousness for Dublin and
provincial audiences, unlike the cosmopolitan Boucicault.

His dramas by and large eschew the comic stage Irishman and attempt
to elevate and dignify the poor and oppressed. John O'Connor's final
speech is redolent with the implied accusations that Ireland was betrayed
by the failure of those in power to alleviate starvation. The stilted for-
mality of its syntax, imitating as it does the formal language properties of
a dialect associated with power and privilege, stylises honour and self-
esteem in an active, articulate, three dimensional form which complemented the Dublin cartoonist's representations of the Irishman as 'angel'.[39]
O'Grady's poor Irish characters do not employ the dialectal idiosyncrasies
of Boucicault's or Whitbread's comic supports; their language and
demeanour reflect the ascribed virtues of their imperial rulers as propagated by the British public school system. John O'Connor when presented
with the opportunity to kill Sackvill soliloquises:

> it would be unmanly and unbecoming of a soldier to shoot a man behind
> his back. No, I'll speak to him face to face, man to man, and ask him to
> release my sister from the madhouse. Then if he refuses, I will shoot him
> dead at my feet.[40]

'O'Grady's native Irish characters do however, utilise the tags and
ritualised stock phrases of ballad discourse. For example, in conversation
with Nelly, John O'Connor speaks of being 'forced into exile'[41] and of
being rescued by 'true-hearted friends',[42] sentiments ironically voiced in
an anglicised speech mode. Father Barry, in conversation with the well-
intentioned Sir Richard in the prologue, provides the pretext for John
O'Connor's remarks which conclude the play. Having learned from Sir

Richard that there are no funds to alleviate starvation but that there are funds to assist emigration, the priest addresses the starving crowd and advises them

> to return quietly to your homes. Let those who are able to work apply for it, and it is the duty of all to assist themselves. Keep up your hearts: brighter days are in store and hope for our country. And I hope we may live to see her with her own Parliament controlling her domestic affairs and 'Eviction', 'Famine', and 'Emigration' banished forever from our native land.[43]

That ideological imperative frames the characterisation and action of the play. It determines the necessity for creating virtuous representations of law-abiding peasant nobility and dictates the minimum of stage violence and sensation. To win self-determination, the native must first learn to become like the ruler, and Father Barry having delivered the message of the hierarchy and set the limits for action and representation, disappears never to return.

Watt and Cheryl Herr,[44] have performed an invaluable function in excavating and examining Irish popular drama of the late nineteenth and early twentieth centuries which preceded and implicitly and explicitly affected the products of the Irish Literary Theatre, the Abbey dramatists and the subsequent twentieth-century evolution of theatre in Ireland.[45] They have demonstrated convincingly the popularity of Boucicault manifest in the repeated stagings of his work over the years for Dublin audiences and the existence and contemporary success and popularity of other non-canonical figures such as J.A. Whitbread, Hubert O'Grady and P.J. Bourke. Their work was performed most often at the (now demolished) Queen's Royal Theatre, a Dublin institution which catered primarily for the lower classes[46] and it was embedded in its repertoire for generations. Their plays reached wider audiences through performance in the repertoire of touring companies. For the most part such texts were written exclusively for Irish audiences and were 'consensus dramas'[47] designed for popular and uncontentious consumption. The political and cultural circumstances of Ireland at the time–fenianism, anti-English feeling, the Land War, nationalism, the Boer War and the centenary of 1798–formed a backdrop against which popular dramatists reversed colonial stereotypes; countered disparaging representations of Ireland and Irishness and substituted alternative, home produced and flattering versions of heroism and hibernian culture. In fashioning success out of historical failure they were however, willingly or unknowingly contributing to the developing discourse of blood sacrifice homologically. Other popular contemporary writers like Joseph Campbell, Ethna Carberry, Nora Hopper, Seumus MacManus, Alice Milligan and Seamus O'Sullivan also fashioned a rhetoric glorifying self-sacrifice, physical courage, heroism and redemption out of Standish O'Grady's redactions of ancient Irish mythology.[48] As Herr puts it, Irish political melodrama was

> a genre that altered its foreign sources to renew itself in terms of local settings, a genre that resisted the inscribed facts of history and thus not only produced some powerful theatrical offspring but also stirred up national feeling throughout Ireland, creating a different kind of revolutionary activity in 1916 and for many years after.[49]

In appropriating melodrama to itself, cultural Ireland was engaging in that 'relentless reciprocity' which characterises the relationship of colonised and coloniser.[50] In one sense it was liberating and ennobling but an appropriation which demands so much from a subject people necessitated the subjugation of the individual to communal aims and ambitions and the sacrifice of personal freedom to nationalism. It was a demand which the Roman Catholic Church in Ireland and the family analogously paralleled in their relentless pressure on individuals to sacrifice independence and freedom of choice to the needs of the wider community, as defined by the elders in the family unit and the ordained in the Church.

PRIESTS AND PEOPLE

The entry of the priest into the forefront of literature towards the end of the nineteenth century mirrored his importance in the social and cultural spheres. Ireland had experienced a 'Devotional Revolution' after the Famine when, as Emmet Larkin suggests, Irish Catholics were affected by an 'identity crisis' as a result of the destruction of much of their traditional culture by the forces of modernisation in the particular forms of commercialisation, anglicisation and emigration. For them, the intensity of their devotion to Catholicism provided 'a substitute symbolic language and offered them a new cultural heritage with which they could identify and through which they could identify with one another'.[51] Sean Connolly suggests that this devotional revolution formed part of a wider process involving the substitution of newly 'invented traditions' for lost and anachronistic symbols of identity.[52] This was a process common to other developing nationalisms throughout Europe[53] and in Ireland associated with the non-violent separatist movement and the philosophy of Irish-Ireland.

The volume of emigration was so great that it demanded explanation and reaction from the spokesmen of the Catholic community. On a superficial level the diaspora was imagined as a spiritual counterpart to the imperialising projects of the european powers, the creation of an Irish empire beyond the seas and it was likened to the monastic missions of the Dark Ages.[54] It led to self-aggrandising references in popular rhetoric to the 'nation beyond the seas', 'Greater Ireland' serving a 'holy mission' and the 'sea-divided Gael' or the 'exiled sons of Erin'. Implicitly and explicitly it allowed the Irish to compare themselves favourably with the imperialists of England whose motives, being temporal and material, lacked the purity and selflessness of the divinely driven missionaries of Hibernia.[55] For the most part however, the Church feared and disapproved of emigration. It was condemned in terms such as Father Barry's, as an evil by clergy and nationalists alike. It was tragic as it deprived Ireland of its young men and women and threatened depopulation. It was seen as disastrous for the emigrants, as morally, materially and physically threatening while America was pictured as the epitome of vice, materialism and selfish individualism. Some critics of emigration accused emigrants of treachery and desertion but more often than not blame for emigration was attributed to the landlord system and British oppression and the emigrants were characterised as 'sorrowing vengeful "exiles"'.[56]

Miller argues that such attribution owed much to traditional motifs and patterns of thought which were deeply rooted in Catholic Irish experience and more specifically that it offered an ideological explanation for contradictory demands and drives within Catholic Ireland. Transferring the responsibility on to the imperialist and the ascendancy enabled the sanctity of 'Holy Ireland' to remain unchallenged from within; threats were externalised, the enemies were the landlord system, Protestant, materialism, atheism and socialism. Therefore, Ireland needed self-government to protect its virtue.[57] For the propagators of 'Holy Ireland' imagery:

> The ideal Irish society was static, organic, and paternalistic, a divinely ordained hierarchy devoid of internal conflicts, insulated by faith from potential 'contamination'. Likewise, to ensure stability and continuity 'holy Ireland's' economy needs to be overwhelmingly agricultural: its fundamental social unit was the peasant family, also paternalistic and static, tilling the soil in secure contentment, hard by the parish Church where its ancestors were buried.[58]

It was unsurprisingly a self-deluding fiction which served the interests of the new developing petty bourgeoisie and grossly misrepresented the needs and desires of the disinherited and dispossessed. As an affective manipulation, it effectively silenced the victims and mandated them to underwrite their own exclusion through the emotional and affective obligations imposed on them to remit large sums of money home to subsidise parents, the homeplace, and to provide the passage money for siblings to emigrate. Moreover, it was woven so intrinsically into the pattern of thought and behaviour of Irish-Irelanders and imaginative fellow travellers, that to challenge the conceptualisation was to exclude oneself from the uncritical majority and to threaten the homogeneity of Catholic nationalist orthodoxy. It was perhaps inevitable then, that those writers bathing in the glow of the Celtic Twilight who were attempting a kind of cultural rapprochement with the Catholic majority should feel unfit or unable to contribute to public debate on the subject.

Watt has indicated how popular newspapers in the late 1890s and early 1900s frequently presented history as melodrama. He also pointed out how journalistic reconstructions of 1798 and Emmet's attempted rebellion of 1803 as their respective centenaries were celebrated at a time of growing nationalist assertiveness, predisposed popular culture to see history as a 'drama of martyrdom and sacrifice'.[59] A drama heightened by the immediacy of the Boer War which of course, to nationalists, acted as an analogue to their as yet unresolved clashes with the might of the Empire in history and in the future. Many Irish nationalists, such as John McBride, fought for the Boers against the imperial forces and many Irishmen were recruited by the British army which in turn stimulated the formation of the Irish Transvaal Committee, a group dedicated to resisting recruitment into the British army. The committee, together with the *United Irishman*, reversed the feminised image of Ireland by maintaining the ineffectuality of Englishmen and their need for more manly Irish recruits to achieve victory.[60] They represented the actions of the army in South Africa as savage, uncivilised and barbaric. Such reversals of the stereotyping prevalent in the imperialist's discourse offered, 'effective counter representation to especially loathsome victorian caricatures of Irishmen'.[61]

The work of popular cultural producers in the mass media and drama was paralleled in the novel by the efforts of Canon Patrick Sheehan, a popular novelist whose work was read throughout the English speaking world and was particularly popular within Ireland itself. Terence Brown says of him, that 'Throughout his career Sheehan had indicated in his fiction that nationalism as a social and cultural movement of high idealism could provide an intellectually aware priesthood with the means whereby it might achieve the leadership of the people in a worthwhile, ennobling cause'.[62] He was active in the promotion of land reform and the material improvement of living conditions for the rural poor, topics he dealt with in *Lisheen* (1907) and *My New Curate* (1900); and emotionally if ambivalently, sympathetic to the spirit of fenianism, a subject he dealt with in his last work *The Graves of Kilmorna* (1915).

Glenanaar, first published in 1905 in London, but clearly addressed to an Irish Catholic audience, enacts many of the concerns, beliefs and value judgements of the Irish priesthood and Irish-Ireland within the conventions of turn-of-the-century popular fiction. The novel is framed within the device of the recorder/reporter, the reliable narrator, who relays the events and emotions as told to him, or divined by him, in his relationship to more adventurous or highly charged characters. This was a convention commonly employed by Conan Doyle, H.G. Wells and Joseph Conrad among many others. Ostensibly it allows distance and detachment and an effective controlling mechanism while denying the unmediated directness and the transparent commitment of the omniscient narrator. Its attraction for many writers was that it allowed for an exploration of the strange, the alien, the exotic; that which challenged the quotidian logic of victorian morality and expectation within a frame that channelled and contained excess and desire.

Set in the 1890s, it utilises the figure of the 'Returned Yank'–itself a contradiction in terms–to review and represent a rural Catholic nationalist version of the nineteenth-century Irish history. This was an appropriation of the well established Anglo-Irish convention of explaining Ireland to an interested outsider–Terence Casey the prosperous 'Yank', a native of the Cork Village of Glenanaar, returns after some twenty-five years in exile (the term is employed unproblematically throughout) in America to his natal home in search of the love he left behind him. His mysterious and unexplained presence excites the curiosity of the villagers and their interest is heightened by his intervention and match winning exploits in a local hurling contest. The unnamed storyteller, the local priest, under the sign of the confessional becomes his confidante and confessor. As the local historian he relates the story of Casey the Hurler's banishment, which necessitates a return to origins, in this case to 1829, the Doneraile Conspiracy and the betrayal of the accused by the informer Cloumper Daly.

Tracing the events of that treachery through the traumatic years of the Whiteboys, the Famine and Fenianism, enables Sheehan to comment, with a notional objectivity, on the cultural formation of the Catholic rural Irish through the juxtaposition of the story of Ann Daly (Cloumper Daly's daughter, a 'waif' abandoned into the care of Edmond Connors one of those accused by Daly but released) her biography and that of her son Terence–'Casey the Hurler'–through to the present. In interweaving the public and the private, Sheehan both implicitly and explicitly promotes and challenges extant images of Irishness. He celebrated what Ashis Nandy has called 'hyper-masculinity'[63] in his description of the 'fighting race' contesting the hurling match;[64] the 'Celtic Temperament' which 'leaps to the weight of a feather'.[65] the nobility of the Irish peasant through the figure of the archetypal Edmond Connors,[66] his son Donal and Redmond Casey, the elemental simplicity of their existence, their piety and attachment to Catholicism and their fatalism. He diffuses sectarian division in an interpolation which forms one of the few references to Protestants in the whole text[67] by relocating allegedly offensive remarks within a more favourable context. He also idealises Irish femininity in images which highlight Madonna-like submissiveness in the figures of Nodlag,[68] love and loyalty in Nora Curtin in her youthful and maternal persona, and alternatively as Kathleen, daughter of Houlihan in the person of Nora's second daughter (a particular favourite of the priest-narrator) who opposes the union of her mother (and mother substitute Tessie) to Casey on the grounds that he is the grandson of an informer.

It is the discovery of his lineage which has caused O'Casey's unhappiness and purgatorial wanderings in the wilderness of America. His unquestioning acceptance of the stain upon his being as the 'breed of an informer'[69] and the almost universal antagonism his mother experiences despite her evident temporal saintliness, is reinforced by Sheehan's authorial stance. It is a position which accepts, through its feeble failure to qualify or seriously question,[70] a domesticated biological determinism.[71] A localised instance of the social Darwinism of high imperialism. At the same time the text contradictorily accepts a culturally conditioned ontology which acknowledges Casey's Anglo-Saxon acculturation and opposes American 'coldness' to Irish 'warmth' and 'Christian charity' to 'pagan exclusiveness'.[72]

The contemporaneity of the text as an articulation of hibernicised victorian stereotypes is further reinforced by the frequent resort to highly stylised melodramatic action and tableau. These include the celebration of victory after the hurling match, the trial scenes, the night ride to Daniel O'Connell, the discovery of Nodlag in the barn on a snowy Christmas day, Donal's rescue of Nodlag in the Great Snow, the conspiracy scene entitled 'A Midnight Synod', the attack on Edmond Connors and Nodlag, the Famine scene and Nodlag's return. All of these are told in flashback which in itself imposes a monocular, conservative, and selective narrative on the flux of events.

The stain (his 'original sin') that Casey carries into exile and the self-torture he endures as a consequence of his pursuit by the 'phantom'[73] of his shame, is also carried into the ludicrous in his description of his trials and tribulations in America. In received images from popular literature Sheehan describes Casey's travails, his encounters with westerners in Nevada and in particular Big Din a caricatured emigrant from 'the ould dart' seeking revenge on Cloumper Daly for informing on a 'mate' to the sheriff.[74] He describes offers of rich marriages he received and refused, his self-education and a gun fight which might have been scripted by Robert Service in which Big Din shoots a card cheat, who it transpires improbably, is Casey's uncle.[75] However, having endured so much, Sheehan resolves that it is time to 'exorcise' the 'old phantom'.[76] The priest-narrator then assumes the role of match-maker enabling Casey to contact Nora Leonard (née Curtin) and to meet Tessie and Kathleen her daughters, who person-ify complementary, but contrasting allegorical perceptions of feminised Ireland.

The encounter with the idealistic nationalist, Kathleen, results in the commonly levelled accusation that Ireland's woes were due to

> you Irish-Americans who fly from your country, and then try to make everyone else fly also ... Tis ye, the recruiting sergeants of England, that are sweeping the people away with your letters; 'come'. Come! For God's sake, leave your cabins, and come out to wealth and comfort! And *ye* are patriots!.[77]

Though these are presented as the opinions of a hot-headed and youthful enthusiast, the space Sheehan devotes to the digression in the following chapter 'An Ancient Rebel' explaining her nationalist genesis, underwrites the priest-narrator's indulgent justification for the trans-gression of the codes of Irish-feminine subservience:

> The children now don't trouble much about Ireland and her nationhood and her welfare ... Whilst the 'American fever' is on them they care little for the motherland. It is some consolation at least that one child has righteous sentiments towards her country.[78]

The chapter concludes with a celebratory panegyric to the spirit of Erin embodied in the person of Kathleen which absolves her of her defiance and acknowledges her maturity and the justice of her cause. The effect of which is to endorse her view of emigration and hence that of conservative Catholic nationalism.

Having created oppositions within the text, the demands of a monologic melodrama written out of a Catholic nationalist need for an homogeneous and obedient unity dictate a happy ending. Divisions are symbolically healed by the marriage of Tessie to Casey, by the mellowing of Kathleen and her role as bridesmaid to her sister.

The marriage represents a healing and an anointing, the culmination of a process of penance, atonement and expiation on the part of Casey and his mother. His sojourn in America is thus depicted as banishment.[79] It is a temporal purgatory which had to be suffered before forgiveness and acceptance could be bestowed by a renewed and virginal Ireland. Coursing through the text is a sense of Catholic triumph which self-confidently proclaims its universalism and totalising cultural and social control. The whole novel is encompassed within the parameters of a priestly patriarchy which exudes a passionate and indulgent paternalism. It presupposes a settled and unchanging social and cultural order. The peasants are in their place, they are quaint, comic and personifications of simplicity and they are constructed linguistically in much the same way as the peasant creations of Somerville and Ross. It is a holistic vision which depends on exclusion to create integrity–in this world there are no alternative orders of creation. Protestantism, the Anglo-Irish and the Celtic Twilight gain no admittance. Irish-America can only enter in the form of one single sinner who has the good grace to repent as, in effect, a troubled conscience whose absolution can only be obtained through submission. That submission is vital to oppose the Manichaen 'Other', the forces of evil manifest in the corrupt materialism of a brutal Anglo-American modernity. As Lloyd puts it:

> The aesthetic formation of the exemplary citizen requires, not alone the selection of an individual sociologically or statistically 'normative', but the representation of that individual's progress from unsubordinated contingency to socially significant integration with the totality.[80]

In this particular narrative ordering, the priests are the epistemological guardians of the purity, essence and soul of Ireland and nationalism is fused seamlessly into the Irish version of Catholicism. Just as the Christian epic charts a progress involving a fall from grace, a journey through a vale of tears and salvation in an ecstatic and heavenly future, so too does *Glenanaar*. After their marriage and return to Lake Shoshone, the narrator shifts from the continuous present into a futuristic and visionary evocation of a semi-mythical Ireland to which Terence Casey, his wife Tessie and all exiled Gaels will return. It is an Irish-Ireland which seems to be saying

> Come back! Come back! Back to the land of your fathers! Let us hear once more the sound of the soft Gaelic in our halls; the laughter of your children beneath our roofs, the skirl of the bagpipe and the tinkle of the harp in our courts, the shout of our young men in the meadows by the river, the old, heart-breaking songs from the fields, the *seanchus* here where our broken windows stare upon weed-covered lawns. Come back! The days are dark and short since ye went; there is no sunshine on Ireland, and the nights are long and dismal! And there in the moonlit Abbey by the river rests the bones of your kindred! There unquiet spirits haunt every mansion and cottage and the wail of their Banshee is over the fields and up along the hills! They shall never rest in peace till your shadows sweep across their tombs and your prayers, like the night winds, stir the ivy on the crumbling walls![81]

The second half of the coda seriously undermines the confident assertion of the first part. It is almost as though the text which has been ordered, controlled and consciously assertive breaks down to reveal its darker fears and preoccupations with an etiolated and devitalised physical landscape and an anorexic cultural and psychic being. It is a bleak, alienating and unnatural inversion of a natural order where the shades inhabit a neo-Gothicised, overgrown, abandoned and exhausted imaginative space and a despairing hope for redemption rests on the emotional and affective pull of dead generations. It is a breakdown which reveals the repressive and ambivalent modes of thinking, feeling and representing the massive haemorrhage of Irish youth and an unspoken recognition that nationalism and Catholicism as ideological forces were of themselves unable to contain the excess of need, aspiration and desire that Ireland–alone–could not satisfy.

WOMEN: REPRESENTATION AND REPRESSION

The representation of young Irish women in the popular tradition continued and perpetuated the stereotypes moulded out of Catholic teaching and patriarchal Gaelic nationalist discourse. They were idealised as beautiful, virtuous, subservient, handmaidens; from whom young men parted, eloped with, or returned to. They were celibate and single and almost totally silent in the discourses surrounding emigration. Yet, they constituted at least half of all those leaving Ireland in the latter part of the nineteenth century and in subsequent years.

Viewed from within Ireland however, the departure of so many young unmarried women inevitably provoked much genuine dismay. It stimulated Fr Guinan the author of *Priests and People in Doon* (1903), (a popular text which ran to numerous editions) to lament the fate of the poor unsuspecting Irish country girl in America:

> How happy, in comparison, and how blessed would have been the lot of an Irish girl the poor betrayed victim of hellish agencies of vice, had she remained at home and passed her days in the poverty, age and wretchedness of a mud wall cabin–a wife and mother, mayhap–her path in life smoothened by the blessed influence of religion and domestic peace until it ended at a green old age in the calm, peaceful repose of God's just.

Joseph Lee, who quotes Fr Guinan in his essay on the topic, goes on to add his own comments which widen the context within which young Irish women made their decision to emigrate:

> The reason that the poor country girl had emigrated was that she saw no chance of becoming wife and mother in the blessed island that so stridently trumpeted its devotion to the idea of the family. Fr Guinan felt deeply for the victims of emigration. He couldn't see that it was the values of the society he cherished that condemned these girls to emigration.[82]

At the forefront of those values was the primacy of patriarchy and the privileging of male interests embedded in the rural economy. Such interests were promoted and sanctioned by a celibate clergy drawn from that same community. It was an effective if intuitive conspiracy of interests which asexualised and depersonalised women by processes of idealisation and marginalisation. Women effectively became ideologically mute, epistemological ciphers and politically powerless.

Women in Ireland were confined within four broad mutually reinforcing phallocentric stereotypes. First of all that of Mary, mother of sorrows whose function was to serve elderly husbands and suffer on behalf of heroic or victim sons like the figure in Patrick Pearse's poem 'The Mother' (1915), Maurya in Synge's *Riders to the Sea* (1902) and Mrs Tancred in *Juno and the Paycock* (1924). Secondly, women who are alone and who 'learn to live with solitude of spirit even before the blow falls' who are 'essentially in harmony with a future eschatology which in some unknown way, contains for them fulfilment, meaning and peace'.[83] An image which slides into and complements that of Mother Ireland as presented by Deasy and the Citizen in *Ulysses*–which in itself informed and buttressed the image of Holy Ireland propagated by the Church and religiose nationalists. The third stereotype is that of the chaste virgin who sacrifices herself for a greater cause, such as the passive female figures in exile songs and the heroines of Dublin melodramas like Eily O'Connor, 'The Colleen Bawn' in Boucicault's play of the same name. Fourthly and finally, women as temptress and/or traitor drawn from reductionist portrayals of women as Eve in Catholic demonology and the clichéd representation of femininity in mass circulation women's magazines and pulp literature of the period.[84]

By contrast the reality of existence for most young Irish women was that they stood in the same relation to Irish men as Irish men stood in relation to their English and Anglo-Irish superiors. James Connolly described the position of Irish women thus:

> The worker is the slave of capitalist society, the female worker is the slave of that slave. In Ireland that female worker has hitherto exhibited in her martyrdom, an almost damnable patience. She has toiled on the farms from her earliest childhood, attaining usually to the age of ripe womanhood without ever being vouchsafed the right to claim as her own a single penny of the money earned by her labour, and knowing that all her toil and privation would not earn her that right to the farm which would go without question to the most worthless member of the family, if that member chanced to be the eldest son.

Her servitude was ordained by the post-Famine conversion to a system of primogeniture and impartable inheritance and underwritten by the social conservatism of 'chapel, church or meeting-house'.[85]

Connolly goes on to consider the fate of the young uneducated female emigrant:

> Everyone acquainted with the lot encountered by Irish emigrant girls in the great cities of England or America, the hardships they had to undergo, the temptations to which they were subject, and the extraordinary proportion of them that succumbed to these temptations must acknowledge that the poetic insight of Kickham correctly appreciated the gravity of the perils that awaited them. It is humiliating to have to record that the overwhelming majority of those girls were sent out upon a conscienceless world, absolutely destitute of training and preparation, and relying solely upon their physical strength and intelligence to carry them safely through.[86]

Fitzpatrick suggests however, that Irish women were not quite so feeble and powerless as Connolly believes. He points to the lack of opportunity in Ireland and the growth of educational resources through the National

School system as providing the motivation and the means by which young women could equip themselves with the basic literacy skills required to find employment in the United States and Australia in particular, and the eagerness with which they took advantage of education and emigration 'to improve their conditions in life beyond that of their mothers'.[87]

Joseph Lee makes the equally interesting, if paradoxical, point that the education system was staffed for the most part by teachers who were themselves drawn from the farming classes and would inevitably have transmitted the values of their class background. Thus the schools, increasingly influenced by clerical authority, reinforced the submissive image and role of women constructed by post-Famine economic and ideological needs:

> Dutiful woman teachers, including many dedicated nuns, taught girls obedience, docility and resignation to the role assigned to them by a male providence, until the more gullible came to believe that the role was a law of universal nature and not simply the product of a peculiar and transient set of local circumstances.[88]

Universal primary education thus provided the means whereby young women could earn their living in the wider English speaking world and overcome the emotional and psychological constraints which prevented them from challenging the role and destiny assigned to them by a society which effectively expelled and silenced them at the same time, by denying them the same kind of honorific exilic martyrdom as that accorded to young male emigrants.

Connolly's text articulates the ambivalence and guilt felt in Ireland most noticeably by Catholic Irish people, at their inability to protect and provide for their young unmarried women. Constrained by that humiliation and the proprieties of his time and culture, Connolly can only allude to the perceptions that many Irish girls abandoned Catholic pieties for prostitution and degradation. Working against the grain of a victorian Catholic bourgeois mind-set that could provoke a riot at the mention of 'shift' in Synge's *Playboy of the Western World* (1907) and exposing the hypocrisy of Irish attitudes to sexuality was probably only possible from the exilic security of Paris or anywhere outside Mother Ireland.

Ambivalence and guilt were endemic in a culture which sanctified chastity but which knew its survival depended on half of its young people leaving in order to subsidise those who remained. It was a community projecting an image of purity onto Irish feminity, while at the same time periodically encouraging 'surplus' young women to leave the protection of the family. Fitzpatrick refers to the exportation of thousands of 'female orphans' at official expense to the Australian colonies in the middle of the century to become servants and wives and how 'Thirty years later, a single philanthropist (with the connivance of almost the entire Roman Catholic clergy of the west of Ireland) was responsible for the emigration of 23,000 girls to take up domestic service in America'.[89]

Faced with the limited options of entering a convent, an arranged marriage or spinsterhood, and a lifelong dependency on parsimonious fathers and brothers rewarded only by unremitting toil, hundreds of thousands of young Irish women evaded the protective clutch of Ireland. They avoided the necessity for dowries, the prospect of having to earn their own dowries (a profoundly shaming reflection on the inadequacy of male provision), and the extended family, and sought their futures willingly abroad, often marrying in exogamous fashion outside the expatriate Irish Catholic community. Their experience of emigration and modernity obviously could not be encompassed in the formulaic and conservative popular song tradition. It was 'censored' out of cultural representation which could not contain the radical challenge their 'independence' signalled. Ignored and suppressed, female access to representation in popular culture was therefore exclusively on male terms in an internal cultural replication of an imperial paradigm. They were corseted in a garment designed by male perceptions of what femaleness was. Their role therefore, was to anchor the affections of exiting Irishmen in Ireland; to that end the idealised image of young women formed an effective counterpart to spiritual, cultural, topographic and material ties. The deployment of romantic feminity expanded the affective hold Ireland had on the emotions of the male emigrant, binding him into a psychological dependency which in many ways left the emigrant unfit to cope with the demands of the New World.

Women's voices and experiences are thus never unmediated, they are almost always positioned and pictured in Ireland, in rural areas and almost as frequently associated linguistically and in an imagistic way with the emigrants' homeplace as in 'Mary From Dungloe' or '(Mary) The Star of Donegal' and 'Katie O'Ryan (On the Banks of the Shannon)'.[90]

When however, the popular tradition does acknowledge the fact of female emigration, it does so in order to admonish, discourage and to deflect attention away from patriarchal Ireland's own responsibility. Connolly, in alluding to Kickham, probably had in mind his very popular 'The Irish Peasant Girl' or as it is more often entitled 'She Lived Beside the Anner' (1859). The song idealises the Irish peasant girl whose 'lips were dewy rose buds' whose teeth were of 'pearls rare', underneath a crown of 'nut brown hair'. She was (of course) 'the loveliest of the throng'. The third verse shifts however, from the stock eulogies of the first two verses into a generalised address to all Irish girls:

> Oh! brave, brave, Irish girls,
>   We well may call you brave;
> Sure the least of all your perils,
>   Is the stormy ocean wave;
> When ye leave our quiet valleys,
>   And cross the Atlantic's foam,
> To hoard your hard own earnings,
>   For the helpless ones at home.

The verse, pregnant with undeclared but potentially horrendous dangers, contrasts the pastoral innocence of Ireland with the corruption of the New World. Yet, at the same time it contains within it a sacrificial sense of selfless obligation to those remaining in Ireland. It thus both justifies and implicitly condemns the emigrant girls simultaneously.

The fourth verse evades the tensions ambiguously established in the third and adopts the speaking voice and persona of the girl herself, now victimised as the object of one (or more) of the unnamed perils referred to previously:

> Write word to my dear mother
>   Say we'll meet with God above;
> And tell my little brothers–
>   I send them all my love;
> May the angels ever guard them,
>   Is their dying sister's prayer,
> And folded in the letter,
>   Was a braid of nut brown hair!

On one level this is another manifestation of Kickham's penchant for the victorian female death scene, sentimentally and mawkishly rendered as with Norah Lahy in *Knocknagow*; on another level it smoothly and stealthily transfers liability for her death onto the plane of the divine–God has called her and she is resigned to the demands of providence. It absolves Ireland therefore of any culpability and sanctions the expression of guilt-free grief. On a third level it acts as a powerful warning or deterrent against the dangers inherent in modernity 'over there' or anywhere beyond the protective shores of a pre-lapsarian 'home'. In this kind of synopsis of the fate of the young Irish female emigrant there is a total absence of the compensatory images of martial valour, physical prowess and worldly success which frequently conclude or pervade songs and ballads about young male emigrants. 'The Irish Peasant Girl' is virtue and victim, support and sacrifice, whose fortunes are mournfully fused with Ireland's own in the shifting lack of specificity of the final verse. The nameless male omniscient narrator sinks into a mood of maudlin self-indulgence which reincorporates the shade of the dead emigrant girl into the spiritless ennui of post-Famine rural Ireland:

> Ah! cold and well night callous,
>   This weary heart has grown,
> For thy hapless fate, dear Ireland,
>   And for sorrows of my own;
> Yet a tear my eye will moisten,
>   When by Anner side I stray,
> For the lily of 'the Mountain Foot',
>   That withered far away.[91]

Those women who did write and were able to publish their material were unable or unwilling to re-write those stereotypes constructed in the interests of men; whether they were men who remained in Ireland or men who left.

Many women writers continued to write under male pseudonyms until the end of the nineteenth century[92] and were thus constrained by the expectations of male authorship and markets which had limited, conservative, affective and emotional needs. Women who succeeded in publishing under their own name such as the female contributors to *The Nation*, whether Catholic or Protestant, nationalist, liberal, home-rulers or unionists were all from relatively privileged backgrounds and unburdened by large numbers of children.

They were remote from the imperatives of forced migration and they were moreover, subsumed in a masculine order. They were obliged by the circumstances and male ordered discourses of patriarchal Ireland– Arnoldian, colonial, Catholic, ascendancy, middle-class and lower-class– to express themselves within the archetypes established by men in terms of form, content and audience. Many women wrote for the nationalist press in the 1890s and in the years prior to Independence. In common with male populist and popular contributors such as Seumus MacManus and Joseph Campbell they employed and deployed a male-oriented rhetoric which feminised, idealised and ruralised Ireland in what unconsciously was to become a contributory element in the developing current of Celtic Twilight, nationalistic and blood-sacrifice hyperbole.

Martin Williams[93] has demonstrated how writers of the time drawing on religious mysticism, the Young Ireland tradition and ancient mythology regularly resorted to themes which highlighted heroic violence and redemption through self-sacrifice. The effect of this restored and reinvigorated resistance in an analeptic manner and in proleptic fashion deferred suffragist demands for equality of status. Women's empowerment, like that of the oppressed male classes, had to be by-passed and subjugated to the homogenising centripetal imperatives of anti-imperialism and nationalism.

Women writers who utilised the vague aspirational and inspirational language of 'Chivalry', 'Sacrifice', 'Heroism', 'History' and 'Joy' in consciously archaic or mock archaic male forms like the epic and the ballad, unconsciously (for the most part) colluded in their own subjection by contributing to the 'hypermasculine' stereotype of the 'Gael' then being developed by male nationalists like D.P. Moran and Michael Cusack in opposition to the imperialist feminised stereotypes of the 'Celt'. The need to boost the Irish nationalist male ego ensured that those women who self-sacrificially promoted the interests of nationalism before female emancipation like *Inghinidhe Na héireann* (the Daughters of Erin) and its successor *Cumann Na mBan*, were celebrated as folk heroines. But, the effect of their self-denial was that 'Cathleen Ní Houlahan's corporeal sisters were marginalised within the political process of the decolonising of Ireland'.[94]

Marginalised and mythicised, Irish women had no effective outlets for expression or audiences willing to listen. Given the monoglossic determinism of the urbanised Gaelic intelligentsia, its heroised monocular romanticisation of the west and its peasantry, it is unsurprising that few spoke out on behalf of those young emigrants from the ranks of the possessing classes. In the meantime the emigrants were leaving in their thousands; silently rejecting and subverting the image of a Gaelic eden.

Even if the social-realist mode of expression had been open in the context of the time to those women writers working within the Gaelicised nationalistic paradigm, their own life experiences would almost certainly have disqualified them from understanding or sympathising with the economic and psychological pressures and attractions determining emigration. In addition to relative economic security most female (and male) writers promoting the political, economic and cultural separation of the period, whether in its most militant or consensual terms, were from

middle-class or ascendancy Protestant backgrounds. Their psychic investment was in a subfusc past devoid of history and an unfocused idealised,
pluralist future which guaranteed their privileged positions. The logic of
their position which foresaw changes in the form of government, but
precluded changes of power position within the existing social formation,
aligned them ironically with writers and interests which underwrote the
position of the existing ruling classes. They might contest the hegemony
of the ascendancy but they were not willing to change forms of power or
to effect any fundamental re-alignments of class and religious-ethnic
groupings.

Intriguingly then, those most vocal in their support for cultural (and/or
political) nationalism, people such as Ethna Carberry and Alice Milligan
the editors of the nationalist *Shan Van Vocht* and Lady Gregory, continued
to share the same interests as those who remained committed to the
Union; writers such as Emily Lawless, the young Edith Somerville and
Martin Ross who agonised over, amused, explored and underscored the
English patriarchal ascendancy.

Irish women writers working out of seemingly contrasting and opposing political and cultural positions were effectively ventriloquising male
preoccupations and perceptions and perpetuating the various forms of
female stereotyping erected to serve male needs and fantasies. They
therefore complemented and reinforced nationalist, Celtic Twilight and
unionist interests and images leaving the millions of young emigrant
women unrepresented and voiceless in the cultural as well as the political
process. Objectified and oppressed, they formed an internalised homo-
logical image of the kind of relationship, representation and power
position then extant between England and Ireland, between masculinity
and feminity, John Bull and Hibernia, imperial overlord and colonised
servant.

RESISTANCE AND RETURN

Padraic Colum, in contrast to the other early contributors to the Revival
and to the drama in particular, was a young, Catholic nationalist and from
a lower middle-class rural background. In his introduction to *three plays by
Padraic Colum* (1963) he outlines the genesis of his three most important
plays: *The Land* (1905), *Thomas Muskerry* (1910) and *The Fiddler's House*
(1907). He also provides a short but fascinating sketch of the tensions
between those who wanted the National Theatre Society to be overtly

nationalist and those who were less enthusiastic for a politically determined and democratically organised theatre. Colum sided with the
former faction against those who were to compose a new directorate:
Yeats, Willie Fay, Lady Gregory and J.M. Synge. At the same time the
Society had acquired the Abbey Theatre where his play *The Land* was
performed, the last production of the society. He goes on:

> It pleased an audience who wanted a theatre that would have political
> orientation; as the people who fought the Land War were shown as coming
> into their own, this was felt as a chapter in the re-conquest, and it had the
> approval of the hundred per cent nationalists. It was accepted too by the
> literary coteries. Indeed 'The Land' was the first popular success the Irish
> Theatre had.[95]

He notes a second reason for its relevance which was 'the revolt of the
young against parental possessiveness'.[96]

The play offers an open, energetic heteroglossic and comprehensive
drama of peasant life. It renders the pride, divisions and generational
aspirations of the Catholic rural classes in a mode of expression which
accords them a dramatic and dialectal dignity denied them by the narrative
distancing and orthographic representations of Kickham's or Sheehan's
peasants. Colum's characters speak in recognisable Hiberno-English
syntax and of course being a play, the text lacks the authorial commentary
and correctness of standard or metropolitan English which does so much
to highlight and undermine the legitimacy of peasant speech silently and
visually in prose texts.

The play is set immediately after the passing of the Wyndham Act of
1903 which enabled the transfer of the land from an alien landlord class
to the farmers themselves. The act signalled the culmination and victory
of the people in the long campaign begun by the Land League. Its
corollary was a diminution in the privileges and power of the landowning
classes and as such it was received enthusiastically by nationalist audiences
and the literati. Aesthetically the play owes more to Ibsen than to the
poeticised dramas of Yeats, and as such it is rooted in the realities of the
midlands; in the world of the contemporary rather than the world of myth
and mysticism. Written in linear time, Colum creates dramatic conflict
through the opposition of the monomaniacally, land obsessed figure of
Murtagh Cosgar and the indigent former fenian, the peasant scholar,
Martin Douras; and through contrasts of youth and age, love and duty,
modernity and tradition.

Murtagh Cosgar, a Lear-like patriarch, and Martin Douras, both of whom have stood serf-like before the arrogance of landlords, voice the sentiments and beliefs of a generation which struggled through to a communal triumph; reclaiming a memorial and spiritual association with the land to assert a new-found pride in their (aged) manhood. The cost, however, has been high, particularly in the case of Cosgar who has succeeded in driving away all but two of his children, Matt and Sally. Colum achieves a kind of dramatic symmetry in creating two children (of an appropriate age) for Martin Douras, Ellen and Cornelius, and romantically links Matt with Ellen and Sally with Cornelius. Dramatic urgency is achieved partly through a fairly strict adherence to the unities, all the action takes place on the same day and in the same location albeit different cottages, and by paring down the cast to six named characters supported by extra unidentified assorted villagers. He avoids further complication by removing additional siblings, a device which in one way provides a history to Cosgar's behaviour but which also suggests the inability of the drama to realistically present the Irish family in its entirety. The most obvious omissions however, are mothers. Neither of the families concerned possess a living mother/wife. The inclusion of a mother would clearly have altered the ambivalent balance of dramatic possibilities as would the on-stage presence of a parish priest. Their absence opens up the opportunity for the young to assert themselves and interestingly it is Ellen who has received an education, who rebels against the harsh servitude to the land and to an outmoded traditionalism which would imprison her as her father's housekeeper and/or her husband's helper on her father-in-law's farm.

In this text the elements which combine to turn the young away from Ireland are intrinsic and extrinsic–customs which insist on the presentation of a dowry and a suitable comparability of wealth and status which preserves power in the hands of the old. The young are condemned to a prolonged dependency on fathers within a society that offers few opportunities for choice and fulfilment outside the family.

In addition, there are compelling counter-attractions which the young have absorbed–images of America which contrast vividly with the oppressive and routine restrictiveness of Irish rurality. The dreams and frustrations of the young are given to us in Act Two in a choral scene when a group of young men and women call on Ellen prior to their departure for America. They allude to their dreams of the sea, great towns, streets of houses, crowds of people, shops, great houses, fine clothes, fine manners and the prospect of money to spend; and the possibility of marriage for all the girls. By contrast 'home' with its old fashioned turf-fires, three-roomed, thatched, mud-walled houses in bogs and fields which are impossible to keep clean seems hopelessly uncivilised. However, they recognise that there will be some heartache in leaving young brothers and sisters they have helped to nurse and rear. The group attempts to persuade Ellen to join them which provokes a brief dialogue which starkly dichotomises the choice Ellen has:

> second girl: she's waiting for her school. It will be a little place by the side of a bog.
>
> third girl: (*going to* ellen): There would be little change in that. And isn't it a life altogether different from this life that we have been longing for? To be doing other work, and to be meeting strange people. And instead of bare roads, and market-towns, to be seeing streets, and crowds, and theatres.[97]

Ellen, an hibernicised version of the late victorian 'new woman' and a threat to the newly established Catholic masculinist order, is quite obviously enamoured of the vision of America presented to her. Its glamour, multiplicity and variousness clearly attract. She goes on however, to articulate a more profound motivation for leaving which is that America offers the possibility of self-realisation of 'a chance of knowing what is in me',[98] a need and an ambition rural Ireland can only suppress. Her refusal to serve challenges the stereotype of the dutiful, selfless Irish daughter and shatters the authoritarian, monoglossic power of Murtagh Cosgar. His victory in gaining possession of the land is ironically made pyrrhic by his own purblind pride and arrogance in refusing to allow the marriage of Matt and Ellen. When, too late, he recognises his need for them, their determination to shape and build a life of their own leads to a rejection of the 'slavery' immanent within a lifetime's subservience to the land. It is an irony heightened and made to appear more ridiculous by the arranged marriage of his daughter Sally to Cornelius Douras. It is a union of the obedient drudge, a girl 'with the expression of a half awakened creature'[99] and a man with an 'expression somewhat vacant' whose own father says of him 'When I'm talking with you Cornelius, I feel like a boy who lends back all the marbles he's won, and plays again, just for the sake of the game'.[100]

It is these who will be inheriting the new Ireland, Colum seems to be intimating, the mindless and the mediocre. The future of an Ireland bereft of the imaginative and the ambitious resides in well-intentioned, likeable, subservient, ill-educated, uninspired, nonentities; a reading reinforced by Colum's ironic placement of second-hand nationalist platitudes in the closing speech delivered by the visionless beneficiary of Matt's renunciation, Cornelius:

> Stay on the land, and you'll be saved body and soul; you'll be saved in the man and in the nation. The nation, men of Ballyhillduff, do you ever think of it at all? Do you ever think of the Irish nation that is waiting all this time to be born?[101]

The silence of Murtagh and Martin registers their sense of loss, foreboding and defeat. Colum's own subsequent emigration to America in 1914 underwrites the lack of opportunity in a colony characterised by what Memmi calls 'petrification'[102] and Joyce, 'paralysis'.[103] For he too, like Conn Hourican the fiddler, heeded the 'call of the road' in the knowledge that 'No man knows how his own life will end, but them that have the gift have to follow the gift'.[104]

T.C. Murray in *Birthright*,[105] written just a few years later in 1910, presents a darker scenario than that painted by Colum in *The Land*. His patriarch, Bat Morrissey is an even more extreme figure than Murtagh Cosgar. Having returned from America with sufficient money to buy his land and having spent some thirty years cultivating and improving, he has after all these years become brutalised and dehumanised by his obsession. His monomania results in the disinheritance of his eldest son Hugh—an idealised portrait of the devoted and dutiful young Irishman, the captain of the local hurling team, favourite of the priest and prizewinning Gaelic language poet—in favour of his youngest son Shane. The latter, a man moulded by the land is a semi-human creation whose imagination and ambitions are circumscribed by the boundaries and the business of the farm.

Bat's decision to deny Hugh and send him to America (rather than Shane) in the belief that Shane will maintain the farm in the fashion that he has created is, Murray implies, an horrifically unnatural act. It is an act which denies the gifted, sensitive and loving a stake in the Ireland of the future, leaving the soul of the country instead of the unimaginative boorish 'grabbers'. It is an inversion of a primal natural order which results in fratricide, tragedy and heartbreak for Maura Morrisey and Mother Ireland, both of whom are condemned to a bleak, hopeless future.

The world of repression, authoritarianism, frustration and loneliness so authentically evoked by writers able to explore Catholic experiences, customs and consciousness is at least superficially the same world J.M. Synge chose to live in (occasionally) and write about. Perhaps as Maurice Harmon suggests, 'To place his work beside any of his contemporaries is to see its greater vitality and imaginative force'.[106] An aesthetic judgement most commentators would readily accept in any consideration of his major dramatic works. Unlike Colum and Murray however, Synge's plays have relatively little to say directly about emigration. There is certainly the same sense of material deprivation, spiritual ennui and absence of communal vitality and hope; a psychic and cultural backdrop which evokes memories of Sir William Wilde's description of Ireland in the post-Famine years. And old Mahon in *The Playboy of the Western World* has, like Murtagh Cosgar, succeeded in driving his children out of Ireland and into hatred. As Christy informs us,

> though he'd sons and daughters walking all great states and territories of the world, and not a one of them, to this day, but would say their seven curses on him.[107]

Direct comment on emigration is reserved for his prose works. He was a sympathetic and diligent cultural anthropologist willing to describe customs, ceremonies, encounters and types in detached detail. In *The Aran Islands* (1907) he says relatively little about the experiences of emigration regarding it seemingly, as an inevitable fact of life. He acknowledges allusively that 'Nearly all the families have relations who have had to cross the Atlantic',[108] briefly describes the return of a native from New York,[109] prints a letter from an island friend referring to the return from America of the correspondent's sister[110] and records the departure of several friends.[111] More space is given to a touching description of how the mother of the family he stayed with reacts to letters received from her two sons Michael, Synge's friend, and another unnamed son who has gone to the United States:

> All evening afterwards the old woman sat in her stool at the corner of the fire with her shawl over her head, keening piteously to herself. America appeared far away, yet she seems to have felt that, after all, it was only the other edge of the Atlantic, and now when she hears them talking of railroads and inland cities where there is no sea, things she cannot understand, it comes home to her that her son is gone for ever. She often tells me how she used to sit on the wall behind the house last year and watch the hooker he worked in coming out of Kilronan and beating up the sound, and what company it used to be to her the time they'd all be out.
>
> The maternal feeling is so powerful on these islands that it gives a life of torment to the women. Their sons grow up to be banished as soon as they are of age, or to live here in continual danger on the sea; their daughters go

away also or are worn out in their youth with bearing children that grow up to harass them in their own turn a little later.[112]

Synge dealt with emigration in more depth in a series of twelve articles written for *The Manchester Guardian* in 1905.[113] His commission was to write about the 'distress' of Mayo and Galway. No doubt the audience he wrote for, the literate, liberal, English middle classes and the form of the newspaper article influenced what he wrote and the way in which he presented his experiences, observations and reflections. He records numerous encounters and conversations with westerners who had travelled variously to America, to Scotland and to England as seasonal migrants.

In the final piece, 'Possible Remedies' Synge acknowledges that one of the principal problems besetting Ireland is emigration. It is, he says, 'probably the most complicated of all Irish affairs, and in dealing with it it is important to remember that the whole moral and economic condition of Ireland has been brought into a diseased state by prolonged misgovernment and many misfortunes'.[114] He goes on to point to the desire for a better life, boredom with what Ireland has to offer, stagnation and hopelessness as motivating factors and concludes:

> one feels but the only real remedy for emigration is the restoration of some national life to the people. It is this conviction that makes most Irish politicians scorn all merely economic or agricultural reforms, for if Home Rule would not of itself make a national life it would do more to make such a life possible than half a million creameries. With renewed life in the country many changes of the methods of government, and the holding property, would inevitably take place, which would all tend to make life less difficult even in bad years and in the worst districts of Mayo and Connemara.[115]

The muted, measured, undemanding reasonableness of this address to a self-consciously superior, albeit, progressive readership, sits oddly with his views expressed privately to Stephen McKenna in a letter written at the same time as the *Guardian* articles. In the letter Synge writes about the commission and the limitations placed on him and he suggests that there were features of life in the west he would like to have written about:

> There are sides of all that western life, the groggy-patriot-publican-general-shop-man who is married to the priest's half-sister and is second cousin once-removed of the dispensary doctor, that are horrible and awful. This is the type that is running the present United Irish League anti-grazier campaign, while they are swindling the people themselves in a dozen ways

and then buying out their holdings and packing off whole families to America.[116]

Synge is of course writing expressively rather than rationally and logically. Nevertheless, this kind of displacement activity, shifting responsibility for emigration onto the shoulders of the native bourgeoisie, alleviates the Protestant landowning classes of their inherited guilt. It was a necessary manoeuvre which allowed the 'nobleman' to side with the 'beggar' in opposition to the materialistic grubby philistinism of the now dominant indigenous middle class. It also allowed the artist to sympathise with the emigrant without, however, acknowledging the conceptualisation of emigration as exile.

Synge, like Yeats and Lady Gregory, was more interested in those who stayed than those who left, while attempting some kind of cultural fusion, and in gathering material for his art. America and England were outside the parameters of their alternative cultural vision, they were the principal destinations of emigrants but they were also a threat to the kind of Ireland they were interested in depicting in literature and outside the frame of their project.[117] In all probability the idea of leaving home as 'exile' would have been strange to relatively wealthy Anglo-Irish Protestants used to travelling frequently to England and elsewhere. It was, moreover, a class committed to a notion of nationalism which presupposed continued shelter under the aegis of English imperialism; one which was opposed to the exclusivist doctrines of Irish-Ireland.

In a letter written in 1907 after the *Playboy* row (but not published until 1966) Synge states his Anglo-Irish credo:

> I believe in Ireland I believe the nation that has made a place in history by seventeen centuries of manhood, a nation that has begotten Grattan and Emmet and Parnell will not be brought to complete insanity in these last days by what is senile and slobbering in the doctrine of the Gaelic League. There was never till this time a movement in Ireland that was gushing, cowardly and maudlin, yet now we are passing England in the hysteria of old women's talk.[118]

In his pantheon of heroes, Synge finds no place for Catholics or sympathy and understanding of the sentiments borne by Gaelic Leaders and others opposed to Anglo-Irish hegemony. It may be inferred that included in the 'hysteria of old women's talk' were the criticisms levelled at the *Playboy* and the Catholic nationalist discourse on exile and emigration.

However, writers from both cultural formations do utilise the figure of the returned emigrant to question, explain and compare. It was a long established narrative device which reflected the geographic and cultural marginality of Ireland in the British Isles, Europe and the Empire–and in relation to North America. It was in many ways a natural corollary of movements out of Ireland since the time of the earliest missionaries. The improvement in communication and transport systems in the latter half of the nineteenth century and the beginning of the twentieth naturally increased the volume of population movement throughout the world. A consequence for Ireland was that many of those who were active in public life at the time were people who had spent considerable periods of their lives outside Ireland.

The wealthy and the Anglo-Irish ascendancy took travel for granted whether it was to properties or interests in England or in the Empire and as Catholics came to acquire education and more political rights in the nineteenth century the ideas and experiences they had acquired abroad were frequently translated, when they returned, into hopes for Ireland's future and criticisms of its past and present. A random list of first and second generation returnees might include John O'Leary, Michael Davitt, Yeats, Griffiths, D.P. Moran, W.P. Ryan, James Connolly, Jim Larkin, George Moore, John McBride, de Valera and Padraic O'Conaire. Martin J. Waters examines the impact of returned emigrants in 'Peasants and Emigrants' (1977) on the development of the Gaelic League and the Irish-Ireland movement. Their experiences abroad he says:

> provided them with an expanded sense of possibility, and it was difficult for them to accept the notion that the established order in Irish country towns represented an unalloyed manifestation of divine wisdom.

Such men (*sic*) challenged the unquestioned dominance of the local clergy in terms of what was acceptable and in terms of social behaviour and they owed allegiance to 'secular and abstract ideals of the nation and its culture'.[119] In spite of their passionate identification with Ireland they remained peripheral figures within their native land. Their importation of patterns of behaviour and ideas which hybridised with what were thought of as purely indigenous ways of thinking and behaving produced in many instances, defensive, ambivalent and hostile responses. In Seamus O'Kelly's *Wet Clay* (1922) for example, the well-intentioned modernising propensities of the Irish-American Brendan Nilan provoke the jealousy of his wastrel cousin Luke Cusack. His violation of the moral code in kissing Luke's wife brings about the melodramatic fight to the death and the grotesque tableau that concludes the novel. In Shan F. Bullock's *Dan the Dollar* (1906) the energy, innovation and adoration of the material, which Daniel Ruddy personifies, is represented as a fundamental threat to both Protestant and Catholics, to a timeless world of unchanging innocence and to the harmonious relationship between the rural poor of both religions. A conservative conclusion which attempts to deflect the dynamics of an inexorably changing world onto the plane of an imagined past and reflected Bullock's own ambivalence as a Protestant brought up amongst a Catholic peasantry he liked, but did not belong to.

George Fitzmaurice, the son of a Church of Ireland minister and a Catholic mother, assumed rights of entry into the culture of the Kerry countryside. He appropriates the figure of the 'returned Yank' Pats Connor, to Anglo-Irish representation of comic peasant life in his play *The Country Dressmaker* (1907). This effectively neutralises and defuses americanisation by mocking Pats mongrelised speech patterns and reducing him to the ineffectual object of competition between the Sheas and the Clohessys.

In broad terms however, the stock figure of the emigrant returning from America was considered the preserve of Catholic writers and the returnee or visitor from England the provenance of the Protestant writer. Thus, Protestants rarely incorporated the 'returned Yank' into their work for he represented a threat to the image of the Celtic peasant constructed by Protestant writers of the Revival and a notion of Irishness which drew on fenianism and anti-colonial rhetoric to challenge the position and status of the Anglo-Irish in the political and in the cultural spheres. Moreover, he was considered by both Protestants and 'Holy Ireland' Irish as crass, loud, vulgar, unsophisticated and materialistic. America served as refuge and threat but above all in cultural terms, it provided a massive market for art from the Old World and rarely distinguished between the works emanating from different traditions within Ireland. America voraciously absorbed 'Culture' and provided extremely lucrative lecture tours and eager, though undiscriminating audiences for writers from whatever background. In the case of Protestant writers that frequently meant suppressing their non-Catholicism in deference to the assumption on the part of their hosts that all Irishmen were Catholic and nationalist.

Less attention has been paid by historians to emigration to Britain than to the USA and most of what has been written focuses on poor Catholic Irish immigrants, but migration across the Irish Sea had been a feature of the colonial relationship for centuries. In 1901 there were about 632,000 Irish-born residents in Britain.[120] The majority of those who went did so as a first step to emigration to the United States, Canada or Australia. Others worked the traditional seasonal pattern as harvesters or worked for relatively short periods as navvies or as factory hands.[121] For the most part they concentrated in urban ghettos 'Little Irelands' and worked at unskilled or semi-skilled occupations and organised their social and cultural activities around the Irish community. As Gearóid Ó Tuathaigh points out there were numerous factors militating against immediate assimilation:

> These currents were in the first instance psychological. The very proximity to home, the disappointment of those whose original aspirations had centred on a passage to America, the high mobility of a section of the Irish labour force; all these factors combined to encourage among many immigrants an attitude of refusal to accept the permanency of their exile. Furthermore, the Irish immigrant communities had, deriving from their historical sense, an unusually ambivalent attitude to their host society. While acknowledging that Britain was providing them with the means to live, and while always ready to acknowledge the better wages and hopes of improvement which prompted emigration in the first place, among the immigrant Irish the sense of obligation or of gratitude for these benefits was nullified, to a considerable extent, by their belief that it was Britain's misgovernment of Ireland which had caused them to be uprooted in the first instance. These attitudes contributed to a situation where the primary loyalty of the immigrant Irish was to their homeland or to the immigrant community itself, and only lastly, if at all, to their new society.[122]

Ó Tuathaigh goes on to describe how those tendencies to self-segregation were complemented by English hostility to Irish immigrants. That opposition was frequently couched in racial terms, sometimes benign and at times of tensions, malign. It was often directed at Irish nationalism and Irish Catholicism both of which represented threats to British imperialism and Protestantism and indicated disloyalty to the 'self-evident' and natural assumptions of superiority inherent in the metropolitan homeland.

Gladstone's conversion to Home Rule in 1886 was a significant turning point for the Irish in Britain in that it legitimised their loyalty to Ireland within the constitutional framework of the Empire and committed them to Liberal politics. Assimilation was also made easier in time by the arrival of newer waves of immigrants from central and eastern Europe and by the increasing secularisation of Britain and consequent indifference to the organised religion.

The Irish in Britain did not however, develop an exile discursive formation along the same lines as their American counterparts for fairly obvious reasons. Most for example, did not see their absence from Ireland as permanent as they could return relatively easily and frequently. America of course, was so much further away and had its own history of opposition to Britain and was thus in dialogic and ideological terms open to the spirit of rebellion against imperialism (of the British variety) and those conditions were clearly inapplicable in Britain itself. Anglo-Irish emigrant discourse could contain the innocuous and nostalgic romanticism of drawing-room sentimentalisation of Ireland as expressed through Moore's *Melodies*. As Fitzpatrick suggests:

> London Irish poets such as Yeats fed upon the illicit glamour attached to John O'Leary, but employed it to manufacture poems rather than bombs. Romantic Ireland had particular appeal for better educated expatriates and their children, providing an attractive image of the Irish past which was not (as in Ireland) seen to be painfully at odds, with the drab materialism of the Irish present. Language classes and bracing lectures on Irish history now supplemented the singing of lachrymose Irish airs round the piano in the parlour of the respectable immigrant household. By 1902 there were 1,500 members of the Gaelic League in London alone, with up to 50 Irish classes weekly in 14 schools. Moist-eyed 'exiles' heard Irish-language sermons on St Patrick's Day at the Dockland Catholic Church, relished 'an atmosphere of the country fireside gatherings' of their boyhoods at League meetings and organised language summer schools in Irish holiday resorts.[123]

It was a context out of which Yeats produced *John Sherman* in 1891, an allegorical analogue of the young poet's relationship with Ireland and England.

Sherman, a 'lounger' and dreamer, leaves his comfortable west of Ireland home Ballah, a semi-mythicised Sligo town, at the behest of his childhood friend the beautiful and unadorned spirit of Anglican Ireland, Mary Carton, to perform his duty and serve God. A move which takes the form of residence in London and employment in his uncle's shipping firm. While there he is romantically attracted by the wealthy, shallow, flirtatious and beguilingly insincere Margaret Leland. He only succeeds in breaking his engagement to Margaret by introducing and uniting her with his friend Howard, an intellectual counterpart to the material superficiality she represents. Their mutual attraction frees him to return to his true home and love in a form of Thoreauesque ecstasy which rejects the lures of modernity in favour of the timeless rhythms of a more natural existence and a forgiving real love in the figure of Ireland/Mary Carton. Having spent his life among 'aliens'[124] his wish fulfilment and dream projection has produced a reintegrated wholeness which reunites the material and the spiritual with the spirit of place.

The novel is in effect a prose equivalent to that most famous of 'exile' poems 'The Lake Isle of Innisfree' (1893) which was written at the same time and under the same circumstances. It was produced out of an inchoate conservative nostalgia which opposed the essential purity and nature of an unspoilt Irish landscape against the corruption and squalor of modern urban and commercial London. It epitomised

> the classic strategy of the Irish Protestant imagination, estranged from the community yet anxious to identify itself with the new patriotic sentiment. While Roman Catholic writers of the Revival period were obsessed with the history of their land, for the Protestant artists that history could only be–a painful accusation against their own people; and so they had recourse to geography in their attempts at impatriation.[125]

And as John Eglinton suggested it is in the presence of Mother Nature herself that 'the poet can forget the squalid animosities of race and creed'.[126]

G.B. Shaw in contrast, worked out of a socialist naturalism, in his case an Ibsenite aesthetic which intellectually revivified the London theatre, challenging the dominant bourgeois complacency of metropolitan audiences in much the same ways that the dramas of Colum and Murray questioned middle-class Catholic nationalist pieties. Shaw, like his Dublin reared contemporary Oscar Wilde, left Ireland more or less as soon as he attained adulthood and like Wilde lived the remainder of his life outside Ireland and for the most part in and around the metropolitan heartland. Shaw and Wilde were of course, brought up in an educational system and a cultural milieu which consciously aped England and as ambitious and talented provincials they accepted that the terms for success were dictated from the centre and that success could only be achieved within the arena of the literary centre of the English-speaking world. Shaw in particular unequivocally outlined his position (and by implication that of all Protestant artists) in an autobiographical fragment written in 1921. In it he refers to his 'abandonment of Dublin' and how many young Irishmen of the time found it difficult to forgive him. He 'had' to go to London as

> London was the literary centre for the English language, and for such artistic culture as the realm of the English language (in which I proposed to be king) could afford. There was no Gaelic League in those days, nor any sense that Ireland had in herself the seed of culture. Every Irishman who

felt that his business in life was on the higher planes of the cultural professions felt that he must have a metropolitan domicile and an international culture: that is, he felt that his first business was to get out of Ireland. I had the same feeling.[127]

Unlike Wilde and to a lesser extent Yeats, Shaw examined his own position with regard to both Ireland and England in overt and explicit terms in numerous articles, pamphlets, speeches and letters over a period ranging from the late 1880s to the late 1940s;[128] and most clearly and paradoxically in the text commissioned by Yeats 'as a patriotic contribution to the repertory of the Irish Literary Theatre' *John Bull's Other Island* (1904). Yeats felt unable or unwilling to stage it. However, Vedrenne and Barker of the Royal Court Theatre in London did stage it as part of their seasons during the period 1904–7 where it proved to be commercially successful. Shaw published the play complete with *Preface for Politicians* in 1906 and in subsequent editions he updated his observations on Ireland and its relationships with England as history moved on. Shaw suggests in the *Preface* that the Irish Literary Theatre refused to perform the play as it 'was uncongenial to the whole spirit of the neo-Gaelic movement'[129] and certainly its demythologising play with stereotypes would have subverted the unreflective heroising symbology of those dedicated to cultural fusion. The emergence of Tom Broadbent, the well-intentioned dreamer and ultimately successful bourgeois liberal 'Gladstonised' entrepreneur as the likeable 'hero', would have offended the anti-materialists of all shades of Irish opinion just as much as it pleased its English audiences who saw in Broadbent a benign and attractive presentation of Englishness and liberal capitalism.

Shaw in fact, seems to be arguing for an alternative kind of fusion or accommodation. In some ways like Tone before him, he is proposing a project which transcends the divisions that separate Irish people. He assumed that the forces of democracy within a federal Home Rule constitutional arrangement will break the power of the English and Roman imperiums, and that the pugnacity and narrowly focused self-interest of Protestantism will fill the leadership vacuum in much the same way that the republican, Tone, assumed that the broadly Protestant leadership of the United Irishmen would liberate the Catholic masses of the late eighteenth century.[130] Shaw however, as an opponent of nationalism and a Fabian Socialist foresees an evolutionary development of Empire into a 'Federal Union of English-speaking commonwealths'.[131] In a specious series of seemingly incontestable claims he comes close to asserting the racial superiority of the Irish Protestant, their historically determined purity, pragmatism and right to rule over all within the Empire:

> When I say that I am an Irishman I mean that I was born in Ireland, and that my native language is the English of Swift and not the unspeakable jargon of the mid-xix century London newspapers. My extraction is the extraction of most Englishmen: that is, I have no trace in me of the commercially imported North Spanish strain which passes for aboriginal Irish: I am a genuine typical Irishman of the Danish, Norman, Cromwellian, and (of course) Scotch invasions. I am violently and arrogantly Protestant by family tradition: but let no English Government therefore count on my allegiance: I am English enough to be an inveterate Republican and Home Ruler ... When I look round me on the hybrid cosmopolitans, slum poisoned or square pampered, who call themselves Englishmen today, and see them bullied by the Irish Protestant garrison as no Bengalee now lets himself be bullied by an Englishman; when I see the Irishman everywhere standing clearheaded, sane, hardily callous to the boyish sentimentalities, susceptibilities, and credulities that make the Englishman the dupe of every charlatan and the idolator of every numskull, I perceive that Ireland is the only spot on earth which still produces the ideal Englishman of history, Blackguard, bully, drunkard, liar, foulmouth, flatterer, beggar, backbiter, venal functionary, corrupt judge, envious friend, vindictive opponent, unparalleled political traitor: all these your Irishman may easily be just as he may be a gentleman (a species extinct in England, and nobody a penny the worse); but he is never quite the hysterical, nonsense-crammed, fact proof, truth–terrified, unballasted sport of all the bogey panics and all the silly enthusiasms that now calls itself 'God's Englishman'. England cannot do without its Irish and its Scots today, because it cannot do without at least a little sanity.[132]

Whether this is to be taken literally or not, it does assert an ancestral linguistic and racial pre-eminence which establishes the Irish Protestant at the very centre of the Empire. The metropolis for Shaw is 'home' and those who do not conform to his notion of the purity of the Irish/English paradigm are 'impure', less wholly 'English' than he, and consequently less important and valued. It is a sub-text which accompanies the satiric iconoclasm and inversion of received images and broadens the possibilities of Irishness, but implicitly refuses simultaneous constructions of 'exile'. In the play itself though nominally a Catholic Larry Doyle, the hard-headed pragmatist, speaks out of a unionist discourse. He is, he informs us, 'made a man of, as you say, by England',[133] whose purpose as a metallurgist and civil engineer is like Broadbent's 'to join countries, not to separate them'.[134]

Shaw and Larry Doyle were of course ultimately embedded in the interstices of Hiberno-English cultural and political relationships and unable to turn elsewhere for psychic refuge. As 'outsiders' and 'insiders' in England and in Ireland they lived the tensions, torsions and contradictions of a fissiparous colonial relationship without the possibility of resolution. As Protestant individualists they conceived their move to England entirely in terms of self-advancement, and as arbiters of their own destiny, they can only celebrate their departure from Ireland and anticipate the future in the home of their choice.

Wilde by contrast, after release from imprisonment did experience exile–it was however exile from England rather than banishment from Ireland. He was in Richard Ellmann's phrase a 'Prisoner at Large',[135] sentenced by society to a peripatetic purposelessness in wandering continental Europe like Maturin's Melmoth, whose name Wilde pseudonymously adopted in a self-ironising counterpoint to the quotidian ignominy of his departure.

Patrick MacGill who came from Donegal just a few miles north of 'Ballah' also expressed longings for home and Ireland in his collections of poetry *Songs of Donegal* (1911) and *Songs of the Dead* (1912)[136] and in his autobiographical novel *Children of the Dead End* (1914). His conventional verse and earthy unromanticised prose forms contrast vividly with the self-indulgent, socially detached etherealism of John Sherman. The poems in particular recall his memories of his peasant upbringing and attachment to place. They contrast the simplicity and innocence of Donegal with the corruption and cruelty of the wider world within the conventions of pre-World War I Georgian versification, Kiplingesque rhythms and the Irish ballad tradition. But it is the novel which retains most impact for its realistic portrayal of the experiences of the Donegal poor in a simple and dignified style which gives voice to the imperatives, trials, obligations and feelings of a hitherto much misrepresented peasant class. It deals with those whose lifestyles incorporated seasonal migration (which often became permanent) into the lived fabric of family and communal existence. And it is told within a recognisable, indigenous shanachie tradition.

The novel works out of a socialist resistance to the power of gombeen men, the casual brutality of the local schoolmaster and the inordinate power of the priest to control social behaviour and levy 'taxes'. Those pressures combined with the need to raise money for the rent, lead Dermod Flynn at the age of twelve to the hiring fair at Strabane, 'the calvary of mid-Tyrone'.[137] Dermod like so many of his contemporaries, was conditioned to believe that he was 'born and bred merely to support my parents'.[138] Eventually, as was common among Donegal people, he joined a gang contracted to harvest potatoes in Scotland for the season. He was also intent on seeing more of the world and making enough money to return to Glenmornan in style. He records descriptions of his adventures in Scotland as a navvy, tramp and railway worker, the begging letters he received from home, his early writings, employment as a journalist and his search for Norah Ryan, his childhood sweetheart in the slums of Glasgow. The search ends in a deathbed scene wherein Norah having been driven to prostitution issues this plea to Dermod:

> Maybe ye'll go home some day. If ye do, go to me mother's home and ask her to forgive me. Tell her that I died on the year I left Mickey's Jim's squad. I was not me mother's child after that; I was dead to all the world. My fault could not be undone–that's what made the blackness of it. Niver let yer own sisters go into a strange country, Dermod. Niver let them go to the potato-squad, for its the place that is evil for a girl like me that hasn't much sense.[139]

Her fate is symptomatic of many young Irish women, a realisation and echo of the warnings issued and reiterated periodically by the moral guardians in (and of) Ireland. Though owing something to the conventions of melodrama, in the context of Flynn/MacGill's developing socialism and the authorial commentary which follows his discovery of her occupation, it should perhaps be read at another level too:

> I stood on the street corner, unable to move or act, and almost unable to think. A blind rage welled up in my heart against the social system that compelled women to seek a livelihood by pandering to the impurity of men. Norah had come to Scotland holy and pure and eager to earn the rent of her mother's croft. She had earned many rents for the landlord who had caused me sufferings in Mid-Tyrone and who was responsible for the death of my brother Dan. To the same landlord Norah had given her soul and purity. The young girls of Donegal came radiantly innocent from their glens and mountains, but often, alas! they fall into sin in a far country. It is unholy to expect all that is good and best from the young girls who lodge with the beasts of the byre and swine of the sty. I felt angry with the social system which was responsibility for such a state of affairs.[140]

MacGill has absorbed here the concerns and writings of the social explorers of victorian and edwardian England, people such as Charles Booth, William Booth, Rider Haggard, Jack London and G.F.G.

Masterman. It was a tradition which mutated with the imported naturalism of French writing to produce the realism of Arthur Morrison's *Tales of Mean Streets* (1894) and *A Child of the Jago* (1896). His own exploration of the abyss has to incorporate his ambivalence about the demands of family and Ireland, and his experience of, and opposition to, the lived social Darwinism of high imperialism and capitalism.

His success through his writing in England and the opposition implicit in socialism towards nationalism brought him into the same zone of discourse as other radical, expatriate Irishmen like Shaw and Wilde, concerns which when taken together with the proximity of Ireland presumably prevented him from romanticising his departure and subsequent life in Scotland and England as banishment and exile. His enrolment in the British army in the First World War also suggests an assimilation into British society, albeit qualified, which is wholly inconsistent with self-imaging exile.

Gerald O'Donovan also served in the British army in the First World War having moved to England after leaving the priesthood in 1908. His most important work, a realist autobiographical novel *Father Ralph*, was published in 1913 shortly after Moore's departure from Ireland and just before the publication of *Portrait Of The Artist As A Young Man* (1916).

His disenchantment with the Irish Catholic Church provided an insider's insight into the Church at a time when its power was virtually unchallengeable and its wealth and the number of its religious was growing, while the population as a whole was diminishing. It described a self-serving monolith concerned primarily with its own status and advancement, an organisation constitutively hierarchic and autocratic which cared little for the intellectual and material development of its lay members. In attempting to empower and enlighten the masses of Bunnahone through self-help and co-operative ventures, Fr Ralph O'Brien antagonises the local tradesmen and their priestly beneficiaries (and ideological benefactors)–a temporal alliance which eventually forces his isolation, disinheritance and alienation. Faced with taking an oath repudiating 'modernist errors' [141] demanded of him by his bishops or suppressing his conscience, Ralph like Stephen Dedalus, refuses to serve. Inevitably that leads to his departure from Holy Orders and Holy Ireland–driven out like the independent minded parishioner Dunne and many before who had resisted the dictates of priestly power and the corruption of gombeen men. He was a victim of malicious gossip, a martyr to mendacity and calculated misrepresentation, a 'traitor' betrayed by his own. However, the novel concludes paradoxically with a punishment that liberates, an expulsion that emancipates and discharges what is in effect a redemptive deliverance:

> He took up his clerical collar and looked at it curiously. He smiled as he thought of how he had dreaded laying it aside. And now, there was only a sense of escape from bondage, of freedom ...
>
> He stood on the deck of the Holyhead mail boat, his eyes fixed on the receding Irish coast. The sands at Merrion, Howth Head, Bray Head, the Wicklow Mountains, recalled youthful dreams. In the blind groping way which is the way of life, he felt that he had been true to them. Life was larger than his vision of it, and where he had read failure life marked advance.
>
> He walked the deck with a springy step, breathing an east wind, that made his face smart, with a sense of victory.
>
> 'I have found myself at last', he said under his breath. Hs blood surged through his veins, and he went back to the stern. The sun, falling slant-wise on the foam in the wake of the boat, made a track of molten silver. On the horizon land had faded to a blue outline. He gazed at it longingly until the last faint grey disappeared and the sea everywhere met the sky.
>
> He turned round and braced himself again to the east wind. Only one dream had faded into the sea, he thought ...
>
> And then? [142]

O'Donovan's closure resists and refuses the psychic and linguistic conventions of Catholic nationalist departure. Instead it accentuates individualism, choice, life-enhancing optimism. The collar and Catholicism which had stood for so long as markers of opposition to secular enslavement in the rhetoric of the colonised had, at least for the spirited and the enlightened, now come to represent a different form of repression, an asphyxiation of the soul and a 'hemiplegia of the will'. [143]

The text lacks the artistic certainties and self-heroising exilic poetics of Stephen Dedalus and the self-celebratory narcissism of Moore, but like his more famous contemporaries O'Donovan emerged from an increasingly self-confident Irish urban educated class. A formation which enabled an articulate, reasoned, humanistic, critique of Irish nationalist and Catholic thought from within. Although the critic could only articulate his criticisms from outside the geographic and ideological borders of Ireland itself, he too had discovered that the quickest way to Tara was via Holyhead.

The language that concludes the novel is a curious adulterated amalgam of simplistic symbolism, reaccentuated exilic discourse and evocative individualism, redolent with the hopes for self-determination and realisation embedded typically in Protestant liberalism. In laying aside the collar he relinquishes the hold the Church has on him. In leaving the scenes of his childhood, he escapes the communal memorialism of nativity and in turning eastwards to face the future he embraces his own creation, to become in effect his own self-made man. He and Joyce entered that state of self-generation that Joyce distinguished from 'economic' exile, that is 'spiritual' exile where Ireland's 'most favourite children ... left her to seek in other lands that food of the spirit by which a nation of human beings is sustained in life'.[144]

CONCLUSION

The Catholic priest and historian, Joseph MacMahon, described the vision of the Church in this period as 'static and hierarchical' where 'Triumphalism was the dominant note'. This meant that 'all foreign ideas were frowned upon' and that 'New social principles were regarded with hostility and there was a tendency to dismiss new ideas without even examining them'.[145] In the secular world of anti-colonial Dublin propaganda D.P. Moran's newspaper *The Leader* formed a complementary site of resistance to modernity, particularly in manifestations emanating from England and America. His key ideas were collected in book form in 1905 under the heading *The Philosophy of Irish Ireland*, where he utilised his experience as an expatriate to observe and criticise Ireland and Irish culture. In the final essay of the collection 'The Battle of Two Civilisations', he addressed himself to literature in Ireland and denies the influence of English literature on Irish sensibilities. He says:

> Tell me of any ordinary man in Dublin, Cork or elsewhere, who professes an appreciation for the best products of English literature, and I will have no hesitation in informing you that he is an intellectual snob, mostly composed of affectation. Literature, to the common Irishman, is an ingenious collection of fine words which no doubt have some meaning, but which he is not going to presume to understand.[146]

He scathingly and sarcastically dismisses Arnoldian 'natural magic', the 'Celtic note', and the 'Celtic Renaissance' as products of mystification which caused 'a little stir amongst minor literary circles in London, but, much less stir in Ireland itself'. The position of Yeats and his followers he says, was challenged and overcome by the Gaelic League which established the criterion that 'Irish literature hence forward was not to be thought of outside the Irish language'.[147] F.S.L. Lyons has described his importance and the views he espoused, as formidable because he refused to admit that a middle ground was possible. Any emanation of what he regarded as English culture, whether it was *Tit-Bits* or the poetry of W.B. Yeats, was suspect because being in the tongue of the foreigner, it was a threat to the survival, and revival of Irish. For him, the battle of two civilisations was the cultural form of the age-old struggle between England and Ireland. In that struggle each individual has to choose which side he or she would be on. Most people, no doubt, were indifferent to, or simply unaware of, Moran's imperatives, but no artist of that generation could ignore them.[148]

Thus, the worlds of Irish Catholicism and secular Irish cultural nationalism manifest in depictions of Holy Ireland, Mother Ireland and organisations like the Gaelic League, the GAA, the Catholic Press, Cuman na nGaedheal, Inginidh na hÉireann and in popular drama, prose and song, formed an overlapping, contingent, contiguous and mobile, intra-molecular discursive formation which came to define itself largely by what it was not and by what it imagined itself to be. It was a world of monocular, ersatz, essences, which excluded what it could not contain. Among those exclusions was the would-be truth teller, the intellectual, the social rebel and, for the most part, the artist of the avant-garde.

In his introduction to Albert Memmi's *The Colonized and the Colonizer* (1990) Liam O'Dowd draws attention to Memmi's modes of escape from the colonial relationship for the colonised. They can either become assimilated to the coloniser's ways of thinking and behaving or they can oppose, resist and ultimately revolt. Within Ireland those processes with modification and variations had determined political, cultural and social forms and relationships since the time of the Tudors. O'Dowd however, points to a third option–emigration for both coloniser and colonised:

> Historically, people could escape the specific antagonisms of the 'settler/ native' relationship in Ireland by joining a wider colonial enterprise abroad. By the time the latter had declined, the escape routes of twentieth-century emigration had opened up. In Ireland, therefore, both coloniser and colonised could 'refuse' by physical escape. While such a strategy eventually led to foreign, especially Irish-American support for Irish independence, it typically reduced the threat to the colonial relationship at home. One strand of emigration, that is to Britain, often ended in assimilation in the long run, while doing little to encourage such unity in Ireland.[149]

Though the experiences of 'settlers' and 'natives' were similar, the perceptions were not. The motivations for, and representations of emigration differed according to origin and destination and were embedded in respective collective consciousnesses differently. Edna Longley the critic, writing in relation to the 1916 Rising and the Battle of the Somme suggests that Irish Catholics and Ulster Protestants

> not only tend to remember different things, but to remember them in different ways. The mnemonic structures: the categories, tropes, rituals. Religion, still the major psycho-cultural force in Ireland, has powerfully influenced the forms of Irish memory.[150]

And what was (is) true of Ulster Protestants, is broadly true too, of Irish Protestants in general. Emigrants, artisans and artists were inevitably imaged and enmeshed in the auricular, the visual and linguistic contours of communal memory and association; frames of reference which were of course, conscious and unconscious, 'watertight' and porous.

CHAPTER FIVE

Exile, Art and Alienation:
George Moore's Irish Writings

INTRODUCTION

EXILE according to Edward Said, is 'predicated on the existence of, love for, and bond with one's native place'.[1] He also assumes that exile carries with it connotations of banishment, of forced removal and that exiles are necessarily prevented from returning home. It was this kind of formulation that characterised pre-modern notions of banishment and exile and produced the prototypical exilic poetry of Ovid. His life in Tomis and the work he produced there, the *Tristia* and *Epistulae ex Ponte* according to Peter Green

> offer an extraordinary paradigm of the fantasies and obsessions that bedevil every reluctant exile: loving evocations of the lost homeland, the personification of letters that one sent to walk the dear familiar streets denied to their writer, the constant parade–and exaggeration–of present horrors, spring *here* contrasted with spring *there* (Tr 111.12), the wistful recall of lost pleasures once taken for granted, the slow growth of paranoia and hypochondria, the neurotic nagging at indifferent friends, the grinding exacerbation of slow and empty time, the fear of and longing for death.[2]

And the only sustaining consolation throughout his indeterminate ordeal is the comfort his writing provides; poetic dispatches which maintain his lifeline to Rome through the re-creation of an increasingly idealised homeland.[3]

The lack of an immediate audience however, produced perhaps the most memorable remark about the condition of the writer in exile, that

> writing a poem you can read to no one
> is like dancing in the dark.[4]

And it may be imagined–dancing in the dark–alone.

That model of exile and its consequences rested on the coercive and proscriptive power of the powerful over the weak, the oppressor over the oppressed. It was a model that would have been understood and felt by the victims of English conquest in Ireland; the followers of the Great O'Neill, the 'Wild Geese'; the expelled and transported United Irishmen; those who fled rather than face imprisonment or execution and those who were forcibly evicted from their homes by landlords and 'emigrated' or those who were expelled to other English speaking colonies elsewhere, or to America. It was what Said distinguishes as an *actual* as opposed to a *metaphorical* condition.[5] His inclusive and expansive diagnosis of the intellectual in exile originates in historical 'dislocation and migration … but is not limited to it'. While his remarks are concerned with the intellectuals in general they are clearly applicable to creative artists. He acknowledges that within a society intellectuals may be 'insiders' or 'outsiders':

> The pattern that sets the course for the intellectual as outsider is best exemplified by the condition of exile, the state of never being fully adjusted, always feeling outside the chatty, familiar world inhabited by natives, so to speak, tending to avoid and even dislike the trappings of accommodation and national well-being. Exile for the intellectual in this metaphysical sense, is restlessness, movement, constantly being unsettled, and unsettling others. You cannot go back to some earlier and perhaps more stable condition of being at home; and, alas, you can never fully arrive; be at one with your new home or situation.

The lecture continues with reflections on the consequences of that broader definition. It produces a habit of mind where 'the intellectual as exile tends to be happy with the idea of unhappiness'[6] and he instances the example of Swift in Ireland, V.S. Naipaul and Theodor Adorno quoting the latter's aphorism: 'For a man who no longer has a homeland, writing becomes a place to live.'[7] This statement of course echoes the predicament of Ovid. But he then proceeds to examine some of the privileges and advantages of exile conceived in this manner.

For the intellectual exile offers 'the pleasures of being surprised',[8] of accommodating himself or herself to new circumstances. Secondly, the exile is advantaged in that he/she 'see things both in terms of what has been left behind and what is actual here and now, there is a double perspective that never sees things in isolation'. That juxtaposition often offers different, unexpected and enlightening perspectives on the familiar and the taken for granted. Thirdly, such an exilic standpoint means that 'you tend to see things not simply as they are, but as they have come to be that way. Look at the situations as contingent, not as inevitable, look at them as the result of a series of historical choices made by men and women, as facts of society made by human beings, and not as natural or god-given, therefore unchangeable, permanent, irreversible.'[9]

And finally he argues, the intellectual as exile is 'always going to be marginal'.[10] It is a liberating condition free from the constraints of conventionality and custom. It aligns the exile with 'the provisional and risky rather than to the habitual, to innovation and experiment rather than the authoritatively given status quo. The *exilic* intellectual does not respond to the logic of the conventional but to the audacity of the daring, and to representing change, to moving on, not standing still.'[11]

This twentieth-century view of exile arises no doubt, out of the experiences of Romanticism, the mass movement of populations (voluntary and compulsory) and resistance to nationalism by many Modernist and Post-Modernist artists and intellectuals. It differs clearly from the pre-modern idea of exile in that it is looser, more ambiguous, voluntarist and concerned with distinguishing the intellectual from the masses.

This chapter acknowledges the mutation of the term within intellectual and artistic discourse and its relatively restricted application to artists and intellectuals. It aims to examine in some detail those texts of George Moore most concerned with Ireland as an exemplary case study of the displaced Irish artist; to relate his experiences and texts to popular conceptions of the term within Ireland and to consider the implications of dislocation and alienation for Moore in particular and for other Irish artists too.

PARIS AND LONDON: VOYAGING IN

Joseph Hone's biography *The Life of George Moore* (1936) provides the most authoritative version of Moore's life we have. The family, he suggests, may have had some links with Sir Thomas More, the author of *Utopia* and an English martyr executed, ironically, for his refusal to impugn the Pope's authority. The family had in all probability, its origins in the Protestant settlement of Ireland in the seventeenth century. What is known is that an ancestor married a Spanish Catholic, Catherine de Killikelly, a product of the expatriate 'Wild Geese' of the late seventeenth century.

The novelist's great-grandfather, a Catholic, returned to Ireland around 1790 with a large fortune, bought about 12,000 acres of Mayo and built Moore Hall. His second son John, the novelist's grand-uncle, interestingly joined the French expedition under Humbert in 1798. He briefly took the title President of the Republic of Connaught, was captured by the forces of the Crown and died soon after.[12] His brother, the third son of the returned 'Wild Goose' was Moore's grandfather. He married Louisa Browne, granddaughter of the first Earl of Atamount and a relative of the Marquess of Sligo, which connected the Moores to the Protestant ascendancy. George Henry Moore, the writer's father, was educated as a Catholic at Oscott, an English boarding school and at Cambridge. As the owner of Moore Hall and the family estate George Henry developed the racing stables which feature in so much of his son's writing. He refused to clear his land of tenants during the Famine and he became an Independent MP for Mayo in 1847. His marriage to Mary Blake of Ballinafad allied the Moores to the Roman Catholic gentry of the west of Ireland.

George Augustus Moore was born in February 1852. He was tutored locally both in the formal sense and, it seems, rather more informally by the servants and stable staff of Moore Hall until 1861, when he too went to Oscott. Oscott as a British Catholic public school 'offered attractions to Irish parents who wanted their children to enjoy the advantages of the system without exposing them to the Protestant atmosphere of the ordinary English public school' according to Joseph Hone. Among the advantages presumably would have been a celebration of the virtues of Englishness, monosexuality and the Empire. In addition, 'there was also the hope that the boys would return without their brogues'.[13] After several unhappy and unproductive years he left Oscott in 1867. His father's political career necessitated frequent family movement between Mayo, Dublin and London and when he was re-elected to Westminster in 1868 (siding with the land reformers) the family moved to London in 1869.

Moore senior had 'a feudal ideal of his relationship with his tenants'. In return for exercising his responsibilities towards them as a landlord 'he expected a return of personal loyalty and affection'.[14] He returned to Mayo to meet demands from his tenants for rent reductions in April 1870 and, while there, died.

His father's death liberated Moore from the necessity of entering the army and provided him with an assured income from the rents of the tenantry for the foreseeable future. Between 1870 and 1873 when at the age of twenty-one he attained full access to his inheritance, he developed his interest in art under the influence of his dilettante uncle Jim Browne. He assumed the persona and life-style of a young man about town, 'turned over the pages of Darwin, Buckle, Mill, Leckey and George Eliot'[15] and developed his friendship with the Bridgers of Old Shoreham in Sussex.

Moore left for Paris in March 1873 (accompanied by his valet William

Maloney) in order to learn how to paint. He dabbled in a desultory manner
with the craft of painting returning 'homesick' to London (*sic*) a year
later.[16] He went back to Paris shortly afterwards, lost his faith in his ability
as a painter and it seems from around September 1876[17] began to turn his
ambitions towards writing as his preferred medium of artistic expression.
He entered into the café life of the Nouvelles Athènes and became
acquainted with the artistic avant-garde of Paris which included: Mallarmé,
Manet, Degas, Monet, Pissarro, Renoir and Sisley. He acquired during his
sojourn in Paris, the sartorial and hirsute accoutrements of the bohemian
artist. As Hone points out however,[18] his personal acquaintance with the
Naturalistic writers was not intimate, although it was during his last years
in Paris that he became a convert to, and a proselytiser for Naturalism.

During the 1870s Moore had travelled between London and Paris on
several occasions spending prolonged periods in London. He returned to
London as his permanent home in 1880 when his uncle Joe Blake, who
had been the agent for his properties, informed him that his tenants were
refusing to pay their rents and that he himself had been subsidising Moore
and now wished to be repaid. Moore visited his estates in the winter of
1880–81 'looking like a caricature of a Frenchman',[19] and met tenants'
deputations who instructed him in the history of confiscation, Irish land
tenure and just why it was they refused to pay rent.

In the spring of 1881 he settled in rooms in the Strand with the intention
of earning his living as a writer. His life in London was lived without the
certainty of a *rentier* income which it seemed, evoked nostalgia for Paris
and induced old friends to remind him that 'he had once been the most
Parisian of all Englishmen'.[20]

Influenced by Zola and dialectically opposed to the fiction of contemporary England he wrote *A Modern Lover* (1883) and *A Mummer's Wife*
(1885). While working on *A Mummer's Wife* in Ireland in the winter of
1883–84 he conceived the idea of writing *A Drama in Muslin* and he spent
the early part of 1884 in Dublin observing and participating in the Dublin
Season.[21] He returned to Ireland for the winter of 1884–85 and wrote some
preliminary sketches for *A Drama in Muslin*. He continued with the story
which was serialised in January 1886 in *The Court and Society Review*, a
struggling periodical. The serialisation was preceded by an advertisement
written by Moore himself which promised 'a picture of Ireland all complete, Castle, landlords, and land leaguers, and *painted* by an Irishman'.[22]

Hone notes that Moore ceased his long annual visit to Ireland after the
publication of *A Drama in Muslin*, partly because of the offence it caused
in Dublin and partly because of his developing social life in London.[23] He

wrote *Terre d'Irland*, a series of Zolaesque portraits for a French audience at the same time as *A Drama in Muslin*. It was published in English in 1887 as *Parnell and his Ireland*. During 1887 Moore prepared *Confessions of A Young Man* and spent some considerable time with his friends the Bridgers in Sussex, a family he came to regard as quintessentially English. *Confessions* was written firstly for *La Revue Independante*, a Parisian avant-garde literary magazine and it was published in book form in 1888.[24]

After the novels *Spring Days* (1888), *Mike Fletcher* (1889), *Vain Fortune* (1891), the play *The Strike at Arlingford* (1893), and his critical work *Modern Painting* (1893) which established Moore as a spokesman for the French Impressionists, he published that most Irish of English novels *Esther Waters* in March 1894.[25]

Hone records only two visits to Ireland by Moore before his attendance at the performance of Yeats' *The Countess Cathleen* at the Antient Concert Rooms in Dublin in May 1899. He was at Moore Hall in August 1890 at the time he was writing *Esther Waters*[26] and he attended his mother's funeral in Mayo in May 1895.

Moore, Jane Chrisler informs us, was, 'A flâneur par excellence' and a 'flâneur', she explains, was a new social type, a product of the growth of new forms of retail establishments, cafés and restaurants which lined the boulevards of Paris in the 1870s. The 'flâneur' 'is a self-conscious observer–he appreciates what he sees and intends that others should see him with the same esteem'.[27] At that time Moore cultivated the appearance and style of a decadent aesthete and dandy, an external signification which suggested a self-absorbed narcissism. He was not immune however, to the prevailing heteroglossia which characterised so much Parisian and european thought and behaviour–social, cultural and aesthetic, including anti-clericalism.

Chrisler describes how Moore observed the transformations of France from a monarchist state making France the first republic among the major european nations. She notes how powerfully the spirit of republicanism had survived since the Revolution of 1789 and how aristocrats throughout the world remembered with fear and horror the power and anger of the masses; and how so many of the Romantic writers (such as Shelley) whom Moore admired were ironically inspired by the democratic idealism of the First Republic. The revolutions of 1830 and 1848 reminded the privileged of the latent and repressed energies of the proletariat which of course manifested themselves in Ireland, in the form of O'Connell's mass protests, Young Ireland and fenianism. She notes that 'The habitués of the Nouvelle Athènes were bourgeois republicans of long standing. Both of his heroes, Manet and Degas, had fought for the government during the Prussian siege of 1870'. She goes on to point out that for artists such as those who frequented the Nouvelle Athènes, 'politics represented more than a lively topic for discussion or the cause of war; it affected their daily lives and their work'.[28] In addition, Chrisler remarks that though they were conservative in terms of their personal lives, their daring lay in the explorations of the processes of creation.

She concludes the article by drawing a specific parallel between the violence of the Paris Commune of 1871 and that of the Phoenix Park murders of 1882 and says:

> The Commune instilled a deep and abiding fear of the urban proletariat in the minds of landholders throughout France; consequently it affected legislation enacted by their representatives. The Land League had the same impact upon Irish landholders.[29]

Earlier in the same paragraph she observes rather innocently that Moore had met John O'Leary, the fenian leader, while in Paris but that he found 'the Fenian and the Irish community in Paris not carefree enough'. As a consequence 'he gravitated towards the *haute* bourgeoisie' with whom no doubt, he had many interests and sympathies.

In London his widening circle of friendships also drew on the upper middle-classes and the minor aristocracy. They too felt threatened by the emergent masses and the extension of the franchise, the inexorability of change and progress and in many cases by the grip of socially applied versions of Darwinism.[30] Naturalism as an aesthetic, evolved out of post-Darwinian biology and highlighted heredity and environment as determining factors in the formation of human character and the societies created by human beings. Moore, as a disciple of Zola, absorbed the tenets of Naturalism and applied the technique to Ireland (albeit imperfectly) in *A Drama in Muslin* and most obviously in *Parnell and his Island*. It was a method and an ideology which perfectly suited the cultural anthropology of the age and the exploration of civilisation's opposite–nature. Ireland had, for the British Protestant and those 'civilising' agents of the ascendancy, long been associated with raw barbarism.[31] Naturalism offered the possibility of a 'scientific' objectivity, an exploration or 'voyage in'[32] to the darkness, degradation, decay and self-deceit of the island he had abandoned. It also provided Moore with a medium behind which he could make a pretence at concealing his interest. The detached authorial pose of the omniscient narrator assumed by Moore in the novel controls, distances and presents events for an audience outside Ireland. It was a useful device therefore for maintaining the illusion of disinterest while assuming a kinship with the non-Irish reader–a pose which allowed him the dual role of insider and outsider.

Ostensibly *A Drama in Muslin* concerns the emergence of five girls from a Catholic boarding school in England after several years schooling, into Irish society, marriage and adulthood. The move from England to Ireland is a movement from normality and security in addition to being a register of the entry into the jungle of the marriage market and the savagery of the west. The anglicised heroine Alice Barton, is the consciousness through which Moore's satire on the Irish gentry is mediated, directly and indirectly. Her lack of physical beauty removes her from the centre of social attention while her intelligence, sensitivity and perception provide a focus for others to confide in and for Moore to speak through. She is perhaps an analogue of the figure Moore aspires to be. Written as a linear narrative the text moves from England to the Mayo social scene, from there to the Dublin season of 1882, back again to the west, then to a second Dublin season. It returns to the west and concludes in London in the mid 1880s.

The gentry both Protestant and Catholic are sketched by Moore as effete, ineffectual, corrupt, self-seeking, vulgar and philistine. They are concerned primarily with the preservation of privileges and the threat to their incomes that the activities of the Land League represent. Women, both mothers and daughters, are overwhelmingly obsessed with making successful, status enhancing marriage contracts. The novel mocks the grotesqueries of the rural gentry through the figures of Mr Ryan and Mr Lynch, both of whom are presented as objects of ridicule; Mr Adair whose intellectual pretensions are exposed by the worldly cynicism of Harding, the writer and Moore surrogate, and through the ludicrous egregiousness of Mr Barton. In a more serious vein, the sinister and immoral are suggested in the person of Lord Dungory and the puritanical proselytising of his daughters, Lady Sarah and Lady Jane. The unmarried Brennan sisters, all of whom were 'dumpty and dark' and in whose 'snub-noses and blue eyes their Celtic blood was easily recognisable',[33] are made to represent the future for the unmarried–that is, the unmarried daughters of an anachronistic order.

Their world, Moore recognises through the persona of Alice, her implied and indirect thought acts and through Moore's authorial inter-ventions, is no longer sustainable. Alice, observing her father and thinking of her sister Olive sees that 'from the imaginative but constantly unhing-ing intelligence of the father, the next step downwards was the weak,

feather-brained daughter'.[34] Alice's liberal instincts express themselves in
the recognition that the peasantry had justice on their side and that there
was 'something wrong in each big house being surrounded by a hundred
small ones, all working to keep it in sloth and luxury'.[35] At the same time
however, Moore resisted the logic of Alice's internal questioning. The
threats and violence of the Land League, the 'occult law that from seventy-
nine to eighty-two governed the island'[36] enables and justifies a shift in
sympathies. The landowning classes become the object of pity. They are
presented as powerless and pitiable, victims of an inexorable, unremitting
march of barbarism. Under pressure from the lawless and their progeny
for their renewed ancestral claim to the land, the oppressors become the
oppressed:

> An entire race, a whole caste, saw themselves driven out of their soft, warm
> couches of idleness, and forced into the struggle of life. The prospect
> appalled; birds with shorn wings could not gaze more helplessly on the high
> trees where they had built, as they thought, their nests out of the reach of
> evil winds. What could they do with their empty brains? What could they
> do with their feeble hands? Like an avenging spirit, America rose above the
> horizon of their vision, and the plunge into its shadowy arms threatened,
> terrified them now, as it had terrified the famine-stricken peasants of Forty-
> nine.[37]

The breakdown of naturalistic impartiality signals on one level the
impossibility of using language purely scientifically or referentially and on
another, Moore's intuitive though tense identification with the class that
spawned him. The determination that has brought his class to this abyss
is reflected in the manoeuvres and ambitions of Mrs Barton in her attempt
to snare Lord Kilcarney for her daughter, Olive. Her pursuit is saturated
throughout in law-of-the-jungle imagery. In the hunt for suitable suitors
'women like to hunt in packs. At the death they may fight among themselves, and the slyest will carry off the prey'.[38] The 'slyest' in this case is
Olive's rival, Violet Sculley.

Violet, one of the five girls educated at St Leonard's, is the daughter of
Mr Sculley, the agent for the Barton's and Mrs Sculley, who we are
informed on every occasion she appears in the text, once worked 'behind
a counter in Galway'.[39] Fred Sculley, Violet's brother, a close approximation to the wastrel son-of-the-squire of melodrama, functions in the
plot as a type illustrative of the obsessive and mindless devotion of the
younger rural gentry to horses and gambling. And it is Fred who seduces
the voluptuous May Gould, an incarnation of the sensuality of Ireland.

May, a child 'of an excellent county family' [40] is seduced and abandoned by this epitome of the crass and heartless new bourgeoisie.

The Sculleys are *arrivistes*, representatives of a new, grasping class not far removed from the peasantry. Moore signals his distaste by caricature and speech representation. Mr Sculley we are told 'having lived all his life among bullocks, partook of their animality'.[41] Mrs Sculley's 'degraded' speech betrays her origins in a portrayal which resonates with echoes of the stage-Irish. Having succeeded in eliciting a proposal from Lord Kilcarney, thus defeating Olive and Mrs Barton, Moore has Mrs Sculley respond in the following manner to Violet's triumph:

> Yes, me choild, me choild, yer have been very good, yer have made me very happy, you'll be a mairchioness. Who wid iver have thought I'd have lived to see all this honour when I served in the little shop at Galway.[42]

Lord Kilcarney, newly engaged and now defeated, agrees to Violet's request to accept Mrs Barton's invitation to Brookfield in order to 'humiliate' them–an act of spite presumably meant to be characteristic of jungle victors and the new ascendancy. The text then sends the marquess on a phantasmagoric odyssey through the Dublin night. It is a stylistic rupture which shifts the narrative into the neo-Gothic. The confused and conflicting demands of duty and desire, the public and private, collide, fuse and contradict in an irresolvable manner in the consciousness of the 'little lord'. Bewitched, entrapped, stripped of an independent will, the Gothic intensity of the prose conflates and conjures images of Catholic jubilation with imminent Anglo-Irish decay. O'Connell's statue provokes the thought that it was 'he who had withdrawn the keystone of the edifice, soon to fall and crush all beneath its ruins'. The Bank of Ireland which had protected him till now would give way to a new power which would 'turn him a beggar upon the world'. Trinity College, 'This ancient seat of wisdom and learning would perish before a triumphant and avenging peasant' and the old race of the Kilcarneys would be doomed to 'poverty and banishment'.

Enwombed in darkness, soaked and shivering with fear, unable to return to his hotel, the darkness fills with the phantasms of his persecutors– Parnell, Davitt and Dillon. Surrounded and overwhelmed by the incomprehensible and haunted by history, the emasculated aristocrat imagines a second coming. 'In the mist and mud of the slum plots and counterplots were hatched, and, breaking their shells, they emerged like reptiles into a terrible and multi-form existence: out of the slime they crawled in strange and formless confusion, and in the twilight of nationhood they fought the obscure and blind battle of birth'. Conspiracy, oaths, informers, secrecy, vengeance, assassination, bodies floating in the Liffey, pistol shots and mysterious cries accompany and inhabit his driven, delusive wanderings until he finds himself standing in the centre of O'Connell bridge where, in the immediacy of the present tense,

> Remorse has followed him–the dreary, unrelenting remorse of those too weak by nature for repentance. Now he remembers for the hundredth time how he has sacrificed the grand old name with all its grand associations. The shades of his ancestors crowd about: and how regretfully they seem to reproach him! At every moment the meaning of the word 'ruin' grows more distinct; and in distorted vision he sees down the long succession of consequences. Since his childhood he had been told that it was his duty to restore by matrimony his ancient name to its ancient prestige and power; and he had sacrificed all for that little thin white face that he could see shining before him–a rare, seductive jewel. If he had never met her he would have done what was right; but having once seen her, he could not but act as he had done. No, it was not his fault–he was not to blame. He could not have lived without her; she was life to him, and to possess life he had to accept ruin.[43]

Transfixed, seduced, mesmerised by this particular manifestation of the beauty of Ireland, Kilcarney is left with nothing but his title, a decrepit and debt-ridden estate and the vestiges of a more noble and civilised past. 'Grace', 'nobility' and 'gentility' now reside, it is implied, in the epicene figure of Violet Scully. Violet is a new Hibernia whose 'almost complete want of a bosom gave her the appearance of a convalescent boy', but who nevertheless had 'a sharp but narrow intelligence … an intelligence that would always dominate weak natures, and triumph in a battle of mean interests'.[44] Within this hermaphroditic discursive configuration, processes of emasculation, transference and displacement interfuse and overlap to excuse and exonerate the 'nobility' who being 'noble' are presumably upright and innocent as well. Kilcarney and Moore, though now ordained as ornamental, are as yet unready or unable to accept the changing order. Reality therefore has to be represented as fragmentary; a series of incongruous juxtapositions, hallucinatory constructions and projections.

Throughout the text the painterly set scenes which Moore sketches, contrast light and dark, day and night. This is particularly evident as Alice and the reader venture further into the darkness of the Irish social and political bog. Scenes of order, custom and civility are permeated with the spoken fears of the landed classes and their demands for new coercive measures are lit within an all encompassing penumbra of threatening darkness and menace. The peasants and the poor who people that unfathomable circumference are invariably described as an amorphous mass. They are undifferentiated, ugly, unshaven, unshod, rootless, dirty, animalistic and superstitious. They grunt, spit, cough and speak in the guttural incomprehensibility of Irish. When they are granted speech as in the scene when abatements of rent are being negotiated,[45] they remain unnamed, their presence signified only by their external appearance and speech patterns.

Moore consciously crafts contrasts for obvious dramatic effect. The tenant's bargaining scene is intercut with the haggling between Mrs Barton and Captain Hibbert over the future of Olive; the privileged within contrast with the poor who have their noses pressed against the window panes during the ball at Ballinasloe. He becomes almost sympathetic towards the crowds who watch the carriages pass into Dublin Castle on the night of the drawing-room reception when the debutantes of Irish (polite) society were presented to the Lord Lieutenant:

> Not withstanding the terrible weather the streets were lined with vagrants, patriots, waifs, idlers of all sorts and kinds. Plenty of girls of sixteen and eighteen come out to see the 'finery'. Poor little things in battered bonnets and draggled skirts, who would dream upon ten shillings a week; a drunken mother striving to hush a child that dies beneath a dripping shawl; a harlot embittered by feelings of commercial resentment; troops of labourers battered and bruised with toil; you see their hang-dog faces; their thin coats, their shirts torn and revealing the beast-like hair on their chests; you see also the Irish-Americans with their sinister faces, and broad brimmed hats, standing scowling beneath the pale flickering gas-lamps … Never were poverty and wealth brought into plainer proximity. In the broad glare of the carriage lights the shape of every feature, even the colour of the eyes, every glance, every detail of dress, every stain of misery were revealed to the silken exquisites who, a little frightened, strove to hide themselves within the scented shadows of their broughams; and in like manner, the bloom on every aristocratic cheek, the glitter of every diamond, the richness of every plume were visible to the avid eyes of those who stood without in the wet and the cold.[46]

It was a relentless thesis and antithesis that could only be resolved for Moore in the deterministic synthesis of defeat for the Castle *habitués*. The guardians of ascendancy privilege, 'the huge, black Assyrian bull-like policemen'[47] and the thousands of military who patrolled the colony, whose officers peopled the pages of so many Anglo-Irish novels were, Moore accepted, temporary impediments to the attainment of some form of self-rule.

Within the fiction itself the position of Alice produced its own dialectic. Her intelligence, agnosticism and plainness precluded her from the likelihood of achieving a satisfactory marriage within her own religion and class formation. Her synthesis was achieved through the intervention of Harding, the iconoclastic, worldly, self-regarding, expatriate journalist and novelist who had returned to Ireland to write a series of descriptive sketches in much the same fashion as Moore himself.

Harding has escaped the entrenched and irreconcilable oppositions of Anglo-Irish and native, Catholic and Protestant, wealth and poverty, by denying natality and transferring his identity and sense of belonging to the world of letters and the arts. In conversation with Alice he imperiously predicts and confirms the direction her life will take. He tells her she will get married and that she will go to live in London. He then says:

> Watch life as it flows and breaks about us: do you not see that man's moral temperament leads him sooner or later back to his connatural home? And we must not confuse home with the place of our birth. There are Frenchmen born in England, Englishmen born in Germany–and you are a Kensingtonian. I see nothing Irish in you.[48]

Alice's adventures in Ireland served to articulate and confirm her developing democratic and liberal impulses. By the time she met Dr Reed she had shed her religious beliefs and any vestigial class prejudices and illusions she may have had. She was disillusioned with the narrow philistinism, imaginative poverty and imprisoning conventions of her social existence and Moore implies, she had begun to develop sympathies with nationalism.[49] But while emancipating her thoughts from the constrictions of Anglo-Irish conservatism she nevertheless, like Moore himself, accepted that 'The present ordering of things may be unjust, but, as long as it exists, had we not better live in accordance with it?'[50]

Alice's marriage, Dr Reed's career, her mother's opposition and her own desire for fulfilment combined to obviate the necessity of commitment within Ireland and to justify the defection of the newly married pair. The couple's paternalistic liberalism is gestured towards in a token manner when they pay the rent of a family about to be evicted. The agents however, in a scene from something Hubert O'Grady might have written, 'laughed coarsely'[51] in the knowledge that there were plenty of alternative victims and that they are assured of the grovelling connivance of half a dozen peasants in identifying them. The scene evokes this unlikely piece of portentous orotundity from Dr Reed:

'And to think', said Dr Reed reflectively, 'that they are the same peasants that we once saw so firmly banded together that it seemed as if nothing would ever again render them cowardly and untrue to each other; is it possible that those wretched hirelings, so ready to betray, so eager to lick the hand that smites them, are the same men whom we saw two years ago united by one thought, organised by one determination to resist the oppressor marching firmly to nationhood? And when one thinks of the high hopes and noble ambitions that were lavished for the redemption of those base creatures, one is disposed to admit in despair the fatality of all human effort, and, hearkening to the pessimist, concede with a Mephistophelian grin that all here is vileness and degradation.'[52]

It is an analysis like that of the Young Irelanders such as Richard D'Alton Williams, Thomas D'Arcy McGee and Thomas Francis Meagher who felt 'betrayed' by the failure of the starving to pick up their swords and drive the Saxon out of Ireland.

Such an analysis absolves the middle-class nationalist of culpability and excuses him (*sic*) from the obligation of responsibility, action and leadership. This is a reading which confirms the unreconstructed colonised consciousness of the masses rendering them unfit for bourgeois freedoms. Such fatalism, of course, then frees the bourgeois nationalist or sympathiser to evacuate Ireland and escape into individuality, alienation and anomie. It also liberates the failed nationalist to embrace the virtues and values of the centre which in this case have triumphed, but within a diminished reality. Alice's dream of the union between King and beggarmaid which pre-figures her return to Ireland realises itself as the monocular, uncomprehending reciprocity of

a King who seemed to regard life as a sensual gratification; and a beggarmaid who looked upon her lover, not kindly, as a new born flower upon the sun, but as a clever huckstress at a customer who had bought her goods at her valuing.[53]

Ireland, the text suggests as it draws to a conclusion, has sunk back into a subservient barbarity, characterised in part by the obsequiousness of a defeated peasantry and by the purblind boorishness of the Sculleys. England, by contrast comes to represent a calmer, more civilised order of being. It came too, to represent escape and renunciation.

The coda which deals with 'Mr and Mrs'[54] two and a half years on, borders on the bathetic. Eschewing the poetic aggrandisement that came to be symptomatic of so many autobiographical and fictive rebels, misfits as well as those who departed, Moore relocates Alice and Dr Reed in

London's suburbia. This represented a move from the grotesque to the genteel, from Mayo to mundanity. Stepping outside the impersonal narrative convention of the detached observer and into the monoglossia of a tourist guide, Moore invites the reader on a Cook's tour of the suburban villa inhabited by the escapees. It is an 'ordinary' ten-roomed habitation with its 'yellow paint and homely vulgarity'. A view from the dining-room window looks on 'a commodious area with dust and coal-holes. The 'slender balcony is generally set with flower-boxes' and the house is 'topped by the mock-Elizabethan gable which enframes the tiny window of a servant's room'. Each house has 'a pair of trim stone pillars' while 'the tender green of the foliage in the crescent seems as cheap and as common as if it had been bought–as everything else is in Ashbourne Crescent–at the stores'.

Ashbourne Crescent represents normality, there is 'neither dissent nor radicalism'. The natives of the male variety go to the city every day while the young ladies 'play tennis, read novels, and beg to be taken to dances at the Kensington Town Hall'. On Sunday, in very orderly fashion the denizens of this 'human warren' proceed to Church: 'the father in all the gravity of umbrellas and prayer-books, the matrons in silk mantles and clumsy ready-made elastic-sides; the girls in all the variety of their summer dresses with lively bustles bobbing, the young men in frock coats which show off their broad shoulders'.

This eulogy to the prosaic, the routine and the heartland of English imperialism is suitably underpinned by an equally homespun philosophy– a hymn to an anglocentric status quo:

> To some this air of dull well-to-do-ness may seem as intolerable, as obscene in its way as the look of melancholy silliness which the Dubliners and their city wear so unintermittently. One is the inevitable decay which must precede an outburst of national energy; the other is the smug optimism, that fund of materialism, on which a nation lives, and which in truth represents the bulwarks wherewith civilisation defends itself against those sempiternal storms which, like atmospheric convulsions, by destroying, renew the tired life of man. And that Ashbourne Crescent, with its bright brass knockers, its white capped maidservant, and spotless oilcloths, will in the dim future pass away before some great tide of revolution that is now gathering strength far away, deep down and out of sight in the heart of the nation, is probable enough; but it is certainly now, in all its cheapness and vulgarity, more than anything else representative, though the length and breadth of the land be searched, of the genius of Empire that has been glorious through the long tale that nine hundred years have to tell ...

Neither ideas nor much lucidity will be found there, but much belief in the wisdom shown in the present ordering of things, and much plain sense and much honesty of purpose.[55]

Moore's self-appointed task like that assigned to the Celt in general and Shaw and Wilde in particular, is to entertain, tease, provoke, challenge and amuse John Bull. Unlike Shaw and Wilde however, Moore had no wish to change him. And John Bull it seems, effortlessly assimilates and accommodates the ambitions and energies of Alice and Olive. Alice significantly as a mother is able to reproduce her kind in England while Olive unmarried, is unable to continue the line in Ireland. Ireland meanwhile, is airbrushed out of their daily existence. Alice's new life as a wife, mother and novelist is now normalised, her art made ordinary. Her fate was perhaps, that which Moore was afraid of. As Wayne Hall comments: 'He may have wished to become John Harding but at times feared that Alice Barton's was the kind of life with which he might have to make do'.[56]

Thematically the novel typifies the strangulated confusion of Irish ideological conflict; in that sense it is orthodox and indicative. In its clash of styles and ambiguity of purpose it is 'marked by a hiatus between the experience it has to record, and conventions available for articulating it'.[57] And like so many novels dealing with Ireland it is framed within the entry / exits storytelling convention, a form which presupposes in dialogic fashion an audience other than the Irish in Ireland; one to whom the unique strangeness of the Celt and the country has to be explained.

Moore's writing is, it is usually alleged, modelled on the work of his French heroes–Flaubert, Balzac and Zola. He is generally credited with the importation of realism into the 'English' novel and with developing innovative methods of representing consciousness. France of course, was the second largest imperial power in the late nineteenth century and the early twentieth century. Its bourgeois artists and intellectuals were just as concerned as the English to exploit, explore, celebrate and condemn the colonised cultures of the Empire and to descend into the abyss of proletarian culture–the jungle within. Moore, in those texts overtly concerned with Ireland is borrowing from and mimicking the forms and preoccupations of the imperial centre, although in this case a metropolis traditionally more acceptable to the subject Irish. It may be that Moore's disregard of the English literary canon is as Terry Eagleton remarks, a sign of 'resistance to ... the cultural forms of its rulers'.[58] It is also possible that Moore's 'condition of Ireland' texts reflected the 'condition of England' novels of writers such as Mrs Gaskell, Dickens, Disraeli and the texts of social explorers like Henry Mayhew, James Greenwood and George Sims, whose work appeared in newspaper articles before being collected in book form.[59] Their publication caused intense and widespread interest reflecting the pervasive fascination in the 1880s and 1890s with the East End of London and the working-class districts of the major conurbations. There was a

> ready made contrast between East and West which could be used to refer simultaneously to both London and the Empire, and this became so popular that it led to what can almost be considered a sub-genre of exploration literature, while the increased activity of the churches at this time in setting up 'missions' and 'settlements' provoked a fresh spate of 'telescopic philanthropy' images.[60]

Moore's *Terre d'Irlande* is a text written by a metropolitan provincial for a metropolitan audience. The restraints imposed by the novel form, and in the case of *A Drama in Muslin* through the developing consciousness of Alice Barton, did not apply. The French title gestures to and echoes Zola's *La Terre* (1887) which Zola was then presumably working on, while the English title–*Parnell and his Ireland*–with its possessive pronoun, signals Moore's intended or felt detachment from Ireland and specifically from the Ireland of contemporary reality. The text was originally published as a series of sketches, generic types in an unmediated Zolaesque, olympian form. In Ireland, he informs the reader early on, 'there is nothing but the land':

> The socialistic axiom that capital is only a surplus value coming from unpaid labour, either in the past or in the present, is in other countries mitigated and lost sight of in the multiplicity of ways through which money passes before falling into the pockets of the rich; but in Ireland the passage direct and brutal of money from the horny hands of the peasant to the delicate hands of the proprietor is terribly suggestive of serfdom.[61]

He continues with a recognition that as a landlord he is implicated in the exploitation of the peasantry and that 'it is a worn-out system, no longer possible in the nineteenth century'.[62] But he is incapable of changing; he is paralysed by his class position yet completely aware too, of its essentially parasitic and philistine nature. His efforts to circumscribe that impasse involve the adoption of a strained, self-ironising mockery and a lyrical evocation of Lord Ardilaun's independence, nobility, generosity and taste. The brewer's wealth, as manifested in his estate and fortified castle on the shore of Lough Corrib, insulates him from the threats of the

Land League. In this world of created beauty 'the poetry of the world is never dead':[63]

> And to awake in the cool spaces of a bedroom, beautiful and bright with Indian curtains, and musical with the rippling sounds of the lake's billow, is also full of gracious charm and delicate suggestion of poetry to him who is alive to the artistic requirements of to-day.[64]

Poetry in this instance is the preserve of the plutocrat. The unprivileged and unpoetic dwell beyond Ardilaun's moat, while he remains picturesquely secure behind the drawbridge, protected by battlements and cannon, safe and a figure to be admired for his patrician virtues, his wealth, Protestantism and conservatism; attributes, Moore seems to be implying, he wished he possessed himself.

Most of the articles in the text however, offer a more offensive view of Ireland, its people and its culture. Micky Moran the typical tenant farmer, is described through external features alone. A crude physiological determinism denies him an inner life, spiritual or imaginative. It anthropomorphisises, reifies and dehumanises simultaneously:

> Micky Moran is a strong built man of forty-five: a pair of corduroy trousers, a frieze coat, a dark discoloured skin with scanty whiskers, a snub nose, blue eyes set deep under a low forehead, receding temples and square-set jaws. His face is expressive of meanness, sullenness, stupidity; he is obviously nearer to the earth than the Saxon; he reminds me of some low earth-animal whose nature has not yet risen from out of the soil. He is evidently of a degenerate race–and should perish, like the black rat perished before the brown and more ferocious species. Micky is not a Celt, he is a Fin.[65]

Moore, it hardly needs saying, is a Saxon. In his racial taxonomy, the peasant breeds prolifically and marries early; daughters attempt to ensnare young men into marriage through pre-marital pregnancy. If the attempt fails, she is abandoned. Subsisting on ten acres, subsidised by emigrant children, seasonal migration and constantly afraid of eviction, the peasant in desperation turns to the Land League. Having succeeded in defying the law the next generation, the sons of the peasant plot (in Irish) violence against their superiors. When finally the land is sold off,

> Micky Moran and his like will terrify with assassination and threats of assassination all intending purchasers away–will, in fine, by an intermitting-ness of effort, win back to the Celt the land that was taken from the Celt.[66]

In a slightly less vicious representation Moore sneers at the figure of the priest. His contempt targets his petit bourgeois origins, duplicity, pretension to learning, his greed, meddling in politics and inability to control the activities of the Land League. The priest like the patriot 'is cunning, selfish, cruel ... his blood is thin with centuries of poverty, damp hovels, potatoes, servility; his passions are dull and sullen as an instinct',[67] and in spite of their efforts, priest and patriot will retain 'The thick greasy brogue ... the soul of the soil'.[68]

In concluding his articles, Moore ensured his enduring unpopularity and lack of credibility within Ireland:

> When I took Ireland in the face, the face I have known since I was a little child, I find myself obliged to admit the existence of a race-hatred–a hatred as intense and as fierce as that which closes the ferret's teeth on the rat's throat. The Saxon heart is a noble heart, a heart that is ever moved by generous aspirations, a heart that is full of a love of truth and justice. It was these qualities that gave the Saxon the greatest empire the world has ever known and it will be these very qualities that will now shatter and destroy the empire. The English heart to-day throbs with an hysterical, with a theoretic love of justice.

And he goes on, this intrinsic Saxon love of justice will result in the near future in a free parliament for Ireland:

> Then the Irish-Americans, those who have subscribed millions of dollars to achieve this, will flock to Ireland, and in seven years all the traces of seven hundred years of Saxon conquest will be effaced.[69]

America for this 'Saxon' and for the landlord class in general meant menace, disturbance and threat. America was useful as a depository of embarrassment; a place to send unwanted peasant concubines and their bastard offspring,[70] or to send those cleared from the land. But Irish-America was a community, an idea, a set of values and feelings that landlords could not sympathise or identify with. The force of the Catholic Irish and Irish-American conceptualisation of exile therefore, simply did not register. England was 'home' for the 'Saxon' and Ireland, Mayo particularly, simply an outpost of the metropolitan homeland. The landlords were an 'alien populace, aping both English and Irish manners',[71] living 'in a land of echoes and shadows'.[72] It was as an 'alien' an Irish 'Saxon' a 'mick on the make'[73] that Moore sought attention in the world he had emigrated into. Like John Leech and R.J. Hamerton, two of the 'most brutal traducers of Irish apishness' in the pages of *Punch*, Moore as a marginalised immigrant 'entered into the process of psychological compensation with an almost unholy gusto'.[74] And he entered the process with what Susan Mitchell referred to as 'all the malignity of kinship'.[75]

Confessions Of A Young Man[76] gave most obvious expression to Moore's self-flaunting narcissism. There are, he declares:

> Two dominant notes in my character–an original hatred of my native country, and a brutal loathing of the religion I was brought up in. All the aspects of my native country are violently disagreeable to me, and I cannot think of the place I was born without a sensation akin to nausea. These feelings are inherent and inveterate in me. I am instinctively averse from my own countrymen; they are at once remote and repulsive.

The passage continues with an assertion of intimacy with the French and a reiteration of his love for England. His love for the English is 'foolish', 'mad', 'limitless' and indeed, more profound than that for the French:

> Dear, sweet Protestant England claims me. Every aspect of it raises me above myself, and there is perhaps no moment in my life more intense then when I stand and gaze admiring the red tiles of the farmhouse, the elms, the great hedgerows and all the rich fields adorned with spreading trees and smock frocks. My soul is cheered by the sight of a windmill or a smock, we find neither in the north; the north is Celtic and I am by ancestry a South Saxon. The country of my instinctive aspiration would be Sussex, the most Saxon of all.[77]

This image of England and Englishness, partial, pastoral and Protestant is complemented by his allegiance to his 'connatural' home, the elysian and elitist land of Art; an anti-democratic eden which is 'the direct antithesis to democracy'.[78] The world of art is built on an infrastructure of inequality and injustice which Moore brazenly proclaims is the condition of existence:

> Injustice we worship; all that lifts us out of the miseries of life is the sublime fruit of injustice. Every immortal deed was an act of fearful injustice; the world of grandeur, of triumph, of courage, of lofty aspiration, was built up on injustice. Man would not be man but for injustice. Hail, therefore, to that thrice glorious virtue injustice! What care I that some millions of wretched Israelites died under Pharoah's lash or Egypt's sun. It was well that they died that I might have the pyramids to look on or to fill a musing hour with wonderment. Is there one amongst us would exchange them for the lives of the ignominious slaves that died?[79]

This adolescent 'sub-Nietzschean'[80] posturing, drawing on the Pavlovian response of an insecure, unwanted and parasitic colonial caste, reflects the discursive reaction of threatened élites throughout a democratising Europe. The sneering cynicism is a retreat into a stereotype of aristocratic style–aloof, disdainful, effortlessly and self-evidently superior:

> All men of inferior genius, Victor Hugo and Mr Gladstone, take refuge in humanitarianism. Humanitarianism is a pigsty, where liars, hypocrites, and the obscene in spirit congregate; it has been so since the great Jew conceived it, and it will be so till the end. Far better the blithe modern pagan in his white tie and evening clothes and his facile philosophy. He says, 'I don't care how the poor live; my only regret is that they live at all;' and he gives the beggar a shilling.[81]

Logic, consistency and a 'theoretic love of justice' in this rhetorical formulation are irrelevant. The truth value of the assertion is axiomatically assumed, it inheres in the utterance, while the non-sequiturs and crude elisions existentially defy rationality and accepted intellectual conventions. Hugo's sympathy with the masses, Gladstone's democratic liberalism and the Christian message of love, hope, charity and forgiveness are anathematised. Style and posture become substance; the superficial, the substantive. Paradoxically, the very rupture Moore is trying to enforce between himself and his patrimony is sutured in the pose he adopts. As Eagleton says:

> Style is also the mark of the privileged sensibility of the very social class Moore is busily detaching himself from, so that he remains bound to that social order by the very medium he deploys to satirise it. If art is a reaction to Ascendancy boorishness, it is also an extension of its leisurely self-indulgence.[82]

Moore, the would-be déclassé aesthete and novice nihilist, revelled in his naughtiness. He was precluded from political or social radicalism by the constituent and atavistic conservatism of his class consciousness and the need to preserve his inherited–though insecure–privileges. His need to be noticed, to create an aura of avant-garde provocativeness, channelled itself into the posturing which characterises and disfigures his autobiographical work and into a displacement onto the plane of the pruriently sexual and religious. Both of which in the late nineteenth-century climate of victorian imperial hypocrisy, could be utilised as vehicles for challenging convention without simultaneously upsetting in any profound sense, the order of things. The image of the artist as iconoclast could be inhabited and enhanced, while the landlord continued to receive his rents. Malcolm Brown suggests that Moore had 'little direct knowledge of Nietzsche ... But the doctrine that the artist is Superman was one that his French tutors had led him to embrace, though in his own dubious and inimitable way'.[83]

Brown also deals at some length with the genesis of what from an English perspective is Moore's most famous work, *Esther Waters* which was first published in 1894. The first edition of *Confessions Of A Young Man* included observations on 'Awful Emma', the servant who cleaned his bedroom in the Strand rooming–house which he lodged in on his return to London. Emma, like Micky Moran, is viewed microscopically as sub-human:

> The lodgers sometimes threw you a kind word, but never one that recognised that you were akin to us, only the pity that might be extended to a dog. And I used to ask you all sorts of cruel questions, I was curious to know the depths of animalism you had sunk to, or rather out of which you have never been raised. And you generally answered innocently and naively enough. But sometimes my words were too crude, and they struck through the thick hide into the quick, into the human, and you winced a little; but this was rarely, for you were very nearly, oh, very nearly an animal; your temperament and intelligence was just that of a dog that has picked up a master, not a real master, but a makeshift master who may turn it out at any moment. Dickens would sentimentalise or laugh over you; I do neither. I merely recognise you as one of the facts of civilisation ... Yes, you are a mule, there is no sense in you; you are a beast of burden, a drudge too horrible for anything.[84]

The relatively sympathetic portrayal of Esther contrasting with the description of Emma may, according to Brown, be explained by the circumstances Moore faced in the early 1890s. At that time he says, his reputation was collapsing. *Esther Waters* was 'a gesture of appeasement to the British reading public'.[85] He was desperate for success and influenced by Mrs Pearl Craigie, an American heiress and novelist whom he was courting at the time and whose approval he sought. His subsequent feelings about the novel are traced by Brown revealing ambivalences according to time and place. At times he delighted in its moral reputation as a tract which drew Gladstonian approval for its attack on gambling and its revelations about baby-farming and infanticide. On other occasions he seemed to regard it as a 'breach of his integrity as an artist'.[86] Walter Allen in his introduction to the Everyman edition of 1962 also comments on the oxymoronic discrepancy between the treatment of Emma and Esther and concludes:

though he was as ambitious as a writer can be, he had little native originality. He was incurably literary, which meant that success–or lack of it–in what he attempted depended very largely on the excellence or otherwise of the writers he took as his models. He had come back to England as the apostle of Naturalism, the advocate and defender of Zola; and Naturalism, however wanting it may seem now as a theory of writing, was his salvation. By offering him something worth emulating, it saved him from his own silliness and vulgarity.[87]

Commentators have drawn attention to Moore's attacks on his English victorian predecessors and contemporaries and their treatment of similar themes, notably that of the fallen woman[88] and in particular to his hostility towards Thomas Hardy's *Tess of the D'Urbervilles*, (1891) which as Brown notes, was published during the gestation of *Esther Waters*.[89] They discuss his attacks in terms of moral and aesthetic fidelity, appealing to undeclared notions of verisimilitude and beauty. Moore himself however, offers a liminal leverage into the psyche which could proclaim *Esther Waters* as a quintessentially 'English' novel while simultaneously castigating 'other' English novelists. In his *Epistle Dedicatory* to T.W. Rolleston, the Irish poet and translator, which first appeared in the 1920 edition,[90] he writes, quixotically:

> My dear Rolleston, it is quite in accordance with the humour of the great Aristophanes above us, that an Irishman should write a book as characteristically English as *Don Quixote* is Spanish, and when the author of *Esther Waters* dedicates his work to another Irishman, it must be plain to all that he is holding the mirror up to nature. But there is another reason why I should dedicate this book to you. You are an Irish Protestant like myself, and you could always love Ireland without hating England, and ... But I am past my patience trying to find logic in a dedication which is an outburst of friendly feeling for an old friend.[91]

J.C. Beckett has identified ambivalence as a particular quality of the Anglo-Irish.[92] This is a local instance of the dialectics of 'exaltation-resentment' which unite the 'colonialist to his homeland' and 'give a peculiar shade to the nature of his love for it'.[93] Moore was working within that psychological paradigm described so clearly by Shaw[94] and assumed the role of a literary avatar and artistic explorer. It seems possible then, to read his overreaction to Hardy and his predecessors as a dialectical resentment against their achievement and an assertion of his own importance as an adventurer into the darker regions of the unspoken. Moore it seemed, always needed an enemy, real or imagined, against whom he could reinvent himself. His particular sense of literary identity however, mediated through the Catholic element within his conditioning, the experience of France, his inadequate education, his ignorance of English literature and his acquired and mutating aesthetics within an English market-place, could not be identical with that of Rolleston, an Irish Protestant from birth who had had the benefit of a university education.

In one sense the dedication clearly delights in the subversive inversion of expectation whereby an Irishman can explain the English to the English more clearly than a native Englishman. The address to Rolleston indicates perhaps that only another Irishman could appreciate the irony of the creation, that an English reader could only read the novel transparently, unaware of the paradoxes and parallels encoded in the text. The specific reference to Rolleston's Protestantism may suggest a further refinement, an assumption that only an Irish Protestant (an educated Irish Protestant) could fully appreciate the rich complexities of a text operating on at least two levels. The sudden halt to the flow of the dedication, the aposiopetic break and abrupt shift into a less complex and a more traditional complimentary formulation signals an inability to force through the consequences of the train of thought he had embarked on. It is possible after having gone so far that he was unable to acknowledge that the 'Nature' he was describing was as Irish as it was English and that the symbiotic coupling of love and hate and Ireland and England, involved an examination of complex and contradictory impulses within the text and within himself that he was incapable of disentangling.

More recent critical opinion accepts that *Esther Waters* draws heavily on Moore's Irish background for portraits of a Big House, racing stables, the characterisation of Mrs Barfield and servant life.[95] Read allegorically however, the text also provides a running commentary on the relationship between the classes in Ireland and the relationship between Ireland and England. Esther, like many young Irish women, is illiterate and religious in a simplistic and unquestioning manner and like most of the poor in Ireland, she comes from a large family who are unable to support her. She is also possessed of a certain elementary physical attraction. Woodview with its obsessive interest in horseracing, is clearly a transposition of the Moore Hall of Moore's youth to the Saxon landscape of Sussex, the home of the Bridgers whom Moore visited often. It may also stand for England itself. The Barfields like the Moores in Mayo, are relatively new arrivals in Sussex. 'The Barfields', we are told, 'were not county from the beginning. They only became county three generations ago. Before that they were in trade–livery stable-keepers'.[96] Mrs Barfield shared a similar background to

Moore's mother, a less elevated farmer/small gentry upbringing and similar, simple, religious virtues. The Latches by contrast, are fallen gentry, natives of the county whose fortunes have been in decline for generations but who 'were once big swells' and as William goes on, 'in the time of my great-grandfather the Barfields couldn't hold their heads as high as the Latches'.[97]

William, like most of Moore's creations, is characterised by a crude physiological determinism. He has 'a low narrow forehead, a small round head, a long nose, a pointed chin, and rather hollow, bloodless cheeks ... The low forehead and the lustreless eyes told of a slight, unimaginative brain, but regular features and a look of natural honesty made William Latch a man that ten men and eighteen women out of twenty would like.[98] Throughout William is acknowledged as vain, well-meaning and profligate, a charming spendthrift though ultimately lawless; a representative of an indigenous class resentful of his superiors. At one point he defends his illegal racing book, with a comparison to the daily gambling on the Stock Exchange, pointing out that there is 'one law for the rich and another for the poor'.[99] The 'poor' in this case, the regulars of William's pub the Kings Head in Soho, are like the Irish, hopeless dreamers, lovers of spectacle, addicted to rumour and prepared to gamble on impossible odds. This class of the dispossessed which William represents, can be ruinous for those above them in the social scale. William's father for example, the former steward of Woodview had defrauded the estate, bringing it to the edge of bankruptcy.[100] It can be ruinous also for those below as in the case of Esther, the innocent and exploited servant girl whom William seduces and very nearly destroys.

Esther's fall and abandonment enables Moore to explore in a picaresque manner, the horrors of London low life. Her descent into squalor, the immoral world of Mrs Spires, the petit bourgeois tyranny of service with those such as the Bingleys is contrasted against the momentary happiness she experienced at Woodview in the full bloom of her youth. Woodview nonetheless, according to Mrs Barfield, 'has been the ruin of the neighbourhood; we have dispensed vice instead of righteousness'.[101] When eventually after some eight years of hardship Esther resumes her relationship with William, he informs her of the decline in the fortunes of Woodview–due of course to gambling. The resumption of their relationship also provides Moore with the opportunity to contrast the hedonism intrinsic in the life of William with the proselytising puritanism of Fred Parsons, a joyless figure reminiscent of the Cullen sisters in *A Drama in Muslin*. Fred, as befits the physiological determinism which informs

Moore's writing is a 'meagre little man ... whose high prominent forehead rose above a small pointed face, a scanty growth of beard, moustache failing to hide the receding chin and the red-sealing wax lips; his faded yellow hair was beginning to grow thin on the crown; and his threadbare frock-coat hung limp from his sloping shoulders'.[102]

The description is no doubt intended to undercut and destabilise the seriousness and authority of Fred's message, emphasising its meanness and lack of appeal. But it is also a self-parodying caricature which testifies to Moore's dissatisfaction with himself and the ambivalence he felt towards those like William, capable of enjoying a sensuous engagement with the present. The consumption which eventually destroys William is symbolic no doubt, of the self-inflicted decline in his fortunes and of his class. Their descent into poverty and their degradation inheres in their composition; it is innate, a reflection of an escapable and indifferent Darwinian ordination 'a see-saw up and above and no more than that'.[103]

The death of William who belatedly recognises that his condition was self-induced, a repentance conventionally rendered in the victorian manner, frees Moore to reunite the virtuous Mrs Barfield with the virtuous Esther; Britannia with Hibernia and the ascendancy with their servants. William's death had taken all that Esther had and she turns to Mrs Barfield after some eighteen years as her last hope and salvation; a saviour from within the extended British family rather than from an external agency. It is a forced conclusion and a departure from the conventions of Naturalism as P.J. Keating notes, producing a peculiar hybrid between Naturalism and the English tradition:

> Esther being saved at the last moment from prostitution by the appearance of Miss Rice and later being sheltered by the deeply religious Mrs Barfield, are Victorian solutions; the working-class issue is not resolved but merely postponed by Moore's recourse to the literary conventions of middle-class paternalism. Moore, the reader feels, was always aware that *he* knew what was best for his characters. In spite of the supposedly inexorable forces at work upon her, Esther is finally rewarded for her 'virtue', and we are left wondering if this is to be the case then why should she be shown to suffer such terrible experiences. The answer is that she belongs to the working classes and such experiences are endemic in working-class life.[104]

Keating's anglocentric observations do not explain however, why Moore forces the reunion of Mrs Barfield and Esther; why Esther returns 'home' and why Moore dwells on the diminished reality of Woodview. The English Big House was then in its heyday as so much literature prior to the First World War testifies.[105] The Irish Big House by the 1880s and 1890s was in decay; while gambling and drinking were considered as endemic and destructive diseases within the fragmented social formation of Ireland in an obvious, overt and starkly unmediated form. Moore Hall itself was a considerably poorer place than it had been in Moore's youth. Moore appears to be driving towards an imagined reconstitution of the bonds between the landowning classes (England) and the poor (Ireland). He seems to be suggesting that they can overcome the barriers of privilege and ignorance through the transcendental unity of shared religious belief and practice, a common love for the land, a recognition of a shared humanity and a mutual love for their children. What hope there is for Ireland (and Anglo-Irish relationships) the text implies, rests with the feminine attributes it embodies. Women remain at home to protect and cultivate as best they can in the hope that their errant masculine offspring will see sense and return safely. When they come home it seems, they inevitably cause disruption. This putative alignment is though, unsurprisingly, a fusion which preserves class differences. Although 'the two women came to live more and more like friends and less like mistress and maid', Esther never 'failed to use the respectful 'ma'am' when she addressed her mistress, nor did they ever sit down to a meal at the same table'.[106]

As a closure this is half-hearted and unconvincing. It is compromised, deflated and downbeat in the same manner as the conclusions to *A Drama in Muslin*, *Parnell and his Island* and *Confessions Of A Young Man*. It is a kind of wish-fulfilment which accepts that Mrs Barfield's absentee son Arthur, a figure in some respects not unlike Moore, has effectively and affectively ceased to regard Woodview as home and that Jack, Esther's son, has a future only as a soldier, a servant of the Empire. His role, that of the poor and of Ireland, is to provide the cannon-fodder for the privileged and the servants to attend them.

Allegory, in this instance, enables the text to evade the immediacy of the political imperatives of Ireland and to comment on the literal level on aspects of the English present. Moore resides in two worlds simultaneously; the metaphoric world of Ireland, refracted through memory, and the actual world of the England which he exists in daily. It was a duality of vision common to all 'exiles' which sanctioned his expedition into English culture as well as into the remembered Ireland of his youth. It also licensed his inquiries into the culture that was being 'revived' in Ireland through the efforts of literary émigrés in the late 1890s and early 1900s.

DUBLIN: VOYAGING OUT

While living in London's Victoria Street in 1897, Moore became involved in his cousin Edward Martyn's plans for an Irish Literary Theatre. The first two plays written for the new venture were Martyn's *The Heather Field* (1899) and W.B. Yeats' *The Countess Cathleen* (1899). Both of these were rehearsed in London with an English cast before opening in Dublin.

Moore's attendance at a performance of *The Countess Cathleen* in 1899 was the first of several visits in which he reconnoitred Dublin before he left London and settled in 4, Ely Place in the Spring of 1901. Malcolm Brown argues that Moore's motivation for returning was an amalgam of several factors. His work since *Esther Waters* had been poorly received; he was searching for new inspiration in terms of subject matter and style; he was also disenchanted with England and Ireland offered artistic opportunities for the avant-garde opportunist. Brown also notes that Moore had recorded an interest in folk aestheticism as early as 1893 but that his participation in the folk movement was delayed by 'his active prejudice against folk and peasants' and his advocacy of folk's opposite, 'exoticism and artificiality'.[107] As in the past Moore sought to position himself in the vanguard of literary aestheticism and in his case, at this time, that meant relocating himself in the second city of the English Empire.

The interest expressed by Standish James O'Grady, Yeats and Lady Gregory among others in folklore, reflected the intense bourgeois concern shown throughout Europe in the cultural complements to developing nationalism in the thirty years prior to the First World War.[108] In the consciousness of Irish cultural nationalism, Ireland was contrasted against England. For Moore this manifested itself in a declared and sudden revulsion against language usage in England, cosmopolitanism and a vehement antipathy towards English involvement in the Boer War. *Hail and Farewell* (1914)[109] describes the pretext for Moore's departure for Ireland. Moore claims he obtained information about a plot by the English military to massacre the Boers, led by De Wit, which he publicised through the medium of the Dublin newspaper the *Freeman's Journal*. The plan having been made public, was disowned by the authorities. His prompt actions he asserts, saved the Boer nation and he saw himself as 'the instrument chosen by God whereby an unswerving, strenuous Protestant people was saved from the designs of the lascivious and corrupt Jew, and the stupid machinations of a nail-maker in Birmingham'.[110]

As 'God's instrument' he hears a voice telling him to 'Go to Ireland' where the 'Messiah Ireland was waiting for was in me and not in another'.

But he remained momentarily doubtful as it 'was hard to abandon my project of going to live in my own country, which was France'. The summons was repeated the next morning and again several weeks later and, 'Doubt was no longer possible. I had been summoned to Ireland'.[111] Whether we are to read this as a tongue-in-cheek account of his 'mission' to Ireland or not, it is a stance he maintains throughout the remainder of the text. In this form the presentation obviates the need to explain himself. It overcomes the objections of those in Ireland on a literary and aesthetic level and elevates his motivation to the plain of the directed and divine. Like the ascetic missionaries of Holy Ireland, Moore is impelled and obedient to the call and deaf to the resistance of those he has been called to redeem. This Pauline posturing in the spiritual domain is undercut, intentionally or otherwise, by the absurd burlesque of his scuffle with a workman who had come to replace his window-sill, the collapse of his dining-room ceiling and the drawn out dispute with the company which held the lease to his flat–events which follow on immediately after his self-authored immaculate conception and messianic rebirth. With the £100 obtained for the purchase of the remaining lease, he moved to Dublin. In leaving London he was forsaking a life which 'had gone dead on him, psychologically and artistically, and the way out was to leave, to go into exile from his dead life and make a new life for himself in the old place'.[112]

Moore's then current views on Ireland, art and authenticity were set out in a speech he gave to an audience of supporters of the Irish Literary Theatre in February 1900. The speech 'Literature and the Irish Language' was published with other papers on the new Ireland by Yeats, Hyde, D.P. Moran, A.E. and Standish O'Grady in a collection edited by Lady Gregory in 1901, entitled *Ideals in Ireland*.[113] The speech outlines the objective of presenting an Irish language play in the forthcoming theatre festival. He announces his decision to produce a translation of Yeats' *The Land of Heart's Desire* (1894) as an original text would at this stage in the development of the Irish Literary Theatre be 'too hazardous an adventure'. Lady Gregory, in a brief preface to Moore's speech and in a footnote signals her disagreement with Moore's view that few would understand an Irish language text pointing to the growth of the language movement in Dublin and to Douglas Hyde's recently written *Casadh an Súgáin* (1901) as a potentially popular success. Her editorial intervention registers the opposition felt within literary circles and by implication, wider indigenous opinion, to Moore's return. In many ways it is symptomatic of the resentment felt by those who remained in Ireland against those who left and then returned.

Moore however had his mission, albeit at this moment unrevealed. The speech identifies the purpose of Moore's involvement in the Irish Literary Theatre; it is to revive the native language so that Ireland may 'preserve her individuality among nations'.[114] Having defined 'Religion, Language, Law' as the distinctive features of nations, the text slides swiftly and evasively over religion and the law to focus on language. 'Fellow country-men' he announces,

> the language is slipping into the grave, and if a great national effort be not made at once to save the language it will be dead in another generation. We must return to the language. It comes we know not whence or how; it is a mysterious inheritance, in which resides the soul of the Irish people. It is through language that a tradition of thought is preserved, and so it may be said that the language is the soul of a race. It is through language that the spirit is communicated, and it is through language that a nation becomes aware of itself.

The speech continues with further exhortations to memorial affection and aspirations, and Moore makes clear his view on the relationship of Ireland, Irish and English. He sees Ireland as a 'bi-lingual country', where English will be used 'as a universal language' and Irish will be 'a medium for some future literature'.[115] The speech devotes considerable space to the development of this notion of the language as the medium and bearer of literary aims and values digressing into arcane analogies with Latin and Greek as bearers of living literature. Returning to the nineteenth century, he refers to Walter Pater's view that English was a decaying language asserting the opinion that 'since his death, we have seen the English language pass through the patty-pans of Stevenson into the pint-pot of Mr Kipling'.[116]

Language he suggests, must be pressed into the service of art, aesthetics and individuality. Drifting into the esoteric, he reflects on the Renaissance, Michelangelo, Reynolds, Gainsborough, Manet, Whistler, Degas, Pater and Ibsen, proclaiming that 'the protest of the artist against the taste of the multitude will become sterner, more energetic'. Attacking commer-cialism and modern barbarism he asserts the view that 'Those who believe that dreams, beauty, and divine ecstasy are essential must pray that all the empires may perish and the world be given back to the small peasant states, whose seas and forests and mountains shall create national aspira-tions and new gods'.[117] Appealing finally for a unity of effort in which everyone can contribute; landlord, peasant, nationalist and unionist; some by 'learning the language, some with sums of money, some by having their children taught the language', he concludes by describing his own proposed contribution:

> I have no children and am too old to learn the language, but I shall at once arrange that my brother's children shall learn Irish. I have written to my sister-in-law telling her that I will at once undertake this essential part of her children's education. They shall have a nurse straight from Aran; for it profits a man nothing if he knows all the languages of the world and knows not his own.[118]

It is difficult to imagine that he was not aware of the irony implicit in his offering but nonetheless, he was serious enough to pursue the issue with his brother and sister-in-law. It was an arrangement it appears, in which the peasants, like the poor wet-nurses of London, have their uses. Just as the peasants exist to serve the élite, the native Irish exist to serve Art–in this formulation the artist does not exist to serve Ireland. Hibernia's role is to perform as a handmaiden to the aesthetic, to nourish the Messiah. This attempt to transpose the values of the landlord system and medieval feudalism into the discourses of artistic service and self-sacrifice was naturally enough, rejected as inappropriate and irrelevant. It was difficult as it was for those artists committed to Ireland to make some impact on the consciousness of cultural nationalism–Moore's attitudinising and his history merely ensured his marginalisation. Nevertheless, at the moment of utterance Hone suggests that 'the evidence of his Irish associates and of his own correspondence between 1895 and 1900 reveals him as a man who was in deadly earnest'.[119] And Declan Kiberd points out that his commitment was enthusiastically pursued in the form of numerous interviews and articles for the press.[120]

Hail and Farewell records Moore's attempts to 'serve' the Gaelic League, the resentment still felt in Ireland towards *Parnell and his Ireland* and his characteristic insensitivity to those he had maligned. His foreshortened recollection dismisses the book as 'mere gabble'[121] and he implies, because it is no longer in print it is incapable of causing offence. *Salve* in fact, inverts the resentment felt by Irish opinion transferring hurt to the mock-naïve consciousness of the hero-narrator, whose altruistic innocence is wounded by the rejection he experiences. In conversation with his 'father-confessor' the narrative voice says:

> All I had hoped for was a welcome and some enthusiasm; no bonfires, torchlight processions, banners, bands, *Céad mílle fáiltes*, nothing of that kind, only a welcome. It may be that I did expect some appreciation of the

sacrifice I was making, for you see I'm throwing everything into the flames. Isn't it strange A.E.?

Word or thought association, the free flow of writing dictated to a secretary provides an answer perhaps. Referring to a comment that the painter Whistler made that: 'nothing matters to you except your writing' he asks himself if 'I were capable of sacrificing brother, sister, mother, fortune friend, for a work of art'.[122] Those who knew him in Ireland at the time would almost certainly have provided an affirmative answer.

Moore rejected the advice of Hyde that he might serve Ireland better in England[123] and A.E.'s suggestion that he adopt the persona of Voltaire to challenge the hegemony of the Catholic hierarchy, a role no Protestant could assume. His resolve was 'to give back to Ireland her language'.[124] At the suggestion of John Eglinton he determined to model his planned volume of short stories about Irish life on Turgenev's *Tales of a Sportsman* (trans. 1855) which was written about Russia from the exilic distance of Paris by a member of the semi-feudal landowning class.[125]

The stories were to be written by Moore, translated into Irish by Pádraig Ó Súilleabháin and Tadgh Ó Donnchadha[126] and published in *The New Ireland Review*, a clerical journal edited by Father Tom Finlay. The intention was that the stories would be collected and published as an intermediate textbook for use in Irish schools. The first stories: 'The Wedding Gown', 'Almsgiving', 'The Clerk's Guest' and 'So On He Fares' were written in 'English rather than Anglo-Irish' as 'that pretty idiom' would be of no use to the translator.[127] In *Hail and Farewell* he claims that absorption in the project led him swiftly into the writing of 'Home Sickness' and 'The Exile', neither of which he judged suitable for *The New Ireland Review* or for a school textbook. These six were published under the Gaelic title *An túr Ghort* (The Untilled Field) in Dublin in 1902.[128] They were 'translated into Irish and published in a very pretty book of which nobody took any notice, and that the Gaelic League could not be persuaded to put in its window'.[129] An English language version was published by Fisher Unwin in London in 1903.[130] It included an additional nine stories: 'A Playhouse In The Waste', 'A Letter To Rome', 'Some Parishioners', 'Patchwork', 'The Wedding Feast', 'The Window' and 'Julia Cahill's Curse'. Commenting on the sequence 'Some Parishioners',[131] Moore said it was a 'pity that some more time was not spent on the writing of them, but the English language was still abhorrent to me; and my text was looked upon by me as a mere foundation for an Irish one'.[132] A publisher's note to the 1931 edition informs us that the first English edition

(1903) also contained two stories: 'In The Clay' and 'The Way Back', which were removed from the edition published in 1914 and rewritten as one story 'Fugitives' for that which was published in 1931.[133]

Kiberd has observed that 'the failure of the Gaelic League to respond to the challenge posed by *An túr Ghort* ... convinced Moore that its writers would never create a major literature'. Such a mood shift helps to explain the radical contrast in sympathies and presentation between the earliest stories and those added to subsequent English editions. As Kiberd says, Moore 'could have endured praise or enjoyed abuse but he had no use for apathy'.[134] Inevitably he reacted against the indifference he provoked to produce in stories like, 'The Wild Goose' and 'Fugitives' more overt and directly targeted criticism of Irish life; criticisms momentarily held in check during the early days of his return:

> His high hopes of finding a waiting audience in Ireland had collapsed. His fellow countrymen had lain too long he said 'under the spell of the magicians' to care for the art that he was prepared to bring them.[135]

'The Wild Goose' was written two years after the others and was first published in the 1914 edition. While writing the story it occurred to him that 'it being impossible to enjoy independence of body and soul in Ireland, the thought of every brave-hearted boy is to cry, now, off with my coat so that I may earn five pounds to take me out of the country'. He also discovered at the same time that the only Irishmen who succeeded were 'policemen, pugilists and priests' and that 'Nature did not intend them to advance beyond the stage of the herdsmen–the finest in the world!'[136]

Moore's tinkering with stories and the order in which they appear obscures to some extent the dynamics of his relationship with Ireland and the Revivalists. Nevertheless, that dialogic dependence on the country and his emotional detachment from it, can be charted thematically, stylistically and narratologically in the publishing history of the collection. Its history both incorporates and comments on *The Lake* (1905) and *Hail and Farewell*, the two additional texts produced during the period of his extended preparation for departure from Ireland. A period in which he had become in effect, an internal exile at odds with dominant cultural, political and artistic impulses; responding in oppositional forms which interiorised his rebellion, channelling his dissent and resentment into experimental explorations of consciousness and exposure.

The 1931 edition of *The Untilled Field* with its fifteen stories in all, remains the authorised version on which comment is based. The order in which the stories are presented moves from 'The Exile' and 'Home Sickness' through the other stories set in the west which deal with peasants and priests to those set in and around Dublin, while the final story 'Fugitives' begins in Dublin and concludes in London. Thus, a movement is suggested which takes the reader from Mayo to the east and ultimately to escape. The journey records a migration from primitivism to civilisation, realism to symbolism, past to present. It also parallels Moore's own self-constructed narrative, a move from the barbarism of the west to Paris, Piccadilly and artifice; from illiteracy to literature.

Moore himself described *The Untilled Field* as 'a dry book' which 'does not claim the affections at once'.[137] The title lays claim to originality, reflecting Moore's belief 'that those who remained in Ireland had written nothing of any worth–miserable stuff, no narrative or any seriousness, only broad farce. Lever and Lover and a rudiment, a peasant whose name it is impossible to remember'.[138] The peasant is presumably William Carleton. Maurice Harmon, noting the similarities between Carleton and Moore says:

> Although Moore's themes are almost the same as Carleton's, the range and intensity of his work are much reduced. Post-famine Ireland is a diminished reality, and the sense of vitality, of masses of people lined up for a faction fight, crowding to Midnight Mass, attending stations, going on pilgrimage, getting married, abducting teachers, drinking, courting, being evicted, emigrating, dying, is missing from Moore's world, as it is from that of his contemporaries.[139]

He goes on to remark that Moore's restricted vision focuses generally on 'one of two characters'.[140] That dryness and 'restricted vision', its 'limp syntax and the consequent limpidity of tone are characteristic of Moore's style' as Deane suggests.[141] Those comments are particularly applicable to the stories dealing with the poor and the clergy but less so to those that describe aspects of Ireland and existence that Moore was more familiar and comfortable with. Moore's detached vision of the west may be attributable to the fact that the knowledge he had of it was to a significant extent that which he remembered from his childhood and the visits he made prior to the publication of *Parnell and his Ireland*.

He had attended his mother's funeral in 1895 and stayed with Edward Martyn at Martyn's Galway castle during their revision of *The Tale of a Town* in 1899. His visit to the chapel at Gort to attend mass at Martyn's insistence evokes memories of the hostility his depiction of the service at nearby Ardrahan in *A Drama in Muslin* had engendered[142] and memories of his churchgoing experiences at Carnacun in the 1860s in Mayo. He recalls 'the herd of peasantry', 'our own serfs' who spoke in 'a great clatter of brogues'.[143] At Gort in 1899 he notes 'surly and suspicious fellows, resolved not to salute the landlord', the survival of superstition and he records his 'great shame' at participating in something he did not believe in.[144] His visit to the Feis in Galway in the company of Martyn, Yeats and Lady Gregory in 1901 provokes him to comment on Irish speakers as 'Creatures of marsh and jungle … sad as the primitive Nature in which they lived', they were barely human. 'I had known them since childhood' he says, but he was, he continues, 'always afraid of them'.[145] There are no records of any further visits to the west in any of his autobiographical pictures or in Hone's account of his life until the visit to Moore Hall in 1911 recorded in the final pages of *Vale*, a visit which preceded his exit from Ireland.

The stories then, were written from the safe and unthreatening distance of Dublin. The memories recorded in *Hail and Farewell* it should be emphasised, were written after the publication of *The Untilled Field* and *The Lake* during the period prior to his departure in 1911. They are not therefore co-terminous with the events and occasions recollected and they are of course unverified by reference to alternative versions by those described in the reminiscences. The explanation for the forensic distaste evident in his treatment of the west is explicit therefore in the texts he wrote about Ireland in the 1880s, and in the confessional *Hail and Farewell* written immediately after the texts usually judged to be most sympathetic to the country and its people. The self-imposed objective of appealing to an Irish audience and overcoming the suspicions created by his previous work necessarily imposed stylistic restraints. Those limitations were inevitably stretched by his prejudices. The earlier stories in *The Untilled Field* are in many ways more successful essays in Naturalism than *A Drama in Muslin*. The first seven are presented through the medium of a disengaged omniscient narrator; the next three through the reportage of Pat Comer, a variation on the 'tale told to a visitor' device; while the remainder evidence a perceptible engagement of authorial consciousness.

As exercises in armchair anthropology the stories evoke 'the diminished reality of Irish life'.[146] They are about emigration, puritanical clerical repression and oppression, frustrated sexuality and obsession, individual fulfilment, art and obligation. In *Esther Waters* Moore attempts a faithful phoneticised representation of cockney speech and syntax. Large sections of the story are conveyed to the reader through the direct speech of characters. We learn about their thoughts and feelings through the interaction of extended dialogue. Moore evidently felt confident about and sufficiently at home with London dialect to give over substantial sections of the narrative to 'showing' rather than 'telling' as perhaps he should, given that he lived in the midst of the dialect at the time. That technical facility is less evident in his representations of Irish peasant speech. The speech he does grant the poor tends to be brief and suggestive of peasant usage rather than faithfully reproductive–at least according to the conventions of orthography. Malcolm Brown points out that,

> At the outset he had scornfully rejected the drift of Yeats, Lady Gregory and Synge towards apotheosis of the so-called Kiltartan dialect of Anglo-Irish, the language of *The Playboy of the Western World* and *Spreading the News*. Synge might think that Kiltartan gave to literature the flavour of nuts and apples, but Moore considered it vulgar, identifying it with the brogue and, in turn, with all his deepest prejudices.[147]

It was he claimed, an 'idiom that had hitherto been used only as a means of comic relief. Tricks of speech a parrot can learn'.[148] He dismissed Lady Gregory's 'beautiful speech' as 'no more than a dozen turns of speech, dropped into pages so ordinary, that redeemed from these phrases it might appear in any newspaper without attracting attention'.[149]

The Preface to *The Untilled Field*[150] claims that the text was a landmark in Anglo-Irish literature and 'Synge could not have passed it by without looking into it'.[151] This is a retrospective assertion of originality which overlooks his own practice in an attempt to establish his pre-eminence. Incongruously perhaps, the very lack of emphasis on dialect confers a degree of dignity. Authorial neutrality in this instance offers his successors a usable model for exploring a comatose culture–from a distance.

The western and agrarian landscapes Moore sketchily summons up as a backdrop to the Mayo and rural stories emphasises the emptiness and loneliness identified by William Wilde and George Petrie,[152] and reiterated in the public discourses of churchmen and politicians which charged Ireland's rulers with systematically depopulating the countryside. The imprecision and vagueness of the descriptions act as a kind of objective correlative to human emotions of sadness, melancholia and spiritual desolation. The ill-defined haziness also acts to suggest the temporal distance of the writer's urban present from that of his experiential past.

Absence and memory edit, select and focus, while the short story form itself tends to preclude heterogeneity. Nonetheless, as Harmon and Deane imply, there is in *The Untilled Field* a particularly narrow vision of life in the west seen through the single optic of remembered prejudice. The four stories most concerned with peasant emigration are 'The Exile', 'Home Sickness'. 'The Wedding Feast' and 'Julia Cahill's Curse'. 'The Exile' sets up an opposition between two brothers Peter and James Phelan, the sons of a small farmer Pat Phelan, for the love of Catherine, a figure who embodies the virtues of Ireland. She perversely, loves the more ineffectual Peter, an indecisive dreamer and failed priest. While in the convent to which she retreated after Peter's entry into Maynooth, Catherine envisions in a kind of inverted *aisling* the departure of James, the son capable of making something of the farm, for America and old Pat Phelan sitting alone without anyone to look after him. Her duty she decides, is to the living, which provokes the Reverend Mother to reflect on Pat Phelan's visit to the convent to plead for the release of Catherine in order to marry Peter and the belief that Catherine's 'mission was perhaps to look after this helpless young man'.[153] Catherine recognises that her destiny will not provide fulfilment as 'she knew that Peter would never love her as well as James, but her vision in the garden consoled her, for she could no longer doubt that she was doing right in going to Peter. that her destiny was with him'.[154]

James Bryden returns from the Bowery in 'Homesickness' to an etiolated Duncannon to restore his health–he is in a sense, sick *for* home. The people and the landscape are even more impoverished than when he first left thirteen years before. His plans to marry Margaret Dirken, a figure emblematic of Irish femininity, founder due to his inability to come to terms with the Ireland he has come 'home' to. His thoughts fly back to New York and recoil against 'the pathetic ignorance of the people' and 'the priest who came to forbid the dancing'; inducing in him a hatred of 'the spare road that led to the village' and 'the little hill at the top of which the village began and he hated more than all other places the home where he was to live with Margaret Dirken'.[155]

In something like a panic he flees Ireland–sick *of* home–and abandons Margaret who nonetheless, continues to exist vestigially in his mind as part of the 'unchanging silent life'[156] of the emigrant.

Kate Kavanagh in 'The Wedding Feast' also rejects Irish customs and piety when she refuses to consummate the marriage made for her by Father Maguire and her mother. Announcing her decision to her mother

> she took the wedding ring off her finger and threw it on the ground. 'I shut the door on him last night, and I'm going to America today. You see how well the marriage that you and the priest made up together has turned out'.

Her spirited individuality is articulated by her remarks to her other suitor, Pat Connex, as she leaves: 'I'm thinking one must go one's own way, and there's no judging for oneself here. That's why I'm going'.[157]

Julia Cahill is another incarnation of independence, sexuality, youth and energy. She resists Father Madden's attempts to tame her by marriage and asserts her right to choose for herself. The priest then forces her father to evict her, whereupon she finds shelter with a blind woman who lives in a cabin on the edge of the bay. After a further two years she leaves to go to America or, as some in the village believe, to join the fairies. Either way she departs having left a curse on the village which was that 'every year a roof must fall in and a family go to America'.[158]

The storyteller in the linked stories 'A Playhouse In The Waste' and 'Julia Cahill's Curse' is Pat Comer, an organiser for Plunkett's Irish Agricultural Organisation Society, and an agent therefore of modernisation. He relates what he saw and heard in Mayo to a group of fellow middle-class Dublin clubmen. It is a narrative device commonly employed in the nineteenth and early twentieth centuries to describe, distance and contain the bizarre, exotic and supernatural. It releases the authorial voice from referential identification and the convention of realism, allowing the venturer into the strange and unknown report back to the centre–to normality. Pat Comer's story, filtered through rumour and communal superstition by the jarvey who drives him around Mayo, concludes with the following comments and exchanges:

> And I noticed that though the land was good, there seemed to be few people on it, and what was more significant than the untilled fields were the ruins for they were not the cold ruins of twenty, or thirty, or forty years ago when the people were evicted and their tillage turned into pasture–the ruins I saw were the ruins of cabins that had been lately abandoned, and I said:
> 'It wasn't the landlord who evicted these people'.
> 'Ah, its the landlord who would be glad to have them back, but there's no getting them back. Everyone here will have to go, and 'tis said that the priest will say Mass in an empty chapel, sorra a one will be there but Bridget, and she'll be the last he'll give communion to. It's said, your honour, that Julia has been seen in America, and I'm going there this autumn. You may be sure I'll keep a look out for her'.[159]

Emigration is thus imagined as escape. America, the destination of all the poor escapees is haven, hope and ambition–it is also the milch cow which sustains the obsessive church building in Ireland.

This kind of specification locates the motivation for emigration clearly and unequivocally within Ireland itself. It is the nature of Ireland, its barrenness, superstition, purposelessness and clerical proscription which drives away the young, talented, ambitious and energetic. The alternative clerical explanation is given by Father MacTurnan, the kindly, well-meaning and ineffectual central figure in 'A Playhouse In The Waste' when he responds to Comer's questioning by saying:

> God has specially chosen the Irish race to convert the world. No race has provided so many missionaries, no race has preached the Gospel more frequently to the heathen; and once we realise that we have to die; and very soon, and that the Catholic Church is the only true Church, our ideas about race and nationality fade from us. We are here not to make life successful and triumphant, but to gain heaven. That is the truth, and it is to the honour of the Irish people that they have been selected by God to preach the truth, even though they lose their nationality in preaching it.[160]

There is a relentless determinism at work in both versions which mirrors Darwinian biologism and which even the benevolent landlords and priests, either individually or in the form of the IAOS, are powerless to prevent. It is also a post-feudal age, unlike the pre-1870 era when the Moores like other landlords 'often sundered wife and husband, sister and brother; and often drove away a whole village to America if it pleased us to grow beef and mutton for the English market'.[161] The volume of emigration was so great at this time, that it was perfectly possible for Moore to visualise two millions as the 'ideal population for Ireland'.[162]

The peasant world of the west that Moore's own sleight of hand conjures up is however, curiously myopic and thinly textured. Physical descriptions are weak and enervated; the landscape, watery, inert, devoid of life, human or natural. The vision is level, fixed and stagnant. There is little impression of the change of seasons, growth, renewal or new birth. Nor is there any sense of human interaction with the land in actual, symbolic or ritualistic forms. The human beings live in isolation. There is an absence of lived social existence represented by fairs, sport, school, songs, music, storytellers, wakes, humour, communal festivities, harvesting, holidays, customs and political meetings. References to the Big House are sorrowful and regretful as though there were none left at all and they imply that their demise has been instrumental in the desolation of the landscape. Work itself is missing; making, mending, training and growing.

Families are oddly deformed; mothers are frequently absent or hardly featured, while siblings are invariably confined to one. Characters like Catherine in 'The Exile', James Bryden and Julia Cahill, exist without brothers and sisters while few protagonists have more than one parent, if they have parents at all. There is a marked omission of children, grand-parents and extended family networks and an absence of social range which might differentiate between occupations and classes. The social and communal events such as parties for homecomers and American wakes are similarly off the page, while the daily acts and communicative events of village and town life are also unrepresented lacunae.

Moore's monocular focus excludes too, the Gaelic language tradition of the *dindshenchas*, the poetry of place and the recognition of the spiritualised genealogical identification of people and topography. The vacant sub-lunar landscapes he nebulously etches are interchangeable; severed of any human investment and personal attachment. An appropriate habitation possibly, for a gallery of deracinated isolates; one from which any would-be emigrant would be glad to escape. There is no room here for the weight of Gaelic Catholic Irish tradition, with its memorial ties and affections; no space for ambivalence, love and heartache or acknowledgement of the emotive and linguistic force of *deorai*. Mother Ireland like Biddy McHale in 'The Window', is infertile, obsessed, in thrall to a monomaniacal vision:

> a god demanding human sacrifices, and everybody, or nearly everybody crying: Take me, Ireland, take me; I am unworthy, but accept me as a burnt offering. Ever since I have been in the country I have heard people speaking of working for Ireland. But how can one work for Ireland without working for oneself? What do they mean? They do not know themselves, but go on vainly sacrificing all personal achievement, humiliating themselves before Ireland as if the country were a god. A race inveterately religious I suppose it must be! And these sacrifices continue generation after generation. Something in the land itself inspires them. And I began to tremble lest the terrible Cathleen ní Houlihan might overtake me. She had come out of that arid plain, out of the mist, to tempt me, to soothe me into forgetfulness that it is the plain duty of every Irishman to disassociate himself from all memories of Ireland–Ireland being a fatal disease, fatal to Englishmen and doubly fatal to Irishmen.[163]

Ireland is primeval, puritanical, a purgatory policed by priests – a near dystopian antinomy to the rough elysium of Moore's contemporaries Somerville and Ross, those most rooted of the Anglo-Irish.

When the locale of the collection transfers to urban Dublin and its environs, Moore maintains 'a strong central preoccupation with loneliness and poverty and various kinds of despair' as John Cronin notes.[164] The stories also acquire a pronounced authorial presence which manifests itself in the form of a more confident and involved omniscient voice in 'The

Clerk's Quest', the existential musings of the first person narrator in 'Alms-Giving', and the sympathetic implied author of the allegory 'So On He Fares'. In 'So On He Fares' the protagonist Ulick Burke is driven from home by his mother's cruelty. When he returns after years of seafaring,

> He could see that his mother wished to welcome him, but her heart was set against him now as it had always been. Her dislike had survived ten years of absence. He had gone away and had met with a mother who loved him, and had done ten years' hard seafaring. He had forgotten his real mother–forgotten everything except the bee and the hatred that gathered in her eyes when she put it down his back; and that same ugly look he could now see gathering in her eyes, and it grew deeper every hour he remained in the cottage.[165]

His mother Catherine, is as Malcolm Brown observes, Ireland, and his surrogate mother, France.[166] Driven away again from home he realises 'In this second experience there was neither terror nor mystery–only bitterness'. He resists thoughts of suicide because 'life had taken hold on him'.[167] As an analogue of his own rejection by the 'terrible Cathleen ní Houlihan', the title prefigures the narrative trajectory of the collection as a whole in proleptic fashion and signals the inevitable over-arching shape of *The Lake* and *Hail and Farewell*. Each of the three texts is some form of voyage or journey into self-realisation.

The 'incessantly intrusive' narrative position Moore comes to adopt in later stories 'directs our thoughts and feelings about the materials and as these authorial personae occupy the front of the stage, the people in the stories get pushed into the background, distanced from us by the general slackness and indecisiveness of the form'.[168] The changes in form and tone however, are based on the circumstances of their composition. By the time Moore came to write 'The Wild Goose' he had broken with Yeats, Lady Gregory and the Gaelic League. Yeats was the undisputed leader of the Revival and the Gaelic League remained suspicious of the intentions and products of the English language literati. Moore having vacated England now found himself spurned by Ireland or at least the Ireland that he aspired to lead. He was, in addition, handicapped by his willingness to continue with his neo-realist investigations and portrayals of Irish social life and relations. What was left to him in Ireland therefore, was an excavation and exploration of his latent or momentarily suspended loathing of Irish culture; the countervailing attractions, his inexhaustible fascination with himself and the way–within a sedentary lifestyle–his mind moved.

Throughout the period of his sojourn in Ireland Moore had maintained close links with France and England and was as ever, preternaturally alert to new ideas and movements in the artistic world. Hone documents numerous visits to France particularly to see Dujardin, to Bayreuth and to England where he frequently stayed with aristocratic friends such as Lord Howard de Walden, Lord Grimthorpe and Lady Cunard.[169] Such associations and contacts provided him with access to avant-garde developments in the arts and images of tradition, order and stability.

'The Wild Goose' is at sixty-three pages by far the longest story in the collection and is in part realistic, in part allegorical and in part symbolist. Ned Carmady, the eponymous 'Wild Goose'–an appellation inadvertently comic in relation to the heroic resonance of the term Wild Geese from which it derives–returns to Ireland to write about it. Moore provides him with a colourful biography. He left Ireland at the age of nine, settled in Manchester with his parents, grew to hate the manifestations of industrialisation and joined a travelling circus at the age of sixteen. When the lion he was responsible for died he was sacked. In Havre (*sic*) he made his living by playing the fiddle and then earned his passage to America in a similar fashion. In the USA he became a map maker (while continuing to play his fiddle), a journalist, an editor, then a war correspondent in Cuba and a participant in the war itself. The war ended before he made the rank of general and he then decided to go to Ireland. The relation of his life story to the representatives of bourgeois Catholic Ireland, the Cronins, elicits contrasting responses. Mr Cronin the inheritor of 'a pretty Georgian house' is a unionist, a guardian of 'tradition and habits that appeal to the wanderer' and evidently satisfied with the status quo. He notes that Carmady came to Ireland as 'a rolling stone' who will one day 'roll out of it'. His daughter Ellen however, is another feminine representation of Ireland in a nationalist/Catholic mould. Her reaction to Carmady's return is to claim him for the nationalist cause. She disagrees with her father saying:

> No father, he is going to stay in Ireland. Ireland wants a new leader, and the leader must come from the outside.[171]

Carmady's earliest impressions of Ireland on his return are of a 'slatten life, touched by the kindness of the people' denied the 'art of verbal expression'[172] and that 'it was a mistake to interfere with the genius of the Irish people "which is herding cattle"'.[173] Beguiled and entranced by Ellen/Ireland, mythology and pre-colonial history, Carmady succumbs to the innocent sexuality of Ellen and the vision she offers him of political

leadership. The vision he subscribes to however, remains oddly unspecified and devoid of content, it exists at a vague level of generality, a desire
to 'regenerate Ireland'[174] which co-exists with his fascination with 'the
charm of tradition'.[175] Their marriage and departure from Brookfield
symbolise a break with the system of received values, while their move to
a 'villa between Kingston and Dublin'[176] signals a shift into the homogenising ordinariness of modernity.

In the absence of the articulation of political ideals Moore offers us
instead symbolism, lyricism in the moonlight; an edenic otherworld,
which binds Carmady to the beauty of Ireland, its past and to Ellen in a
momentary communion of body and soul in which he says 'I feel that a
spell is upon me'.[177] The paradisal moment climaxes in their discussion of
Carmady's forthcoming trip to America, the concern Ellen/Eve expresses
about her loss of physical appeal during her pregnancy and Ned's
constancy; a discussion which takes place under their favourite apple tree.
When Carmady shakes the tree we are told that 'their apple gathering
seemed portentous'. In narrative terms this pivotal moment or *peripeteia*
marks Carmady's psychic, if acknowledged, break with Ireland. The spell
it is implied, has been broken.

Ellen's ethereal, semi-divine appeal which had bewitched him, is after
the moment of birth dispelled onto the plane of the domestic, the physical
and the prurient; while her decision to baptise the child as a Catholic
effectively estranges Carmady's affections. That estrangement from the
child, Ellen and Ireland grows and is compounded by his increasingly
virulent anti-clericalism, his plan to use her money to found a newspaper
called *The Heretic* and Ellen's consultation with Fr Brennan. The consequences of their diminishing emotional attachment are to weaken the
attractiveness and stature of Ellen and to liberate Carmady from 'the
sensual coil that had bound them'.[179] It is a severance Moore underwrites
with a philosophy of inevitability. Carmady musing on the breakdown of
his relationship with Ellen says that there are three periods within a
relationship:

> a year of mystery and passion, then some years of passion without mystery,
> and a period of resignation, when the lives of the parents pass into the
> children and the mated journey on, carrying their packs. Seldom, indeed,
> do the man and woman weary of the life of passion at the same time and
> turn instinctively into the way of resignation like animals.

Moore's intimate identification with the thought processes and
behaviour of Carmady absolve the 'wanderer' of responsibility for the

breakdown of the marriage. Ellen, we are informed through the consciousness of Carmady, 'brought herself to betray the man she loved to a priest' and that 'he had laid no trap; she had walked into one and must pay for her indiscretion'.[180] A fact she herself recognises when she says, 'But, Ned, you could not live with anyone, at least not always'. Carmady reassures himself with the thought that 'Another would not have satisfied her instinct; constancy is not everything'.[181]

The narrative resolves itself in actual and symbolic terms with an exposition on the paralysing power of the parish priest, yet the closest Carmady/Moore comes to laying a specific charge against the priesthood is the suggestion which fuses the failure to develop an indigenous art tradition with the power of the priest–a lacuna which conveniently overlooks the intervening centuries of conquest and colonisation. In the absence of the particular the text slides into the symbolic. While strolling on the hill of Howth, a landscape redolent with pre-Christian associations, Carmady is disturbed by an image of flight; he hears

> a whirring sound, and high overhead he saw three geese flying through the still air. War had broken out in South Africa; Irishmen were going out to fight once again the stranger abroad.

The vision vanishes, shrouded in mist, which also obscures the flute player whose 'dolorous melody' he categorises as 'The Wailing … of an abandoned race'.[182] A melody which 'is the song of the exile, the cry of one driven out into a night of wind and rain, a prophetic echo'.[183]

The epiphanic revelation, shared with Ellen, evokes from her a gesture of release; a self-sacrificing abnegation which absolves Carmady of obligation and guilt, whilst assuring him nevertheless of her life-long commitment to her vows. Moore also attempts to overcome the amorality of Carmady's abandonment of his son by suggesting that in bringing up the child as a Catholic she had effectively severed the links of parental love and responsibility; the Church it is implied, will act as a surrogate father. The moment of separation between father and son is also a moment of denial; a moment when the self-evident radiance of Carmady's conviction blinds the boy whose vision is impaired by his saturation in Catholic obscurantism. On being awoken to say farewell:

> He put up hands into his eyes and looked at his father, and then hid his face in his mother's neck, for the light blinded him.[184]

The coda both employs and transforms the convention of the hero sailing away from Ireland. In the ballads of popular literature the hero (*sic*) left regretfully, driven out by others. Carmady leaves voluntarily 'possessed by the great yearnings of the wild goose when it rises from the warm marshes, scenting the harsh north through leagues of air, and goes away on steady wing-beats'. In this kind of representation the leaving of Ireland is imaged as a form of elementalism, an instinctual drive determined by natural forces.

It is also an intensely individualistic act, volitional, self-determined; an act of symbolic liberation and a declaration of freedom. In venturing out of the womb of Mother Ireland into the infinity of sky and sea, the iconoclast also severs the umbilical cord in a gesture of self-delivery and self-definition. Unlike the exiles of nationalist symbology however, the self-aggrandising intellectual exile faces up to the future. In this instance Carmady faces the 'what is to come' ambivalently, glad to be free of the 'base moral coinage in circulation' (no matter how ill-defined). He is 'at one moment ashamed of what he had done, at the next overjoyed that he had done it'.[185] John Wilson Foster has remarked that:

> What we have in Carmady's return to Ireland, period of enchantment, and disillusionment is a vision of Moore's own adventure with the revival, and it suggests that the adventure was over by the time the story was written. The three stages of Ned's involvement are those Moore later entitled 'Ave', 'Salve', and 'Vale' when recounting his own story. Interestingly enough, they are the three phases of marriage, as Ned sees them.[186]

Moore's play with the tropes of Irish femininity in the works written in Ireland between 1901 and 1911 (including those subsequent re-writings and additions) confirms and defies traditional portrayals of Ireland and feminine individuality. She is variously figured as hag and harridan, seductress and enchantress in prose echoes of pre-nineteenth-century representations. Fictive formations, no doubt, drawn in part from Yeatsian formulations and the redactions of Lady Gregory and Standish O'Grady. At the same time however, Moore creates in the characters of Kate Kavanagh, Julia Cahill, Nora Glynn and Lucy Delaney individuals whose defiance of priests and patriarchy contrasts with the moral ambivalence and aphasic departures of Bryden, Carmady, Fr Oliver Gogarty and the 'I' consciousness of *Hail and Farewell*. But denied an enabling and textually dense existence in a complex and multifarious social and political reality, their rebellion is represented principally in terms of sexuality and repression. There is a kind of voyeurism pervading the images which is perhaps, as partial and imprisoning as that which the texts ostensibly defy.

Moore's continued interest in self-realisation led to the novel *The Lake* and to the novelised autobiography *Hail and Farewell*, the first volume of which was published in 1911. Both of course, explore the growth of consciousness against the background of Ireland and both conclude with the departure of the principal protagonist. Each work like the final story in the 1931 edition of *The Untilled Field*, 'Fugitives' views departure as escape, while all three texts are muted in their expression of leaving as exile. Oliver Gogarty, the priest whose consciousness is explored in *The Lake* fakes his own suicide and escapes into anonymity in America. Moore himself, portrays his own departure as an act of sacrifice. Referring to *Hail and Farewell* he says that he felt that:

> I must leave my native land and my friends for the sake of the book; a work of liberation I divined it to be–liberation from ritual and priests, a book of precept and example, a turning point in Ireland's destiny.[187]

It was a religiose compulsion which led to his unheroic exit from Ireland 'On a grey windless morning in February'[188] prior to the publication of 'Ave' in 1911, which he knew would cause offence amongst those portrayed. Rodney, the sculptor, abandons Ireland after his sculpture of Lucy Delaney is broken. His despair at the philistinism of Ireland induces an apostrophe in which he declares:

> There is no place in Ireland for an artist ... nor yet for a poor man who would live his life in his own way. The rich leave Ireland for pleasure, and the young fellow who would escape from the priests puts it differently. 'Off with me coat' he says, 'to earn five pounds that'll take me out of Ireland'.[189]

The destination for each of these escapees is freedom. It becomes difficult therefore to present their flight as exile. The term is employed ironically in 'Fugitives' when Rodney, Carmady and Harding meet in Piccadilly, the hub of the English imperium. Yet, it does not feature in any text of Moore's in the same form, carrying the meanings, as that utilised in the discourses of Gaelic, nationalist, Catholic Ireland. Moore's paradoxical position as a Catholic and a landlord gives him entry into peasant life and Catholic consciousness which few Protestant writers felt fully capable of. However, his ineffable indifference to those he knew and wrote about, his antipathy towards the aspirations of the unemancipated and his affiliation with the culture of the English effectively excluded his full affective identification with those he described in Ireland–Catholic or Protestant.

The upset the trilogy generated–'a work of stylish malignance'[190]– inevitably provoked angry responses. Susan Mitchell's *George Moore* (1916) spoke for many in its hostility. She writes of him as a man who has 'profaned his home, his parents, his most sacred ties, to whom writing is father, mother, home, lover, friend, life itself, who when he ceases to write will cease to live and will crumple up shapeless, nameless, mortal'.[191] 'He is', she asserts, in a later chapter, a 'primitive, indeed, infantile man, as sure of himself as the baby is. He has escaped all altruism wherewith the guardians of our youth so early confound our confidence in ourselves ... Mr Moore, has never got beyond babyhood in his character, and few women can have known him long without that desire to slap him that is the normal woman's attitude toward an aggravating baby.'[192] Yeats in 'Dramatis Personae' (1935) gains revenge on Moore for the mocking portrayal of himself in *Hail and Farewell*. Moore he suggests, had the qualities of a peasant, for he 'sacrificed all that seemed to other men good breeding, honour, friendship, in pursuit of what he considered the root facts of life'.[193] He emerged 'from a house where there was no culture'.[194] He was 'a man carved out of a turnip ... he spoke badly and much in a foreign tongue, read nothing, and was never to attain the discipline of style'.[195] Moore's friend, John Eglinton in his *Irish Literary Portraits* (1935) refers to him rather more sympathetically as one who 'remained outside all companionship of causes and crusades, a pathetically lonely figure, lonely both as artist and man'.[196] And he remembers him in his old age in London as 'a die-hard Britisher of the old type'.[197]

It is perhaps more fitting then to view Moore, not as an exile from Ireland in terms of its commonly understood meaning within Ireland at the time, but as an isolate, estranged and alienated from his filial home and family; an anomic affiliate of English culture. His abandonment of Ireland may then be read as an escape from the consequences of his artistic exhibitionism, exploitation and a re-entry into a marginal form of Englishness.

CONCLUSION

Moore, in many ways, came to typify important aspects of the image of artistic exile in the late nineteenth and early twentieth centuries. He was déclassé, deracinated and iconoclastic in terms of his cultural origins and inherited cultural practices. His art proclaimed an exclusivity, a concern with itself and the opinions of a similar self-selecting coterie of thinkers, painters, musicians and writers. This was a position which his independence, freedom from financial and material want, and his inexperience of the world beyond the boundaries of Art, underwrote. Like other early modernists, he opposed and broke from the restraints of established hegemonic conventions. In his case these were Catholicism, patrician obligation, family and duty and emergent nationalism. He opposed too, in conventional modernist manner, the commercialisation and massification of western industrialised democracies. In imitation of his Parisian heroes he sought new kinds of signification, rebelling against and rejecting forms of sentiment and expression embedded in received and dominant (in his case) anglophone cultures.

Moore's journey however, through Naturalism, Realism, Symbolism and autobiography was never merely technical or solely in a dialectical reaction against the already existent. As Raymond Williams observes, the reality of opposition and estrangement which so characterised modernist thought and behaviour was made possible by

> the availability within a new kind of social formation of social relationships which eventually corresponded to the practical initiatives. These were found within the social form of the metropolis: typically the imperial metropolis of Paris, London and eventually New York. An extraordinary number of the innovators were not so much exiles and émigrés, though that was how they started, but immigrants which is where the conditions of their practice formed. Distanced from, though often still preoccupied by, more local cultures, they found the very materials of their work–their language, which writers had once fully shared with others; their visual signs and representations, which shared ways of life had carried–insufficient yet productive in one crucial way: that writers, artists and intellectuals could share this sense of strangeness with others doing their kind of work but who had begun from quite different familiarities.[198]

Out of that shared dislocation and cultural plurality, heteroglot and polyglot though by and large eurocentric, emerged versions of trans-national and transcendent artistic hybridity and community, of artistic universality which superseded the particular. Williams goes on to assert that in time these metropolitan centres come to acquire a dominance over influential groups of intellectuals and artists and says 'what began in isolation and exposure ended, at many levels, in an establishment'.[199] A corollary of that dominance was the indiscriminate elision of terms of displacement, imaging virtually all supra-national or extraterritorial artists, in Steiner's term[200] as exiles, regardless of the circumstances of their actual removal or departure from the culture that bore them. It was a world-view that metaphorised the exile, the emigrant and the émigré as citizens of 'the modern country of the arts ... a country that has come to acquire its landscape, geography, focal communities, places of exile', where 'The writer himself (*sic*) becomes a member of a wandering, culturally inquisitive group–by enforced exile ... or by design and desire'.[201] But Malcolm Bradbury's figurative aggrandisement in that last formulation, his inflation and conflation of degrees of separation, fails to distinguish between the psychic weight and cultural force of terms within the lexicon of dislocation. The experiences of those who fled tyranny, torture, death sentences, starvation and eviction *is* qualitatively different from those who *choose* to flee ennui, provincialism, and communal conformity. Similarly, there are distinctions of reality and authenticity to be made between those psychically, culturally and artistically formed within a metropolitan centre and those shaped by a colonial experience.

The terms in which Moore couched his notion of exile are understated, individualistic, narcissistic, solipsistic and modernist. There is no recognition of his work of communal affinity or acknowledgement of the elements within Ireland or England that authored him. He is, in a sense, self-defined and that definition slips and shifts according to time, place and his imagined audience. Radically unconnected to home, community, history or belief, Moore came to exist perceptually in language and posture alone. It is a posture of self-creation, characterised by absorption, confession, reverie, digression, memory, meditation, protest, egotism, self-ironising autobiography and betrayal. In Moore, as Eagleton puts it,

> style becomes a kind of willed repression or amnesia, a scrupulously externalising medium which sets its face against portentous metaphysical depth and operates as suavely ironic detachment from historical reality.[202]

Moore is perhaps, ultimately marooned in an ontogenic emptiness: sign and symbol signifying absence; a vicarious voyeuristic, antinomian nothingness whose presence registered his irrelevance and anachronistic prescience. His departure appropriately, was barely noticed and his return to England received with indifference. It was in fact a repatriation to 'normality', 'civility' and 'home'. His gestures were the return of an 'exile' and the defection of an artistic apostate, a faithless renegade. *Hail and Farewell* then, that work of 'liberation', 'the sacred text', memorialises betrayal, it stands as a monument or testament to egocentricity and the perfidy of the self-obsessed, self-made artificer.

He was nonetheless, an important though now neglected figure in the development of Irish writing. His experimentalism 'was to prove ... attractive to Irish writers, for whom such interrogation was a necessity if they were to write at all'.[203] His preoccupation with Ireland, the role of the artist, sexual repression and individual freedom prefigured the work and concerns of others such as James Joyce, Frank O'Connor, Seán Ó Faoláin, Eimer O'Duffy and Brinsley McNamara. In rendering 'exile' aesthetic he was also instrumental–although unintentionally–in transmuting the idea from its commonly understood Catholic/Nationalist meaning with its rooted opposition to external rule into an infinitely more ambiguous and elastic conceptualisation which came to stand for any resistance to established authority, internal or external, English or Irish while simultaneously carrying with it heavy traces of its history in the discourses of popular resistance. The infusion of the discourse of 'Art' into the discourse of 'exile' in Ireland in the early twentieth century, adulterated the narrow semantic force of Catholic/Nationalist usage. Exile in the domain of Art became synonymous with rebellion against Ireland rather than a punishment imposed by an oppressive imperialism.

Moore with his aptitude for excess became a triple 'exile', alienated from Ireland, France and England, displaying and living out all the characteristics of Said's intellectual exile. He existed in a metaphorical exile as an 'outsider', one who never fully adjusted to the trappings of 'accommodation and national well-being'. He was restless, unsettled, one who succeeded in unsettling others and one who could not return 'home'. He was an artist for whom writing becomes a place to live. Moore's art was predicated on dissatisfaction, on 'the idea of unhappiness' and a duality of vision, a hybrid and dialogic presupposition of comparison and conflict between Ireland, France and England, between the quotidian and the élite.

Finally, as the evidence of his contemporaries suggests, his marginality was ensured by his lack of attachment to and belief in anything but his devotion to Art and his belief in himself. In that sense, within the narrow perceptual boundaries of the self-serving and self-ordained transnational community of Art, he deified himself–perhaps ironically–as the archetypal 'exile'.

The Exiles Write Back: Artists, Escape, Representations and Exilic Studies

INTRODUCTION

IN 1916 there were two seminal print texts published by Irish authors which apotheosised the exile and the artist: *The Proclamation of the Republic* and *A Portrait Of The Artist As A Young Man*. A third text, equally important, was performative–the Battle of the Somme in July 1916. Each of these texts was of course, authored out of male psychologies.

The Proclamation of the Republic was delivered outside the General Post Office on 24 April 1916 by Patrick Pearse on behalf of the Provisional Government of Ireland. It triggered events which, viewed retrospectively, were the culmination of years of nationalist rhetoric; events which, in many ways typified the eurocentric preoccupation with sacrifice and bloodletting in the era of competing imperialisms before the First World War.[1] *The Proclamation* also however, enshrines the idea of exile in nationalist symbology in an axiomatic equation of those in America with involuntary and forced removal. The opening paragraph reads:

> Irishmen and Irishwomen: In the name of God and of the dead generations from which she receives her old tradition of nationhood, Ireland through us, summons her children to her flag and strikes for her freedom.
>
> Having organised and trained her manhood through her secret revolutionary organisation, the Irish Republican Brotherhood, and through her open military organisations, the Irish Volunteers and Irish Citizen Army, having patiently perfected her discipline, having resolutely waited for the right moment to reveal itself, she now seizes that moment, and, supported by her exiled children in America and by gallant allies in Europe, but relying in the first on her own strength, she strikes in full confidence of victory.[2]

The document like most foundational texts, elevates unquestioned premisses into a universal and timeless schema. Its assumptions are mediated through powerful and all embracing western political and philosophical ideas which assert inherent human rights within a liberal democratic framework. It draws on fundamental and 'self-evident' beliefs in rootedness which equate possession and entitlement with precedent, territory, language and longevity. In addition to the messianic tone which pervades the first four paragraphs, and the implicit acknowledgement in the final paragraph that their final venture is bound to fail militarily, the text's 'unconscious' testifies to the colonial and conservative formations which shaped it. Ireland throughout is feminised. The pronouns 'she'and 'her' dialogise with idealised images of *Kathleen Ní Houlihan* in assertive and submissive moods and the consistent references to Irishmen and Irishwomen as 'children' undermine the overt obeisance to citizenship in the fourth paragraph.[3] It assumes a protective and ultimately patriarchal patrimony; offering security in exchange for obedience in a hierarchy underwritten by divinity, at least as it was conceived by Irish Catholicism.

In utilising the image of the family as propagated in the Catholic Church's teachings and in its iconography, the text unavoidably casts those in America as supportive and obedient children, whose function is to finance and enable, but not to question or interfere. In highlighting those emigrants who settled in America, while remaining silent about those who went elsewhere, the *Proclamation* effectively disowns those 'children' over-seas in the British dominions and colonies and those thousands, if not hundreds of thousands, resident in Britain itself. They are in effect erased from the Irish extended family; outside the representative frames available to the authors–orphaned and outcast. The text while registering an all-inclusive generosity and gesturing towards all those who would lay an affective claim to Ireland–a stake in its future and a share in its past–rejects, dispossesses and denies those whose existence complicates and transforms simplistic, essentialist, constructions of Irishness.

As an inaugural text it informed and reflected the narrow censorious-ness of the triumphant native bourgeoisie whose interest it served. Their view of the nature of Ireland and its future shaped the cultural conditions and levels of permissibility; and of course, their vision was manifested in legislative and non-legislative forms which effectively outlawed the non-conformist.[4]

Three of the signatories to the *Proclamation* were poets. Patrick Pearse, Joseph Plunkett and Thomas McDonagh. James Joyce and Stephen Dedalus, like Pearse, Plunkett and McDonagh, rebelled against the domi-nant orthodoxies of their time–without however, resort to arms. In a celebrated passage from *A Portrait Of The Artist As A Young Man* Stephen declares:

> I will not serve that in which I no longer believe, whether it call itself my home my fatherland, or my church: and I will try to express myself in some mode of life or art as freely as I can and as wholly as I can, using for my defence the only arms I allow myself to use–silence, exile, and cunning.[5]

Stephen's proclamation of independence has been seen as a manifesto for the western bourgeois artist in the early part of the twentieth century. It has also been seen as a conceptualisation of the artistic imperative which transcends the nets of nationality, language and religion. It is a construction derived largely from Romanticism which tends to minimise Joyce's Irishness by relocating him into a wider european pantheon of transnational artistic heroes; above and apart from the petty national and imperialistic difference of late nineteenth and early twentieth-century Europe. Liberal humanists could thus celebrate his artistic vision and originality in a kind of re-contextualised european tradition; one that reached back to ancient Greece and made artistic sense synchronically, of the flux and fragmentation of modern experience and that of course, applied particularly to *Ulysses*.

Stephen Dedalus though, clearly acknowledges the cultural formations which shaped his psyche when he says to Davin: 'This race and this country and this life produced me ... I shall express myself as I am'.[6] His self-awareness and Joyce's world-view quite explicitly recognise the formative influence of Ireland's position as a predominantly rural and relatively undeveloped colony speaking in the language of the imperialist conqueror. It is a view which encompasses an aggregation of anti-colonial and pro-nationalist ideas and assumptions–linked to an adherence by the majority of the inhabitants–to a conservative, Catholic church with all that entailed, in terms of obedience, family life and separation from the non-Catholic Irish. To be more precise, Stephen's aims and 'weapons' derive specifically from a discourse constructed over several hundred years of opposition to English rule; while silence, exile and cunning as self-imaging terms, have been metaphorically appropriated by artists since the early nineteenth century, to explain and justify artistic alienation and the poet's feeling of difference.

Joyce's employment of the terms may be seen from outside Ireland as archetypal, even 'european'; a construction which in Edward Said's words 'affiliates' him with other migratory artists of Modernism; migratory in the literal and the metaphoric modes in a loose, transnational association of highly self-conscious artists, imposing their own narrative order on culture and experience. But, seen from within the perceptual perimeters of Irish cognitive and cultural comprehension, departure may be interpreted rather more problematically.

Stephen's diary entry for April 14, with its reflections on Mulrennan's encounter with the old peasant in the west of Ireland, may then be read as an expression of the profoundly ambivalent oppositions felt by most Irish emigrants. It represents the pull of hearth and home, the security of familiarity, love and loyalty to the place (imagined or not) that formed him, and on the other hand, the push of incapacitating conservatism and the allure of new places and opportunities.

The stated rationalisation for his departure however, inflates his decision to the level of the heroic as he sees himself going into exile *for* the old man and *for* the people of Ireland. His missionary, aesthetic imperative is paradoxically in the service of Ireland. By leaving he serves, desertion becomes devotion, 'betrayal' self-sacrifice, as he goes 'to forge in the smithy of my soul the uncreated conscience of my race'.[7] In appropriating and re-working discursive practices derived from Irish tradition and the art world of Europe, Joyce images Stephen as a poète maudit, seer, prophet, 'a priest of the eternal imagination'.[8] He is, as the diary form signals, a self-constructed hero of consciousness, subject and object, author and text, Irish and european, singular and plural. The ontological duality which Joyce as text and creator came to represent paradigmatically, set the imaginative boundaries for most Irish artists who succeeded him, and the terms of their acceptance of the categories he rewrote or their opposition to, or discomfort with, such configurations. After Joyce exile and art in written forms ceased to signify individually. They fused symbiotically with discourses emanating out of neo-realist Catholic practices and perhaps, just as importantly, in critical commentary on all Irish writing in the English language.

More recent criticism originating within Ireland[9] draws on postcolonial theorists such as Fanon, Memmi, Said and Homi Bhabha to relocate Joyce and indeed, the other major literary artists, within the context of a colonised and post-colonial culture and the assertiveness of Irish political and cultural nationalism. Such criticism notes the theme of exile as a characteristic of all post-colonial literatures.[10] This book argues that the idea of exile has an etymological, cultural and psychic history in Ireland which can be traced back to the monastic traditions of early Irish Christianity with its attendant notions of exile as a type of martyrdom. This involved forms of inner exile such as an ascetic anchoritic state as well as missionary activity outside Ireland. Such conceptualisations in turn, were linked to love of place, family and community. Attachments such as these found early expressions in the myths, legends and sagas of Gaelic Ireland particularly in their christianised manifestations.

Successive waves of invasion by Vikings, Normans, Tudors and Cromwellians produced recurrent patterns of flight and banishment, most notably of literate opinion formers, and reinforcement in poetic and linguistic expression of dislocation–internal and external–as exile. Exile was thus incorporated into a complex of compensatory, oppositional associations in the Gaelic language which were further reinforced throughout the era of the Penal Laws by the proscription of those exemplary exiles, poets and priests, and the transposition of literary concerns into the oral tradition. It was however, a literary and oral tradition which subjected women to male perceptions and preoccupations.

The early English language tradition while also drawing on the Judaeo-Christian imagery of exile, viewed Ireland as a place to be exiled *to* rather than exiled *from*. For such users Britain was home, and at least in eighteenth-century America, the Promised Land. That very different notion of exile came to co-exist, if only in repressed form, with the Gaelic, Catholic, nationalist conceptualisation, when in the post-Famine period Ireland came to be largely English speaking. Both the coloniser and the colonised came to absorb the effects of the American and French revolutions and the discursive practices of Romanticism in different ways in the latter half of the nineteenth century.

The argument continues with an examination of the relationship of the concept of exile with that of nationalism in the work of Young Ireland, Mangan, Mitchell, Kickham and in popular culture; relating the personal to the political, form to theme, in the circumstances of the post-Famine exodus and literary fenianism. It suggests that there was an inevitable concentration on the communal at the expense of the individual, and that literature was subordinated to a more dominant and over-arching imperative which necessitated the elimination of difference in sectarian, gender and class terms as well as the suppression of differing exilic experiences.

The needs of political and cultural nationalism were underwritten by the power, discourses and iconography of the Irish version of Catholicism. It drew on centuries of leadership and identification with the Catholic masses to view emigration as forced exclusion. In constructing a mythicised 'Holy Ireland', Catholicism also employed inherited perceptions form popular culture which fused and interacted with ideas and images derived from the Gaelic language tradition and from the construction of an 'Irish-Ireland' complex of representations. The effect was to create a nexus of imaginary essences which broadly defined those who belonged and those who did not; those who were 'truly' Irish and those who were outsiders. In this kind of formulation the individual had to submit to, or to separate himself (*sic*) from the prevailing hegemony. The artist therefore, was faced with the prospect of accepting and articulating the fictions of a Catholic nationalist self-portraiture – refracted as it was through the 'cracked looking glass of a servant'.[11] S/he might evade the simplicities of the present, create alternative fictions excavated out of a mythicised past, retreat into silence, or escape into other, more liberating conditions of creativity.

Stephen Dedalus the exilic avatar of Irish art, in many ways exemplifies the oxymoronic estrangement of the 'voluntary' exile. Cranly says of him 'your mind is supersaturated with the religion in which you say you disbelieve'.[12] It is unsurprising then that Stephen, like the vast majority of Irish Catholics, employs exile as a metaphorical construct for all departure 'voluntary' or involuntary–it had acquired the linguistic and experiential encrustations of hundreds of years of oppressed understanding. In the psyche of Catholic Ireland it engendered an heroic habitualisation, a routine, male, equation, which Protestants, women and other diasporic peoples used with greater discrimination. The self-imagery of the Irish artist in exile fused in the era of Modernism with the self-aggrandisement of the western artist as a man apart predestined to break the bonds of narrow nationalism. It was an image underwritten by a supportive critical tradition which, for the most part, saw its role as handmaiden of Art; intent on working with the grain, explicating and explaining the Artist and his (*sic*) work in a circular self-enclosed aestheticism.

The conjunction of events in 1916, the Rising and The Battle of the Somme, epitomised the radical choices which those attached to Ireland faced. The question of belonging and identity and subscription to the narratives of a new order had to be answered (or evaded) by all who laid claim to the name of Irishman (or woman). 1916, The Rising, The War of Independence and the Civil War accelerated a process of Protestant realignment which had been growing throughout the previous decades. L.P. Curtis has identified two key elements in the Anglo-Irish predicament. The first was a 'chronic ambivalence' between two homes 'one historic (Ireland) the other atavistic (England), two loyalties–one immediate (Crown and Empire), and two cultures–one improvised (Anglo-Irish) the other absolute (English)'.[13] This produced a state which F.S.L. Lyons categorises as 'congential schizophrenia'.[14] The second element Curtis describes was 'gradual deracination' resulting in 'severing of the roots of Anglo-Ireland and the increasing withdrawal of the Anglo-Irish gentry from the mainstream of Irish life to the point that emigration or exile became the logical extreme'.[15]

Daniel Corkery's *Synge and Anglo-Irish Literature*, first published in 1931, listed thirty-six non-resident Irish writers. It included such names as: Padraic Colum, Thomas McGreevy, Gerald O'Donovan, John Eglinton, Austin Clarke, James Joyce, James Stephens, Sean O'Casey, Patrick MacGill, George Moore, G.B. Shaw and Liam O'Flaherty. It would be relatively easy to add significantly to that list in a consideration of the period from the 1930s to the present. Absence from Ireland then, can be taken as an enduring and recurring given in any examination of the development and interaction of literary activities in the English language tradition in the twentieth century. The dialectics between 'home' and 'abroad', consciously or unconsciously, pervaded the cultural and artistic consciousness of those who stayed, and those who left. The fact of emigration and expatriation covertly permeated all aspects of national life, for all Irish people in one way or another.

After the traumas of war, partition and the establishment of two separate polities, each ossified in sectarianism, there was little room for, or tolerance of dissent. Art as Corkery exemplified, was expected to serve the 'national being'.[16] Irish or English as the case may be. Censorship and censoriousness within Ireland effectively closed off much of the matter of Irish life from artistic comment and exploration. Inevitably artists such as Samuel Beckett, Elizabeth Bowen, Frank O'Connor, Louis MacNeice, Denis Johnston, Oliver St John Gogarty, George Russell (A.E.) and Kate O'Brien left during the 1930s, 1940s and 1950s. There were of course those who remained. Individuals such as Brinsley McNamara, George Fitzmaurice, Lennox Robinson, F.R. Higgins, Edith Somerville, Molly Keane, Flann O'Brien, Patrick Kavanagh, Michael McLaverty, Peader O'Donnell, Mary Lavin and Mervyn Wall. Some like Seán Ó Faoláin both left and resettled in Ireland.

Further investigation into the nature, form and consequences of 'exile' or expatriation would clearly have to take into account the effects of changed circumstances–political, social, cultural and artistic, as well as inherited patterns of thought, motifs, tropes and expressive forms. Andrew Gurr has provided a useful post-colonial framework within which texts produced by those who leave and those who remain might be studied. He distinguishes between 'colony' and 'metropolis' suggesting that in the former 'colony' or small community 'art tends to be conservative, traditional, conformist' and that 'Artistic freedom rules only in the metropolis'.[17] He goes on to claim that 'An artist born in a colony is made conscious of the culturally subservient status of his home and is forced to go into exile in the metropolis as a means of compensating for that sense of cultural subservience'.[18] He argues that the 'search for identity ... is probably the most characteristic preoccupation in twentieth-century literature'[19] and that the exile has a 'stronger sense of home' and a 'clearer sense of his own identity'.[20] He also claims that for the colonial exile 'the search for identity and the construction of a vision of home amount to the same thing'.[21]

His notion of exile, like that of Edward Said, is capacious. It embraces compulsion, self-determination and flight. It complements Salman Rushdie's observation that writers in his position 'exiles, or emigrants or expatriates, are haunted by some sense of loss, some urge to reclaim, to look back even at the risk of being mutated into pillars of salt'. The consequence however for Rushdie, is that he, and those like him will 'create fictions, not actual cities or villages, but invisible ones, imaginery homelands, Indias of the mind'.[22] Gurr notes that Joyce, the archetypal artist-exile 'spent his life obsessively rebuilding his home in his art'.[23] He distinguishes between expatriates and exiles; the former he describes as those like Scott Fitzgerald and Hemingway who would come and go freely, whereas Joyce was unable to return to Ireland because he says, the conditions there prevented him from writing. He notes too, that many expatriate writers like Pound, Eliot and Auden were poets who did not need the explicitness of prose. In an interesting comparison he argues that Yeats in contrast to Joyce, stands as the archetype of the home based writer[24] and that poetry and drama tend to be employed by those remaining at home as forms which engage more easily with the present. On the other hand prose tends to be a more flexible medium which to create or re-create history and home. It is a distinction however, which overlooks Yeats' frequent absences from Ireland. Other features of displacement he points to include

> the awkward equation between deracination and freedom, the tension between the motives for escape and the nostalgias of exile, the compulsion to write about the familiar with the help of distance, the reality of the inward life which becomes stronger and more tangible as the outward life becomes alien, the chronic need for stasis in a changing world a need which only memory can satisfy, and ultimately the question of homecoming.[25]

Towards the end of his book Gurr returns to the 'pose of detachment'

as being 'the clearest hallmark of the exile, and yet a paradox since exile
directly implies loss and a yearning for home'.[26] The posture of objectivity
or detachment is invariably positioned outside, in this case, Ireland, of
necessity. It has implications therefore, in terms of what may be dealt
with by the writer in exile, for theme and content and how the writer
chooses to represent memories, evocations, impressions, descriptions and
for whom. It is striking for example, how often absent Irish writers resort
to the architectonics of the *bildungsroman*, autobiography and travel
writing.

Gurr's analysis then, may provide a useful conceptual framework
within which Irish writing between the early 1920s and the late 1950s
might be reviewed. In examining who stayed and who left attention might
be paid to material issues such as class, status and gender; opportunities
for publication and performance; the forms those who stayed chose to
employ; the audiences they appealed to implicitly or explicitly; the constraints they inevitably worked under and the ways in which they
represented themselves and their subjects. Gurr, like Said and Rushdie,
dwells on the enabling aspects of exile; by and large they see it as liberating
and empowering. In the context of Irish writing and artistic emigration
that needs clarification and qualification. There were writers who contributed to the Revival for example who, having left Ireland wrote little if
anything, or who found it necessary to employ preferred forms differently,
and there were those who chose to resort to alternative expressive
mediums entirely. James Stephens for instance, wrote prolifically and
enthusiastically on behalf of Ireland prior to Independence. Yet after his
move to London in 1925 he wrote little of consequence, devoting himself
to lecture tours and BBC broadcasts. Similarly, Denis Johnston virtually
ceased to write creatively after taking up employment with the BBC in the
late 1930s. Furthermore, as has often been noted, the dramatic work of
O'Casey changed radically while his later years were given over to strident
autobiographical self-justification. In some instances therefore, 'exile'
might prove emasculating.

Terence Brown has commented that 'Alienation, deracination, loss of
religious faith, emigration, identity crisis were the experience of several
literary generations of Protestant Irishman in this century'.[27] What was
true of Brown's subjects, C.S. Lewis, Beckett and MacNeice, is equally true
too, of Catholics such as Joyce, O'Connor, O'Donovan, O'Duffy and a host
of other emigrants.

Literary criticism tends to remain silent with regard to those writers
who effectively ceased to produce literary texts after leaving Ireland.

Questions therefore remain as to why such writers became creative mutes and in some cases why they resorted to other forms of expressivity. There is a similar aphonic emptiness in literary representation and the mass media about the experience of emigration for ordinary men and women. Peter Feeney, the producer/director of the RTE television series 'The Age of de Valera' (1982), notes in the preface to the book that accompanied the series that when he and his team came to research emigration for the programme, they were unable to find any film recording the experience of leaving Ireland at all.[28] The novelist Joseph O'Connor, in his introduction to the anthology *Ireland in Exile* (1993) remarks on a similar absence of representation in writing during the same period:

> Emigration is as Irish as Cathleen Ní Houlihan's harp, yet it is only since the sixties and the generation of Edna O'Brien that Irish writers have written about the subject at first hand. That seems staggering I know, but I think it's true. It has been taken as read that Exile is an important theme in Irish writing, like the Big House or The Catholic Church. But if it is, it's an inconsistent and entirely intermittent preoccupation. Where are the first-person texts of Irish emigrant life in the later part of the last century and the earlier part of this? With one or two exceptions–Robert Tressell's *Ragged Trousered Philanthropist*, say and the bleak spare poems of Patrick MacGill–they're not there. At the heart of the Irish emigrant experience there is a caution, a refusal to speak, a fear of the word.[29]

The sociologist Liam Ryan, attributes this 'refusal to speak' to 'the defence mechanism of traditional categories of thought' which enabled opinion formers 'to interpret twentieth-century emigration in comforting ways'[30] and to a class consciousness and a culture of shame which stigmatised those families whose sons and daughters emigrated.[31] Those reactive mechanisms, cultivated in times of nationalist struggle, led dominant opinion forming forces to subscribe to what Kiberd calls 'the notion of Irish exceptionality' which in turn meant that 'they often failed to regard Irish experience as representative of human experience, and so they remained woefully innocent of the comparative method, which might have helped them more fully to possess the meaning of their lives.'[32]

Comparative studies of the Irish emigrant experience with that of other dispersed cultures, colonised or otherwise, and examination of narrative structures and representations might serve to internationalise Irish migration, to connect, contextualise and highlight commonalities. Rushdie has claimed that Indian writers in England belong to two traditions, Indian, clearly and 'the culture and political history of the phenomena of migration, displacement, life in a minority group'.[33] If that is true of the Indian writer, it must be true too of the Irish artist.

Within the area of literary studies, analyses of the exilic experience of those writers who fled the tyrannies of european dictatorships or the oppressive life-threatening regimes of newly independent states, might help to re-establish the discriminatory force between such terms as exile, expatriation, refugee, emigrant and (inner) émigré. Comparisons between artistic representations of emigration and texts produced out of more prosaic circumstances, such as the Blasket Island memoirs, John Healy's journalistic accounts *Nineteen Acres* (1978), *Death of an Irish Town* (1968), Walter Macken's, *I Am Alone* (1949), and Donal MacAmlaigh's *An Irish Navvy: The Diary of an Exile* (1964), could contribute to a fuller under-standing, as would comparisons between men and women, northerners and southerners, those from the city and those from the country.

Examination of institutional representations of exile in popular anthologies and histories, the perpetuation of exilic imagery in popular and traditional music and the evaluation of exile in the past, compared to emigration in the present, might well require reassessment and re-classification of traditional categories of thought. Such studies would no doubt dispel, demythologise and place into meaningful perspective the actualities of absence. Shorn of aesthetic accretions and nationalist symbology, it may be possible to challenge what Deane has referred to as the 'fetish of exile, alienation and dislocation' which characterised the work of Joyce and Beckett[34] and to re-think migration in more precise and metonymic terms. Deane has also written of Joyce, Beckett, Francis Stuart and Louis MacNeice as figures who 'seek in the world beyond an alterna-tive to their native culture, (and who) have come to regard their exile from it as a generic feature of the artist's rootless plight rather than a specifically Irish form of alienation'.[35] Perhaps a close examination of literary migrants and others from the 1960s onwards would reveal a shift in the semantics of departure.

Edna O'Brien for example, eschews the term 'exile' in favour of 'escape'[36] and the poet Michael O'Loughlin has written:

> I have always found it amusing to hear people, including literary scholars, refer to James Joyce's 'exile'. Exile from what? By leaving Ireland he found readers, publishers, collaborators, patrons, a sympathetic milieu. If he had stayed in Ireland, that would have been a true exile: exile from himself, from the James Joyce he became.[37]

Later in the same pamphlet, he points out that:

It has once again become clear that emigration is a structural factor in Irish society, the most important subject on our hidden curriculum. Its continued existence undermines the entire basis of Irish culture, and reduces questions of Irish identity and traditions, Anglo-Irish and peasant, Planter and Gael to the status of a sideshow, a divertissement, and not always an innocent one.[38]

The Irish imigrant experience since the 1960s has taken place within a communications revolution in terms of air travel, road transport and telecommunications which has, as Anderson remarks 'profoundly affected the subjective experience of migration'.[39] And that revolution has also created 'a transnational ethnicity'[40] which challenges simple nineteenth-century notions of nationality and promotes an extension of, in this case, Irishness to include successive generations of the diaspora. This 'Long-distance nationalism' of the type Anderson refers to[41] incorporative rather than exclusive, necessitates revision of established ways of thinking about identity, belonging, being, indigene and exile.

Joseph O'Connor speaks perhaps, for the inhabitants of this Greater Ireland, this fifth province, when he says:

Silence, exile and cunning, Joyce maintained, were the true weapons of the writer. But the exiles have been silent too long. And we have too frequently left cunning to the politicians who translate into platitude the part they have played in our marginalisation. Well, don't think we have gone away, those of us who have gone. When the voting rights come through, we who have so rarely spoken will be remembering the fervent promise of Coriolanus, 'Long my exile, sweet my revenge'.[42]

And, after pointing to the proliferation and fecundity of Irish writing throughout the world, he comments:

This energetic new wave of fiction writers is claiming the right to celebrate an Ireland that is various also, in terms that are primarily aesthetic, but also, by implication, profoundly political. The silence of the Irish exile is over now.[43]

In addition to those who live elsewhere but visit(ed) regularly, 'exiles' like Joseph O'Connor himself, Edna O'Brien, Matthew Sweeney, Tom Paulin, Paul Muldoon, Bernard MacLaverty, Brian Moore, William Trevor and Derek Mahon, there are a growing number of literary figures who though based in Ireland, spend considerable periods working in England, America or elsewhere. Such individuals include Seamus Heaney, Hugh Leonard, John Montague, Benedict Kiely and the playwrights Brian Friel and Tom Murphy whose work is staged frequently in other English speaking societies. Such exposure to other expectations, needs, perceptions and histories, must surely add to the forms of hybridity they acquired in their own cultural formation and contribute to an already porous and mutating social, psychic and historical ferment. The migrations of these artisans of the arts, literary spalpeens, intellectual itinerants, replicate in many ways the 'nomadism' characteristic of other Irish emigrants and as Anderson suggests, much of post-industrial capitalism.[44]

In similar vein the Antrim born, London based poet, Cahal Dallat has questioned the continued applicability of repression in Ireland and exilic writing 'home thoughts from abroad', as typifying signifiers, and argues that what now distinguishes Irish writing from outside Ireland is 'otherness'. Referring specifically to five poets, first and second-generation Irish, based in England he says that they are

> voices independent of belief-system, history or duty. Freed from unitary interpretations of (Southern) Irishness or binary interpretations of (Northern) Irishness, in, but not quite of, the world of English letters, these writers, and no doubt many others who trade, or whose parents have, of necessity, traded permanence for flux, are privileged to be able to write across frontiers which will come to seem increasingly jingoistic, fundamentalist, regional, hidebound.[45]

Further studies of those abroad might pay attention to the 'cultural remittances'.[46] Such voyagers contribute to evolving ideas of Ireland and Irishness; to their relationship with other migrant groups; to cultures which provide some kind of sustenance, permanent or temporary, and to 'Otherness' in relation to those in the host community and to those at home. Studies of indigenous writers might also examine the metaphoric nature of 'Otherness' such as Heaney's claim to be:

> An inner émigré, grown long haired
> And thoughtful: a wood kerne
>
> Escaped from the massacre,
> Taking protective colouring
> From bole and bark, feeling
> Every wind that blows:[47]

Exilic studies, situated within a broader cultural studies programme dealing with inside and outside, centre and periphery, home and abroad, the present and the past, may offer opportunities to re-conceptualise Irish history, identity and representation.[48]

To emigrate is to change, to become 'Other', different, plural. Eavan Boland the poet, has affirmed the repressed centrality of emigration in the formation of the Irish mind. In a moving re-definition of the borders of affectivity and identity she invites the emigrants home. Implicitly and simultaneously she suggests, that those who left over the centuries embarked on the voyage to an imaginative expansion of knowing, being and feeling. Exploration and settlement in expanded domains of epistemology, sentiment and consciousness would—indeed did produce new—narratives told in appropriate forms:

'The Emigrant Irish'

Like oil lamps we put them out the back,
of our houses, of our minds. We had lights
better than, newer than and then

a time came, this time and now
we need them. Their dread, makeshift example.

They would have thrived on our necessitites.
What they survived we could not even live.

By their lights now it is time to
imagine how they stood there, what they stood with
that their possessions may become our power.

Cardboard. Iron. Their hardships parcelled in them
Patience. Fortitude. Long-suffering
in the bruise-coloured dusk of the New World.
And all the old songs. And nothing to lose.[49]

References

CHAPTER 1

1. See for example Harry Levin, 'Literature and Exile', in *Refractions: Essays in Comparative Literature* (New York, 1966), pp. 62–81; Paul Tabori, *The Anatomy of Exile* (London, 1972); Claudio Guillen, 'On the Literature of Exile and Counter Exile', in *Books Abroad* 50, Spring 1976, pp. 271–80; Andrew Gurr, *Writers in Exile. The Identity of Home in Modern Literature* (Sussex, 1981); Michael Seidel, *Exile and the Narrative Imagination* (New Haven, 1986); María-Inés Lagos-Pope (ed.), *Exile in Literature* (London, 1988).

2. Edward W. Said, *The World, The Text And The Critic* (London, 1984), p. 39.

3. The term is incorporated into Vol. II of Seamus Deane (ed.), *The Field Day Anthology of Irish Writing* (Derry, 1991), in a section headed 'The London Exiles: Wilde and Shaw' by Declan Kiberd.

4. See for example Donald H. Akenson, *Half the World from Home: perspectives on the Irish in New Zealand 1860–1950* (Wellington, New Zealand, 1991); Mary Clancy, John Cunningham, Alf Maclochlainn (eds), *...the emigrant experience ...* (Galway, 1991); Chris Curtin, Riana O'Dwyer, Gearóid Ó Tuathaigh, 'Emigration and Exile', in Thomas Bartlett et al. (eds), *Irish Studies: A General Introduction* (Dublin, 1988), pp. 60–86; Graham Davis, *The Irish in Britain 1815–1914* (Dublin, 1991); David N. Doyle, 'The Irish in Australia and the United States: Some Comparisons, 1800–1939', in *Irish Economic and Social History XVI*, 1989, pp. 73–93; 'The Irish in North America, 1776–1845', in W.E. Vaughan (ed.), *A New History of Ireland: Vol. V, Ireland Under the Union, 1801–1870* (Oxford, 1989), pp. 682–725; P.J. Drudy (ed.) *The Irish in America: Emigration, Assimilation and Impact. Irish Studies 4* (Cambridge, 1985); Bruce Elliot, *Irish Migrants in the Canadas: A New Approach* (Belfast, 1988); David Fitzpatrick, 'Irish Emigration in the Later Nineteenth Century', in *Irish Historical Studies*, Vol. 22, No. 86, Sept. 1980, pp. 126–43; *Irish Emigration, 1801–1921* (Dublin, 1984); 'Emigration, 1801–70', in W.E. Vaughan (ed.), *A New History of Ireland: Vol. V, Ireland Under the Union, 1801–1870*, pp. 562–620. '"A peculiar tramping people" the Irish in Britain 1801–70' in W.E. Vaughan (ed.), *A New History of Ireland: Vol. V, Ireland Under the Union, 1801–1870*, pp. 621–60. R.F. Foster, *Modern Ireland, 1600–1972* (Harmondsworth, 1989), Chapter 15; Colm Kiernan (ed.), *Australia and Ireland: Bicentenary Essays, 1788–1988* (Dublin, 1988); Joseph Lee, *Ireland, 1912–1985: Politics and Society* (Cambridge, 1989); Kerby Miller,

Emigrants and Exiles: Ireland and the Irish Exodus to North America (Oxford, 1985); John O'Brien and Pauric Travers (eds), *The Irish Emigrant Experience in Australia* (Swords, 1991); Patrick O'Farrell, *The Irish in Australia* (New South Wales, 1986); Gearóid Ó Tuathaigh, 'The Irish in Nineteenth-Century Britain: Problems of Integration'. *Transactions of the Royal Historical Society 5th Series* 31, 1981, pp. 149–74. Roger Swift and Sheridan Gilley (eds), *The Irish in Britain, 1815–1939* (London, 1989).

5. Daniel Corkery, *Synge and Anglo-Irish Literature* (Cork, 1931), p. 4.
6. *Synge and Anglo-Irish Literature*, p. 14.
7. *Synge and Anglo-Irish Literature*, p. 19.
8. *Synge and Anglo-Irish Literature*, p. 2.
9. Benedict Anderson, *Imagined Communities: Reflections on the Origin and Spread of Nationalism* (London, 1983).
10. *Synge and Anglo-Irish Literature*, p. 3.
11. *Synge and Anglo-Irish Literature*, pp. 3–4.
12. *Synge and Anglo-Irish Literature*, p. 5.
13. *Synge and Anglo-Irish Literature*, p. 4.
14. *Synge and Anglo-Irish Literature*, p. 3.
15. *Synge and Anglo-Irish Literature*, p. 8.
16. *Synge and Anglo-Irish Literature*, p. 9.
17. *Synge and Anglo-Irish Literature*, pp. 9–10.
18. David Lloyd, 'Adulteration and the Nation', in *Anomalous States: Irish Writing and the Post-Colonial Moment* (Mullingar, 1993), pp. 88–124.
19. See for example Terence Brown, *Ireland: A Social and Cultural History, 1922–1985* (London, 1981); David Cairns and Shaun Richards, *Writing Ireland: colonialism, nationalism and culture* (Manchester, 1988); Seamus Deane, *A Short History of Irish Literature* (London, 1986); Maurice Goldring, *Pleasant the Scholar's Life: Irish Intellectuals and the Construction of the Nation State* (London, 1993).
20. Benedict Kiely, *Modern Irish Fiction: A Critique* (Dublin, 1950), Foreword p. xii.
21. *Modern Irish Fiction*, Chapter VII, pp. 108–30.
22. *Modern Irish Fiction*, p. 109.
23. *Modern Irish Fiction*, p. 110.
24. *Modern Irish Fiction*, p. 111.
25. *Modern Irish Fiction*, p. 111.
26. *Modern Irish Fiction*, p. 111.
27. *Modern Irish Fiction*, p. 112.
28. *Modern Irish Fiction*, p. 119.
29. *Modern Irish Fiction*, p. 120.
30. *Modern Irish Fiction*, p. 120.
31. *Modern Irish Fiction*, p. 121.
32. *Modern Irish Fiction*, p. 122.
33. *Modern Irish Fiction*, p. 123.
34. *Modern Irish Fiction*, p. 124.
35. *Modern Irish Fiction*, p. 125.
36. *Modern Irish Fiction*, p. 127.

37. *Modern Irish Fiction*, p. 128.
38. Jean-Paul Sartre, Introduction to Albert Memmi's, *The Colonizer and the Colonized* (London, 1990), p. 26.
39. *Modern Irish Fiction*, p. 129.
40. Seamus Deane, 'Heroic Styles: The tradition of an idea' in Field Day Theatre Company, *Ireland's Field Day* (London, 1985), p. 57.
41. Peter Costello, *The Heart Grown Brutal: The Irish Revolution in Literature from Parnell to the Death of Yeats, 1891–1939* (Dublin, 1978), p. 246.
42. *The Heart Grown Brutal*, p. 246.
43. *The Heart Grown Brutal*, p. 255.
44. *The Heart Grown Brutal*, p. 257.
45. *The Heart Grown Brutal*, p. 269.
46. Roger McHugh and Maurice Harmon, *A Short History of Anglo-Irish Literature: From its origins to the present day* (Dublin, 1982), p. 249; A. Norman Jeffares, *Anglo-Irish Literature* (London, 1982), p. 62; Seamus Deane, *A Short History of Irish Literature*, pp. 13, 168, 172, 196; David Cairns and Shaun Richards, *Writing Ireland: colonialism, nationalism and culture*, pp. 74, 75, 134, 137; Norman Vance, *Irish Literature: A Social History, Tradition, Identity and Difference* (Oxford, 1990), pp. 56, 165, 196, 197; Maurice Goldring, *Pleasant the Scholar's Life: Irish Intellectuals and the Construction of the Nation State* pp. 41, 51, 108, 153, 161.
47. Paul Hyland and Neil Sammells (eds), *Irish Writing: Exile and Subversion* (London, 1991).
48. James Cahalan, *The Irish Novel: A Critical History* (Dublin, 1988), pp. 33, 35, 61, 69, 70, 102, 109, 111, 124, 125, 179, 185, 186, 211, 257, 271, 274; Charles Fanning (ed.), *The Exiles of Erin: Nineteenth-Century Irish-American Fiction* (Indiana, 1987); Richard Fallis, *The Irish Renaissance: An introduction to Anglo-Irish Literature* (Dublin, 1978), Chapter 12, pp. 233–63.
49. *The Irish Renaissance*, p. 262.
50. *The Irish Renaissance*, p. 263.
51. *The Irish Renaissance*, p. 263.
52. *The Irish Renaissance*, p. 263.
53. George O'Brien, 'The Muse of Exile: Estrangement and Renewal in Modern Irish Literature', in María-Inés Lagos-Pope (ed.), *Exile in Literature*, pp. 82–101.
54. 'The Muse of Exile', p. 83.
55. 'The Muse of Exile', p. 84.
56. 'The Muse of Exile', p. 85.
57. 'The Muse of Exile', p. 86.
58. Hallvard Dahlie, 'Brian Moore and the Meaning of Exile', in Richard Wall (ed.), *Medieval and Modern Ireland* (Gerrards Cross, 1988), pp. 91–107.
59. 'Brian Moore and the Meaning of Exile', p. 92.
60. 'Brian Moore and the Meaning of Exile', p. 93.
61. 'Brian Moore and the Meaning of Exile', p. 93.
62. Chris Curtin, Riana O'Dwyer and Gearóid Ó Tuathaigh, 'Emigration and Exile', in Thomas Bartlett et al. (eds), *Irish Studies*, pp. 60–86.
63. 'Emigration and Exile', p. 80

64. 'Emigration and Exile', p. 80
65. See Note 1.
66. Edward W. Said, *The World, The Text, And The Critic*, pp. 1–30.
67. Edward W. Said, 'The Mind of Winter: Reflections on life in exile', *Harpers Magazine*, Vol. 269, No. 161, Sept. 1984, pp. 49–55.
68. 'The Mind of Winter', p. 49.
69. 'The Mind of Winter', p. 50.
70. 'The Mind of Winter', p. 51.
71. 'The Mind of Winter', p. 52.
72. 'The Mind of Winter', p. 52.
73. 'The Mind of Winter', p. 53.
74. 'The Mind of Winter', p. 53.
75. 'The Mind of Winter', p. 54.
76. 'The Mind of Winter', p. 55.
77. See Note 3.
78. Kerby Miller, *Emigrants and Exiles*.
79. Kerby Miller, 'Emigration, Capitalism and Ideology in Post-Famine Ireland', in Richard Kearney (ed.), *Migrations: The Irish at Home and Abroad* (Dublin, 1990), pp. 91–108.
80. 'Emigration, Capitalism and Ideology', p. 92.
81. 'Emigration, Capitalism and Ideology', p. 93.
82. 'Emigration, Capitalism and Ideology', p. 95.
83. Joseph Lee, *Ireland, 1912–1985*, p. 324.
84. 'Emigration, Capitalism and Ideology', p. 96.
85. 'Emigration, Capitalism and Ideology', p. 101.
86. 'Emigration, Capitalism and Ideology', p. 102.
87. 'Emigration, Capitalism and Ideology', p. 105.
88. Homi Bhabha, 'DissemiNation: time narrative and the margins of the modern nation', in Homi Bhabha (ed.), *Nation and Narration* (London, 1990), pp. 291–322.
89. 'DissemiNation', p. 292.
90. 'DissemiNation', p. 293.
91. 'DissemiNation', p. 292.
92. Timothy Brennan, 'The national longing for form', in *Nation and Narration*, pp. 44–70.
93. 'Heroic styles', p. 57
94. Edward W. Said, *Culture and Imperialism* (London, 1992), p. 380.

CHAPTER 2

1. Frederick Jameson, *The Political Unconscious: Narrative as a Socially Symbolic Act* (London, 1981), p. 9.
2. Accounts are given in Edmund Curtis, *A History of Ireland* (London, 1950), p. 13 and Henry Boylan, *A Dictionary of Irish Biography* (Dublin, 1978), p. 63.
3. A fuller account of the doctrine may be found in Robin Flower, *The Irish Tradition* (Oxford, 1947), pp. 19–23.

4. See Tómas Ó Fiaich, 'The Beginnings of Christianity', in T.W. Moody and F.X. Martin (eds), *The Course of Irish History* (Cork, 1967), p. 74.
5. Liam de Paor, *The Peoples of Ireland: From prehistory to modern times* (London, 1986), p. 62.
6. *The Irish Tradition*, p. 1.
7. *The Irish Tradition*, pp. 38–9.
8. Thomas Kinsella (Trans.), *The Tain* (Oxford, 1970), p. 15.
9. *The Tain*, p. 58.
10. Seamus Heaney, *Sweeney Astray* (London, 1984), Introduction.
11. *Sweeney Astray*, p. 10.
12. *Sweeney Astray*, p. 20–21.
13. *Sweeney Astray*, p. 66.
14. Seamus O'Neill, 'Gaelic Literature', in Robert Hogan (ed.), *The Macmillan Dictionary of Irish Literature* (London, 1980), p. 32.
15. *The Irish Tradition*, p. 79.
16. Thomas Kinsella (ed.), *The New Oxford Book of Irish Verse* (Oxford, 1989), Introduction, p. xxv.
17. James Carney, 'Literature in Irish, 1169–1534', in Art Cosgrove (ed.), *A New History of Ireland: Vol. 11, Medieval Ireland, 1169–1534* (Oxford, 1987), p. 689.
18. 'Gaelic Literature', p. 32.
19. *The Irish Tradition*, p. 89.
20. *The Peoples of Ireland*, p. 104.
21. *Modern Ireland, 1600–1972*, p. 35.
22. See John J. Silke, 'The Irish Abroad, 1534–1691', in T.W. Moody et al. (eds), *A New History of Ireland: Vol. 111, Early Modern Ireland, 1534–1691* (Oxford, 1976), p. 592.
23. 'The Irish Abroad, 1534–1691', p. 591.
24. David Cairns and Shaun Richards, *Writing Ireland: colonialism, nationalism and culture*, p. 17.
25. Brian Ó Cuív, 'The Irish language in the early modern period', in T.W. Moody et al. (eds), *A New History of Ireland: Vol. III*, p. 521.
26. 'The Irish language in the early modern period', p. 510.
27. Seán Ó Faoláin, *The Great O'Neill: A Biography of Hugh O'Neill Earl of Tyrone, 1550–1616* (Cork, 1970), p. 267.
28. *New Oxford Book of Irish Verse*, p. 162.
29. *Modern Ireland*, p. 40.
30. *A Short History of Irish Literature*, p. 18.
31. *Modern Ireland*, p. 43. It is a comment which might also of course, be applied to Foster's own project in rewriting Irish history for the 1990s emphasising as he does 'varieties of Irishness'. See Chapter 1, in *Modern Ireland*.
32. Brian Friel, *Making History* (London, 1989), p. 67.
33. *Making History*, p. 65.
34. *The Great O'Neill*, Introduction, p. vi.
35. *Making History*, p. 16.
36. *Making History*, p. 27.
37. Tom Dunne, 'The Gaelic Response to Conquest and Colonisation: The Evidence of the Poetry', *Studia Hibernia*, Vol. xx, 1980, p. 17.

38. Nicholas Canny, 'The Formation of the Irish Mind: Religion, Politics and Gaelic Irish Literature, 1580–1750', in *Past and Present*, No. 95, p. 107.
39. Patrick J. Corish, 'The Cromwellian regime, 1650–60', in T.W. Moody et al. (eds), *A New History of Ireland: Vol. III*, p. 362.
40. 'The Cromwellian regime, 1650–60', p. 364.
41. Conor Cruise O'Brien, *States of Ireland* (London, 1972), p. 65.
42. 'The Cromwellian regime, 1650–60', p. 364.
43. 'The Cromwellian regime, 1650–60', p. 373.
44. Seán Ó Tuama and Thomas Kinsella (eds), *An Duanaire, 1600–1900: Poems of the Dispossessed* (Portlaoise, 1981), p. 105.
45. 'The Cromwellian regime, 1650–60', p. 376.
46. *Modern Ireland*, p. 115.
47. From the Irish *toirdhe*, raider.
48. From the Irish *rapairidhe*, pike.
49. *An Duanaire, 1600–1900*, p. 95.
50. 'The Cromwellian regime, 1650–60', p. 384.
51. 'The Formation of the Irish Mind', p. 96.
52. Quoted in, 'The Cromwellian regime, 1650–60', p. 357.
53. Peter Berresford Ellis, *Hell or Connaught! The Cromwellian Colonisation of Ireland, 1652–1660* (London, n.d.), p. 25.
54. Brian Ó Cuív, 'Irish language and literature, 1691–1845', in T.W. Moody and W.E. Vaughan (eds), *A New History of Ireland: Vol. IV, Eighteenth Century Ireland, 1691–1800* (Oxford, 1986), p. 397.
55. *A History of Ireland*, pp. 272–3.
56. J.G. Simms, 'The Irish on the Continent, 1691–1800', in T.W. Moody and W.E. Vaughan (eds), *A New History of Ireland: Vol. IV*, p. 637.
57. Richard Murphy, *Selected Poems* (London 1979), p. 36.
58. 'The Gaelic Response to Conquest and Colonisation', p. 20.
59. Quoted in Brian Ó Cuív, 'The Irish language in the early modern period', p. 535.
60. *The Peoples of Ireland*, p. 175.
61. *The New Oxford Book of Irish Verse*, Introduction, p. xxv.
62. Quoted in Proinsias McCana, 'Early Irish ideology and the Concept of Unity', in Richard Kearney (ed.), *The Irish Mind: Exploring Intellectual Traditions* (Dublin, 1985), p. 77.
63. 'The Irish language in the early modern period', p. 543.
64. 'The Gaelic Response to Conquest and Colonisation', p. 26.
65. 'The Gaelic Response to Conquest and Colonisation', p. 26.
66. 'The Gaelic Response to Conquest and Colonisation', p. 27.
67. Richard Kearney, 'Myth and Motherland', in Field Day Theatre Company, *Ireland's Field Day*, p. 77.
68. 'Irish language and literature, 1691–1845', p. 402.
69. *An Duanaire*, p. 181.
70. Gearóid Ó Tuathaigh, 'The Role of Women in Ireland under the new English Order', in Margaret MacCurtain and Donncha Ó Corráin (eds), *Women in Irish Society: The historical dimension* (Dublin, 1978), p. 34.
71. Jerrold Casway, 'Irish Women Overseas, 1500–1800', in Margaret Mac-

Curtain and Mary O'Dowd (eds), *Women in Early Modern Ireland* (Edinburgh, 1991), p. 114.

72. 'Irish language and literature, 1691–1845', p. 407.
73. 'Irish language and literature, 1691–1845', p. 409.
74. Bernadette Cunningham, 'Women and Gaelic Literature, 1500–1800', in Margaret MacCurtain and Mary O'Dowd (eds), *Women in Early Modern Ireland*, p. 153.
75. P.L. Henry (ed.), *Dánta Bán: Poems of Irish Women: early and modern* (Cork, 1990).
76. *Dánta Bán*, pp. 113, 139.
77. See Máire Cruise O'Brien, 'The Female Principle in Gaelic Poetry', in S.F. Gallagher (ed.), *Women in Irish Legend, Life and Literature* (Gerrards Cross, 1983), p. 29; and Katherine Simms, 'Bardic poetry as a historical source', in Tom Dunne (ed.), *The Writer As Witness: literature as historical evidence* (Cork, 1987), p. 60.
78. *A Short History of Irish Literature*, p. 24.
79. 'The Formation of the Irish Mind', p. 111.
80. Breandán Ó Buachalla, 'Irish Jacobite Poetry', in Kevin Barry et al. (eds), *The Irish Review*, No. 12, Spring/Summer 1992, p. 45.
81. 'The Formation of the Irish Mind', p. 114.
82. Louis Cullen, *The Hidden Ireland: Reassessment of a Concept* (Mullingar, 1988).
83. *Modern Ireland*, p. 207.
84. Frantz Fanon, *The Wretched of the Earth* (Harmondsworth, 1967), p. 66.
85. *The Wretched of the Earth*, p. 40.
86. *Emigrants and Exiles*, p. 148.
87. *Modern Ireland*, p. 216.
88. *Emigrants and Exiles*, p. 160.
89. *Emigrants and Exile*, p. 156.
90. Albert Memmi, *The Colonizer and the Colonized*, p. 131.
91. J.C. Beckett, *The Anglo-Irish Tradition* (Belfast, 1982), p. 144.
92. P.F. Sheeran, 'Colonists and Colonised: Some Aspects of Anglo-Irish Literature from Swift to Joyce', in *Yearbook of English Studies*, Vol. 13 (1983), p. 106.
93. Full text in *The New Oxford Book of Irish Verse*, pp. 186–7.
94. From *Verses on the Death of Dr Swift*. Full text in *The New Oxford Book of Irish Verse*, pp. 193–4.
95. J.C. Beckett, 'Literature in English, 1691–1800', in T.W. Moody and W.E. Vaughan (eds), *A New History of Ireland: Vol. IV*, p. 434.
96. Joseph McMinn (ed.), *Swift's Irish Pamphlets: an Introductory Selection* (Gerrards Cross, 1991). p. 80.
97. *Swift's Irish Pamphlets*, p. 81.
98. *Swift's Irish Pamphlets*, pp. 19–20.
99. *A Short History of Irish Literature*, p. 47.
100. In Heinz Kosok (ed.), *Studies in Anglo-Irish Literature* (Bonn, 1982), p. 33.
101. *A Short History of Irish Literature*, p. 28.
102. 'Celts, Carthaginians and constitutions: Anglo-Irish literary relations, 1780–1820', in *Irish Historical Studies*, Vol. 22, No. 87, March 1981, pp. 230–31.
103. 'Celts, Carthaginians and constitutions', p. 231.

104. Patrick Fagan (ed.), *A Georgian Celebration: Irish Poets of the Eighteenth Century* (Dublin, 1989).

105. *The Colonizer and the Colonized*, p. 127.

106. Wolfe Tone in Seán Ó Faoláin (ed.), *The Autobiography of Theobald Wolfe Tone* (London, 1937), p. 37.

107. Marianne Elliott, *Partners in Revolution: The United Irishmen and France* (New Haven, 1982), p. 72.

108. *The Autobiography of Theobald Wolfe Tone*, p. 78.

109. *The Autobiography of Theobald Wolfe Tone*, pp. 79–80.

110. *Partners in Revolution*, p. 365.

111. *Emigrants and Exiles*, pp. 187–8.

112. David N. Doyle, 'The Irish in North America, 1776–1845', in W.E. Vaughan (ed.), *A New History of Ireland: Vol. V*, p. 688.

113. 'The Irish in North America, 1776–1845', p. 687.

114. 'The Irish in North America, 1776–1845', p. 684.

115. *Emigrants and Exiles*, pp. 228–9.

116. *Emigrants and Exiles*, p. 2232.

117. *Modern Ireland*, p. 281.

118. *Modern Ireland*, p. 283.

119. Full text in Brendan Kennelly (ed.), *The Penguin Book of Irish Verse* (Harmondsworth, 1970), pp. 126–7.

120. Tom Dunne, 'Popular ballads, revolutionary rhetoric and politicisation', in Hugh Gough and David Dickson (eds), *Ireland and the French Revolution* (Dublin, 1990), pp. 143–5.

121. *Partners in Revolution*, p. 239.

122. See Robert Kee, *The Most Distressful Country* (London, 1976), pp. 97–100.

123. Robert Hughes, *The Fatal Shore* (London, 1988), p. 181.

124. Patrick O'Farrell, *The Irish in Australia* (New South Wales, 1986), p. 26.

125. 'Irish language and literature, 1691–1845', p. 384.

126. Maureen Wall, 'The Decline of the Irish Language', in Brian Ó Cuív (ed.), *A View of the Irish Language* (Dublin, 1969), p. 89.

127. Michelle O'Riordan, 'Historical Perspectives on the Gaelic Poetry of *The Hidden Ireland*', in Kevin Barry et al. (eds), *The Irish Review*, No. 4, Spring, 1988, p. 79.

128. 'Historical Perspectives on the Gaelic Poetry of *The Hidden Ireland*', p. 79.

129. 'Historical Perspectives on the Gaelic Poetry of *The Hidden Ireland*', p. 80.

130. 'Popular ballads, revolution rhetoric and politicisation', p. 142.

131. George-Denis Zimmerman, *Songs of Irish Rebellion: political street ballads and rebel songs, 1780–1900* (Dublin, 1967), p. 12.

132. Dáithí Ó hÓgáin, 'Folklore and Literature, 1700–1850', in Mary Daly and David Dickson (eds), *The Origins of Popular Literacy in Ireland: Language Change and Educational Development, 1700–1920* (Dublin, 1990, p. 8.

133. 'Folklore and Literature, 1700–1850', p. 9.

134. See Louis Cullen, 'Patrons, Teachers and Literacy in Irish, 1700–1850', in Mary Daly and David Dickson (eds), *The Origins of Popular Literacy in Ireland*, pp. 15–44.

135. *Songs of Irish Rebellion*, p. 23.

136. *Songs of Irish Rebellion*, p. 133.
137. *Songs of Irish Rebellion*, p. 34.
138. *Songs of Irish Rebellion*, p. 46.
139. *Songs of Irish Rebellion*, p. 64.
140. *Modern Ireland*, p. 298.
141. 'Irish language and literature, 1691–1845', p. 380.
142. Brian Friel, *Translations* (London, 1981), pp. 25–6.
143. Irish language and literature, 1691–1845', p. 381.
144. Seamus Heaney, 'The Interesting Case of John Alphonsus Mulrennan', *Planet*, Vol. 41, 1978, p. 35.
145. *Songs of Irish Rebellion*, p. 173.
146. *Songs of Irish Rebellion*, p. 193.
147. *Songs of Irish Rebellion*, pp. 101–2.
148. *Songs of Irish Rebellion*, p. 295.
149. *Songs of Irish Rebellion*, p. 301.
150. *Emigrants and Exiles*, p. 228.
151. Seamus Deane, 'Irish National Character, 1790–1900', in Tom Dunne (ed.), *The Writer As Witness*, p. 101.
152. *Irish Literature: A Social History*, p. 106.
153. Seamus Deane, *The Field Day Anthology of Irish Writing*, Vol. 1, p. 1054.
154. Thomas Moore, *Irish Melodies* (London, 1843), p. 266.
155. Terence Brown, 'Thomas Moore: A Reputation', in *Ireland's Literature: Selected Essays* (Mullingar, 1988), p. 21.
156. Tom Dunne, 'Haunted by history: Irish romantic writing 1800–50', in Roy Porter and Mikulas Teich (eds), *Romanticism In National Contexts* (Cambridge, 1988), p. 69.
157. 'Haunted by history', p. 87.
158. *Irish Melodies*, p. 274.
159. *Irish Melodies*, p. 275.
160. 'Thomas Moore: A Reputation', p. 19.
161. Seamus Deane, *The Field Day Anthology of Irish Writing*, Vol. 1, p. 1055.
162. Seamus Deane, *The Field Day Anthology of Irish Writing*, Vol. 1, p. 1054.
163. 'The Interesting Case of John Alphonsus Mulrennan', p. 36.
164. *Irish Melodies*, pp. 182–3.
165. *Emigrants and Exiles*, p. 105.
166. Walter J. Ong, *Orality and Literacy: The Technologising of the Word* (London, 1982), p. 34.
167. *Orality and Literacy*, p. 45.
168. *Orality and Literacy*, p. 47.

CHAPTER 3

1. Seamus Deane, General Introduction, *The Field Day Anthology of Irish Writing*, Vol. 1, p. xxii.
2. Seamus Deane, General Introduction, *The Field Day Anthology of Irish Writing*, Vol. 1, p. xxii.

3. The term is based on the notion of 'hegemony' employed by Antonio Gramsci in *Selections from the Prison Notebooks* (London, 1971), p. 52 onwards.

4. Cormac Ó Gráda, *The Great Irish Famine* (London, 1989), p. 65.

5. Mary Daly, *The Famine In Ireland* (Dublin, 1986), p. 117.

6. *Emigrants and Exiles*, p. 291.

7. *The Famine In Ireland*, p. 99.

8. Cecil Woodham Smith, *The Great Hunger* (London, 1977). See for example pp. 157–8.

9. See *The Great Irish Famine*, p. 66 and the *Famine In Ireland*, p. 69.

10. *The Great Irish Famine*, p. 63.

11. *The Famine In Ireland*, p. 68.

12. *Emigrants and Exiles*, p. 297.

13. David Lloyd, *Nationalism and Minor Literature: James Clarence Mangan and the Emergence of Irish Cultural Nationalism* (London, 1987), p. 76.

14. *Nationalism and Minor Literature*, p. 76.

15. *Modern Ireland*, p. 311.

16. *A Short History of Irish Literature*, p. 77.

17. *Nationalism and Minor Literature*, p. 77.

18. Christopher Morash (ed.), *The Hungry Voice: The Poetry Of The Irish Famine* (Dublin, 1989), p. 18.

19. *Nationalism and Minor Literature*, p. 60.

20. In *The Hungry Voice*, p. 91.

21. Complete text in *The Hungry Voice*, pp. 54–5.

22. *The Hungry Voice*, p. 220.

23. Complete text in *The Hungry Voice*, p. 199.

24. *Nationalism and Minor Literature*, p. 69.

25. See *Nationalism and Minor Literature*, p. 206.

26. *The Hungry Voice*, p. 22.

27. *Nationalism and Minor Literature*, p. 190.

28. See *Nationalism and Minor Literature*, pp. 190–91.

29. Quoted in *The Hungry Voice*, p. 22.

30. *Nationalism and Minor Literature*, p. 196.

31. *Nationalism and Minor Literature*, p. 195.

32. The introduction is reproduced in D.J. Donoghue (ed.), *Poems of James Clarence Mangan* (Dublin, 1903), p. xxviii.

33. *Poems of James Clarence Mangan*, p. xxviii.

34. *Poems of James Clarence Mangan*, p. xxviii.

35. *Poems of James Clarence Mangan*, p. xxxv.

36. *Poems of James Clarence Mangan*, p. xxxvii.

37. *Poems of James Clarence Mangan*, p. xiii.

38. *Poems of James Clarence Mangan*, p. xiv.

39. *Poems of James Clarence Mangan*, p. 6.

40. *Poems of James Clarence Mangan*, p. 16.

41. *Poems of James Clarence Mangan*, p. 27.

42. *Poems of James Clarence Mangan*, p. 52.

43. *Poems of James Clarence Mangan*, p. 3.

44. *Poems of James Clarence Mangan*, p. 63.

45. *Poems of James Clarence Mangan*, p. 74.
46. *Poems of James Clarence Mangan*, p. 8.
47. *Poems of James Clarence Mangan*, p. 13.
48. *Poems of James Clarence Mangan*, p. 17.
49. *Poems of James Clarence Mangan*, p. 24.
50. *Poems of James Clarence Mangan*, p. 41.
51. *Poems of James Clarence Mangan*, p. 48.
52. *Poems of James Clarence Mangan*, p. 49.
53. *Poems of James Clarence Mangan*, p. 54.
54. *Poems of James Clarence Mangan*, p. 67.
55. *Poems of James Clarence Mangan*, p. 70.
56. *Poems of James Clarence Mangan*, p. 80.
57. *Poems of James Clarence Mangan*, p. 38.
58. *Poems of James Clarence Mangan*, p. 72.
59. *Poems of James Clarence Mangan*, p. 80.
60. *The Field Day Anthology of Irish Writing*, Vol. II, p. 29.
61. *Poems of James Clarence Mangan*, p. xl.
62. *Poems of James Clarence Mangan*, p. 151.
63. Full text in *The Field Day Anthology of Irish Writing*, Vol. II, p. 25–26.
64. *The Hungry Voice*, p. 23.
65. *The Hungry Voice*, p. 132.
66. See 'The Woeful Winter: Suggested by the Accounts of Ireland in December 1848', in *The Hungry Voice*, p. 199 and Meagher's speech extolling the virtues of the sword quoted in *Modern Ireland*, p. 312.
67. *Nationalism and Minor Literature*, p. 208.
68. Seamus Deane, introduction to 'The Petrie Collection of the Ancient Music of Ireland', in *The Field Day Anthology of Irish Writing*, Vol. II, pp. 160–61.
69. Seamus Deane, *The Field Day Anthology of Irish Writing*, Vol. II, p. 6.
70. John O'Rourke, *The History of the Great Irish Famine of 1847 with Notices of Earlier Irish Famines* (Dublin, 1875).
71. *The History of the Great Irish Famine of 1847*, p. 488.
72. *The History of the Great Irish Famine of 1847*, p. 443.
73. *The History of the Great Irish Famine of 1847*, p. 444.
74. Terry Eagleton, 'Emily Bronte and the Great Hunger', in Kevin Barry et al. (ed.), *The Irish Review*, No. 12, Spring/Summer 1992, p. 113.
75. *The Hungry Voice*, p. 18.
76. *The Hungry Voice*, p. 37.
77. 'Emily Bronte and the Great Hunger', p. 112.
78. Roger McHugh, 'The Famine in Irish oral tradition', in R. Dudley Edwards and T. Desmond Smith (eds), *The Great Famine: Studies in Irish History, 1845–52* (Dublin, 1956), p. 391.
79. 'The Famine in Irish oral tradition', pp. 413–14.
80. 'The Famine in Irish oral tradition', p. 435.
81. 'The Famine in Irish oral tradition', pp. 431–2.
82. *The History of the Great Irish Famine of 1847*, p. 504.
83. See Matthew Arnold, *On the Study of Celtic Literature* (London, 1867).
84. Patrick O'Farrell, *The Irish in Australia* (New South Wales, 1986), p. 50.

85. *A Short History of Irish Literature*, p. 73.
86. Thomas Flanagan, 'Literature in English, 1801–91', in W.E. Vaughan (ed.), *A New History of Ireland: Vol. V*, p. 507.
87. W. Dillon, *Life of John Mitchel* (2 vols. London, 1888), ii, pp. 104–5. Quoted in Thomas Flanagan, 'Literature in English, 1801–91', p. 508.
88. *Nationalism and Minor Literature*, p. 49.
89. John Mitchel, *Jail Journal* (London, 1983), p. 16.
90. 'Literature in English, 1801–91', p. 507.
91. *Nationalism and Minor Literature*, p. 50.
92. 'Literature in English, 1801–91', p. 507.
93. *Jail Journal*, p. 67.
94. *Jail Journal*, p. 342
95. Oliver MacDonagh, 'Ideas and institutions, 1830–1845', in W.E. Vaughan (ed.), *A New History of Ireland: Vol. V*, p. 199.
96. Malcolm Brown, *The Politics of Irish Literature from Thomas Davis to W.B. Yeats* (London, 1972), p. 174.
97. *The Politics of Irish Literature*, p. 208.
98. Full text in *The Field Day Anthology of Irish Writing*, Vol. II, p. 106.
99. The original title was *O'Donovan Rossa's Prison Life: Six Years in Six English Prisons* (1874).
100. Jeremiah O'Donovan Rossa, *Irish Rebels in English Prisons* (Dingle, 1991), p. 283.
101. *Emigrants and Exiles*, p. 468.
102. A.M. Sullivan, *The Story of Ireland* (Dublin, n.d.), p. 566.
103. *The Story of Ireland*, p. 567.
104. *The Politics of Irish Literature*, p. 415.
105. Benedict Kiely, in James Maher (ed.), *Sing a Song of Kickham: Songs of Charles J. Kickham* (Dublin, 1965), p. 7.
106. Seamus Deane, *The Field Day Anthology of Irish Writing*, Vol. II, p. 248.
107. 'Literature in English, 1801–91', p. 510.
108. 'Literature in English, 1801–91', p. 510.
109. Charles J. Kickham, *Knocknagow or, The Homes of Tipperary* (Dublin, 1988), p. 481.
110. *Knocknagow*, p. 223.
111. *Knocknagow*, p. 613.
112. *Knocknagow*, p. 581.
113. James Joyce, *Ulysses* (Harmondsworth, 1960), p. 328.
114. *Knocknagow*, p. 584.
115. *Knocknagow*, p. 600.
116. *Knocknagow*, p. 617.
117. *Knocknagow*, p. 478.
118. L. Perry Curtis, *Apes and Angels: The Irishman in Victorian Caricature* (Newton Abbot, 1971).
119. *Apes and Angels*, p. 75.
120. See Michael Toolan, 'The signification of representing dialect in writing', in *Language and Literature: Vol. 1, No. 1*, 1992, pp. 29–46, for a discussion on the constraints and implications in the reporting of speech, and dialect

in particular.
121. *Knocknagow*, p. 620.
122. John Cronin, *The Anglo-Irish Novel: The Nineteenth Century* (Belfast, 1980), p. 111.
123. *Emigrants and Exiles*, p. 128.
124. *Imagined Communities*, p. 19.
125. *Imagined Communities*, p. 20.

CHAPTER 4

1. *Emigrants and Exiles*, p. 346.
2. *Irish Emigration, 1801–1921*, p. 5.
3. *Emigrants and Exiles*, p. 353.
4. *Irish Emigration, 1801–1921*, p. 11.
5. *Irish Emigration, 1801–1921*, p. 8.
6. Sir William Wilde, *Ireland, past and present: the land and the people*. Quoted in David Fitzpatrick, 'Irish Emigration in the Later Nineteenth Century', p. 126.
7. *Emigrants and Exiles*, p. 350.
8. *Irish Emigration, 1801–1921*, p. 13.
9. Full text in Robert L. Wright (ed.), *Irish Emigrant Ballads and Songs* (Ohio, 1975), p. 131.
10. Seamus Deane, *The Field Day Anthology of Irish Writing*, Vol. II, p. 76.
11. See *John McCormack in Irish Song*, Harp Records, HPC 669.
12. See William H.A. Williams, 'From Lost Land to Emerald Isle: Ireland and the Irish in American Sheet Music 1800–1920', in *Éire-Ireland*, No. 26, Spring 1991, pp. 19–45, for a survey of Irish-American popular songs and developing representations of Ireland.
13. Colm O'Lochlainn (ed.), *The Complete Irish Street Ballads* (London, 1984), Introduction, p. x.
14. Robert L. Wright (ed.), *Irish Emigrant Ballads and Songs*, p. 11.
15. Full text in Mrs De Burgh Daly (ed.), *Percy French: Prose, Poems and Parodies* (Dublin, 1980), p. 146.
16. Full text in Mrs De Burgh Daly (ed.), *Percy French: Prose, Poems and Parodies*, p. 6.
17. Full text in Mrs De Burgh Daly (ed.), *Percy French: Prose, Poems and Parodies*, p. 1.
18. Full text in Mrs De Burgh Daly (ed.), *Percy French: Prose, Poems and Parodies*, p. 5.
19. Full text in Mrs De Burgh Daly (ed.), *Percy French: Prose, Poems and Parodies*, p. 3.
20. Stephen Watt, *Joyce, O'Casey, and the Irish Popular Theater* (New York, 1991), p. 4.
21. *Joyce, O'Casey and the Irish Popular Theater*, p. 6.
22. *Joyce, O'Casey and the Irish Popular Theater*, p. 21.
23. *Joyce, O'Casey and the Irish Popular Theater*, p. 47.

24. David Krause (ed.), *The Dolmen Boucicault* (Dublin, 1964), p. 26.
25. Andrew Parkin (ed.), *Selected Plays of Dion Boucicault* (Gerrards Cross, 1987), p. 19.
26. *The Dolmen Boucicault*, p. 33.
27. *Selected Plays of Dion Boucicault*, p. 19.
28. *Apes and Angels*, Chapter iv.
29. *Joyce, O'Casey and the Irish Popular Theater*, p. 72.
30. *Joyce, O'Casey and the Irish Popular Theater*, pp. 75–6.
31. Dion Boucicault, 'Arrah-Na-Pogue', in *The Dolmen Boucicault*, p. 115.
32. 'Arrah-Na-Pogue', p. 134.
33. David Krause, 'The Theatre of Dion Boucicault', in *The Dolmen Boucicault*, p. 33.
34. *Joyce, O'Casey and the Irish Popular Theater*, p. 87.
35. See Edward W. Said's 'Secular Criticism', in *The World, The Text, and The Critic*, p. 16, for a discussion of filiation and affiliation.
36. *Joyce, O'Casey and the Irish Popular Theater*, p. 57.
37. Hubert O'Grady, 'The Famine: A Drama in Prologue and Four Acts', in Stephen Watt (ed.), *Journal of Irish Literature*, 14, Jan. 1985, p. 30.
38. 'The Famine', p. 49.
39. *Apes and Angels*, Chapter vi.
40. 'The Famine', pp. 39–40.
41. 'The Famine', p. 44.
42. 'The Famine', p. 45.
43. 'The Famine', p. 27.
44. Cheryl Herr (ed.), *For The Land They Loved: Irish Political Melodramas, 1890–1925* (New York, 1991).
45. See Richard Pine, 'After Boucicault–Melodrama and the Modern Irish Stage', in Irish Theatre Archives, *Prompts*, No. 6, Sept. 1983, pp. 39–50.
46. *For The Land They Loved*, p. 5.
47. *For The Land They Loved*, p. 5.
48. See Martin Williams, 'Ancient Mythology and Revolutionary Ideology in Ireland, 1878–1916', *Historical Journal*, Vol. xxvi, No. 2, 1983, pp. 307–28.
49. *For The Land They Loved*, p. 64.
50. See Jean-Paul Sartre's introduction to Albert Memmi's *The Colonizer and the Colonized*, p. 26.
51. Emmet Larkin, 'The Devotional Revolution in Ireland 1850–75', in the *American Historical Review*, Vol. xxvii, No. 3, June 1972. Quoted in Sean Connolly, *Religion and Society in Nineteenth-Century Ireland* (Dundalk, 1985), p. 60.
52. *Religion and Society in Nineteenth-Century Ireland*, p. 60.
53. See Eric Hobsbawm and Terence Ranger (eds), *The Invention of Tradition* (Cambridge, 1983), pp. 263–307.
54. Sheridan Gilley, 'The Roman Catholic Church and the Nineteenth-Century Irish Diaspora', *Journal of Ecclesiastical History*, Vol. 35, No. 2, April 1984, p. 188.
55. *Emigrants and Exiles*, p. 455.
56. *Emigrants and Exiles*, p. 457.

57. *Emigrants and Exiles*, p. 464.
58. *Emigrants and Exiles*, p. 463.
59. *Joyce, O'Casey, and the Irish Popular Theater*, p. 59.
60. *Joyce, O'Casey, and the Irish Popular Theater*, p. 62.
61. *Joyce, O'Casey, and the Irish Popular Theater*, p. 64.
62. Terence Brown, 'Canon Sheehan and the Catholic Intellectual', in *Ireland's Literature*, p. 72.
63. Ashis Nandy, *The Intimate Enemy: Loss and Recovery of Self under Colonialism* (Delhi, 1983), p. 52.
64. Canon Sheehan, *Glenanaar* (Dublin, 1989), p. 4.
65. *Glenanaar*, p. 70.
66. *Glenanaar*, pp. 74–5.
67. *Glenanaar*, p. 70.
68. *Glenanaar*, pp. 166–7.
69. *Glenanaar*, p. 234.
70. *Glenanaar*, p. 218.
71. *Glenanaar*, p. 254.
72. *Glenanaar*, pp. 15–16.
73. *Glenanaar*, p. 249.
74. *Glenanaar*, pp. 252–3.
75. *Glenanaar*, p. 258.
76. *Glenanaar*, p. 259.
77. *Glenanaar*, p. 269.
78. *Glenanaar*, pp. 274–5.
79. *Glenanaar*, p. 304.
80. *Anomalous States*, p. 110.
81. *Glenanaar*, p. 320.
82. Joseph Lee, 'Women and the Church since the Famine', in Margaret MacCurtain and Donncha Ó Corráin (eds), *Women in Irish Society*, p. 43.
83. Margaret MacCurtain, 'Towards an Appraisal of the Religious Image of Women', in Mark P. Hederman and Richard Kearney (eds), *The Crane Bag*, Vol. 4, No. 2, 1980, p. 542.
84. See Anne Bernard, 'Creativity and Procreativity', in Mark P. Hederman and Richard Kearney (eds), *Crane Bag Book of Irish Studies* (Dublin, 1982), p. 550.
85. James Connolly, in Peter Berresford Ellis (ed.), *James Connolly's Selected Writings* (Harmondsworth, 1973), p. 191.
86. *James Connolly's Selected Writings*, p. 193.
87. David Fitzpatrick, '"A Share of the Honeycomb': Education, Emigration and Irishwomen', in Mary Daly and David Dickson (eds), *The Origins of Popular Literacy in Ireland*, p. 175.
88. 'Women and the Church since the Famine', pp. 41–2.
89. 'A Share of the Honeycomb', p. 175.
90. See *Irish Emigrant Ballads and Songs*, Chapter vi, for the full text of each song and for numerous additional examples.
91. Full text in *Irish Emigrant Ballads and Songs*, p. 619.
92. A.A. Kelly (ed.), *Pillars of the House: An Anthology of Verse by Irish Women from 1690 to the Present* (Dublin, 1987), p. 11.

93. 'Ancient Mythology and Revolutionary Ideology in Ireland, 1878–1916'.
94. David Cairns and Shaun Richards, 'Tropes and Traps: Aspects of "Woman" and nationality in twentieth-century Irish drama', in Toni O'Brien Johnson and David Cairns (eds), *Gender in Irish Writing* (Milton Keynes, 1991), p. 131.
95. Padraic Colum, *three plays by Padraic Colum* (Dublin, 1963), p. 6.
96. *three plays by Padraic Colum*, p. 7.
97. *three plays by Padraic Colum*, p. 31.
98. *three plays by Padraic Colum*, p. 32.
99. *three plays by Padraic Colum*, p. 11.
100. *three plays by Padraic Colum*, p. 14.
101. *three plays by Padraic Colum*, p. 74.
102. *The Colonizer And The Colonized*, p. 168.
103. James Joyce, *Dubliners* (St Albans, 1977), p. 7.
104. *three plays by Padraic Colum*, p. 109.
105. Full text in *The Field Day Anthology of Irish Writing*, Vol. II, pp. 659–74.
106. Maurice Harmon, 'Cobwebs before the Wind: Aspects of the Peasantry in Irish Literature from 1800 to 1916', in Daniel J. Casey and Robert E. Rhodes (eds), *Views of the Irish Peasantry, 1800–1916* (Hamden, Connecticut, 1977), p. 155.
107. J.M. Synge, *Plays, Prose and Poems* (London, 1941), p. 123.
108. J.M. Synge, *Collected Works: II, Prose* (Gerrards Cross, 1982), p. 60.
109. *Collected Works: II, Prose*, p. 96.
110. *Collected Works: II, Prose*, p. 104.
111. *Collected Works: II, Prose*, p. 106.
112. *Collected Works: II, Prose*, p. 108.
113. *Collected Works: II, Prose*, p. 283.
114. *Collected Works: II, Prose*, p. 341.
115. *Collected Works: II, Prose*, pp. 342–3.
116. *Collected Works: II, Prose*, p. 283.
117. See 'Colonists and Colonised: Some Aspects of Anglo-Irish Literature from Swift to Joyce', p. 114.
118. *Collected Works: II, Prose*, pp. 399–400.
119. Martin J. Waters, 'Peasants and Emigrants: Considerations of the Gaelic League as a Social Movement', in Daniel J. Casey and Robert E. Rhodes (eds), *Views of the Irish Peasantry, 1800–1916*, p. 174.
120. Graham Davis, *The Irish in Britain, 1815–1914* (Dublin, 1991), p. 52.
121. *The Irish in Britain, 1815–1914*, p. 53.
122. Gearóid Ó Tuathaigh, 'The Irish in Nineteenth-Century Britain: Problems of Integration', *Transactions of the Royal Historical Society*, 5th Series, 31, 1981, p. 159.
123. David Fitzpatrick, 'A curious middle place: The Irish in Britain, 1871–1921', in Roger Swift and Sheridan Gilley (eds), *The Irish in Britain, 1815–1939* (London, 1989), p. 35.
124. W.B. Yeats, *John Sherman & Dhoya* (Dublin, 1990), p. 47.
125. Declan Kiberd, 'Yeats, Childhood and Exile', in *Irish Writing: Exile and Subversion*, p. 134.
126. John Eglinton, *Anglo-Irish Essays* (Dublin, 1917), p. 9.

127. G.B. Shaw in David H. Greene and Dan H. Laurence (eds), *The Matter with Ireland* (London, 1962), p. 10.
128. Collected in David H. Greene and Dan H. Laurence (eds), *The Matter with Ireland*.
129. G.B. Shaw, *Preface for Politicians, John Bull's Other Island, How He Lied to Her Husband, Major Barbara* (London, 1931), p. 13.
130. *Preface for Politicians, John Bull's Other Island*, p. 30.
131. *Preface for Politicians, John Bull's Other Island*, p. 31.
132. *Preface for Politicians, John Bull's Other Island*, pp. 15–16.
133. *John Bull's Other Island*, p. 87.
134. *John Bull's Other Island*, p. 88.
135. Richard Ellmann, *Oscar Wilde* (Harmondsworth, 1988), p. 495.
136. Collected in *The Navvy Poet: The Collected Poetry of Patrick MacGill* (London, 1984).
137. Patrick MacGill, *Children of the Dead End: The Autobiography of a Navvy* (London, 1985), p. 30.
138. *Children of the Dead End*, p. 48.
139. *Children of the Dead End*, p. 304.
140. *Children of the Dead End*, p. 269.
141. Gerald O'Donovan, *Father Ralph* (Dingle, 1993), p. 364.
142. *Father Ralph*, pp. 376–7.
143. James Joyce, *Stephen Hero* (London, 1991), p. 199.
144. James Joyce, *Exiles* (Harmondsworth, 1973), p. 129.
145. Joseph MacMahon, 'The Catholic Clergy and the Social Question in Ireland, 1891–1916', *Studies*, Vol. 1xx, No. 280, 1981, pp. 280–1.
146. D.P. Moran, *The Philosophy of Irish-Ireland* (Dublin, 1905), p. 103.
147. *The Philosophy of Irish-Ireland*, pp. 104–5.
148. F.S.L. Lyons, *Culture and Anarchy in Ireland, 1890–1939* (Oxford, 1982), p. 61.
149. Liam O'Dowd, Introduction to *The Colonized and the Colonizer*, p. 52.
150. Edna Longley, 'The Rising, The Somme and Irish Memory', in Máirín Ní Dhonnchada and Theo Dorgan (eds), *Revising the Rising* (Derry, 1991), p. 30.

CHAPTER 5

1. 'The Mind of Winter', p. 55.
2. Peter Green, Introduction to *Ovid: The Poems of Exile* (Harmondsworth, 1994), p. xxxi.
3. Introduction to *Ovid: The Poems of Exile*, p. xxxviii.
4. *Ovid: The Poems of Exile*, p. 176.
5. Edward W. Said, 'Intellectual Exile: Expatriates and Marginals', in *Representations of the Intellectual: The 1993 Reith Lectures* (London, 1994), p. 39.
6. 'Intellectual Exile', p. 39.
7. 'Intellectual Exile', p. 43.
8. 'Intellectual Exile', p. 44.
9. 'Intellectual Exile', p. 45.
10. 'Intellectual Exile', p. 46.

11. 'Intellectual Exile', p. 47.
12. Joseph Hone, *The Life of George Moore* (London, 1936), p. 16.
13. *The Life of George Moore*, pp. 21–2.
14. *The Life of George Moore*, pp. 36–7.
15. *The Life of George Moore*, p. 42.
16. *The Life of George Moore*, p. 47.
17. *The Life of George Moore*, p. 59.
18. *The Life of George Moore*, p. 74.
19. *The Life of George Moore*, p. 86.
20. *The Life of George Moore*, p. 90.
21. *The Life of George Moore*, p. 100.
22. *The Life of George Moore*, p. 117.
23. *The Life of George Moore*, pp. 123–4.
24. *The Life of George Moore*, p. 143.
25. *The Life of George Moore*, p. 193.
26. *The Life of George Moore*, p. 166.
27. Jane Chrisler, 'George Moore's Paris', in Janet Dunleavy (ed.), *George Moore in Perspective* (Gerrards Cross, 1983), p. 47.
28. 'George Moore's Paris', p. 53.
29. 'George Moore's Paris', p. 55.
30. See Eric Hobsbawm, *The Age of Empire, 1875–1914* (London, 1987), Chapters 9 and 10 in particular.
31. See Seamus Deane, 'Civilians and Barbarians', in *Ireland's Field Day*, pp. 33–42 for a discussion of the terms and background.
32. The term is Edward W. Said's and used in *Culture and Imperialism* (London, 1993), p. 295. It has been adopted and freely adapted by this writer to suit his own purposes.
33. George Moore, *A Drama In Muslin* (Gerrards Cross, 1981), p. 57.
34. *A Drama In Muslin*, p. 38.
35. *A Drama In Muslin*, p. 68.
36. *A Drama In Muslin*, pp. 94–5.
37. *A Drama In Muslin*, p. 95.
38. *A Drama In Muslin*, p. 157.
39. *A Drama In Muslin*, p. 106.
40. *A Drama In Muslin*, p. 76.
41. *A Drama In Muslin*, p. 125.
42. *A Drama In Muslin*, p. 216.
43. *A Drama In Muslin*, pp. 218–19.
44. *A Drama In Muslin*, p. 3.
45. *A Drama In Muslin*, pp. 123–30.
46. *A Drama In Muslin*, p. 171.
47. *A Drama In Muslin*, p. 172.
48. *A Drama In Muslin*, p. 198.
49. *A Drama In Muslin*, p. 293.
50. *A Drama In Muslin*, p. 199.
51. *A Drama In Muslin*, p. 323.
52. *A Drama In Muslin*, p. 324.

53. *A Drama In Muslin*, p. 13.
54. *A Drama In Muslin*, p. 324.
55. *A Drama In Muslin*, pp. 325–6.
56. Wayne E. Hall, *Shadowy Heroes: Irish Literature of the 1890s* (New York, 1980), p. 95.
57. Terry Eagleton 'The Anglo-Irish Novel' in *Heathcliff and the Great Hunger: Studies in Irish Culture* (London, 1995), p. 224.
58. 'The Anglo-Irish Novel', p. 224.
59. For an account of the work of the social explorers see P.J. Keating (ed.), Introduction, *Into Unknown England, 1866–1913: Selections from the Social Explorers* (Glasgow, 1976). For a general account of the English working classes in literature at the time see P.J. Keating, *The Working Classes in Victorian Fiction* (London, 1971).
60. *Into Unknown England, 1866–1913*, p. 20.
61. George Moore, *Parnell and his Island* (London, 1887).
62. *Parnell and his Island*, p. 7.
63. *Parnell and his Island*, p. 181.
64. *Parnell and his Island*, p. 182.
65. *Parnell and his Island*, p. 96.
66. *Parnell and his Island*, p. 112.
67. *Parnell and his Island*, p. 141.
68. *Parnell and his Island*, p. 146.
69. *Parnell and his Island*, p. 253.
70. *Parnell and his Island*, p. 86.
71. *Parnell and his Island*, p. 95.
72. *A Drama In Muslin*, p. 159.
73. An ugly term coined by Roy Foster, the Irish-born Professor of Irish History at the University of Oxford for the title of an essay. See 'Marginal Men and Micks on the Make', in *Paddy and Mr Punch: Connections in Irish and English History* (Harmondsworth, 1995), pp. 281–305.
74. *Paddy and Mr Punch*, p. 178.
75. Susan Mitchell, *George Moore* (Dublin, 1916), p. 59.
76. George Moore, *Confessions Of A Young Man* (London, 1888).
77. *Confessions Of A Young Man*, pp. 95–6.
78. *Confessions Of A Young Man*, p. 100.
79. *Confessions Of A Young Man*, p. 118.
80. 'The Anglo-Irish Novel', p. 216.
81. *Confessions Of A Young Man*, p. 217.
82. 'The Anglo-Irish Novel', p. 218.
83. Malcolm Brown, *George Moore: A Reconsideration* (Seattle, 1955), p. 58.
84. *Confessions Of A Young Man*, pp. 126–7.
85. *George Moore: A Reconsideration*, p. 127.
86. *George Moore: A Reconsideration*, p. 132.
87. George Moore, *Esther Waters* (London, 1962), p. vii.
88. Malcolm Brown, *George Moore: A Reconsideration*, p. 133. Richard Cave, *A Study of the Novels of George Moore* (Gerrards Cross, 1978), p. 72.
89. *George Moore: A Reconsideration*, p. 134.

90. *The Life of George Moore*, p. 288. Rolleston, like Moore, was by 1920 resident in England.

91. *Esther Waters*, p. 1.

92. *The Anglo-Irish Tradition*, pp. 144–5.

93. *The Colonizer And The Colonized*, p. 131.

94. See Chapter 4, pp. 172–3.

95. *Shadowy Heroes*, p. 101.

96. *Esther Waters*, p. 29.

97. *Esther Waters*, p. 43.

98. *Esther Waters*, p. 6.

99. *Esther Waters*, p. 282.

100. *Esther Waters*, p. 13.

101. *Esther Waters*, p. 185.

102. *Esther Waters*, p. 74.

103. *Esther Waters*, p. 29.

104. *The Working Classes in Victorian Fiction*, p. 135.

105. Moore's forecast of war with Russia at the end of *Parnell* reflects the growing tension between the major imperial powers in the last quarter of the nineteenth century and the sense of impending Armageddon. In that context the unease of the Irish landlord may have anticipated Forsterian intimations of doom.

106. *Esther Waters*, p. 357.

107. *George Moore: A Reconsideration*, pp. 146–7.

108. See Eric Hobsbawn, *Nations and Nationalism since 1870: Programme, myth, reality* (Cambridge, 1990), pp. 103–4.

109. George Moore, Richard Cave (ed.), *Hail and Farewell* (Gerrards Cross, 1985).

110. *Hail and Farewell*, p. 256. Richard Cave in his notes identifies the 'Jew' as Viscount George Joachim Goschen, the First Lord of the Admiralty and the 'nail-maker' as Joseph Chamberlain, the Secretary of State for the Colonies, p. 705.

111. *Hail and Farewell*, pp. 257–8.

112. Robert Welch, 'Moore's Way Back: The Untilled Field and The Lake', in Robert Welch (ed.), *The Way Back: George Moore's The Untilled Field and The Lake* (Dublin, 1982), p. 31.

113. George Moore, 'Literature and the Irish Language', in Augusta Gregory (ed.), *Ideals in Ireland* (New York, 1973).

114. 'Literature and the Irish Language', p. 46.

115. 'Literature and the Irish Language', p. 47.

116. 'Literature and the Irish Language', p. 49.

117. 'Literature and the Irish Language', p. 50.

118. 'Literature and the Irish Language', p. 51.

119. *The Life of George Moore*, p. 218.

120. Declan Kiberd, 'George Moore's Gaelic Lawn Party', in Robert Welch (ed.), *The Way Back: George Moore's The Untilled Field and The Lake*.

121. *Hail and Farewell*, p. 266.

122. *Hail and Farewell*, p. 269.

123. *Hail and Farewell*, p. 266.

124. *Hail and Farewell*, p. 343.
125. *Hail and Farewell*, p. 345.
126. Richard Cave, Notes, *Hail and Farewell*, p. 715.
127. George Moore, *The Untilled Field* (Gerrards Cross, 1976), Preface, p. xvii.
128. *The Life of George Moore*, p. 243.
129. *The Untilled Field*, Preface, p. xviii.
130. T.R. Henn, *The Untilled Field*, Foreword, p. v.
131. In *The Life of George Moore* Joseph Hone identifies the sequence as 'Some Parishioners', 'Patchwork', 'The Wedding Feast' and 'The Window', p. 244.
132. *Hail and Farewell*, p. 347.
133. *The Untilled Field*, Publisher's Note, p. xxv.
134. 'George Moore's Gaelic Lawn Party', p. 25.
135. *George Moore: A Reconsideration*, p. 166.
136. *Hail and Farewell*, p. 349.
137. *The Life of George Moore*, p. 246.
138. *Hail and Farewell*, p. 57.
139. 'Cobwebs before the Wind', p. 147.
140. 'Cobwebs before the Wind', p. 148.
141. *A Short History of Irish Literature*, p. 170.
142. *Hail and Farewell*, p. 195.
143. *Hail and Farewell*, p. 199.
144. *Hail and Farewell*, p. 201.
145. *Hail and Farewell*, p. 331.
146. 'Cobwebs before the Wind', p. 149.
147. *George Moore: A Reconsideration*, p. 156.
148. *The Untilled Field*, Preface, p. xxi.
149. *Hail and Farewell*, pp. 550–1.
150. 1914 edition, reprinted in the 1931 edition.
151. *The Untilled Field*, Preface, p. xxii.
152. See Chapter 2.
153. George Moore, 'The Exile', in *The Untilled Field*, p. 27.
154. 'The Exile', p. 29.
155. George Moore, 'Homesickness', in *The Untilled Field*, p. 46.
156. 'Homesickness', p. 49.
157. George Moore, 'The Wedding Feast', in *The Untilled Field*, p. 99.
158. George Moore, 'Julia Cahill's Curse', in *The Untilled Field*, p. 165.
159. 'Julia Cahill's Curse', pp. 171–2.
160. George Moore, 'A Playhouse In The Waste', in *The Untilled Field*, p. 160.
161. *Hail and Farewell*, p. 634.
162. *Hail and Farewell*, p. 293.
163. *Hail and Farewell*, p. 43.
164. John Cronin, 'George Moore: The Untilled Field', in Patrick Rafroidi and Terence Brown (eds), *The Irish Short Story* (Gerrards Cross, 1979), p. 122.
165. George Moore, 'So On He Fares', in *The Untilled Field*, pp. 215–16.
166. *George Moore: A Reconsideration*, p. 169.
167. 'So On He Fares', p. 216.
168. 'George Moore: The Untilled Field', p. 123.

169. *The Life of George Moore*, Chapter vii.
170. George Moore, 'The Wild Goose', in *The Untilled Field*, p. 234.
171. 'The Wild Goose', p. 237.
172. 'The Wild Goose', p. 217.
173. 'The Wild Goose', p. 220.
174. 'The Wild Goose', p. 247.
175. 'The Wild Goose', p. 248.
176. 'The Wild Goose', p. 249.
177. 'The Wild Goose', p. 254.
178. 'The Wild Goose', p. 255.
179. 'The Wild Goose', p. 221.
180. 'The Wild Goose', p. 272.
181. 'The Wild Goose', p. 273.
182. 'The Wild Goose', p. 276.
183. 'The Wild Goose', p. 277.
184. 'The Wild Goose', p. 279.
185. 'The Wild Goose', p. 280.
186. John Wilson Foster, *Fictions of the Irish Literary Revival: A Changeling Art* (Dublin, 1987), p. 132.
187. *Hail and Farewell*, p. 643.
188. *Hail and Farewell*, p. 644.
189. George Moore, 'Fugitives', in *The Untilled Field*, p. 295. The same sentiment, expressed in very nearly the same words, occurs in *Hail and Farewell*, p. 349.
190. *A Short History of Irish Literature*, p. 175.
191. Susan Mitchell, *George Moore* (Dublin, 1916), p. 48.
192. *George Moore*, p. 117.
193. W.B. Yeats, 'Dramatis Personae', in *Autobiographies* (London, 1955), p. 403.
194. 'Dramatis Personae', p. 404.
195. 'Dramatis Personae', p. 405.
196. John Eglinton, *Irish Literary Portraits* (London, 1935), p. 13.
197. *Irish Literary Portraits*, p. 104.
198. Raymond Williams, *Writing in Society* (London, n.d.), p. 222.
199. *Writing in Society*, p. 223.
200. George Steiner, 'Extraterritorial', in *Extraterritorial Papers on Literature and the Language Revolution* (New York, 1971), p. 3.
201. Malcolm Bradbury, 'The Cities of Modernism', in Malcolm Bradbury and James McFarlane (eds), *Modernism* (Harmondsworth, 1976), p. 101.
202. 'The Anglo-Irish Novel', p. 216.
203. *A Short History of Irish Literature*, p. 174.

CHAPTER 6

1. See Paul Fussell's *The Great War and Modern Memory* (Oxford, 1977).
2. Full text in Roy Foster's *Modern Ireland*, pp. 597–8.
3. Declan Kiberd offers an interesting analysis of childhood within the colonial enterprise in *Inventing Ireland: The Literature of the Modern Nation* (London,

1995), pp. 101–14.

4. See Terence Brown's *Ireland: A Social and Cultural History, 1922–1985*, for a full account of the cultural conditions and artistic responses in the years following 1922.

5. James Joyce, *A Portrait Of The Artist As A Young Man* (Harmondsworth, 1960), p. 247.

6. *A Portrait Of The Artist As A Young Man*, p. 202.

7. *A Portrait Of The Artist As A Young Man*, p. 253.

8. *A Portrait Of The Artist As A Young Man*, p. 221.

9. See the work of *Field Day* in particular.

10. See Bill Ashcroft et al., *The Empire Writes Back: Theory and Practice in Post-Colonial Literatures* (London, 1989), p. 19.

11. *Ulysses*, p. 13.

12. *A Portrait Of The Artist As A Young Man*, p. 240.

13. L. Perry Curtis, 'The Anglo-Irish Predicament', in *Twentieth Century Studies*, Nov. 1970, p. 61.

14. F.S.L. Lyons, *Culture and Anarchy in Ireland 1890–1939* (Oxford, 1982), p. 71.

15. 'The Anglo-Irish Predicament', p. 61.

16. *Synge and Anglo-Irish Literature*, p. 19.

17. Andrew Gurr, *Writers in Exile: The Identity of Home in Modern Literature* (Brighton, 1982), p. 7.

18. *Writers in Exile*, p. 8.

19. *Writers in Exile*, p. 10

20. *Writers in Exile*, p. 9.

21. *Writers in Exile*, p. 11.

22. Salman Rushdie, 'Imaginary Homelands', in *Imaginary Homelands: Essays and Criticism, 1981–1991* (London, 1991), p. 10.

23. *Writers in Exile*, p. 15.

24. *Writers in Exile*, p. 20.

25. *Writers in Exile*, p. 32.

26. *Writers in Exile*, p. 145.

27. Terence Brown, 'Louis MacNeice's Ireland', in Terence Brown and Nicholas Grene (eds), *Tradition and Influence in Anglo-Irish Poetry* (Basingstoke, 1989), p. 81.

28. Joseph Lee and Gearóid Ó Tuathaigh (eds), *The Age of de Valera* (Dublin, 1982), p. 9.

29. Joseph O'Connor in Dermot Bolger (ed.), *Ireland in Exile: Irish Writers Abroad* (Dublin 1993), p. 16. O'Connor however, overlooks Pádraic Ó Conaire's *Deoraíocht* the first Irish language novel which was published in 1904.

30. Liam Ryan, 'Irish Emigration to Britain since World War II', in Richard Kearney (ed.), *Migrations*, p. 66.

31. 'Irish Emigration to Britain since World War II', p. 50.

32. Declan Kiberd, *Inventing Ireland*, p. 641.

33. 'Imaginary Homelands', p. 20.

34. 'Heroic Styles', p. 58.

35. Seamus Deane, *Celtic Revivals: Essays In Modern Irish Literature* (London, 1985), p. 156.

36. Edna O'Brien, in *Mother Ireland* (Harmondsworth, 1978), p. 87.

37. Michael O'Loughlin, *Frank Ryan: Journey to the Centre* (Dublin, 1987), p. 10.

38. *Frank Ryan*, p. 18.

39. Benedict Anderson, 'Exodus', in *Critical Enquiry*, Winter 1994, p. 322.

40. 'Exodus', p. 325.

41. 'Exodus', p. 327.

42. *Ireland In Exile*, p. 16.

43. *Ireland In Exile*, p. 17.

44. 'Exodus', p. 322.

45. Cahal Dallat, 'Other Irish Writing: A New Poetics of Exile', *Verse*, Vol. 9, No. 3, Winter 1992, p. 31.

46. The term is quoted in Patrick O'Sullivan (ed.), *The Creative Migrant* (London, 1994), Introduction, p. 19.

47. Seamus Heaney, 'Exposure', in *North*, p. 72.

48. See Declan Kiberd's 'Imagining Irish Studies', in *Inventing Ireland* for a stimulating discussion of the possibilities of a cultural studies programme, pp. 641–53.

49. Eavan Boland, 'The Emigrant Irish', in *The Field Day Anthology of Irish Writing*, Vol. 111, p. 1,397.

Bibliography

PRIMARY TEXTS

Bolger, Dermot (ed.), *Ireland In Exile: Irish Writers Abroad* (Dublin, 1993).
Boucicault, Dion, David Krause (ed.), *The Dolmen Boucicault* (Dublin, 1964).
—— Andrew Parkin (ed.), *Selected Plays of Dion Boucicault* (Gerrards Cross, 1987).
Bowen, Elizabeth, *The Last September* (Harmondsworth, 1942).
—— *Bowen's Court and Seven Winters: Memories of a Dublin Childhood* (London, 1984).
Bullock, Shan, *Dan the Dollar* (Dublin, 1905).
Casey, Daniel J. and Rhodes, Robert E. (eds), *Modern Irish American Fiction: A Reader* (New York, 1989).
Colum, Padraic, *three plays by Padraic Colum* (Dublin, 1963).
Connolly, James, Peter Berresford Ellis (ed.), *Selected Writings* (Harmondsworth, 1973).
Deane, Seamus (ed.), *The Field Day Anthology of Irish Writing* (Derry, 1991).
Delaney, Frank (ed.), *Silver Apples, Golden Apples: Best Loved Irish Verse* (Belfast, 1987).
Fagan, Patrick (ed.), *A Georgian Celebration: Irish Poets of the Eighteenth Century* (Dublin, 1989).
Fallon, Peter and Mahon, Derek (eds), *The Penguin Book of Contemporary Irish Poetry* (Harmondsworth, 1990).
Fanning, Charles (ed.), *The Exiles of Erin: Nineteenth-Century Irish-American Fiction* (Indiana, 1987).
Fitzmaurice, George, *The Plays of George Fitzmaurice: Realistic Plays* (Dublin, 1970).
French, Percy, Mrs De Burgh Daly (ed.), *Percy French: Prose, Poems and Parodies* (Dublin, 1980).
Friel, Brian, *Translations* (London, 1981).
—— *Making History* (London, 1989).
Gantz, Jeffrey (ed.), *Early Irish Myths and Sagas* (Harmondsworth, 1981).
Glassie, Henry (ed.), *Irish Folk Tales* (Harmondsworth, 1987).
Greene, David and O'Connor, Frank (eds), *A Golden Treasury of Irish Poetry* A.D. *600–1200* (Dingle, 1990).
Gregory, Augusta (ed.), *Ideals in Ireland* (New York, 1973).
Healy, John, *Nineteen Acres* (Galway, 1978).
Heaney, Seamus, *North* (London, 1975).
—— *Sweeney Astray* (London, 1984).

Henry, P.L. (ed.), *Dánta Bán: Poems of Irish Women; early and modern* (Cork, 1990).

Herr, Cheryl (ed.), *For the Land they Loved: Irish Political Melodramas, 1890–1925* (New York, 1991).

Jackson, Kenneth, H. (ed.), *A Celtic Miscellany: Translations from the Celtic Literatures* (Harmondsworth, 1971).

James Joyce, *A Portrait Of The Artist As A Young Man* (Harmondsworth, 1960).

—— *Ulysses* (Harmondsworth, 1969).

—— *Exiles* (Harmondsworth, 1973).

—— *Dubliners* (St Albans, 1977).

—— *Stephen Hero* (London, 1991).

Keane, Molly, *Mad Puppetstown* (London, 1985).

Kelly, A.A. (ed.), *Pillars of the House: An Anthology of Verse by Irish Women from 1690 to the Present* (Dublin, 1987).

Kennelly, Brendan (ed.), *The Penguin Book of Irish Verse* (Harmondsworth, 1970).

Kickham, Charles J., James Maher (ed.), *Sing A Song of Kickham: Songs of Charles J. Kickham* (Dublin, 1965).

—— *Knocknagow or, The Homes of Tipperary* (Dublin, 1988).

Kinsella, Thomas (Trans.), *The Tain* (Oxford, 1970).

____ (ed.), *The New Oxford Book of Irish Verse* (Oxford, 1989).

Lampe, David (ed.), *The Legend of Being Irish: A Collection of Irish American Poetry* (New York, 1989).

MacAmlaigh, Dônal, *An Irish Navvy: The Diary of an Exile* (Trans. Valentin Iremonger) (London, 1964).

MacGill, Patrick, *The Navvy Poet: The Collected Poetry of Patrick MacGill* (London, 1984).

—— *Children of the Dead End: The Autobiography of a Navvy* (London, 1985).

Macken, Walter, *I Am Alone* (London, 1977).

MacNamara, Brinsley, *The Clanking of Chains* (Tralee, 1965).

—— *The Valley of the Squinting Windows* (Dublin, 1984).

Mangan, James Clarence, *Poems of James Clarence Mangan*, D.J. Donoghue (ed.) (Dublin, 1903).

McMahon, Sean (ed.), *Rich and Rare: A Book of Ireland* (Swords, 1987).

—— (ed.), *Poolbeg Book Of Irish Ballads* (Swords, 1991).

Mitchel, John, *Jail Journal* (London, 1983).

Montague, John (ed.), *The Faber Book of Irish Verse* (London, 1974).

Moore, George, *Esther Waters* (London, 1962).

—— *The Untilled Field* (Gerrards Cross, 1976).

—— *The Lake* (Gerrards Cross, 1980).

—— *A Drama in Muslin* (Gerrards Cross, 1981).

—— Richard Cave (ed.), *Hail and Farewell* (Gerrards Cross, 1985).

—— *Confessions Of A Young Man* (London, 1886).

—— *Parnell and his Ireland* (London, 1887).

Moore, Thomas, *Irish Melodies* (London, 1843).

Moran, D.P., *The Philosophy of Irish Ireland* (Dublin, 1905).

Morash, Christopher (ed.), *The Hungry Voice* (Dublin, 1989).

Murphy, Richard, *Selected Poems* (London, 1979).

O'Brien, Edna, *Mother Ireland* (Harmondsworth, 1978).

O'Connor, Frank (ed.), *Kings, Lords and Commons: An Anthology from the Irish* (Dublin, 1959).

O'Donovan, Gerald, *Father Ralph* (Dingle, 1993).

O'Duffy, Eimar, *The Wasted Island* (London, 1919).

—— *King Goshawk and the Birds* (London, 1926).

O'Grady, Hubert, *Emigration*, Stephen Watt (ed.), *Journal of Irish Literature*, 14 Jan. 1985, pp. 14–25.

—— *The Famine: A Drama in Prologue and Four Acts*, Stephen Watt (ed.), *Journal of Irish Literature*, 14 Jan. 1985, pp. 25–49.

O'Kelly, Seamus, *Wet Clay* (Dublin, 1922).

Ó Lochlainn, Colm (ed.), *The Complete Irish Street Ballads* (London, 1984).

O'Rourke, John, *The History of the Great Irish Famine of 1847, with Notices of Earlier Irish Famines* (Dublin, 1875).

Ó Tuama, Seán and Kinsella, Thomas (eds), *An Duanaire 1600–1900: Poems of the Dispossessed* (Portlaoise, 1981).

Ovid, Peter Green (ed.), *Ovid: The Poems of Exile* (Harmondsworth, 1994).

Rossa, Jeremiah O'Donovan, *Irish Rebels in English Prisons* (Dingle, 1991).

Shaw, George Bernard, *John Bull's Other Island, How He Lied To Her Husband, Major Barbara* (London, 1931).

—— David, H. Green and Dan H. Laurence (eds), *The Matter with Ireland* (London, 1962).

Sheehan, Canon, *Glenanaar* (Dublin, 1989).

Somerville, Edith and Ross, Martin, *The Big House of Inver* (London, 1978).

Spirit of the Nation: Ballads and Songs with Original Ancient Music (Dublin, 1981).

Sullivan, A.M., *The Story of Ireland* (Dublin n.d.).

Swift, Jonathan, Joseph McMinn (ed.), *Swift's Irish Pamphlets: An Introductory Selection* (Gerrards Cross, 1991).

Synge, John Millington, *Plays, Poems and Prose* (London, 1941).

—— *Collected Works: II, Prose* (Gerrards Cross, 1982).

Tone, Theobald Wolfe, Seán Ó Faoláin (ed.), *The Autobiography of Theobald Wolfe Tone* (London, 1937).

Wright, Robert L. (ed.), *Irish Emigrant Ballads and Songs* (Ohio, 1975).

Yeats, W.B., *Autobiographies* (London, 1955).

—— *John Sherman and Dhoya* (Dublin, 1990).

Zimmerman, George-Denis (ed.), *Songs of Irish Rebellion: political street ballads and rebel songs, 1780–1900* (Dublin, 1967).

SECONDARY TEXTS

Adams, J.R.R., *The Printed Word and the Common Man: Popular Culture in Ulster, 1700–1900* (Belfast, 1987).

Ahmad, Aijaz, 'Jameson's Rhetoric of Otherness and the "National Allegory"', *Social Text*, 17, Fall 1987, pp. 3–25.

Akenson, Donald H., *Half the World from Home: perspectives on the Irish in New Zealand, 1860–1950* (Wellington, New Zealand, 1991).

—— *Small Differences: Irish Catholics and Irish Protestants, 1815–1922* (Dublin, 1991).

Anderson, Benedict, *Imagined Communities: Reflections on the Origin and Spread of Nationalism* (London, 1983).

—— 'Exodus', *Critical Inquiry*, Winter 1994, pp. 314–27.

Andrews, K., Canny, N. and Hair, P.E.H. (eds), *The Westward Enterprise: English Activities in Ireland, the Atlantic and America, 1480–1650* (Liverpool, 1978).

Arnold, Matthew, *On the Study of Celtic Literature* (London, 1867).

Ashcroft, Bill, Griffiths, Gareth and Tiffin, Helen, *The Empire Writes Back: Theory and Practice in Post-Colonial Literatures* (London, 1989).

Bakhtin, Mikhail, *The Dialogic Imagination: Four Essays*, Michael Holquist (ed.), Caryl Emerson and Michael Holquist (trans.) (Austin, Texas, 1981).

Barker, Francis, Hulme, Peter, Iversen, Margaret and Loxley, Diana (eds), *Literature, Politics and Theory: Papers from the Essex Conference, 1976–84* (London, 1986).

Bartlett, Thomas, Curtin, Chris, O'Dwyer, Riana and Ó Tuathaigh, Gearoid (eds), *Irish Studies: A General Introduction* (Dublin, 1988).

Beckett, J.C., *The Anglo-Irish Tradition* (Belfast, 1982).

—— 'Literature in English, 1691–1800', in T.W. Moody and W.E. Vaughan (eds), *A New History Of Ireland: Vol. IV, Eighteenth Century Ireland, 1691–1800* (Oxford, 1986), pp. 424–70.

Bennington, Geoff, Bowlby, Rachel and Young, Robert (eds), *Colonialism and Other Essays: The Oxford Literary Review*, Vol. 9, Nos 1–2, 1987.

Bernard, Anne, 'Creativity and Procreativity', in Mark P. Hederman and Richard Kearney (eds), *Crane Bag Book of Irish Studies* (Dublin, 1982), pp. 544–54.

Bhabha, Homi K., 'Representation and the Colonial text. A Critical Exploration of Some Forms of Mimeticism', in Frank Gloversmith (ed.), *The Theory of Reading* (Brighton, 1984), pp. 93–121.

—— 'Of Mimicry and Man. The Ambivalence of Colonial Discourse', *October*, No. 28, 1984, pp. 125–33.

—— 'Signs Taken for Wonders: Questions of Ambivalence and Authority under a Tree outside Delhi, May 1817', *Critical Inquiry*, 12, Autumn 1985, pp. 144–64.

—— 'The other question: difference, discrimination and the discourse of colonialism', in Francis Barker et al. (eds), *Literature, Politics and Theory, Papers from the Essex Conference 1976–84* (London, 1986), pp. 148–72.

—— (ed.), *Nation and Narration* (London, 1990).

Blake, John W., 'Transportation from Ireland to America, 1653–60', *Irish Historical Studies 3*, No. 11, March 1943, pp. 267–81.

Bliss, Alan, 'The English language in early modern Ireland', in T.W. Moody et al. (eds), *A New History Of Ireland: Vol. III, Early Modern Ireland, 1534–1691* (Oxford, 1976), pp. 546–60.

—— and Long, Joseph, 'Literature in Norman French and English to 1534', in Art Cosgrove (ed.), *A New History Of Ireland: Vol. II, Medieval Ireland, 1169–1534* (Oxford, 1987), pp. 708–36.

Bolton, G.C., 'The Anglo-Irish and the Historians, 1830–1980', in Oliver Mac-Donagh et al. (eds), *Irish Culture and Nationalism, 1750–1950* (London, 1983), pp. 239–57.

Bradbury, Malcolm and McFarlane, James (eds), *Modernism* (Harmondsworth, 1976).

Bradshaw, Brendan, 'Native reaction to the Westward Enterprise: A case-study in Gaelic ideology', in K.R. Andrews et al. (eds), *The Westward Enterprise: English Activities in Ireland, the Atlantic and America, 1480–1650* (Liverpool, 1978), pp. 66–80.

Brady, Ciaran and Gillespie, Raymond (eds), *Natives and Newcomers: Essays on the Making of Irish Colonial Society, 1534–1641* (Dublin, 1986).

Brasted, H.V., 'Irish Nationalism and the British Empire in the late Nineteenth Century', in Oliver MacDonagh et al. (eds), *Irish Culture and Nationalism, 1750–1950* (London, 1983), pp. 83–103.

Breatnach, R.A., 'The End of a Tradition: A Survey of Eighteenth-Century Gaelic Literature', *Studia Hibernica*, Vol. 1, 1961, pp. 128–50.

Brennan, Timothy, 'The national longing for form', in Homi K. Bhabha (ed.), *Nation and Narration* (London, 1990), pp. 44–70.

Brown, Malcolm, *George Moore: A Reconsideration* (Seattle, 1955).

—— *The Politics of Irish Literature from Thomas Davis to W.B. Yeats* (London, 1972).

Brown, Terence, *Ireland: A Social and Cultural History, 1922–1985* (London, 1981).

—— *The Whole Protestant Community: the making of a historical myth*, A Field Day Pamphlet, No. 7, Derry, 1985.

—— *Ireland's Literature: Selected Essays* (Mullingar, 1988).

—— and Grene, Nicholas (eds), *Tradition and Influence in Anglo-Irish Poetry* (London: 1989).

Cahalan, James, *The Irish Novel: A Critical History* (Dublin, 1988).

Cairns, David and Richards, Shaun, *Writing Ireland: colonialism, nationalism and culture* (Manchester, 1988).

—— 'Tropes and Traps: Aspects of "Woman" and nationality in twentieth-century Irish drama', in Toni O'Brien Johnson and David Cairns (eds), *Gender in Irish Writing* (Milton Keynes, 1991).

Callahan, Bob, *The Big Book of American Irish Culture* (Harmondsworth, 1989).

Canny, Nicholas P., 'The Ideology of English Colonisation: From Ireland to America', *William and Mary Quarterly*, Vol. 30, 1973, pp. 575–98.

—— 'The Formation of the Irish Mind: Religion, Politics and Gaelic Irish Literature, 1580–1750', *Past and Present*, No. 95, 1982, pp. 91–116.

—— 'Identity Formation in Ireland: The Emergence of the Anglo-Irish', in Nicholas Canny and Anthony Pagden (eds), *Colonial Identity in the Atlantic World, 1500–1800* (Princeton, 1987), pp. 159–212.

Carney, James, 'Literature in Irish, 1169–1534', in Art Cosgrove (ed.), *A New History of Ireland Vol. 11, Medieval Ireland, 1169–1534* (Oxford, 1987), pp. 688–707.

Carpenter, Andrew (eds), *Place, Personality and the Irish Writer* (Gerrards Cross, 1977).

Casey, Daniel J. and Rhodes, Robert E. (eds), *Views of the Irish Peasantry, 1800–1916* (Hamden, Connecticut, 1977).

—— (eds), *Modern Irish-American Fiction: A Reader* (New York, 1989).

Casway, Jerrold, 'Irish Women Overseas, 1500–1800', in Margaret MacCurtain and Mary O'Dowd (eds), *Women in Early Modern Ireland* (Edinburgh, 1991), pp. 112–32.

Cave, Richard, *A Study of the Novels of George Moore* (Gerrards Cross, 1978).

Césaire, Aimé, *Discourse on Colonialism* (London, 1972).

Chatterjee, Partha, *Nationalist Thought and the Colonial World: A Derivative Discourse* (London, 1986).

Clancy, Mary, Cunningham, John and MacLochlain, Alf (eds), ... *the emigrant experience* ... (Galway, 1991).

Coleman, Terry, *Passage to America* (Newton Abbot, 1973).

Connolly, Peter (ed.), *Literature and the Changing Ireland* (Gerrards Cross, 1982).

Connolly, Sean, *Religion and Society in Nineteenth-Century Ireland* (Dundalk, 1985).

—— 'Popular Culture in Pre-Famine Ireland', in Cyril J. Byrne and Margaret Harry (eds), *Talamh An Eisc: Canadian and Irish Essays* (Halifax, Nova Scotia, 1986), pp. 12–28.

Corish, Patrick J., 'The Cromwellian regime, 1650–60', in T.W. Moody et al. (eds), *A New History Of Ireland: Vol. III, Early Modern Ireland, 1534–1691* (Oxford, 1976), pp. 353–86.

Corkery, Daniel, *Synge and Anglo-Irish Literature* (Cork, 1931).

—— *The Hidden Ireland: A Study of Gaelic Munster in the Eighteenth Century* (Dublin, 1967).

Cosgrove, Art (ed.), *A New History Of Ireland: Vol. II, Medieval Ireland, 1169–1534 (Oxford, 1987)*.

Costello, Con, 'The Convicts: Transportation from Ireland', in Colm Kiernan (ed.), *Australia and Ireland Bicentenary Essays, 1788–1988* (Dublin, 1986), pp. 111–20.

—— *Botany Bay: The Story of the Convicts transported from Ireland to Australia, 1791–1853* (Cork, 1987).

Costello, Peter, *The Heart Grown Brutal: The Irish Revolution in Literature from Parnell to the Death of Yeats, 1891–1939* (Dublin, 1978).

Cronin, John, 'George Moore: The Untilled Field', in Patrick Rafroidi and Terence Brown (eds), *The Irish Short Story* (Gerrards Cross, 1979), pp. 113–25.

—— *The Anglo-Irish Novel: The Nineteenth Century* (Belfast, 1980).

Cullen, Louis, *The Hidden Ireland: Reassessment of a Concept* (Mullingar, 1988).

—— 'Patrons Teachers and Literacy in Irish: 1700–1850', in Mary Daly and David Dickson (eds), *The Origins of Popular Literacy in Ireland: Language Change and Educational Development, 1700–1920* (Dublin, 1990), pp. 15–44.

Cunningham, Bernadette, 'Native Culture and Political Change in Ireland, 1580–1640', in Ciaran Brady and Raymond Gillespie (eds), *Natives and Newcomers: The Making of Irish Colonial Society, 1534–1641* (Dublin, 1986), pp. 148–70.

—— 'Women and Gaelic Literature, 1500–1800', in Margaret MacCurtain and Mary O'Dowd (eds), *Women in Early Modern Ireland* (Edinburgh, 1991), pp. 147–159.

Curtin, Chris, O'Dwyer, Riana and Ó Tuathaigh, Gearóid, 'Emigration and Exile', in Thomas Bartlett et al. (eds), *Irish Studies: A General Introduction* (Dublin, 1988), pp. 60–86.

Curtis, Edmund, *A History of Ireland* (London, 1950).

Curtis, Liz, *Nothing But The Same Old Story* (London, 1984).

Curtis, L. Perry, *Anglo-Saxons and Celts: A Study of Anti-Irish Prejudice in Victorian England* (Connecticut, 1968).

—— 'The Anglo-Irish predicament', *20th Century Studies*, November 1970, pp. 37–63.

—— *Apes and Angels: The Irishman in Victorian Caricature* (Newton Abbot, 1971).

Dahlie, Hallvard, 'Brian Moore And The Meaning Of Exile', in Richard Wall (ed.), *Medieval and Modern Ireland* (Gerrards Cross, 1988), pp. 91–107.

Dallat, Cahal, 'Other Irish Writing: A New Poetics of Exile', *Verse*, Vol. 9, No. 3, Winter 1992, pp. 23–33.

Dalton, G.F., 'The Tradition of Blood Sacrifice to the Goddess Éire, *Studies*, Vol. LXII, 1974, pp. 343–54.

d'Alton, Ian, 'Southern Irish Unionism: A Study of Cork Unionists, 1884–1914', *Transactions of the Royal Historical Society, 5th Series*, 23, 1973, pp. 71–88.

—— 'A contrast in crises: southern Irish Protestantism, 1830–43 and 1885–1910', in A.C. Hepburn (ed.), *Minorities in History* (London, 1978), pp. 70–83.

Daly, Mary, *The Famine in Ireland* (Dublin, 1986).

—— and Dickson, David (eds), *The Origins of Popular Literacy in Ireland: Language Change and Educational Development, 1700–1920* (Dublin, 1990).

Davis, Graham, *The Irish in Britain, 1815–1914* (Dublin, 1991).

Dawe, Gerald and Longley, Edna (eds), *Across a Roaring Hill: The Protestant imagination in modern Ireland* (Belfast, 1985).

Deane, Seamus, 'Civilians and barbarians', in Field Day Theatre Company, *Ireland's Field Day* (London, 1985), pp. 33–42.

—— 'Heroic styles: the tradition of an idea', in Field Day Theatre Company, *Ireland's Field Day* (London, 1985), pp. 45–58.

—— *Celtic Revivals: Essays in Modern Irish Literature, 1880–1980* (London, 1985).

—— *A Short History of Irish Literature* (London, 1986).

—— 'Irish national character 1790–1900', in Tom Dunne (ed.), *The Writer as Witness: literature as historical evidence* (Cork, 1987), pp. 90–113.

de Paor, Liam, *The Peoples of Ireland: From prehistory to modern times* (London, 1986).

Dickson, R.J., *Ulster Emigration to Colonial America 1718–1775* (Belfast, 1988).

Doyle, David N., 'The Irish in Australia and the United States: Some Comparisons, 1800–1939', in *Irish Economic and Social History XVI*, 1989, pp. 73–93.

—— 'The Irish in North America, 1776–1845', in W.E. Vaughan (ed.), *A New History of Ireland: Vol. V, Ireland Under the Union, 1801–1870* (Oxford, 1989), pp. 682–725.

Drudy, P.J. (ed.), *The Irish in America: Emigration, Assimilation and Impact, Irish Studies 4* (Cambridge, 1985).

Duffy, Patrick, 'Literary Reflections on Irish Emigration in the nineteenth and twentieth centuries', in Russell King et al. (eds), *Writing Across Worlds: Literature and Migration* (London, 1995).

Dunleavy, Janet (ed.), *George Moore in Perspective* (Gerrards Cross, 1983).

Dunne, Tom, 'The Gaelic Response to Conquest and Colonisation: The Evidence of the Poetry', *Studia Hibernica*, Vol. XX, 1980, pp. 7–30.

—— 'Maria Edgeworth and the Colonial Mind', *The 26th O'Donnell Lecture* (Cork, 1984).

—— (ed.), *The Writer as Witness: literature as historical evidence* (Cork, 1987).

—— 'Haunted by history. Irish romantic writing, 1800–1850', in Roy Porter and Mikulas Teich (eds), *Romanticism in National Contexts* (Cambridge, 1988), pp. 68–91.

—— 'Popular ballads, revolutionary rhetoric and politicisation', in Hugh Gough and David Dickson (eds), *Ireland and the French Revolution* (Dublin, 1990), pp. 139–55.

—— 'New Histories: Beyond 'Revisionism', in Kevin Barry et al. (eds), *The Irish Review*, No. 12, Spring/Summer 1992, pp. 1–12.

Eagleton, Terry, *Exiles and Émigrés: Studies in Modern Literature* (London, 1970).

—— *Nationalism, Colonialism and Literature, Nationalism: Irony and Commitment, A Field Day Pamphlet*, No. 13, Derry, 1988.

—— *Ideology: An Introduction* (London, 1991).

—— 'Emily Bronte and the Great Hunger', in Kevin Barry et al. (eds), *The Irish Review*, No. 12, Spring/Summer 1992, pp. 108–19.

—— *Heathcliff and the Great Hunger: Studies in Irish Culture* (London, 1995).

—— *Crazy John and the Bishop and Other Essays on Irish Culture* (Cork, 1998).

Edwards, John, *Language, Society and Identity* (Oxford, 1985).

Edwards, Ruth Dudley, *An Atlas of Irish History* (London, 1973).

Edwards, R. Dudley and Williams, T. Desmond (eds), *The Great Famine: Studies in Irish History, 1845–52* (Dublin, 1956).

Eglinton, John, *Anglo-Irish Essays* (Dublin, 1917).

—— *Irish Literary Portraits* (London, 1935).

Elliott, Bruce, *Irish Migrants in the Canadas: A New Approach* (Belfast, 1988).

Elliott, Marianne, *Partners in Revolution: The United Irishmen and France* (New Haven and London, 1982).

—— *Watchmen in Sion: The Protestant idea of liberty, A Field Day Pamphlet*, No. 8, Derry, 1985.

Ellis, Peter Berresford, *A History of the Irish Working Class* (London, 1985).

—— *Hell or Connaught! The Cromwellian Colonisation of Ireland, 1652–1660* (London, n.d.).

Ellman, Richard, *Oscar Wilde* (Harmondsworth, 1988).

Fallis, Richard, *The Irish Renaissance: An Introduction to Anglo-Irish Literature* (Dublin, 1978).

Fanon, Frantz, *The Wretched of the Earth* (Harmondsworth, 1967).

Field Day Theatre Company, *Ireland's Field Day* (London, 1985).

Fitzpatrick, David, *Politics and Irish Life, 1913–1921: Provincial Experience of War and Revolution* (Dublin, 1977).

—— 'Irish Emigration in the Later Nineteenth Century', *Irish Historical Studies*, Vol. 22, No. 86, Sept. 1980, pp. 126–43.

—— *Irish Emigration, 1801–1921* (Dublin, 1984).

—— 'Emigration, 1801–70', in W.E. Vaughan (ed.), *A New History Of Ireland: Vol. V, Ireland under the Union, 1810–1870* (Oxford, 1989), pp. 562–620.

—— '"A peculiar tramping people": the Irish in Britain, 1810–70', in W.E. Vaughan (ed.), *A New History of Ireland: Vol. V, Ireland under the Union, 1801–1870* (Oxford, 1989), pp. 621–60.

—— 'A curious middle place: the Irish in Britain, 1871–1921', in Roger Swift and Sheridan Gilley (eds), *The Irish in Britain, 1815–1939* (London, 1989), pp. 10–59.

—— '"A Share of the Honeycomb": Education, Emigration and Irishwomen', in Mary Daly and David Dickson (eds), *The Origins of Popular Literacy in Ireland: Language, Change and Educational Development, 1700–1920* (Dublin, 1990), pp. 167–87.

Flanagan, Thomas, 'Literature in English, 1801–91', in W.E. Vaughan (ed.), *A New History of Ireland: Vol. V, Ireland under the Union, 1810–1870* (Oxford, 1989), pp. 482–522.

Flower, Robin, *The Irish Tradition* (Oxford, 1947).

Fogarty, Michael, Ryan, Liam and Lee, Joseph, *Irish Values and Attitudes* (Dublin, 1984).

Foster, John Wilson, *Forces and Themes in Ulster Fiction* (Dublin, 1974).

—— 'The Revival of Saga and Heroic Romance during the Irish Renaissance: The Ideology of Cultural Nationalism', in Heinz Kosok (ed.), *Studies in Anglo-Irish Literature* (Bonn, 1982), pp. 126–36.

—— *Fictions of the Irish Literary Revival: A Changeling Art* (Dublin, 1987).

—— *Colonial Consequences: Essays in Literature and Culture* (Dublin, 1991).

Foster, R.F., *Modern Ireland, 1600–1972* (Harmondsworth, 1989).

—— *Paddy and Mr Punch: Connections in Irish and English History* (Harmondsworth, 1995).

Fussell, Paul, *The Great War and Modern Memory* (Oxford, 1977).

Gallagher, S.F. (ed.), *Women in Irish Legend, Life and Literature* (Gerrards Cross, 1983).

Gallagher, Thomas, *Paddy's Lament: Ireland, 1846–1947 Prelude to Hatred* (Swords, 1988).

Garvin, Tom, 'The Return of History: Collective Myths and Modern Nationalisms', in Kevin Barry et al. (eds), *The Irish Review*, No. 9, Autumn 1990, pp. 16–30.

Gibbons, Luke, 'Montage, Modernism, and the City', in Kevin Barry et al. (eds), *The Irish Review*, No. 10, Spring 1991, pp. 1–6.

—— 'Race Against Time: Racial Discourse and Irish History', in Robert Young (ed.), *The Oxford Literary Review: Neocolonialism*, Vol. 13, Nos. 1–2, 1991, pp. 95–117.

Gilley, Sheridan, 'English Attitudes to the Irish in England, 1780–1900', in Colin Holmes (ed.), *Immigrants and Minorities in British Society* (London, 1978), pp. 81–109.

—— 'The Roman Catholic Church and the Nineteenth Century Irish Diaspora', *Journal of Ecclesiastical History*, Vol. 35, No. 2, April 1984, pp. 188–207.

Glynn, Sean, 'Irish Immigration to Britain, 1911–1951: Patterns and Policy', *I.E.S.H.*, Vol. viii, 1981, pp. 50–69.

Goldring, Maurice, *Pleasant the Scholar's Life: Irish Intellectuals and the Construction of the Nation State* (London, 1993).

Gough, Hugh and Dickson, David (eds), *Ireland and the French Revolution* (Dublin, 1990).

Gramsci, Antonio, *Selections from the Prison Notebooks* (London, 1971).

—— *Selections from Cultural Writings* (London, 1985).

Green, E.R.R. (ed.), *Essays in Scotch-Irish History* (Belfast, 1992).

Guha, Ranajit and Spivat, Gayatri Chakravorty (eds), *Selected Subaltern Studies* (Oxford, 1988).

Guillen, Claudio, 'On the Literature of Exile and Counter Exile', *Books Abroad*, 50, Spring 1976, pp. 271–80.

Gurr, Andrew, *Writers in Exile: The Identity of Home in Modern Literature* (Brighton, 1981).

Gwynn, Aubrey, 'Early Irish Emigration to the West Indies', *Studies*, September 1929, pp. 377–93.

—— 'Cromwell's Policy of Transportation, Pt. I', *Studies*, 1930, pp. 607–23.

—— 'Cromwell's Policy of Transportation, Pt. II', *Studies*, Vol. XX, No. 78, June 1931, pp. 291–305.

Hall, Wayne, E., *Shadowy Heroes: Irish Literature of the 1890s* (New York, 1980).

Hannan, Damian, *Rural Exodus: A Study of the forces influencing the large scale migration of Irish rural youth* (Dublin, 1970).

Harmon, Maurice, 'Cobwebs before the Wind: Aspects of the Peasantry in Irish Literature from 1800 to 1916', in Daniel J. Casey and Robert E. Rhodes (eds), *Views of the Irish Peasantry, 1800–1916* (Hamden, Connecticut, 1977), pp. 129–59.

—— (ed.), *Images and Illusion: Anglo-Irish Literature and its Contexts* (Dublin, 1979).

Heaney, Seamus, 'The Interesting Case of John Alphonsus Mulrennan', *Planet*, Vol. 41, 1978, pp. 34–40.

—— *Preoccupations: Selected Prose, 1968–78* (London, 1980).

Hechter, Michael, *Internal Colonialism: The Celtic Fringe in British National Development, 1536–1966* (London, 1975).

Hederman, Mark P. and Kearney, Richard (eds), *Crane Bag Book of Irish Studies, 1977–81* (Dublin, 1982).

—— (eds), *Crane Bag Book of Irish Studies*, Vol. 2, Dublin, 1987.

Herr, Cheryl, *Joyce's Anatomy of Culture* (Urbana, 1986).

Hickey, Des and Smith, Gus (eds), *A Paler Shade of Green* (London, 1972).

Hobsbawm, Eric, *The Age of Empire* (London, 1987).

—— *Nations and Nationalism since 1780: Programme, myth, reality* (Cambridge, 1990).

—— and Ranger, Terence (eds), *The Invention of Tradition* (Cambridge, 1983).

Hogan, Robert (ed.), *The Macmillan Dictionary of Irish Literature* (London, 1980).

Hone, Joseph, *The Life of George Moore* (London, 1936).

Houston, Cecil J. and Smyth, William J., *Irish Emigration and Canadian Settlement: Patterns, Links and Letters* (Belfast, 1990).

Hughes, Robert, *The Fatal Shore* (London, 1987).

Hutchinson, John, *The Dynamics of Cultural Nationalism: The Gaelic Revival and the Creation of the Irish Nation State* (London, 1987).

Hyland, Paul and Sammells, Neil (eds), *Irish Writing: Exile and Subversion* (London, 1991).

Ilie, Paul, *Literature and Inner Exile: Authoritarian Spain, 1939–75* (Baltimore, 1980).

Innes, C.L. (ed.), *Woman and Nation in Irish Literature and Society, 1880–1935* (Hemel Hempstead, 1993).

Irish Theatre Archive, 'Dion Boucicault and the Irish Melodrama Tradition', *Prompts 6*, September 1983, pp. 30–7.

Jackson, Rosemary, *Fantasy: The Literature of Subversion* (London, 1981).

Jameson, Fredric, *The Political Unconscious: Narrative as a Socially Symbolic Act* (London, 1981).

—— 'Third World Literature in the Era of Multinational Capitalism', *Social Text*, 15, Fall 1986, pp. 65–87.

—— *Nationalism, Colonialism and Literature, Modernism and Imperialism, A Field Day Pamphlet*, No. 14, Derry, 1988.

JanMohamed, Abdul R., 'The Economy of Manichaen Allegory: The Function of Racial Difference in Colonialist Literature', *Critical Inquiry*, 12, Autumn 1985, pp. 59–87.

Jeffares, A. Norman, *Anglo-Irish Literature* (London, 1982).

Johnson, Toni O'Brien and Cairns, David (eds), *Gender in Irish Writing* (Milton Keynes, 1991).

Journal of Irish Literature, 13, Jan.–May 1984, Bourke-de-Burca double number.

Journal of Irish Literature, 14, Jan. 1985, Hubert O'Grady number.

Kain, Richard M., *Dublin in the Age of William Butler Yeats and James Joyce* (Newton Abbot, 1972).

Kearney, Richard, 'Faith and Fatherland', in Mark P. Hederman and Richard Kearney (eds), *The Crane Bag*, Vol. 8, No. 1, 1984, pp. 55–66.

—— 'Myth and Motherland', in Field Day Theatre Company, *Ireland's Field Day*, London 1985, pp. 59–80.

—— (ed.), *The Irish Mind: Exploring Intellectual Traditions* (Dublin, 1985).

—— *Transitions: Narratives in Modern Irish Culture* (Dublin, 1988).

—— (ed.), *Migrations: The Irish at Home and Abroad* (Dublin, 1990).

Keating, P.J., *The Working Classes in Victorian Fiction* (London, 1971).

—— (ed.), *Into Unknown England: Selections from the Social Explorers, 1866–1913* (Glasgow, 1976).

Kee, Robert, *The Green Flag* (London, 1976).

Kennedy, Dennis, *The Widening Gulf: Northern attitudes to the independent Irish State, 1919–49* (Belfast, 1988).

Kennedy, Jr. Robert E., *The Irish: Emigration, Marriage and Fertility* (Los Angeles, 1973).

Kenner, Hugh, *A Colder Eye: The Modern Irish Writers* (Harmondsworth, 1984).

Kenny, Vincent, 'The Post-Colonial Personality', in Mark P. Hederman and Richard Kearney (eds), *The Crane Bag*, Vol. 9, No. 1, 1985, pp. 70–82.

Kershner, R.B., *Joyce, Bakhtin and Popular Literature: Chronicles of Disorder* (Chapel Hill, 1989).

Kiberd, Declan, *Synge and the Irish Language* (London, 1979).

—— 'Story-telling: The Gaelic Tradition', in Patrick Rafroidi and Terence Brown (eds), *The Irish Short Story* (Gerrards Cross, 1979), pp. 13–25.

—— 'The Fall of the Stage Irishman', in Ronald Schleifer (ed.), *The Genres of the Irish Literary Revival* (Dublin, 1980), pp. 39–60.

—— 'The Perils of Nostalgia: A Critique of the Revival', in Peter Connolly (ed.), *Literature and the Changing Ireland* (Gerrards Cross, 1982), pp. 1–24.

—— 'George Moore's Gaelic Lawn Party', in Robert Welch (ed.), *The Way Back: George Moore's The Untilled Field and The Lake* (Dublin, 1982), pp. 13–27.

—— 'Inventing Irelands', in Mark P. Hederman and Richard Kearney (eds), *The Crane Bag*, Vol. 8, No. 1, 1984, pp. 11–23.

—— 'Anglo-Irish Attitudes', in Field Day Theatre Company, *Ireland's Field Day* (London, 1985), pp. 83–105.

—— 'Yeats, Childhood and Exile', in Paul Hyland and Neil Sammels (eds), *Irish Writing: Exile and Subversion* (London 1991), pp. 126–45.

—— *Inventing Ireland: The Literature of the Modern Nation* (London, 1995).

Kiely, Benedict, *Modern Irish Fiction: A Critique* (Dublin, 1950).

Kiernan, Colm, 'Anglo-Irish Literature and Australia', in Heinz Kosok (ed.), *Studies in Anglo-Irish Literature* (Bonn, 1982), pp. 474–80.

—— (ed.), *Australia and Ireland: Bicentenary Essays, 1788–1988* (Dublin, 1986).

Kilroy, Thomas, 'The Irish Writer: Self and Society, 1950–1980', in Peter Connolly (ed.), *Literature And The Changing Ireland* (Gerrards Cross, 1982), pp. 175–87.

Kinsella, Thomas, 'The Divided Mind', in Seán Lucy (ed.), *Irish Poets in English* (Cork, 1975), pp. 208–18.

Kosok, Heinz (ed.), *Studies in Anglo-Irish Literature* (Bonn, 1982).

Lagos-Pope, María-Inés (ed.), *Exile in Literature* (London/Ontario, 1988).

Lee, Joseph, *The Modernisation of Irish Society, 1848–1918* (Dublin, 1973).

—— 'Women and the Church since the Famine', in Margaret MacCurtain and Donncha Ó Corráin (eds), *Women in Irish Society: the historical dimension* (Dublin, 1978), pp. 37–45.

—— (ed.), *Ireland, 1945–1970* (Dublin, 1979).

—— and Gearóid Ó Tuathaigh, *The Age of de Valera* (Dublin, 1982).

—— (ed.), *Ireland: Towards a Sense of Place* (Cork, 1985).

—— *Ireland, 1912–1985: Politics and Society* (Cambridge, 1989).

Lees, Lynn H., *Exiles of Erin: Irish Migrants in Victorian London* (Manchester, 1979).

Levin, Harry, 'Literature and Exile', in *Refractions: Essays in Comparative Literature* (New York, 1966), pp. 68–81.

Lloyd, David, *Nationalism and Minor Literature: James Clarence Mangan and the Emergence of Irish Cultural Nationalism* (California, 1987).

—— *Anomalous States: Irish Writing and the Post-Colonial Moment* (Mullingar, 1993).

Longley, Edna, 'The Rising, the Somme and Irish Memory', in Máirín Ní Dhonnchadha and Theo Dorgan (eds), *Revising the Rising* (Derry, 1991), pp. 29–49.

Lucy, Seán (ed.), *Irish Poets in English* (Cork, 1973).

Lyons, F.S.L., *Ireland since the Famine* (London, 1973).

—— *Culture and Anarchy in Ireland, 1890–1939* (Oxford, 1982).

—— 'Yeats and the Anglo-Irish Twilight', in Oliver MacDonagh et al. (eds), *Irish Culture and Nationalism, 1750–1950* (London, 1983), pp. 212–38.

MacCurtain, Margaret, 'Women, the Vote and Revolution', in Margaret MacCurtain and Donncha Ó Corráin, (eds), *Women in Irish Society: the historical dimension* (Dublin, 1978), pp. 46–57.

—— 'Towards An Appraisal of the Religious Image of Women', in Mark P. Hederman and Richard Kearney (eds), *The Crane Bag*, Vol. 4, No. 1, 1980, pp. 539–43.

—— and Ó Corráin, Donncha (eds), *Women in Irish Society: the historical dimension* (Dublin, 1978).

—— and O'Dowd, Mary (eds), *Women in Early Modern Ireland* (Edinburgh, 1991).

MacDonagh, Oliver, 'Irish Emigration To The United States Of America And The British Colonies During The Famine', in R. Dudley Edwards and T. Desmond Williams (eds), *The Great Famine: Studies in Irish History 1845–52* (Dublin, 1956), pp. 317–87.

—— *States of Mind: A Study of Anglo-Irish Conflict, 1780–1980* (London, 1983).

—— Mandle, W.F. and Travers, Pauric (eds), *Irish Culture and Nationalism, 1750–1950* (London, 1983).

—— 'Ideas and Institutions, 1830–45', in W.E. Vaughan (ed.), *A New History of*

Ireland: Vol. V. Ireland under the Union, 1801–1870 (Oxford, 1989), pp. 193–217.

Maclaughlin, Jim, *Ireland: The Emigrant Nursery And the World Economy* (Cork, 1994).

—— (ed.), *Location and Dislocation in Contemporary Irish Society: Emigration and Irish Identities* (Cork, 1997).

MacMahon, Joseph A., 'The Catholic Clergy And The Social Question In Ireland, 1891–1916', *Studies*, Vol. LXX, No. 280, 1981, pp. 263–88.

MacManus, Seumus, *The Story of the Irish Race: A Popular History of Ireland* (Connecticut, 1921).

Malcolm, Elizabeth, 'Popular Recreation in Nineteenth-Century Ireland', in Oliver MacDonagh et al. (eds), *Irish Culture and Nationalism, 1750–1950* (London, 1983), pp. 40–50.

Mandle, W.F., 'The Gaelic Athletic Association and Popular Culture, 1884–1924', in Oliver MacDonagh et al. (eds), *Irish Culture and Nationalism, 1750–1950* (London, 1983), pp. 104–21.

McCaffrey, Lawrence J., 'Fictional images of Irish-America', in Tom Dunne (ed.), *The Writer as Witness* (Cork, 1987), pp. 227–44.

—— *Textures of Irish America* (New York, 1992).

McCana, Proinsias, 'Women in Irish Mythology', in Mark P. Hederman and Richard Kearney (eds), *The Crane Bag Book Of Irish Studies* (Dublin, 1982), pp. 520–24.

—— 'Early Irish Ideology and the Concept of Unity', in Richard Kearney (ed.), *The Irish Mind: Exploring Intellectual Traditions* (Dublin, 1985), pp. 56–78.

McCartney, Donal, 'The Quest for Irish Political Identity: the Image and the Illusion', in Maurice Harmon (ed.), *Image and Illusion: Anglo-Irish Literature and its Contexts* (Dublin, 1979), pp. 13–22.

McCartney, Robert, *Liberty and Authority in Ireland: A Field Day Pamphlet*, No. 9, Derry, 1985.

McCormack, W.J., *Ascendancy and Tradition in Anglo-Irish Literature* (Oxford, 1985).

McDonald, Peter, 'The Fate of "Identity" John Hewitt, W.R. Rodgers and Louis MacNeice', in Kevin Barry et al. (eds), *The Irish Review*, No. 12, Spring/Summer 1992, pp. 72–86.

McHugh, Roger, 'The Famine in Irish Oral Tradition', in R. Dudley Edwards and T. Desmond Williams (eds), *The Great Famine: Studies in Irish History, 1845–52* (Dublin, 1956), pp. 391–436.

—— and Harmon, Maurice, *A Short History of Anglo-Irish Literature: From its origins to the present day* (Dublin, 1982).

Memmi, Albert, *The Colonizer and the Colonized* (London, 1990).

Mercier, Vivian, *The Irish Comic Tradition* (Oxford, 1962).

—— *Beckett/Beckett* (London, 1990).

Miller, Kerby, *Emigrants and Exiles: Ireland and the Irish Exodus to North America* (Oxford, 1985).

—— 'Emigration, Capitalism and Ideology in Post-Famine Ireland', in Richard Kearney (ed.), *Migrations: The Irish at Home and Abroad* (Dublin, 1990), pp. 91–108.

Mitchell, Susan, *George Moore* (Dublin, 1916).

Moody, T.W. and Martin, F.X. (eds), *The Course of Irish History* (Cork, 1967).

—— Martin, F.X. and Byrne, F.J. (eds), *A New History Of Ireland: Vol. III, Early Modern Ireland, 1534–1691* (Oxford, 1976).

—— and Vaughan, W.E. (eds), *A New History Of Ireland: Vol. IV, Eighteenth-Century Ireland, 1691–1800* (Oxford, 1986).

Moretti, Franco, *Signs Taken for Wonders: Essays in the Sociology of Literary Forms* (London, 1988).

Nandy, Ashis, *At the Edge of Psychology: Essays in Politics and Culture* (Delhi, 1980).

—— *The Intimate Enemy: Loss and Recovery of Self Under Colonialism* (Delhi, 1983).

Nelson, James M., 'From Rory And Paddy To Boucicault's Myles, Shaun And Conn: The Irishman On The London Stage, 1830–1860', in *Éire-Ireland*, 13, Fall 1978, pp. 79–105.

Ngũgĩ, Wa Thiong'o, *Decolonising the Mind: The Politics of Language in African Literature* (London, 1986).

Ní Brolcháin, Muireann, 'Women in Early Irish Myths and Sagas', in Mark P. Hederman and Richard Kearney (eds), *The Crane Bag Book Of Irish Studies* (Dublin, 1982), pp. 525–32.

Ní Dhonnchadha, Máirín and Dorgan, Theo (eds), *Revising The Rising* (Derry, 1991).

Nolan, Janet A., *Ourselves Alone: Women's Emigration from Ireland, 1885–1920* (Kentucky, 1989).

O'Brien, Conor Cruise, *States Of Ireland* (London, 1972).

O'Brien, George, 'The Muse of Exile: Estrangement and Renewal in Modern Irish Literature', in María-Inés, Lagos-Pope (ed.), *Exile in Literature* (London/Ontario, 1988), pp. 82–101.

O'Brien, John and Travers, Pauric (eds), *The Irish Emigrant Experience in Australia* (Swords, 1991).

O'Brien, Máire C., 'The Female Principle In Gaelic Poetry', in S.F. Gallagher (ed.), *Women in Irish Legend, Life and Literature* (Gerrards Cross, 1983), pp. 26–37.

Ó Buachalla, Breandán, 'Irish Jacobite Poetry', in Kevin Barry et al. (eds), *The Irish Review*, No. 12, Spring/Summer 1992, pp. 40–9.

O'Callaghan, Margaret, 'Language, nationality and cultural identity in the Irish Free State, 1922–7: *The Irish Statesman* and *The Catholic Bulletin* reappraised', *I.H.S.* XXIV, No. 94, Nov. 1984, pp. 226–45.

Ó Cíosáin, Niall, 'Printed Popular Literature in Irish, 1750–1850: Presence and Absence', in Mary Daly and David Dickson (eds), *The Origins of Popular Literacy in Ireland: Language Change and Educational Development, 1700–1920* (Dublin, 1990), pp. 45–57.

O'Connor, Kevin, *The Irish In Britain* (Dublin, 1974).

O'Connor, Noreen, 'Exile and Enrootedness', in *Seminar 11* (Cork, 1978), pp. 53–5.

O'Connor, Nuala, *Bringing It All Back Home: The Influence Of Irish Music* (London, 1991).

O'Connor, Ulick, *Celtic Dawn: A Portrait of the Irish Literary Renaissance* (London, 1985).

Ó Cuív, Brian, 'Ireland in the Eleventh and Twelfth Centuries (c. 1000–1169), in T.W. Moody and F.X. Martin (eds), *The Course of Irish History* (Cork, 1967), pp. 107–22.

—— (ed.), *A View Of The Irish Language* (Dublin, 1969).

—— 'The Irish language in the early modern period', in T.W. Moody et al. (eds), *A New History Of Ireland: Vol. III, Early Modern Ireland, 1534–1691* (Oxford, 1976), pp. 509–45.

—— 'Irish language and literature, 1619–1845', in T.W. Moody and W.E. Vaughan (eds), *A New History Of Ireland: Vol. IV, Eighteenth-Century Ireland, 1691–1800* (Oxford, 1986), pp. 374–423.

Ó Danachair, Caoimhín, 'Oral Tradition and the Printed Word', in Maurice Harmon (ed.), *Image and Illusion: Anglo-Irish Literature and its Contexts* (Dublin, 1979), pp. 31–41.

O'Dowd, Liam, 'Intellectuals in 20th Century Ireland: And the case of George Russell (A.E.)' in Mark P. Hederman and Richard Kearney (eds), *The Crane Bag*, Vol. 9, No. 1, 1985, pp. 6–25.

—— 'Neglecting the Material Dimension: Irish intellectuals and the problem of identity', in Kevin Barry et al. (eds), *The Irish Review*, No. 3, 1988, pp. 8–17.

Ó Faoláin, Seán, *The Great O'Neill: A Biography of Hugh O'Neill Earl of Tyrone, 1550–1616* (Cork, 1970).

—— *The Irish* (Harmondsworth, 1980).

O'Farrell, Patrick, *The Irish in Australia* (New South Wales, 1986).

—— 'The Irish in Australia and New Zealand, 1791–1870', in W.E. Vaughan (ed.), *A New History Of Ireland: Vol. V, Ireland Under The Union, 1801–1870* (Oxford, 1989), pp. 661–81.

Ó Fiaich, Tómas, 'The Beginnings of Christianity (5th and 6th Centuries), in T.W. Moody and F.X. Martin (eds), *The Course of Irish History* (Cork, 1967), pp. 61–75.

—— 'The Language and Political History', in Brian Ó Cuív (ed.), *A View of the Irish Language* (Dublin, 1969), pp. 101–11.

Ó Gráda, Cormac, 'Some Aspects of Nineteenth-Century Irish Emigration', in Louis Cullen and T.C. Smout (eds), *Comparative Aspects of Scottish and Irish Economic and Social History, 1600–1900* (Edinburgh, 1977), pp. 65–73.

—— *The Great Irish Famine* (London, 1989).

O'Halloran, Clare, *Partition and the Limits of Irish Nationalism: An Ideology under Stress* (Dublin, 1987).

Ó hÓgáin, Dáithí, 'The Visionary Voice: A Survey of Popular Attitudes to Poetry in the Irish Tradition', in Maurice Harmon (ed.), *Image and Illusion: Anglo-Irish Literature and its Contexts* (Dublin, 1979), pp. 44–61.

—— 'Folklore and Literature, 1700–1850', in Mary Daly and David Dickson (eds), *The Origins of Popular Literacy in Ireland: Language, Change and Educational Development, 1700–1920* (Dublin, 1990), pp. 1–13.

Olinder, Britta, 'John Hewitt: Ulsterman of Planter Stock', in Heinz Kosok (ed.), *Studies in Anglo-Irish Literature* (Bonn, 1982), pp. 376–98.

O'Loughlin, Michael, *Frank Ryan: Journey to the Centre* (Dublin, 1987).

O'Neill, Seamus, 'Gaelic Literature', in Robert Hogan (ed.), *The Macmillan Dictionary of Irish Literature* (London, 1980), pp. 17–64.

Ong, Walter J., *Orality and Literacy: The Technologising of the Word* (London, 1982).

Oram, Hugh, *The Newspaper Book: A History of Newspapers in Ireland, 1649–1983* (Dublin, 1983).

O'Riordan, Michelle, 'Historical Perspectives on the Gaelic Poetry of The Hidden

Ireland', in Kevin Barry et al. (eds), *The Irish Review*, No. 4, Spring 1988, pp. 73–81.

O'Sullivan, Patrick, 'A literary difficulty in explaining Ireland: Tom Moore and Captain Rock, 1824', in Roger Swift and Sheridan Gilley (eds), *The Irish in Britain, 1815–1939* (London, 1989), pp. 239–74.

—— (ed.), *The Irish World Wide Series: History, Heritage, Identity, Vol. 3, The Creative Migrant* (London, 1994).

O'Toole, Fintan, *A Mass for Jesse James: A Journey through 1980s Ireland* (Dublin, 1990).

—— *The Ex-Isle of Erin: Images of Global Ireland* (Dublin, 1997).

Ó Tuama, Seán, 'Stability and Ambivalence: Aspects of the Sense of Place and Religion in Irish Literature', in Joseph Lee (ed.), *Ireland: Towards A Sense Of Place* (Cork, 1985), pp. 21–33.

Ó Tuathaigh, Gearóid, *Ireland before the Famine, 1798–1848* (Dublin, 1972).

—— 'The Role of Women in Ireland under the new English Order', in Margaret MacCurtain and Donncha Ó Corráin (eds), *Women in Irish Society: the historical dimension* (Dublin, 1978), pp. 26–35.

—— 'Language, Literature and Culture in Ireland since the War', in Joseph Lee (ed.), *Ireland, 1945–70* (Dublin, 1979), pp. 111–23.

—— 'The Irish in Nineteenth-Century Britain: Problems of Integration', *Transactions of the Royal Historical Society*, 5th Series, 31, 1981, pp. 149–74.

—— 'de Valera and the Irish People', in Joseph Lee and Gearóid Ó Tuathaigh, *The Age of de Valera* (Dublin, 1982), pp. 165–201.

—— 'The historical pattern of Irish emigration: some labour aspects', in Mary Clancy et al. (eds), *... the emigrant experience ...* (Galway, 1991), pp. 9–28.

Outram, Dorinda, 'Holding the Future at Bay: The French Revolution and modern Ireland', in Kevin Barry et al. (eds), *The Irish Review*, No. 6, Spring 1989, pp. 1–6.

Pine, Richard, 'After Boucicault – Melodrama and the Modern Irish Stage', in Irish Theatre Archives, *Prompts*, No. 6, Sept. 1983, pp. 39–50.

Póirtéir, Cathal (ed.), *The Great Irish Famine* (Cork, 1995).

—— *Famine Echoes* (Dublin, 1995).

Porter, Roy and Teich, Mikulas (eds), *Romanticism In National Contexts* (Cambridge, 1988).

Potts, Lydia, *The World Labour Market: A History Of Migration* (London, 1990).

Rafroidi, Patrick, 'Imagination and Revolution: The Cuchulainn Myth', in Oliver MacDonagh etc. (eds), *Irish Culture and Nationalism, 1750–1950* (London, 1983), pp. 137–48.

—— and Brown, Terence (eds), *The Irish Short Story* (Gerrards Cross, 1979).

—— and Harmon, Maurice (eds), *The Irish Novel In Our Time* (Lille, 1976).

Rodgers, W.R., *Irish Literary Portraits* (London, 1972).

Rushdie, Salman, *Imaginary Homelands: Essays and Criticism, 1981–1991* (London, 1991).

Ryan, Liam, 'Irish Emigration to Britain since World War II', in Richard Kearney (ed.), *Migrations: The Irish at Home and Abroad* (Dublin, 1990), pp. 45–67.

Saakana, Amon Saba, *The Colonial Legacy In Caribbean Literature* (London, 1987).

Said, Edward W., 'The Mind of Winter: Reflections on life in exile', *Harpers Magazine*, Vol. 269, No. 161, Sept. 1984, pp. 49–55.

—— *The World, The Text And The Critic* (London, 1984).

—— *Orientalism* (Harmondsworth, 1985).

—— *Nationalism, Colonialism and Literature: Yeats and Decolonization, A Field Day Pamphlet*, No. 15, Derry, 1988.

—— 'Representing the Colonized: Anthropology's Interlocutors', *Critical Inquiry*, Vol. 15, No. 2, Winter 1989, pp. 205–25.

—— *Culture and Imperialism* (London, 1993).

—— *Representations Of The Intellectual: The 1993 Reith Lectures* (London, 1994).

Saunders, Norah and Kelly, A.A., *Joseph Campbell: Poet and Nationalist, 1879–1944* (Dublin, 1988).

Schleifer, Ronald (ed.), *The Genres of the Irish Literary Revival* (Dublin, 1980).

Seidel, Michael, *Exile and the Narrative Imagination* (New Haven, 1986).

Sharkey, Sabina, *Ireland and the Iconography of Rape: Colonisation, Constraint and Gender*, Irish Studies Centre, Occasional Papers Series Four (London, 1994).

Sheeran, P.F., 'Colonists and Colonised: Some Aspects of Anglo-Irish Literature from Swift to Joyce', *Yearbook of English Studies*, Vol. 13, 1983, pp. 97–115.

—— 'The Irish Tradition and Nineteenth-Century Fiction: A Review', in Thomas Bartlett et al. (eds), *Irish Studies: A General Introduction* (Dublin, 1988), pp. 87–114.

—— 'The Idiocy of Irish Rural Life Reviewed', in Kevin Barry et al. (eds), *The Irish Review*, No. 5, Autumn 1988, pp. 27–33.

Silke, John J., 'The Irish Abroad, 1534–1691', in T.W. Moody et al. (eds), *A New History Of Ireland: Vol. III, Early Modern Ireland, 1534–1691* (Oxford, 1976), pp. 587–633.

Simms, J.G., 'The Irish on the Continent, 1691–1800', in T.W. Moody and W.E. Vaughan (eds), *A New History Of Ireland: Vol. IV, Eighteenth-Century Ireland, 1691–1800* (Oxford, 1986), pp. 629–56.

Simms, Katherine, 'Bardic poetry as a historical source', in Tom Dunne (ed.), *The Writer as Witness* (Cork, 1987), pp. 58–75.

Sloan, Barry, *The Pioneers of Anglo-Irish Fiction, 1800–1850* (Gerrards Cross, 1986).

Smith, Cecil Woodham, *The Great Hunger* (London, 1975).

Smyth, Ailbhe, 'The Floozie in the Jacuzzi', in Kevin Barry et al. (eds), *The Irish Review*, No. 6, Spring 1989, pp. 7–24.

Smyth, William J., 'Explorations of Place', in Joseph Lee (ed.), *Ireland: Towards A Sense Of Place* (Cork, 1985), pp. 1–20.

Spivak, Gayatri Chakravorty, *In Other Worlds: Essays in Cultural Politics* (London, 1988).

Steiner, George, 'Extraterritorial', in *Extraterritorial: Papers on Literature and the Language Revolution* (New York, 1971), pp. 3–11.

Swift, Roger and Gilley, Sheridan (eds), *The Irish in the Victorian City* (London, 1985).

—— (eds), *The Irish in Britain, 1815–1939* (London, 1989).

Tabori, Paul, *The Anatomy of Exile* (London, 1972).

Thompson, William, *The Imagination of an Insurrection: Dublin 1916* (London, 1967).

Toolan, Michael, 'The significance of representing dialect in writing', *Language and Literature*, Vol. 1, No. 1, 1992, pp. 29–46.

Todd, Loreto, *The Language of Irish Literature* (London, 1989).

Vance, Norman, 'Celts, Carthaginians and constitutions: Anglo-Irish literary relations, 1780–1820', in *Irish Historical Studies*, Vol. 22, No. 87, March 1981, pp. 216–38.

—— *Irish Literature: A Social History, Tradition, Identity and Difference* (Oxford, 1990).

Vaughan, W.E. (ed.), *A New History of Ireland: Vol. V, Ireland Under The Union, 1801–70* (Oxford, 1989).

Viney, Ethna, 'Women In Rural Ireland', in *Christus Rex*, 22, 1968, pp. 333–42.

Wall, Maureen, 'The Decline Of The Irish Language', in Brian Ó Cuív (ed.), *A View of the Irish Language* (Dublin, 1969), pp. 81–90.

Wall, Richard (ed.), *Medieval and Modern Ireland* (New Jersey, 1988).

Waters, Martin J., 'Peasants and Emigrants: Considerations of the Gaelic League as a Social Movement', in Daniel J. Casey and Robert E. Rhodes (eds), *Views of the Irish Peasantry, 1800–1916* (Hamden, Connecticut, 1977), pp. 160–77.

Watson, George, *Irish Identity And The Literary Revival: Synge, Yeats, Joyce and O'Casey* (London, 1979).

Watt, Stephen M., 'Boucicault and Whitbread: The Dublin Stage At The End Of The Nineteenth Century', in *Éire-Ireland*, 18, Fall 1983, pp. 23–53.

—— *Joyce, O'Casey and the Irish Popular Theater* (New York, 1991).

Welch, Robert (ed.), *The Way Back: George Moore's The Untilled Field and The Lake* (Dublin, 1982).

Williams, David, 'The Exile as Uncreator', *Mosaic*, 8, Nos. 3–4, 1975, pp. 1–14.

Williams, Martin, 'Ancient Mythology and Revolutionary Ideology in Ireland, 1878–1916', *Historical Journal*, Vol. XXVI, No. 2, 1983, pp. 307–28.

Williams, Raymond, *Writing in Society* (London n.d.).

Williams, William, 'From Lost Land To Emerald Isle: Ireland And The Irish In American Sheet Music, 1800–1920', in *Éire-Ireland*, No. 26, Spring 1991, pp. 19–45.

Wills, Clair, 'Language Politics, Narrative, Political Violence', in Robert Young (ed.), *Oxford Literary Review: Neocolonialism*, Vol. 13, Nos. 1–2, Oxford 1991, pp. 20–60.

Young, Robert (ed.), *Oxford Literary Review: Neocolonialism*, Vol. 13, Nos 1–2, Oxford 1991.

Zach, Wolfgang, 'Oliver Goldsmith On Ireland and the Irish: Personal Views, Shifting Attitudes, Literary Stereotypes', in Heinz Kosok (ed.), *Studies in Anglo-Irish Literature* (Bonn, 1982), pp. 23–35.

Index